The Economies of Africa and Asia in the Inter-war Depression

The Economies of Africa and Asia in the Inter-war Depression

Edited by

Ian Brown

ROUTLEDGE
London and New York

First published 1989 by Routledge
11 New Fetter Lane, London EC4P 4EE
29 West 35th Street, New York, NY 10001

Printed in Great Britain by
T.J. Press (Padstow) Ltd, Padstow, Cornwall

British Library Cataloguing in Publication Data
The economies of Africa and Asia in the inter-war depression.
1. Africa. Economic conditions 1900-1945
2. Asia. Economic conditions 1905-1945
330.96′031

Library of Congress Cataloging in Publication Data
The Economies of Africa and Asia in the inter-war depression / edited by Ian Brown.
p. cm.
Includes bibliographies and index.
1. Africa — Economic conditions — 1918-1945 — Congresses.
2. Asia — Economic conditions — 1918- — Congresses.
3. Depressions — 1929- —Africa — Congresses.
4. Depressions — 1929 — Asia — Congresses.
I. Brown, Ian, 1947-
HC800.E3 1989
330.95′041 — dc 19 88-268 12

ISBN 0-415-00377-6

CONTENTS

ACKNOWLEDGEMENTS

The essays in this volume were originally presented at a conference held at the School of Oriental and African Studies, University of London, in December 1985. I am very grateful to the Economic and Social Research Council, the Nuffield Foundation, the British Academy, the British Council and the School of Oriental and African Studies for financing that conference so generously. The School has also provided the funds which now bring the papers to publication.

In the academic organisation of the conference, which frequently took me far beyond my own regional expertise, I relied heavily on the advice of colleagues throughout the School, although none more than Richard Rathbone and Peter Robb, who gave generously of their time and wisdom. In the practical organisation of that gathering, Martin Daly was unfailingly resourceful. And in preparing the papers for publication I have been assisted magnificently by three people whose talents were exceeded only by their patience and good humour: Doris Johnson, who undertook the copy-editing, Joyce Hutchinson, who set the text, and Susan Harrop, who drew the maps.

Ian Brown

CONTRIBUTORS

David Anderson is Lecturer in History, Birkbeck College, University of London

Marie-Claire Bergère is Professor at l'Institut National des Langues et Civilisations Orientales and Director of Studies at l'École des Hautes Études en Sciences Sociales, Paris

Ian Brown is Lecturer in Economic History with reference to South East Asia, School of Oriental and African Studies, University of London

Neil Charlesworth was Lecturer in Economic History, University of Glasgow, 1973-1986

Gervase Clarence-Smith is Lecturer in the History of Africa, School of Oriental and African Studies, University of London

Wolfgang Döpcke is a Research Associate in history at the University of Hanover

Susan Martin is Lecturer in the History of West Africa, School of Oriental and African Studies, University of London

Ramon H. Myers is Senior Fellow and Curator-Scholar of the East Asian Collection of the Hoover Institution on War, Revolution and Peace, Stanford, California

Norman G. Owen is Lecturer in History, University of Hong Kong

Roger Owen is Faculty Lecturer in the Economic History of the Middle East and Fellow of St Antony's College, University of Oxford

Kaoru Sugihara is Lecturer in the Economic History of Japan, School of Oriental and African Studies, University of London

David Throup is Lecturer in Politics, University of Keele

Ann Waswo is University Lecturer in Modern Japanese History and Fellow of St Antony's College, University of Oxford

INTRODUCTION

IAN BROWN[1]

For some considerable time economic historians of the non-European world have been moving towards a more sophisticated appreciation of the impact of the inter-war depression on the economies of Africa, Asia and Latin America. The conventional view has in essence argued that these economies, having developed a highly specialised dependence on primary export production from the early and mid-nineteenth century, were cruelly exposed by the very sharp contraction in the value and volume of world commodity trade which took place from the end of the 1920s, with the most severe consequences for indigenous economic welfare. Agricultural and mining populations in the non-European world faced primarily an unprecedented fall in money incomes, subsequently reinforced by a severe tightening of local credit markets and by intense pressure from the state for the full payment of land and capitation taxes, fixed in monetary terms. Thus the inter-war world depression, in this view, was a major economic disaster for the peoples of Africa, Asia and Latin America: following the confident expansion of world primary production and trade from the mid-nineteenth century, it constitutes a major turning-point in the modern economic history of the non-European world.

The main thrust of the revisionist literature, thus far, has been to argue that the impact of the depression on the non-European economies was by no means wholly damaging - specifically that the collapse of export earnings (reinforced by the sharp contraction in capital inflows), in reducing real import capacity, provided an important stimulus for substantial industrial growth in a number of primary exporting economies in the 1930s.[2] A more recent revisionist focus has been to argue that in a number of ways (for example, by a partial return to subsistence production, by the employment of violent resistance against the cash demands of moneylenders, landlords and the state) many primary producing communities in the non-European world were able to mitigate the full impact of sharply contracting money income on their level of material welfare.[3] It might also be argued here (although the argument is still to be fully explored) that the real incomes of primary producers in Africa and Asia were also sustained by the sharp falls in the prices of manufactured imports (and of foodstuffs) which accompanied the collapse of primary export prices: a crucial influence here was the striking penetration of markets throughout Asia and Africa by very low cost Japanese manufactures (principally textiles) which occurred from the opening of the 1930s.

The essays collected here seek to further the process of revision and refinement. The volume was conceived and contributions invited on the principle (firmly borne out by the resulting essays) that the impact of the inter-war depression on the economies of Africa and Asia was considerably more diverse and complex than has hitherto been acknowledged. Thus each of the papers is a closely detailed empirical study, drawing out the distinctive complexity of a specific aspect of economic change in a particular state or district during the depression period. No attempt at geographical or thematic comprehensiveness has been made in the volume. A rough balance has been achieved between the Asia and Africa papers, but it would be difficult to justify (in terms of scale of production and trade or complexity of economic experience), for example, the exclusion from the Asia contributions of the Netherlands East Indies, or the inclusion of two papers on the Philippines yet only one on India. Similarly, although thematically there is an emphasis on the rural sector (reflecting a relative neglect in the earlier revisionist literature) even here important lacunae remain. There is no discussion, for example, of the experience of rural non-agricultural production during the depression years, no attempt to assess the extent to which an increase in such production may have compensated for falling import capacity. Beyond the rural sector, still more substantial omissions may be admitted, notably discussion of the impact on internal economic conditions of exchange-rate policy and administration. In terms of the primary objective of this volume, these omissions should cause no concern. What is attempted here is a preliminary detailed exploration, a series of test bores, into the experience of the economies of Africa and Asia during the depression of the inter-war decades.

It follows that this introduction will not attempt to bring together the conclusions of the main contributions into a rounded, concluding statement. The diversity and complexity of the impact of the depression in these continents and the still preliminary state of scholarship in this field mean that it is premature to establish a new orthodoxy. Rather, the remaining pages of this introduction will sketch in a number of general themes, fix a number of points of reference, which may guide the reader through the detailed explorations which follow.

It would be valuable at the outset to establish a rather simple point about chronology and cause. It is erroneous to see the depression of the inter-war decades as a single event, cleanly delineated in time and origins. There were indeed three principal contractions in world production and trade in this period: in the early 1920s as the post-first World War boom broke (this is the focus of Marie-Claire Bergère's paper in this volume); at the close of the 1920s extending through to the early or mid-1930s, clearly the most severe contraction (and the principal concern here); and in 1937, as the recovery from that severe contraction temporarily faltered. All three contractions may be said to have their principal, immediate origins in the industrial world, being transmitted to the primary economies of Africa and Asia principally through plunging commodity demand. But for the African and Asian economies there was a further depression in this period, one notably deep-rooted and persistent. This was an agricultural depression whose origins, naturally varying from commodity to commodity, included long-term overproduction and deteriorating market preference. Its clearest manifestation was a sustained movement in the terms of trade against primary producers, sustained through the inter-war decades but in certain commodities and regions beginning before the first World War and continuing beyond the second. This 'long depression' is the principal focus of Susan Martin's essay on West Africa: but it also constitutes an important element in other papers, notably Norman Owen's consideration of the economic experience of the abaca province of Bicol in the Philippines during the slump and in particular of Ann Waswo's analysis of the long origins of the 1930s crisis in Japan's sericulture districts. In brief, for the primary economies of Asia and Africa *the* great contraction from the end of the 1920s does not mark a decisive break with a long era of expansion. There had been a comparably sharp (if not as severe) contraction at the beginning of that decade: more importantly, by this period many if not most primary economies were already well drawn into a distinctly separate agricultural depression.

For the internal economy of China (Ramon Myers argues) the great world contraction of the early 1930s signalled no significant break at all. It is true that the real value of China's exports fell by almost 40 per cent between 1928 and 1932 and indeed that a sharp domestic deflation set in from late 1931 as falling world prices (reinforced by an appreciating exchange) were transmitted into Chinese markets. But those same years (1931-6) also saw GDP grow in real terms, at 1.55 per cent per annum, with particularly impressive growth in the manufacturing sector but also notable growth in agriculture. And Ramon Myers is thus able to conclude that China simply did not experience internal economic depression as the world depression took hold. A comparable argument is advanced in Marie-Claire Bergère's paper on the consequences of the depression of the early 1920s for the China treaty-port economy. Although the contraction struck hard at those interests tied to foreign trade, the increasingly important Chinese industrial sector - drawing largely on local raw materials and serving principally the local market - maintained a vigorous growth, essentially unaffected by falling prices and falling foreign demand. And beyond the treaty ports, the peasant and his world, with rare exceptions, remained largely untouched by the international contraction. Ramon Myers and Marie-Claire Bergère provide intricate explanations for the essential immunity of the Chinese economy from the depressions of the early 1920s and early 1930s (and indeed it should be noted that there are significant variations of emphasis and direction between these two authors) but the fundamental consideration here is that during this period external transactions comprised only a very small part of total economic activity. The basic rhythms of the Chinese economy (Marie-Claire Bergère's phrase) were internally driven.

China's essential immunity may well be unrivalled in the African and Asian world. Yet her experience does bring into focus an important consideration of wide applicability. Even for those economies in Africa and Asia closely dependent on the world economy and thus notably vulnerable to external contraction, the internal dynamics of economic change continued to exert their powerful influence. This point is explicitly recognised by Neil Charlesworth when he argues that 'against the vast size, weight and stability of the agricultural economy [in Bombay Presidency], external pressures for change, even when in the shape of a massive international depression, were weak'. There is a crucial argument to be developed from here. The internal dynamics of economic change were clearly unique in each district and region in Africa and Asia, being determined by a diverse range of distinct influences - export cropping patterns, the structure of landownership relations, the balance between subsistence food production and export crop cultivation, the opportunities for non-agricultural employment, demographic pressures, ecological conditions. These unique internal dynamics then shaped comparably distinct responses to the inter-war depressions (distinct from district to district and from region to region), even (it must be strongly emphasised) as between economies comparably integrated into world markets.

To summarise, the impact of the inter-war depression on the economies of Africa and Asia was markedly diverse and complex for three principal reasons: the depression itself was an extremely intricate phenomenon, involving a number of contractions of differing severity, cause, character and timing; there was wide variation in the degree to which individual African and Asian economies were dependent on external trade and investment during this period and thus vulnerable to external contraction; and external contraction was transmitted to economies in Africa and Asia each of unique internal structure and dynamic and thus of response. With these preliminary statements it is now possible to add brief comment on two of the principal foci of the papers which follow - the prospects for industrialisation in Africa and Asia during the 1930s and (more prominently) the impact of the depression on the African and Asian rural economy.

A wide range of industrial experience is in evidence in the following papers. Thus in Japan, an industrial power as the depression took hold, rapid industrial expansion constituted the principal part of the Japanese recovery. That expansion has traditionally been explained in terms of a very marked increase in both the export of Japanese consumer manufactures and of government expenditure (notably military expenditure) from the early 1930s. But Kaoru Sugihara seeks an important shift of emphasis, drawing attention to the importance of rising rural incomes to Japan's industrial recovery. Within the primary economies of Africa and Asia, quite notable (if geographically and sectorally focused) industrialisation took place even in such an apparently unpromising region as equatorial and central Africa as well as in a more advantaged Egypt: in the Philippines, industrial expansion was weak (and was, incidentally, inspired by considerations essentially unrelated to the world contraction of the early 1930s). Two principal (but by no means mutually exclusive) approaches to primary economy industrialisation are discernible. Gervase Clarence-Smith explains the varying extent and character of industrialisation achieved in equatorial and central Africa primarily in terms of the balance of class forces both in Africa and in the colonial metropoles. The prospects for industrialisation were most secure where European settler populations (eager to create local commercial opportunities) and metropolitan companies (eager to relocate to cheap labour economies) exercised effective political power. My own paper emphasises instead the importance of an economy's external relationships, and the degree to which during the 1930s they provided (or failed to provide) protection to indigenous industrialisation.

Turning to the rural economy during the depression, three broad (but again not mutually exclusive) approaches are in evidence in the papers which follow. Norman Owen, in his study of the Bikol region of the Philippines, considers the ways in which Bikolanos, committed to the production of abaca for external markets, were able to protect their material welfare as cash income sharply contracted in the slump. They did so principally by reducing unnecessary expenditures, by defaulting on tax payments and by reallocating their labour away from abaca cultivation and towards construction work, mining, lumbering and cattle-ranching (which commonly implied migration) and towards the cultivation of other crops, including rice, maize and sweet potatoes. Susan Martin's paper on West Africa identifies a further important survival strategy for peasant communities heavily dependent on fragile external markets. This involved producers expanding cultivation (of ground-nuts, cocoa and palm-oil) in an attempt to compensate for declining export prices, although for some communities (as the author firmly emphasises) that option was restricted by the emergence of acute pressures on land and labour resources. She also draws attention to a longer-term, more radical response - in which rural communities began to direct their investment resources away from export agriculture and towards a primarily urban world of commerce, education and government employment. The second approach draws attention to the sharply varied impact of the depression as between different socio-economic classes in rural Africa and Asia. Norman Owen suggests that in Bikol the depression struck hardest at the smallholder, while (for a range of reasons) the wealthier landlords, tenants and the landless poor were either less vulnerable to market contraction or had the resources to mitigate its more severe consequences. Neil Charlesworth, concerned with Bombay Presidency, offers a contrasting insight: 'in the short term the depression severely afflicted the landlord and rich peasant [although] its more long-term and substantive impact was to weaken the ability of labourers and the poor to earn good wages'.

The final approach draws attention to the success of certain rural communities (defined by geographical location as much as by class) in sustaining an earlier pace of agricultural expansion through the crisis of the 1930s. This argument is pursued by Wolfgang Döpcke, as he explores the vigour with which the peasants in Chiweshe Reserve in colonial Zimbabwe, in contrast to communities elsewhere in the colony, fought to maintain their socio-economic position as produce markets disintegrated. An important extension of this argument is sketched in by Norman Owen but fully developed by David Anderson and David Throup. In Central Province, Kenya, the latter suggest, the Kikuyu did not simply maintain their socio-economic position through the crisis of the 1930s but used that crisis to increase their economic power at the expense of commercially and ecologically weaker neighbours. By the late 1930s they were sufficiently strong to challenge the privileged economic position of the white settlers. Thus for the Kikuyu the depression was not a disaster but an opportunity. It was indeed the midwife of Kikuyu capitalism.

This last approach offers a possibly radical new direction for research, taking enquiry still further from the deeply pessimistic generalisations referred to in the opening of this introduction. It is a direction which pays less attention to the consequences of the depression for the immediate material welfare of peasant producers but focuses instead on its impact on the structure of indigenous socio-economic power in rural Africa and Asia and on the balance of economic interest between the rural and urban world. It sees the depression not as a deeply tragic experience but as an intervention which permitted certain communities and classes to strengthen greatly their economic position, a process which had substantial implications for subsequent economic (and possibly political) change both in the rural districts and in the urban centres. And it might be noted that this new direction restores the inter-war depression as a major turning-point in the modern economic history of Africa and Asia, although for radically different reasons from those maintained by the now discarded orthodoxy.

NOTES

1 Gervase Clarence-Smith, Susan Martin, Peter Robb and Kaoru Sugihara each offered valuable comment on an earlier draft of this essay. The usual caveat applies.

2 See for example C.H. Lee, 'The effects of the depression on primary producing countries', *Journal of Contemporary History*, *4*, 4 (1969), pp.139-55; R. Thorp (ed), *Latin America in the 1930s: the role of the periphery in world crisis* (Macmillan, London, 1984); C. Baker, 'Debt and the depression in Madras, 1929-1936' in C. Dewey and A.G. Hopkins (eds), *The imperial impact: studies in the economic history of Africa and India* (Athlone Press, London, 1978), pp.233-42. This is an appropriate point to make reference to Christopher Baker's *An Indian rural economy 1880-1955: the Tamilnad countryside* (Oxford University Press, Delhi, 1984), which provides an extensive (and revisionist) consideration of

the impact (in all its aspects) of the depression on rural South India.

3 See for example I. Brown, 'Rural distress in Southeast Asia during the world depression of the early 1930s: a preliminary reexamination', *Journal of Asian Studies*, *45*, 5 (1986), pp.995-1025.

1

THE AGRARIAN ECONOMY OF CENTRAL PROVINCE, KENYA, 1918 TO 1939

DAVID ANDERSON AND DAVID THROUP

The rise and fall of the settler economy in Kenya between 1918 and 1939 reflected the extent to which white farmers had come to depend upon the export of their agricultural produce. In the buoyant markets of the 1920s, Kenya's white settlers could afford to be optimistic, bolstered by rising cereal prices and by the consolidation of coffee and sisal production. By the early 1930s their prosperity lay in tatters. Cereal farmers worked the soil as intensively as they could manage, yet even with heavy government subsidy few could make it pay. Sisal producers saw the value of their exports fall by nearly half during the course of 1931, while coffee planters watched a steady decline in market prices from the early months of 1930.[1] This crisis heralded the restructuring of Kenya's economy, as the colonial state struggled to balance revenue and expenditure. In broad terms, the frailty of the settler economy had been exposed, and in the process the comparative strength and stability of African production had been revealed. It was the African agricultural producer and tax-payer who carried the colonial state in Kenya through the crisis of the 1930s.[2]

This essay will examine the experience of the Kikuyu of Central Province, Kenya, during this crucial middle phase of colonial rule. Both in spatial and in economic terms the Kikuyu stood close to the heart of the settler farming economy. The Kikuyu Native Reserves were bounded on three sides by the major area of white farms, and lay close to the colony's commercial centre, Nairobi. Kikuyu labourers worked the settler coffee plantations and cereal farms, while Kikuyu squatters occupied European-owned lands throughout the White Highlands. Interlocked in this close relationship with European agricultural production, the Kikuyu economy was inevitably influenced by fluctuations in the economic fortunes of settler farming.[3]

However, many Kikuyu producers were better placed to weather the 1930s depression than were the heavily mortgaged settler farmers. At moments of economic crisis, there were distinct advantages in not being fully incorporated into the capitalist economy. Peasant cultivators could sell their produce at prices which the European producers found uneconomic, because production for the market was peripheral to peasants' subsistence requirements. Production and exchange within the African agrarian economy, as distinct from African economic activity linked directly to the settler farming sector, is therefore a critical dimension in understanding the Kikuyu experience during the world economic depression. The complex pattern of accumulation which had begun during the 1920s, stimulated by the internal dynamics of Kikuyu society, was sustained through the years of economic crisis. In the 1930s the Kikuyu continued to exploit local market opportunities, increasingly to diversify and expand their production of food crops, accumulate larger numbers of livestock, and take up the cultivation of lucrative cash crops. While not all Kikuyu families either on the settler farms or in the Reserves experienced the 1930s as a decade of prosperity, an underlying trend of growth and diversification is clear. By the late 1930s the Kikuyu were beginning to emerge into the modern capitalist economy, and were sufficiently strong to challenge the privileged economic position of the settler community. European and Kikuyu were on a collision course as they scrambled for land, lucrative cash crops, and the position of Kenya's first indigenous bourgeoisie. It was a conflict that was to be resolved only by the Mau Mau Emergency of the 1950s.[4]

DEPRESSION AND THE STATE

After the years of uncertainty and speculation before 1914, the settler community emerged from the first World War looking confidently towards a brighter and more secure future.[5] The war years had seen a move towards the more efficient working of European farms, and this economic advance was given further impetus by an influx of new settlers under the post-war Soldier Settlement Scheme. Despite the difficulties in the operation of this scheme, in particular the need for government to improve already very favourable terms in order to attract and retain new settlers, it was an important political signal to the European community; it indicated a commitment to white settlement that, prior to 1914, had seemed lacking.[6] The soldier settlers swelled the ranks of European landowners to 1,183 in 1920 and to 1,386 in 1922, although the depression of the early 1920s removed some of their number.[7] But the slump of 1921 to 1923 did more than reveal the vulnerability of the colony's more inexperienced and under-capitalised farmers; it also demonstrated the impact of world recession upon the colony's revenues. The budget deficits of those years, although they quickly gave way to a buoyant recovery, were a sign of things to come. Throughout the 1920s the colony's revenue, which doubled between 1922 and 1929, remained heavily dependent upon customs duties and upon the African Hut and Poll Tax. With customs duties accounting for approximately 30 per cent of revenue, the financial security of the colonial state was based upon the export of settler agricultural products and upon the settler communities' continuing ability to purchase imports. African producers were left to supply their own domestic markets, and to pay taxes for services that, by and large, were geared to develop export-orientated settler production.[8]

FIGURE 1: The Kikuyu Reserves and the White Highlands

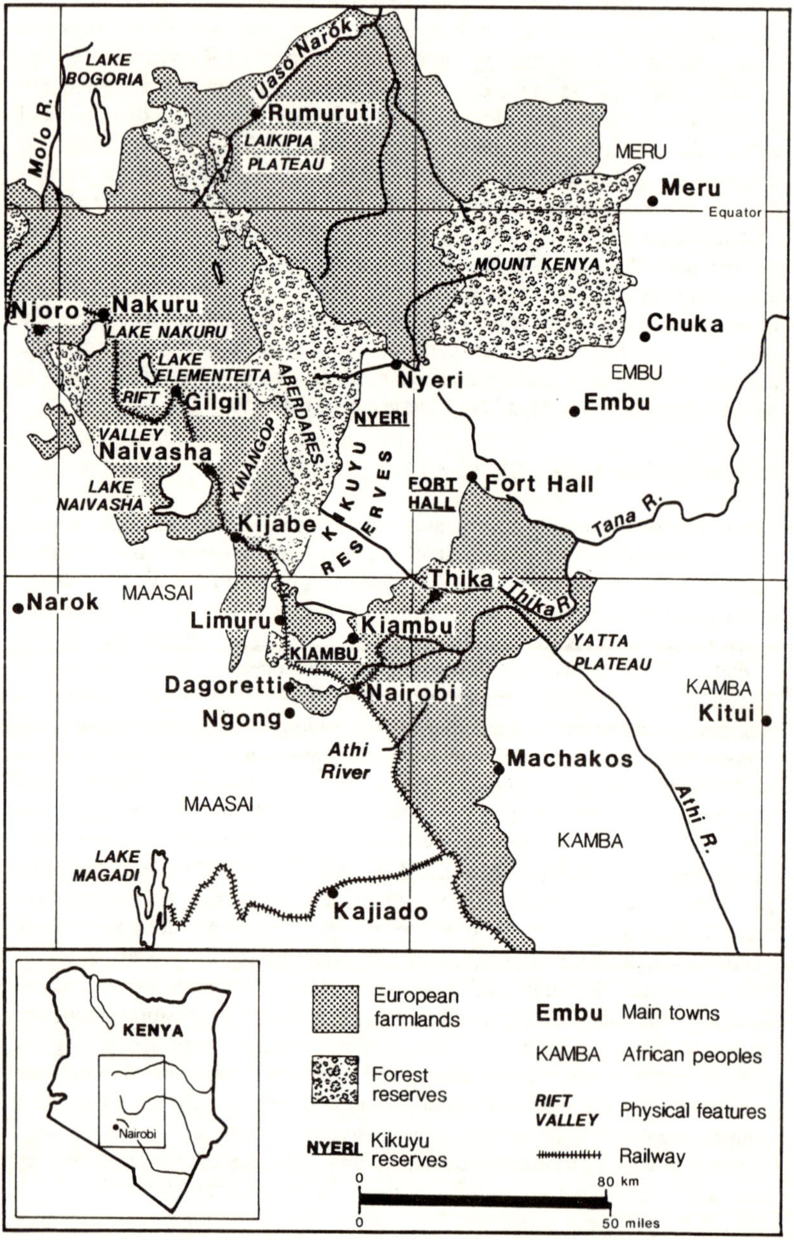

In the 1920s commitment to settler production was most clearly demonstrated in the willingness of the colonial state to assist in establishing the infrastructure required by settler farmers for the marketing of their crops. Between 1921 and 1933 the Kenya government raised loans totalling £17,205,600, mainly for construction of over 1,000 miles of railway line (necessary to link outlying farming areas to the coast) and the expansion of deep-water facilities at the port of Mombasa.[9] These constructions gave a considerable boost to settler production, but left the colony with a very heavy burden of debt. Interest charges on these loans amounted to over £1 million per annum by 1933, £226,000 being drawn from the general revenues (the remainder payable from the railways account). In the midst of economic recession, such high levels of debt repayment were to prove crippling.[10] The colony's high dependence upon customs duties, coupled with the substantial debts accumulated in the 1920s to develop the transport infrastructure, worked to accentuate the impact of the depression in the early 1930s. The slump in world trade from 1929 dragged Kenya into a fiscal crisis. Customs revenue fell from £949,724 in 1929 (28.47 per cent of total general revenue) to £581,770 in 1933 (18.63 per cent), and did not recover the 1929 level until 1939. With loan repayments to be met, the government had little choice but to adopt a policy of retrenchment. Government expenditure was cut from £3,505,073 in 1929 to £3,119,723 in 1932, but even this was not sufficient to prevent budget deficits in every year from 1929 to 1933. The basis of the 1920s boom, the construction of an infrastructure to assist settler exports, had become the burden of the 1930s. Significantly, the contribution of the African Hut and Poll Tax to the revenues was maintained at above £500,000 per annum throughout the years of depression.[11]

To Kenyan settlers, the revenue position of the colony was of less immediate significance than their own difficulties in raising credit to tide them over the depression. The prosperity of the 1920s had been achieved through the support of the state, and settlers looked to the same quarter for assistance in the darker days of the early 1930s. Always politically vocal, the settler community demanded from the government subsidies and loans. While the level of government investment in settler export production meant that this commitment could not be lightly tossed aside, further support for the settlers could be provided after 1929 only at the cost of an increasing budget deficit. If the Nairobi administration was inclined to this course, London certainly was not. The colony could not be run at a deficit, least of all a deficit incurred in order to ease the settlers through their difficulties.[12] All the same, the plight of the settler agricultural sector was indeed severe.

The storm of the depression came upon the European farmers out of a clear blue sky. The 1920s had witnessed the very rapid development of settler agriculture. Between 1918 and 1929 the number of European farmers almost doubled, climbing to over 2,000 on the eve of the depression. Where large tracts of the White Highlands had previously been in settler ownership without being farmed on a commercial basis, these lands were now placed under cultivation. The total area of European farmland under cultivation multiplied more than threefold during the 1920s. Coffee, sisal and cereals, mainly maize and wheat, were the basis of this expansion. Substantial planting of coffee had taken place during the first World War. By 1921 over 30,000 acres were under coffee; by 1929 over 90,000 acres. In the mid-1930s, half of Kenya's settler farmers grew coffee, with the coffee estates of Central Province accounting for two-thirds of the total coffee acreage.[13] Many fewer settlers were concerned with sisal, but the increase in production was comparably dramatic; from 30,396 acres in 1920 to over 100,000 acres in 1929, from which 15,000 tons were produced for export.[14] But the most startling developments were in cereal production. Cereals were the mainstay of settler prosperity in the 1920s. Farmers in the Rift Valley and in Western Kenya put ever larger areas under cereals as the construction of railways and roads opened up greater export opportunities. European farmers grew only 32,167 acres of maize in 1920. In 1929 that figure had climbed above 200,000 acres, from which more than one million bags of maize were produced.[15]

Inefficiencies in settler production, notably fluctuating and poor yields, were disguised between 1924 and 1929 by the generally high prices received for the colony's exports. Market prices for coffee, which represented almost half the total value of agricultural exports from the White Highlands, remained high throughout this period. Coffee exports were an average £951,585 per annum between 1924 and 1930, and in 1928 the average export price was over £5 per cwt. Sisal planters, who needed a price of above £25 per ton to produce at a profit, were realising £39 15s per ton in the early months of 1929.[16] But it was the high prices in the world cereal markets that brought particular confidence to Kenya's settlers. With maize fetching over 13 Kenya shillings per bag, f.o.b. Mombasa in 1929, few could have anticipated the dramatic fall which was to occur over the following few years. The impact of the 1929 slump was devastating. Export prices for maize were to fall to 8 Kenya shillings per bag in 1931, and to under 7 Kenya shillings in 1933.[17] In January 1930 sisal prices began to slide, and by December had fallen to £21 10s per ton, substantially below the Kenya planters' profit threshold. The fall continued in 1931, the year's average declared values on shipment from Mombasa being only £14 10s 10d. Kenya coffee was selling at £6 4s 0d per cwt early in 1930, but had slumped to £2 14s 0d by July. A partial recovery to £3 19s 11d per cwt in 1932 was followed by further falls in 1933 and 1934.[18] The total value of sisal, coffee and maize exports had reached a peak of approximately £2.5 million in 1930. In 1934 the combined value of these principal settler exports was less than £1 million.[19]

With many settlers already heavily mortgaged to the commercial banks, and with further credit curtailed by the slump, some form of government assistance was imperative if a rash of settler bankruptcies was to be averted. The financial aid offered by the government was less than the settlers had hoped, yet it represented a significant intervention. Cereal farmers, whose plight was the most serious, received refunds on grading, inspection and storage charges, and rebates on railway freight charges. Loan subsidies were granted on the 1929-30 cereals crop, and an Agricultural Advances Ordinance was rushed through in May 1930, releasing £100,000 for loan to the most needy farmers.[20] In a more far-reaching move, the government established a Land Bank, which began operations in July 1931 with an initial capital of £240,000. In 1933 a further £500,000 was added to its capital, and in 1936 another £250,000. This was loaned to farmers at an interest rate of 6.5 per cent per annum; many of the loans were made contingent upon the borrower moving away from cereal monoculture towards mixed farming. By the end of 1936, the Land Bank had assisted one in four of Kenya's settler farmers, with loans totalling £631,260.[21]

Reluctant though the Kenya government was to increase its budget deficit in order to bail out the settler farmers, the importance of settler exports to the revenues and the simple immediacy of the crisis compelled action. In the short term, at least, this action provided the settlers with the crutch they so badly needed. In the longer term, the colonial state had to consider a re-structuring of the economy that would avoid a repetition of this predicament. The high dependence upon customs duties for revenue meant that the colonial state could not completely relinquish its commitment to settler production, but the depression did demonstrate that certain sectors of the European farming economy were more of a liability than an asset. Established producers of high-value crops (such as coffee) were better able to survive these difficult years, and along with those settlers who moved into other plantation crops at this time, notably tea, they emerged at the end of the 1930s having proved their resilience and their worth.[22] The same could not be said of the majority of settler cereal farmers, or of those in marginal areas who had moved into coffee in response to the high prices of the late 1920s. Although fewer than 300 settlers were permanently forced off the land by the depression, many more were forced to abandon their farm temporarily during the worst years.[23] Cereal farmers in Nakuru and in parts of Western Kenya were most prominent among those absentees. Recovery from the depression came very slowly for these white farmers; indeed many continued to struggle until wartime subsidies brought them another period of prosperity built upon artificially high prices.[24]

This vulnerability was thrown into relief by the comparative success of African cereal producers over the same period. By the onset of the depression, it was becoming clear that the African cultivator could produce cereals more cheaply than the European farmer.[25] A realisation of the weakness of European cereal producers was implicit in the policies adopted by the colonial state in the depression; settlers were pushed away from cereal production into higher value plantation crops or towards a mixed regime of cereals and dairying, while the further expansion of African cereal production was encouraged. This marked the beginning of the re-structuring of the Kenya economy. When the first official encouragement to increased African cultivation was announced in 1930, amid settler demands for greater state support for their own agricultural production, the response of the European community was predictably hostile.[26] However African cultivators needed little encouragement from the colonial state to move down a road along which they were already travelling at some speed.

DEPRESSION AND THE KIKUYU AGRARIAN ECONOMY

With the fall in prices for the main settler crops, the Department of Agriculture was called upon to preserve the fiscal resources of the colonial state by encouraging increased African cultivation and exports. During the 1920s capitalist forces had penetrated deep into Kikuyuland, following the extension of the railway to Nyeri and the expansion of motor transport. As Gavin Kitching has shown, throughout the decade District Commissioners commented upon the expansion of peasant production and the diffusion of African-owned shops and itinerant traders in the Kikuyu Reserves. Despite the concentration of government assistance on settler production, by 1929 the foundation of Kikuyu cash-crop production had been laid. The onset of the depression compelled the colonial state to reassess its attitude towards African peasant cultivators, who now demonstrated a much greater ability than the settlers to withstand the collapse of commodity prices. Building upon the expansion of their agrarian economy in the 1920s, the Kikuyu were able in the 1930s to move into self-sustaining growth, at a time when their settler rivals were laid low.[27]

African subsistence producers were protected from the worst effects of the depression. Those who had been enticed into the capitalist economy, and had become migrant labourers in Nairobi or casual workers on settler farms, were less fortunate. European businessmen and farmers had first reduced wages, and when more drastic economies were required had dismissed many labourers. This contraction was greatest on the wheat farms and sisal plantations. The acreage under wheat declined each year, falling from 82,951 acres in 1928-9 to only 30,114 four years later. A similar contraction occurred in the sisal industry, and by 1932 planting had been virtually discontinued.[28] Initially the Kikuyu had responded to wage reductions by refusing to work on the settler farms, coffee estates or sisal plantations, in the expectation that this would compel the settlers to restore their wages. But as the depression deepened, these labour boycotts became increasingly ineffective. Labourers in Nairobi and on the European farms returned to the Reserves and, with few new employment opportunities outside, remained there. The number of Africans in wage employment fell in 1930, in 1931 and in 1932. There was little demand for coffee pickers, and even on the Kericho tea estates, which survived the depression relatively unscathed, the number of workers was reduced by 20 per cent between 1931 and 1933. Many sisal estates were forced to dismiss virtually their entire staff, and many coffee farms were reduced to maintenance levels.[29]

This was most serious for those African households which had come to rely upon wage labour to meet the annual demand for the Hut and Poll Tax. Payment of these taxes, and to a lesser extent the rates levied by Local Native Councils in the Reserves, was the greatest problem confronting most Kikuyu during the 1930s. Subsistence producers, although cushioned from the dislocations of the capitalist economy, could not easily evade these exactions. Colonial taxation had been the lever with which capitalist forces had prised open the Native Reserves, bringing even the remotest area into contact with imperial authority and economy. In the early 1930s most Kikuyu households could make up for the temporary loss of cash income from wage labour by selling surplus produce, and in this way meet their tax obligations. Those Africans who had little or no surplus, and in the lower-lying semi-arid regions of Meru, Embu, Machakos and Kitui there were many such people, had to sell their livestock, often at highly unfavourable prices.[30]

The years 1933 and 1934 were the most difficult for the African taxpayers of Central Province, for the contraction of the labour market was now compounded by adverse cropping seasons. The long rains of 1933 failed almost completely in South Nyeri, in Embu, and in Meru. In the four months from March to June, which were normally the wettest, less than five inches fell in Nyeri, the lowest figure ever recorded. This produced a complete failure of the local peasant grain crops, and of the coffee harvest on the European farms in neighbouring North Nyeri. The latter removed an important source of additional income in coffee picking. The long drought and the low prices for agricultural produce created a severe slump in local trade. Indian merchants and shopkeepers were forced to close, and the District Administration found it extremely difficult to collect taxes.[31] The colonial government, however, could not afford to grant the widespread remissions from tax that would normally have been allowed in conditions of drought and local crop failure. With the fiscal crisis of the colonial state at its most severe in these years, the revenue from African taxation was the crucial component in the colony's strategy for survival. African tax payments were the only reliable ballast left on board as the colonial state lurched its way through the storm. Quite simply, Africans had to be compelled to pay whatever they could. If they failed to pay, their property was seized. During 1933 the District Court in South Nyeri heard 143 cases for non-payment of taxes; in the same period still larger numbers were prosecuted before Native Tribunals. Between October and December 1933, there were on average 90 people held in the local detention camp for failure to pay tax. The great majority were from the central areas of South Nyeri, around Tambaya, where the effects of the drought had been most severe and where the peasantry had been able to survive only by spending their tax money on food from neighbouring districts. All the same, the District Administration gave considerable energy to tax collection, and managed to secure 517,219 shillings during 1933, a shortfall of only 6,500 on the previous year. This was the unacceptable face of colonialism.[32]

While the contraction of the settler economy squeezed those Kikuyu who were employed in the European farming sector, this fall in cash income was offset by the continued expansion of African agricultural production in the Kikuyu Reserves. Although the total value of exports from all the African Reserves fell over the early 1930s, from £543,240 in 1929 to £355,500 in 1933, this ignores the significant growth of the internal market - given its impetus by local crop failures and droughts - and disguises the fact that the fall in exports was due almost entirely to a decline in the trade in hides and skins from the pastoralist Reserves. Valued at £307,000 in 1929, hides and skins then accounted for 56 per cent of African export earnings. By 1933 the value of this trade had fallen by half, and now accounted for less than 40 per cent of African exports. Most of the commodities exported from the African Reserves had held their total value over this period, which of course meant that they had increased considerably in volume. The Kikuyu were, therefore, producing and exporting more crops during the depression, while they also engaged in the 'unofficial' local marketing of surplus produce.[33]

The continued expansion of the Kikuyu agrarian economy during the 1930s is clearly illustrated by the increased export of a new cash crop, wattle. Earnings from wattle provided many of the emerging proto-capitalists in Kikuyuland with the financial resources to take full advantage of the economic opportunities arising in this period. The export of wattle bark and extract, for use in the manufacture of tanning, was dominated in Kenya by the multi-national company Forrestal. Cultivation had begun in the Kikuyu Reserves during the 1920s, and for Kikuyu households then expanding into a network of economic activities linked to agrarian production, it held many attractions. As a tree crop, wattle required little attention after the initial effort of planting, and was therefore an ideal crop for the families of those engaged in wage labour. Wattle provided not only cash income but also fuel and building materials; and it could be planted on steep or eroded hillsides where other crops would not grow. It was even encouraged by the Department of Agriculture, who argued that it helped to reduce erosion and to replenish the nitrogen content of the soil. The Department's extension services offered advice to potential cultivators to establish the crop.[34]

Although wattle was not a high-value crop like tea or coffee, which were monopolised by European planters, it did enable the Kikuyu peasantry to generate additional income without disrupting their agricultural cycle, and at the same time use land on which subsistence crops could not be cultivated. Earnings from wattle increased dramatically over the worst years of the depression, rising from £35,000 in 1929 to £79,500 in 1932. The cultivation of this new African export crop was concentrated in the higher areas of Kikuyuland and Embu, but its impact was undoubtedly most marked in Kiambu. By 1933, the value of dried wattle bark exported from that district had increased to £10,000 from £2,000 the previous year. In the three Kikuyu districts of Nyeri, Muranga and Kiambu the quantity of wattle passing through official inspection centres increased by 700 per cent during the course of 1933.

In 1929 only 62 tons had been railed from Muranga Town; in 1937 nearly 12,000 tons passed through that station, worth £25,000. In 1935 the total wattle acreage over Kikuyuland increased by approximately one-half, to 100,000 acres.[35]

In supporting the expansion of wattle cultivation, the government was deliberately fostering African production of export crops. It was hoped that this would generate additional income in the Reserves, and thus facilitate the payment of the Hut and Poll Tax; it would also subsidise the shipment of settler-grown maize and other low-value bulky exports. The settler option still dominated the policies of the colonial state, but the longer-term benefits to the African peasant were clear. It was the cultivation of this new crop that enabled many Kikuyu households to emerge from the depression relatively unscathed, having kept open 'the peasant option'.[36]

The government also encouraged the expansion of African food production. Food shortages in some parts of the colony during the late 1920s had made famine relief measures necessary, and it was in order to avoid further claims of this sort upon the over-stretched financial resources of the colonial state that the Department of Agriculture and the Local Native Council farms began experimenting with drought-resistant crops and higher yielding strains. The new seeds were distributed to African farmers. This drive for local self-sufficiency in food also led the government to pay greater attention to the husbandry and land-use methods employed in the African Reserves. In the drought-hit regions of South Nyeri and Embu the government pushed ahead with a scheme to reclaim and drain areas of swampland. The Chiefs and Local Native Councils were mobilised to support this project, and eight miles of drains were cut by compulsory labour in two months. Chiefs Murigo and Kareithi in South Nyeri forced 100 people to work each day for six weeks on reclaiming 2,000 acres of potentially rich land in a densely populated area hit by the drought. Crops grown on these reclaimed lands, combined with wattle exports, enabled that district to survive until the long rains of 1934, when the grain stores were replenished.[37]

The expansion and improvement of African agrarian production was viewed with pleasure by District Administrators preoccupied with local self-sufficiency and the need to maintain the level of tax payments; and it was welcomed by the Department of Agriculture, which extended its activities more deeply into the Kikuyu Reserves in the 1930s than ever before. But the settlers still held a monopoly on the high-value cash crops, such as Arabica coffee. The Official Mind in Whitehall and in the Nairobi Secretariat deemed it essential, for political and strategic reasons, to sustain 'the White Man's Country' in Kenya; but the attractions of stimulating additional African revenue by establishing a high-value cash crop in the Reserves were all too obvious. The Kenya government toyed with the idea, and then elected to break the settler monopoly on coffee production, although not without retaining strict controls on African production. Africans in areas adjacent to the main European estates in Kiambu were not to be encouraged to grow coffee. Instead, coffee was to be planted in the fertile but remote, and economically under-exploited, Reserves of Meru, Embu, and Kitui. However, settler political influence effectively prevented even those distant tentative proposals from getting off the ground, and the African area under coffee remained less than 100 acres. Yet the principle of a settler monopoly on coffee production had been undermined, and this was of considerable significance for the future of both African and European agriculture. The official willingness to develop the African agricultural sector reflected the need to broaden the fiscal base of the state, and was indicative of a loss of confidence in the ability of settler production to secure the colony's revenue in the future.[38]

In Central Province, and elsewhere, the government's support for the African agrarian economy became increasingly apparent in the 1930s. The Department of Agriculture strove to improve the quality of African produce and to ensure that African producers secured a premium price on the London market. Under the Crop Production and Live Stock Ordinance of 1929, the marketing of ground-nuts, wattle, simsim and maize was controlled. The three Kikuyu Local Native Councils attempted to increase African production, and they erected stores and appointed buying agents to operate the new regulations. A new system of inspection and grading (by the buying agent) produced a marked improvement in the quality of the maize exported from Kikuyuland. African maize growers were encouraged to select only white seed for planting, which produced a better-quality crop suitable for export. In South Nyanza, for example, all produce had to be passed by official inspectors before it was declared suitable for sale outside the district. Initially the inspection system had been introduced for ground-nuts, maize, simsim and beans, but later it was also applied to other produce. During 1932 special attention was given to the improvement of wattle bark. Badly prepared and immature bark was rejected, with the result that the reputation of 'East African fair average quality' increased considerably.[39]

In 1935 these controls were institutionalised under the Marketing of Native Produce Ordinance. In Central Province, wattle, maize, beans and potatoes were brought under closer supervision, and in Nyanza the inspection service now covered maize, beans, ground-nuts and sesame. The various effects of the new ordinance on African entrepreneurs were contradictory. Itinerant traders and middlemen were squeezed as the settler-controlled Kenya Farmers' Association and Forrestal (the wattle extract multinational) established, with official encouragement, a virtual monopoly on transactions at the gazetted market centres. In contrast, peasant cultivators benefited from the improved prices now secured on the international market as the quality of African-grown wattle and maize improved and was standardised. By 1935, for example, the American market quotation for Kenya wattle bark was equal to that for Natal bark; two years earlier the latter had enjoyed a premium of between twenty and thirty Kenya shillings per ton. The cost of the inspection services, which had secured this transformation, was equivalent to only thirty cents per ton.[40]

These efforts to improve the quality of African production had less relevance for the domestic market. There the Kikuyu were able to take advantage of market opportunities without the direct assistance of government. Ecological adversity had a greater impact upon the African domestic economy during the 1930s than international economic recession. A series of natural disasters affected many parts of Kenya from the mid-1920s to the mid-1930s, with widespread drought in 1927-9, 1931 and 1933, and visitations of locusts in each year from 1928 to 1931. While the neighbouring lowland pastoralist areas of the Rift Valley and Ukambani were severely hit by these droughts and plagues, only certain parts of the Kikuyu areas in Central Province were badly affected. While their neighbours suffered, the Kikuyu agriculturalists, by and large, escaped. A district administrator in Kikuyuland noted in 1931 that ' the general prosperity of the natives of the Reserves has not decreased to the extent that one might expect'.[41] The Kikuyu peasants had only limited financial resources, of course, but the expanding trade in wattle and the opening up of new areas for cultivation had partly offset this. Moreover, the succession of droughts in the pastoral areas surrounding Central Province between 1926 and 1936 had the effect of lowering the price of cattle, sheep and goats in those areas. The terms of trade between the agricultural Kikuyu and their pastoralist neighbours had moved decisively in favour of the former. The pastoralists' hardship was a Kikuyu opportunity.[42]

Official figures on livestock numbers and trade are notoriously unreliable in Kenya, invariably under-estimating the reality; but even these indicate a significant trend. During 1928, with the Kamba area in the grip of drought, there was a substantial increase in the number of livestock entering Murangu from Ukambani - 9,242 cattle and 43,723 sheep and goats according to the official figures. Many more entered illegally without the necessary veterinary permits. The Kamba were desperate to acquire money to buy food, and livestock prices thus dropped dramatically. Heifers which in 1927 had been worth 100 shillings a head, fetched only 30 during the worst months of May and June 1928. Bullocks fell from 60 to 20 shillings a head; and goats from 25 to 4 shillings. This collapse in the price of imported livestock had important repercussions in Central Province, for it enabled households to liquidate any long-standing debts in livestock at a fraction of the original exchange, much to the dissatisfaction of their creditors. The money price of goats in 1931, for example, was less than one-third the price in 1915. Ties of obligation and dependence were thus undermined; and those with a surplus could acquire additional land and wives, to increase the inequalities within Kikuyu society.[43]

African societies had always taken advantage of their neighbours' crises. Indeed, the structure of Kikuyu society, with its age grades and lineage ties related to ownership of and access to land, was designed not only to minimise the risks of economic and social dislocation during the periodic famines which afflicted pre-colonial Africa but also to exploit the opportunities created by social dislocation. Famines were highly localised; consequently disaster in one area might compel one sub-clan (*mbari*) to cast off its dependent clients, yet be the stimulus for another, perhaps only 20 miles away, to construct a new system of obligations and dependence, and on favourable terms.[44] The penetration of the market simply transformed this process of exploitation into new, capitalist, modes. The transport revolution expanded economic exploitation into more distant provinces. Rich peasants with a surplus over subsistence requirements could now transport maize, sweet potatoes and other food crops to the lower, more arid, parts of Kiambu and to the Rift Valley in the early 1930s; and to Embu and Ukambani during the droughts later in the decade and during the second World War. Thus, they were able to maximise the return on their crops. Indeed, as exposure to the vagaries of the market grew, a Kikuyu form of 'futures speculation' emerged. Peasants in Muranga or Nyeri would sell their maize reserves to benefit from high famine prices in a neighbouring district, in anticipation that when they later turned to the market to meet their own deficiencies, the price would have fallen as supplies became available from the White Highlands or from Nyanza, areas remote from the famine. As one District Commissioner lamented, the economic rationale of these Kikuyu speculators was impeccable. Capitalising upon the greater ecological security of production in Central Province, the Kikuyu peasant elite played the market with considerable success.[45]

The Kikuyu were particularly well placed to take advantage of these shifting terms of exchange because of their extensive contacts on the European farms in the White Highlands. Before 1918, Kikuyu families had been enticed to these farms by promises of as much land as they required for cultivation and grazing. In the first two decades of European settlement, the settler farming community had lacked the financial resources to work more than a small fraction of their land. Nor could they pay the high wages that would attract Africans into the migrant labour market. Money was a scarce resource; land was not. Enterprising Kikuyu, once their frontiers in Kiambu and Nyeri had been frozen by European tea and coffee plantations and by European stock ranches, began to expand to the west from where the colonialists had expelled the Maasai. The White Highlands were not simply opened for European settlement but also provided a new frontier for Kikuyu expansion. In the 1920s, however, this Kikuyu 'El Dorado' had begun to disintegrate.[46] European farmers had now accumulated sufficient capital to work their farms more intensively. Many had invested in expensive herds of pure-bred or high-grade dairy or beef cattle. The Kikuyu squatters, with their large plots and diseased herds, had ceased to be an asset and were now a dangerous threat. The incidence of rinderpest and East Coast fever increased, as more European farmers abandoned their scrub stock for new dairy herds which were highly susceptible to African livestock diseases. By the late 1920s a confrontation between the 2,000 white farmers and their 200,000 Kikuyu squatters appeared inevitable.[47]

These pressures evaporated with the onset of the depression. Kikuyu squatters in the three main European dairy and stock farming areas, Naivasha, Nakuru and the Aberdares, were granted a reprieve. During this, the Kikuyu diaspora, like the Kikuyu in Central Province, seized the opportunity to increase their cultivation and to evade the restrictions which the settlers had placed on their ownership of livestock. As we have shown, many European farmers, over-capitalised and with 8 per cent mortgages from the commercial banks, were unable to continue farming; they temporarily abandoned their estates, much to the benefit of the squatters who continued to use the land, now free from settler control.[48] The contraction in European agriculture enabled the Kikuyu squatters, who had been producing primarily to satisfy their family subsistence requirements, to increase cultivation and to keep more sheep and goats. Despite the low price of maize, which had fallen to four shillings per 200 lb bag in 1931 and 1932, and of other crops such as potatoes and vegetables, squatters could still make a profit selling surplus produce. Their overheads were even lower than those of Kikuyu in Central Province. Although prices were at an uneconomic level for settler farmers, they did not prevent Kikuyu subsistence producers from expanding cultivation or from increasingly entering the market economy, to supply Nairobi and Nakuru with vegetables and grain.[49]

The cultivation of food crops - increasingly for the market rather than for household subsistence - dominated the agricultural cycle of most Kikuyu peasant households in Central Province and in the Rift Valley. As the 1930s progressed, market forces penetrated deeply into these peasant societies, a process facilitated by the increasing mileage of road and the increasing number of lorries operating in the Reserves. As land became a scarce resource, because of increasing population and expanded cultivation, the reciprocal obligations of 'tribal' life began to disintegrate, especially among the Kikuyu. Dependent labourers, *ahoi* and *ndungata*, became as great a hindrance to the emerging proto-capitalists among the Kikuyu in Central Province as the squatters were to the more prosperous European farmers. Both proto-capitalists and farmers, who were struggling to become Kenya's first local bourgeoisie, appreciated that the economic rewards of capitalist relations were being diminished by these earlier ties of economic clientage. Before the first World War the mechanisms which had attracted dependent labour had been extremely useful; but as Kenya emerged from the depression and the rewards of individualism became evident, such dependants were now an economic liability, a remnant from an earlier era.[50] Increased production for the market provided the financial resources for some peasants to expand their landholdings, and to increase their cultivation of other crops by hiring labourers from among poorer neighbours who were being squeezed. The reciprocal ties of obligation to the marginal lineages of the sub-clan were weakened, and *ahoi*, *athoni* and *ndungata* dependants were transformed into wage labourers, to work on the plots of the emerging Kikuyu commercial farmers. During the depression this process of social differentiation, which had just begun, gathered momentum. The expansion of wattle cultivation in the early 1930s had been the vital first stage in the emergence of Kikuyu proto-capitalists. Although depressed commodity prices had prevented the accumulation of sufficient capital to secure a major advance in Kikuyu entrepreneurship, the future 'big men' of Kikuyu society had prepared the essential foundation for further development.[51]

One index of Kikuyu prosperity was the increasing breakdown of the traditional order under the pressure of entrepreneurs and proto-capitalists, as reflected in the incidence of litigation over land in the Native Tribunals. The burden on the courts increased throughout the early 1930s.[52] Moreover, the locust infestations and the droughts hastened the process of social differentiation within African, and particularly Kikuyu society. Rich peasants with surplus resources were not only able to survive: they also laid the foundation for further expansion. Famine in the pastoral reserves enabled Kikuyu cultivators to exchange surplus food for livestock on very favourable terms; and this subsequently enabled them to acquire more wives and household labour and thus increase cultivation even further.[53] These 'big men' were able to acquire even more land from their poor neighbours, who were desperate for money to pay taxes, school fees and their other financial obligations to the colonial state. The government encountered considerable hostility whenever it attempted to restrict Kikuyu entrepreneurs from taking advantage of high famine prices. Interference with the free market (under the 1929 Foodstuffs Ordinance) became a popular target of criticism for the Kikuyu Central Association, the fledgling political organisation which voiced the discontent of those itinerant traders and emerging commercial farmers who were not allied to the favoured elite around the chiefs and their clients.[54]

CONCLUSION

The depression had a profound impact upon settler agriculture. It contributed to a major restructuring of the economy as, encouraged by the Land Bank, European farmers began to diversify from a maize monoculture into mixed farming, to build up their herds of high-grade livestock, and to concentrate upon the production of high-value crops. These changes deeply affected the Kikuyu agrarian economy, increasing not only the conflict between Kikuyu squatters and settler farmers in the White Highlands but also that between Kikuyu in the Reserves. They enabled peasant farmers in Central Province to become the dominant producers of maize for the domestic market, and to expand their cultivation of cash crops, such as wattle, which could easily be integrated into the household labour cycle. The damaging impact of the depression upon the Kikuyu agrarian economy was, therefore, offset by the internal dynamics of local African trade and exchange. In particular, the drought-prone areas of neighbouring Ukambani, Embu and Meru gave Kikuyu entrepreneurs a market for their surplus produce, and thus the resources to invest in increased cultivation. The dynamic of the domestic economy is crucial to our understanding of the Kikuyu experience during the inter-war years.

The expansion of the 1930s was based upon: the foundations laid in the 1920s when more land had been brought under cultivation in the high bracken zone; the opportunities created in the early 1930s by the collapse of European agricultural competition and by the attempts of the Department of Agriculture to increase peasant production (in order to finance the colonial state and to subsidise the settler economy); and the opportunities opened for the Kikuyu 'big men' by the droughts and locust infestations of the early 1930s, which so disrupted food production in the neighbouring Reserves. Kikuyu society was already becoming highly differentiated by the 1930s; consequently a wide range of strategies was available to African entrepreneurs, the 'big men' or 'proto-capitalists' of Central Province.

At first sight it may appear as if most Kikuyu were running hard to stand still during the depression. However, the evolving pattern of accumulation in Kikuyuland was founded upon a longer trend of agrarian expansion, which had emerged in the 1920s, was sustained in the 1930s, and in the 1940s and 1950s was to lead to political, and ultimately violent conflict with the European settlers. The depression was a crucial period, marking the emergence not only of a mounting confrontation with the settlers over their privileged economic position within the colonial state (a conflict which was to culminate in Mau Mau 20 years later), but also of a series of internal conflicts within Kikuyu society; conflicts between proto-capitalists and poor peasants; between marginal lineages and their dependants; and between the established African elite, who had already secured the rewards of political and economic incorporation into the colonial state, and their opponents who were knocking on the door. When their efforts to secure admission were rebuffed, after the second World War, these men, the proto-capitalists who had seized the opportunities offered by the depression, were to turn to Kenyatta and the Kenya African Union. The poor peasants' rebellion, Mau Mau, provided them with a battering ram that would enable them to replace the settlers as the dominant capitalist force in independent Kenya. The depression of the 1930s not only witnessed their birth, but could be said to have been the midwife of Kikuyu capitalism.

APPENDIX 1: European agricultural production in Kenya, 1920-38

	a	b	c	d	e	f	g	h	i	j	k	l
				Coffee			Sisal			Maize		
	No. of European farmers	Acreage occupied	Acreage cultivated	Acres	Prod. (cwt)	Exports (value £)	Acres	Prod. (tons)	Exports (value £)	Acres	Prod. (200lb bags)	Exports (value £)
1920	1,183	3,157,440	176,209	27,813	71,970		30,396	5,124		32,167	317,525	
1921	1,346	3,333,106	206,959	33,813	89,889		31,050	6,191		30,846	164,722	
1922	1,386	3,804,158	234,055	43,359	52,965		37,118	4,677		57,131	338,837	
1923	1,466	3,985,371	274,319	52,249	93,357	491,416	39,625	6,924	236,044	74,747	517,877	249,545
1924	1,715	4,443,180	346,988	60,054	144,952	799,420	45,223	8,454	396,777	108,556	833,640	381,144
1925	1,695	4,420,573	392,628	65,140	115,530	723,180	35,610	11,091	531,129	129,647	893,108	424,528
1926	1,809	4,587,817	463,854	68,950	153,729	747,453	60,197	13,026	579,499	155,751	926,614	318,652
1927	1,901	4,737,920	512,543	74,562	151,545	1,140,459	71,213	15,006	468,974	177,987	1,314,643	544,323
1928	1,971	4,996,406	592,741	84,073	246,292	1,119,894	91,909	14,737	495,959	177,009	1,088,706	354,768
1929	2,035	5,000,648	635,590	90,205	136,371	703,158	109,375	15,809	553,572	204,945	1,099,317	326,660
1930	2,097	5,111,161	643,644	96,042	233,086	1,427,536	138,012	17,321	437,269	233,973	1,858,586	586,851
1931	2,106	5,389,965	659,380	96,689	277,725	986,988	137,299	18,858	232,564	200,926	1,649,728	425,041
1932	2,107	5,119,093	613,557	98,874	180,915	1,214,392	145,660	14,674	186,575	160,546	762,622	119,133
1933	2,102	5,206,264	593,988	100,387	317,914	832,353	139,834	17,369	249,868	164,018	1,139,616	218,514
1934	2,027	5,138,324	556,182	102,023	268,335	493,343	141,495	20,127	311,371	112,949	746,893	130,509
1935						934,923			423,112			204,967
1936	1,807	4,580,029	502,497	101,234	435,296	969,804	128,565	32,185	690,459	117,848	1,011,863	254,087
1937						732,684			673,719			228,068
1938	1,890	5,053,448	546,602	93,772	328,986	767,789	166,517	31,817	436,259	113,103	968,076	289,212

Sources: Columns **a, b, c, d, e, g, h, j, k**: *Kenya Colony Agricultural Census*, 1919-34, 1936, 1938. Columns **f, i, l**: compiled from *Dept of Agriculture Annual Report*, 1938, *Kenya Colony Agricultural Census*, 1934, and *Kenya Colony Annual Report*, 1927 and 1929.

NOTES

1 *Kenya Colony A[nnual] R[eport]*, 1930 and 1931, pp.16-17 and 19-31 respectively. *Kenya Colony Agricultural Census, 1934*, appendix 2, p.49, presents a table of the approximate values and quantities of agricultural exports between 1929 and 1933. C.C. Wrigley, 'Kenya: the patterns of economic life, 1902-45' in V. Harlow and E.M. Chilver (eds), *History of East Africa* (Clarendon Press, Oxford, 1965), pp.239-60, remains a valuable study of the period. See also E.A. Brett, *Colonialism and underdevelopment in East Africa: the politics of economic change, 1919-39* (Heinemann, London, 1973), ch.6; and for an important recent revision, J.M. Lonsdale, 'The depression and the second World War in the transformation of Kenya' in D. Killingray and R. Rathbone (eds), *Africa and the second World War*, (Macmillan, London, 1986), pp.97-142.

2 This essay develops part of the argument set out in D.M. Anderson and D.W. Throup, 'Africans and agricultural production in colonial Kenya: the myth of the War as a watershed', *Journal of African History, 26* ,4, (1985), pp.327-45. Much valuable information on African production in Kenya during the inter-war period has been collected and analysed by G. Kitching, *Class and economic change in Kenya: the making of an African petite-bourgeoisie, 1905-1970* (Yale University Press, New Haven, 1980). Another important recent study is P. Mosley, *The settler economies: studies in the economic history of Kenya and Southern Rhodesia 1900-1963* (Cambridge University Press, Cambridge, 1983).

3 J.M. Lonsdale, 'The depression and the second World War', pp.97-119. On Kikuyu labour and squatters, see R.M.A. Van Zwanenberg, *Colonial capitalism and labour in Kenya, 1919-39* (East African Literature Bureau, Kampala, 1975), especially ch.8; S. Stichter, *Migrant labour in Kenya: capitalism and African response, 1895-1975* (Longman, London, 1982), chs.3 and 4; T. Kanogo, *Squatters and the roots of Mau Mau* (James Currey, London, 1987), *passim.*

4 For a fuller examination, see D.W. Throup, 'The origins of Mau Mau', *African Affairs, 84*, 336 (1985), pp.399-434; for an overview of the mounting pressures on land-use in the 1930s, see D.M. Anderson, 'Depression, dust bowl, demography and drought: the colonial state and soil conservation in East Africa during the 1930s', *African Affairs, 83*, 332 (1984), pp.321-44.

5 For the first World War and settler farming, see J.D. Overton, 'War and economic development: settlers in Kenya 1914-18', *Journal of African History, 27*, 1 (1986), pp.79-103.

6 C.C. Wrigley, 'Kenya: the patterns', pp.232-9.

7 *Kenya Colony Agricultural Census*, 1927, Table 1.

8 For colonial revenue and expenditure, see *Kenya Colony AR*, 1922-39, and E.A.Brett,*Colonialism and underdevelopment* pp.143-7. The commitment to export-orientated settler production was maintained despite the difficulties in securing reliable markets for settler produce. For the example of the livestock industry, see I.R.G. Spencer, 'Pastoralism and colonial policy in Kenya, 1895-1929' in R.I. Rotberg (ed), *Imperialism, colonialism and hunger: East Central Africa* (Lexington Books, D.C. Heath, Lexington, Mass., 1983), pp.113-40.

9 C.C. Wrigley, 'Kenya: the patterns', pp.239-41; E.A. Brett, *Colonialism and underdevelopment*, pp.145-6 and 199-202; *Kenya Colony AR*, 1933, p.48, for the loan position of the Colony at the end of 1933. Also S. Constantine, *The making of British colonial development policy, 1914-1940* (Frank Cass, London, 1984), *passim.*

10 J.M. Lonsdale, 'The depression and the second World War', pp.104-5; E.A. Brett, *Colonialism and underdevelopment*, p.146.

11 *Kenya Colony AR*, 1929-39.

12 For example, see the *Report of the Economic Development Committee, 1934* (Government Printer, Nairobi, 1935), especially pp.168-70.

13 This expansion is documented in the *Kenya Colony Agricultural Census, 1920-9*. A summary of these statistics, along with others for the 1930s, is presented as Appendix 1. On the expansion of coffee planting prior to 1920, see J.D. Overton, 'War and economic development', pp.91-7. 'Register of Coffee Estates, 1st January 1936', K[enya] N[ational] A[rchives], Agricultural Department 85/935, provides details of all European coffee growers.

14 *Kenya Colony Agricultural Census, 1922* and *1929*; *Kenya Colony AR*, 1929, p.35.

15 *Kenya Colony Agricultural Census, 1920* and *1929*; *Kenya Colony AR*, 1929, pp.30-3. Wheat production also increased very substantially between 1924 and 1929; but in 1929 there was a shift away from wheat towards maize and barley, primarily due to difficulties in developing a rust-resistant wheat.

16 *Kenya Colony AR*, 1926,1927,1929 and 1930, pp.17-21, 36-8, 28-37 and 17 respectively; N.J. Westcott, 'The East African sisal industry, 1929-1949: the marketing of a colonial commodity during the depression and the war', *Journal of African History, 25*, 4 (1984), pp.445-61.

17 P. Mosley, *The settler economies*, Table 3.6b, pp.94-5; *Kenya Colony AR*, 1930, pp. 13-14; V. Liversage, 'Official economic management in Kenya, 1930-45', typescript, Rhodes House Library, Mss.Afr.s.510. For detailed surveys of the crisis of European maize production, see *Dept of Agriculture Annual Reports, 1929-36.*

18 For sisal, see *Kenya Colony AR*, 1930 and 1931, pp.17 and 30 respectively. For coffee, *Kenya Colony AR*, 1930, 1931 and 1934, p.16, p.30 and p.26 respectively.

19 Calculated from the approximate values of exports given in the *Kenya Colony Agricultural Census, 1930* and *1934*. Figures in Appendix 1.

20 *Kenya Colony AR*, 1930, pp.6-8; C.C. Wrigley, 'Kenya: the patterns', pp.247-9.

21 *Kenya Colony AR*, 1936, p.44; P. Mosley, *The settler economies*, pp.178-80.

22 Tea was the great success of the 1930s. Production in 1928 was only 33,403 lb, but by 1934 had climbed to over 3 million lb. Pyrethrum also emerged in the late 1930s as an important export crop. *Kenya Colony Agricultural Census, 1928-34, 1936, 1938.*

23 J.M. Lonsdale, 'The depression and the second World War', p.103, citing M. Salvadori, *La colonisation européenne au Kenya* (Larose, Paris, 1938). Settlers who left their farms took whatever temporary work they could find. Some 600 Europeans were employed in the Kakamega goldfields at the peak of production in 1935. See H. Fearn, 'The gold-mining era in Kenya colony', *Journal of Tropical Geography, 11* (1958), pp.43-58.

24 V. Liversage, 'Official economic management', chs 3 and 4, deals with the forms of assistance offered to cereal farmers, notably the controls on maize marketing instituted through the Kenya Farmers' Association (KFA). See also P. Mosley, 'Protecting the "core" of the settler economy: pricing and marketing policies for wheat, maize and dairy products, 1929-52', paper presented to the conference on the 'Political Economy of Kenya Colony 1929-52', Trinity College, Cambridge, 1975. On the important divisions between cereal farmers and planters among the settlers, see P. Mosley, *The settler economies*, ch.5. On the wartime settler boom, see I.R.G. Spencer, 'Settler dominance, agricultural production and the second World War in Kenya', *Journal of African History, 21*, 4 (1980), pp.497-514; but also, D.M. Anderson and D.W. Throup, 'Africans and agricultural production', *passim.*

25 G. Kitching, *Class and economic change*, pp.33-56; P. Mosley, *The settler economies*, ch.3.

26 'Greater production in Kenya: government campaign in the Native Reserves', *East African Weekly*, 26 November 1931; D.M. Anderson and D.W. Throup, 'Africans and agricultural production', *passim.*

27 *Native Affairs Dept AR, 1929*, pp.38-40; 'Kiambu AR 1929', pp.8-9 and 15, KNA DC/KBU 1/22; 'Fort Hall AR, 1929', pp.16-17 and Appendix xvii, KNA DC/FH 1/8; G. Kitching, *Class and economic change*, pp.33-9 and 156-69.

28 *Dept of Agriculture AR, 1932*, pp.24-34.

29 S. Stichter, *Migrant labour in Kenya*, pp.94-6; *Native Affairs Dept AR, 1932* and *1933*, pp.54-5 and 126-8 respectively; *Dept of Agriculture AR, 1933*, pp.18-21.

30 *Native Affairs Dept AR, 1933*, p.144; 'South Nyeri AR, 1933', pp.2-4 and 30-3, and 'South Nyeri AR, 1934', pp.3-4 and 36-7, KNA DC/NYI 1/3.

31 'South Nyeri AR, 1933', pp.2-7, and 'South Nyeri AR, 1934', pp.3-6 and 34-7, KNA DC/NYI 1/3; 'Fort Hall AR, 1934', pp.25 and 45-6, KNA DC/FH 1/13.

32 'South Nyeri AR, 1933', pp.2-4 and 26-33, KNA DC/NYI 1/3.

33 For estimated values of agricultural exports of African origin over the years 1928 to 1933, see *Kenya Colony AR*, 1933, p.17. G. Kitching, *Class and economic change*, pp.62-73, outlines the expansion of Kikuyu production over the 1930s.

34 M. Cowen, 'Capital and household production: the case of wattle in Kenya's Central Province, 1903-64', unpublished PhD thesis, University of Cambridge, 1979, especially pp.44-7; G. Kitching, *Class and economic change*, pp.62-7; Senior Agricultural Officer, Central Province to Assistant Agricultural Officers, 26 June 1944, 'Wattle rules and marketing, 1942-46', KNA Agri.4/220.

35 *Native Affairs Dept AR, 1933* and *1935*, pp.48-9 and pp.58 and 100 respectively; 'Central Province AR, 1937', pp.57-60, KNA PC/CP 4/3/1; 'Fort Hall AR, 1929', appendix xviii, KNA DC/FH 1/8; *Dept of Agriculture AR, 1933*, p.99. During 1933 the tonnage of wattle passing through the inspection centres in Central Province increased as follows:

	1932	1933
South Nyeri	80 tons	1,584 tons
Muranga	159 tons	2,315 tons
Kiambu	564 tons	2,557 tons
Total	803 tons	6,456 tons

36 *Dept of Agriculture AR, 1933*, pp.3, 21 and 82-6.

37 *Dept of Agriculture AR, 1933*, pp.84 and 98-101; 'South Nyeri AR, 1933', pp.5-7 and 'South Nyeri AR, 1934', pp.3-4, KNA DC/NYI 1/3; 'Kikuyu and Akamba Provinces AR, 1933', pp.638-9, KNA PC/CP 4/1/2.

38 *Dept of Agriculture AR, 1934*, p.84; *Native Affairs Dept AR, 1935*, p.105; 'Central Province AR, 1935', p.46, KNA PC/CP 4/3/1.

39 *Dept of Agriculture AR, 1932, 1933* and *1935*, pp.64-5, 69, 73-4, and pp.82-3 and pp.81-2 respectively; *Native Affairs Dept AR, 1931* and *1932*, pp.46-8 and pp.55-6 respectively; I.D. Talbott, 'Agricultural innovation and policy changes in Kenya in the 1930s', unpublished PhD thesis, University of West Virginia, 1976, summarised in G. Kitching, *Class and economic change*, pp.100-4.

40 *Dept of Agriculture AR, 1935*, p.81.

41 'Fort Hall AR, 1931', p.4, KNA DC/FH 1/10. Prices of food crops in the domestic market of Central Province and its neighbouring areas show enormous fluctuations throughout the 1930s, primarily correlated with variations in local climate and ecology. District reports and correspondence files are littered with references to these fluctuations. G. Kitching, *Class and economic change*, pp.70-3, has provided a summary of a sample from Kikuyuland.

42 G. Kitching, ibid., pp.217-23.

43 'Fort Hall AR, 1929', pp.2-3, KNA DC/FH 1/8. For data on livestock prices, see P. Dalleo, 'Trade and pastoralism: economic factors in the history of the Somali of N.E. Kenya, 1895-1948', unpublished PhD thesis, Syracuse University, 1975; R.D. Waller, 'Uneconomic growth: the livestock economy of the Maasai 1914-29', paper presented to the conference on the 'Political Economy of Kenya Colony 1929-52', Trinity College, Cambridge, 1975.

44 P. Rogers, 'The British and the Kikuyu, 1890-1905', *Journal of African History, 20*, 2 (1979), pp.262-5.

45 For food shortages and Kikuyu marketing opportunism in the drought of 1927-9, see 'Food Control Ordinance 1929', minute by Eastwood, 11 April 1929, P[ublic] R[ecords] O[ffice], Kew, CO 533/384/2; and *Kenya Colony AR*, 1929, pp.28-9. On similar practices during the 1943 food shortage, see D.M. Anderson and D.W. Throup, 'Africans and agricultural production', pp.337-42; and 'Machakos AR, 1943', pp.1-3, KNA DC/MKS 1/1/29.

46 T. Kanogo, *Squatters and the roots of Mau Mau, passim.*

47 Ibid. and also T. Kanogo, 'The Kikuyu squatter phenomenon in the Nakuru District of the Rift Valley', History Staff Seminar Paper, University of Nairobi, May 1977.

48 *Dept of Agriculture AR, 1932* and *1933*, pp.7-9 and 8-9 respectively. The removal of squatters and their livestock from the White Highlands was a prominent political issue throughout the 1930s. The settlers finally gained the political power to expel unwanted squatters in 1937. D.M. Anderson and D.W. Throup, 'Africans and agricultural production', pp.332-3. See also R.M.A. Van Zwanenberg, *Colonial capitalism and labour*, pp.259-67.

49 T. Kanogo, *Squatters and the roots of Mau Mau, passim*; D.W. Throup, *The economic and social origins of Mau Mau* (James Currey, London, 1987), ch.5.

50 Ibid; and G. Kitching, *Class and economic change*, pp.282-97.

51 J.M. Lonsdale, 'The depression and the second World War', p.109; 'Fort Hall AR, 1935', pp.6-7, KNA DC/FH 1/14; 'South Nyeri AR, 1933', pp.4-5, KNA DC/NYI 1/3; M. Cowen, 'Capital and household production', pp.68-74. *Kenya Land Commission: Evidence and Memoranda* (Government Printer, Nairobi, 1934), vol.1, contains considerable material on the agrarian economy of Kikuyuland in the early 1930s; see especially pp.971-1039, S.H. Fazan, 'An economic survey of the Kikuyu Reserves'.

52 'Fort Hall AR, 1929-39', KNA DC/FH 1/8 to 1/18; 'South Nyeri AR, 1931-8', KNA DC/NYI 1/3; 'Kiambu AR, 1929-39', KNA DC/KBU 1/22 to 1/30.

53 G. Kitching, *Class and economic change*, pp.218-26.

54 D.W. Throup, *The economic and social origins of Mau Mau*, ch.7.

2

'MAGOMO'S MAIZE': STATE AND PEASANTS DURING THE DEPRESSION IN COLONIAL ZIMBABWE

WOLFGANG DÖPCKE

INTRODUCTION[1]

Interpretations of the impact of the Great Depression on peasant societies at the periphery of the world economy divide into two broad approaches. One line of thought stresses the destructive impact of world market forces, exacerbated by the policies of the colonial state, on the reproduction of peasant societies. C. Coquery-Vidrovitch identifies the Depression as a major turning-point in the underdevelopment of African peasantries in the French colonial empire. Rapidly deteriorating terms-of-trade, rural impoverishment and increased fiscal repression, led to intensified social differentiation and the disintegration of the remaining 'traditional' social relations.[2] Whereas in Coquery-Vidrovitch's analysis, the Great Depression served as the agent for structural change in peasant societies, in Scott's work on South-East Asian peasantries, the 1930s saw the culmination of a long-term destruction of pre-colonial society and ethics. 'The depression delivered the coup de grâce to an agrarian order already weakened by structural changes well before 1930'.[3]

In contrast, a second body of literature points to the successful struggle of peasant societies against the threat directed at their mode of existence by the breakdown of the international and local economies during the crisis. The contributions on West Africa and Kenya in this volume show the strength of peasant societies, their flexibility, room for manoeuvre and their survival techniques during a period of severely worsening terms of participation in produce markets.

The dominant interpretations of peasants' experience in southern Africa, and specifically in colonial Zimbabwe, clearly fall into the first category. A major school of thought suggests a periodisation of the peasant history of southern Africa in which an initial peasant prosperity in the early phase of white colonisation was superseded by destruction and 'delayed proletarianisation' of peasant societies. From the enforcement of state-aided white agricultural settlement, the peasants were fighting a losing battle against the settler societies.[4]

The period of the Great Depression has a prominent place in this approach: it saw the final collapse of peasant viability in the face of increased white protectionist policies.

> By the end of the 1930s, the agricultural economy of the Shona and Ndebele, like that of the Kikuyu and most South African peoples, had been destroyed. The struggle between the European farmer seeking to reduce the African to a proletarian and the African seeking to retain the maximum amount of economic independence had been won exclusively by the Europeans.[5]

These provocative sentences initiated a debate which provides the background to this paper.[6] But it is not an attempt to contribute to the full width of that debate: for this paper considers only a small section of Zimbabwean society, the peasants in Chiweshe Reserve, and only part of their experience during the 1930s.

This paper focuses on a marketing scheme for African-grown maize ('Magomo's maize') which Major Wane, the Native Commissioner for Mazoe District, established in Chiweshe Reserve to counteract the adverse impact of the depression. In the 'Prologue' the Africans voice their grievances over the rapidly deteriorating terms of exchange with the capitalist markets. From this descriptive part the paper moves on to an analysis of the growth of peasant production in Chiweshe Reserve up to the depression. In 'Motives', the reasons for the establishment of state-controlled marketing for African maize producers are discussed. While the Africans' interest in better terms of participation in the produce market seems obvious, the motivation of the representatives of the state necessitates a more complex explanation. In this part 'Magomo's maize' is set in a wider context, and is analysed against the background of a conservative 'roll-back' which aimed at restructuring the colonial mode of control in the Reserves. Consequently the paper assesses the impact of Wane's scheme on the peasantry of Chiweshe. In 'Conclusions' the possibility of generalisation from this case study is discussed.

PROLOGUE

As the Native Board meeting progressed, the crowd of 300 to 400 Africans became what the Native Commissioner of Mazoe District, Major Wane, later described as 'somewhat unruly'. During his 30 years of service in the Southern Rhodesian Native Affairs Department he had never 'heard Natives so strongly or so openly display such a spirit of antagonism to any law as they did to the Maize Control Act and the Cattle Levy Act'.[7]

This Native Board meeting in 1934 saw the culmination of African protest against the price they received for their maize, and the conditions of sale they were forced to accept in Chiweshe Reserve in the 1930s. The protest began in 1931 when the price of African-produced maize dropped. The Maize Control Act, which regulated maize marketing in the colony, was passed in that year, and its impact was clearly reflected at the Native Board meeting in Chiweshe Reserve a year later:

> Marufu asked why it was that no white man except traders were allowed to buy mealies [maize] in the reserve. He said that formerly many farmers in the Umvukwes used to come and buy mealies for money but last year they did not do so in any numbers; consequently they had to sell their mealies to the traders who gave them very little for them and would only buy generally for goods and not for cash.[8]

Major Wane's attempts to persuade traders to buy African grain for cash had had little impact. Joseph Gusha, whom the Native Commissioner labelled the representative of the 'more advanced people', and who later became an outspoken advocate of African capitalism, linked the absence of buyers other than traders to Maize Control:

> He thought it [Maize Control] was a very bad thing for them as they were not in a position to send their mealies away in big lots like the white farmers and had to take goods not money for their mealies.[9]

Wane's reply was cynical and contrary to his own convictions:

> [He] said that the Government had made this Maize Control to try and make the price of mealies better . . . That probably if it had not been for what the Government had done they would not have been able to get even as much as they did last year.[10]

The truth was that as trade turned into barter, they received hardly anything in terms of cash. The Board remained hostile and voted unanimously, with 3,000 people silently watching: 'That Maize Control was a bad thing for them'.[11]

The same year a modification to the original Act slightly eased the situation. Farmers and ranchers were now allowed to buy part of their requirements directly from the African peasants. Wane praised this minor change as a major achievement of the Native Boards. But the Africans' position in the grain market did not alter substantially. They turned their anger against the store-keepers, the most visible agents of unequal exchange.

Headman Musarara believed it would be of great benefit to the Natives if

> Jews and other storekeepers in the Reserve were to be expelled therefrom and Government-controlled stores established instead, as existing stores charged exorbitant prices and were otherwise a constant source of irritation to the natives.[12]

Storekeepers were accused of assaulting women and forcing them to barter. Joseph Gusha connected the several local half-caste children to Jewish trading enterprises in the Reserve, knowing well that Wane shared his attitude towards rural traders. As a remedy, Wane suggested a co-operative store.

At the 1934 meeting Maize Control dominated the Board's agenda. Wane had the thankless task of explaining both the amendment to the 1931 Maize Control Act and the new Cattle Levy Act. Both meant a further deterioration in the Africans' economic position. Marafu:

> Why does the Government do everything to help the white farmer and nothing to help us? Even the white farmer's dogs can ride in motorcars and are better treated than we are. The Government is killing us by this Act which we do not understand . . . It is put on us by force.[13]

The open antagonism forced Wane to act. He appointed an agent at Rosa, a small central village on the main road in the Reserve, to buy African-grown maize. Wane was able to offer an initial cash payment of 4 shillings per bag, which in his view was a big improvement on the barter terms offered by the 'Jewish' storekeepers. This system of state-marketing was expanded over the next five years and also introduced into the Bindura and Shamva Subdistricts under Wane's supervision. As a consequence, most of the traders were forced to pay cash again. The Africans applauded and requested that the scheme be extended to the more distant parts of the Reserve and to other crops. Amidst great acclamation from about 2,000 people, the Board unanimously approved a resolution proposed by Headman Ndazambo and seconded by Chief Makope:

> It is the desire of this meeting that the Native Commissioner make arrangements to take over the entire grain and nuts crop of the Reserve, and that a store of a co-operative nature be started so that we will no longer be forced to pay big prices to the Jews who rob us and take our women.[14]

Wane tried to meet both demands. Consequently Maize Control came to be seen by the Africans in a very different light. 'Magomo's maize', as the scheme was called, became part of the historical tradition in Chiweshe, and marked a turning point for the Africans in their relations to the institutions of the state.[15]

FIGURE 1: Mazoe District in the 1930s

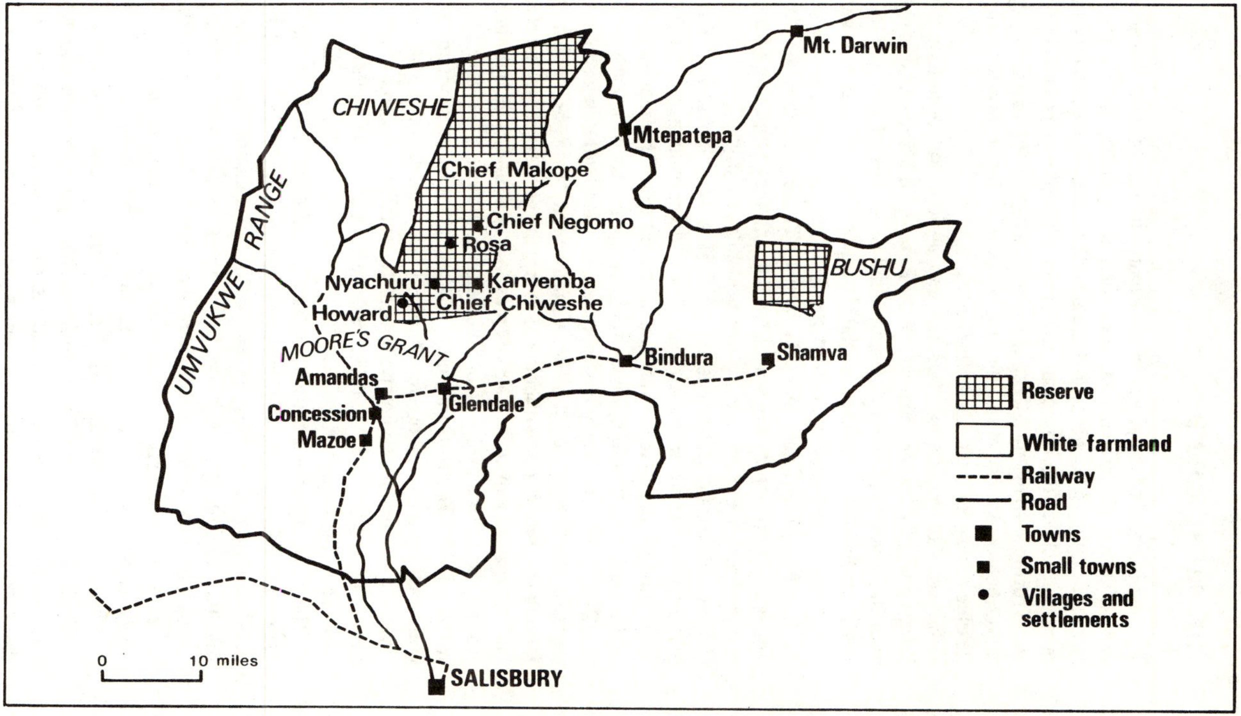

THE BACKGROUND

The involvement of the peasantry of that area in the agricultural market is a long story of a struggle to sustain and reinforce their position, in the face of threats from the capitalist economy and the colonial state. The peasantry suffered the same setbacks as the European farmers in times of economic decline, but they were further adversely affected by state support for capitalist agriculture. Nevertheless African peasants in Chiweshe Reserve proved competent and flexible in responding to these challenges.

In terms of population, acreage and agricultural production, Chiweshe Reserve was by far the most important Reserve in Mazoe District. Compared with the other Reserves in colonial Zimbabwe, it had a favourable physical environment. The absolute rainfall is higher and its long-term variability is lower than in most other African areas. Most soils in the Reserve consist of moderate shallow sands to sandy loams. These soils are easy to work and inherently fertile, but they very soon demand the restoration of their organic components under a regime of permanent cultivation.[16]

Colonial peasantisation depended on the activities of nascent white capitalism in the region. There are indications of an early peasant market production when local Africans began to convert their 'normal surplus' from domestic production into a market commodity, for example by trading with the early prospectors in the District.[17] This early barter trade was completely dislocated, as in other parts of the Colony, by the first *Chimurenga* of 1896-7 and its aftermath. During this first major anti-colonial rising, the greater part of the Ndebele state and the majority of the Shona peoples fought a bitter - though unsuccessful - war to liberate themselves from the colonial intruders. As a result of the war, mining in the District, the main market for peasant production, collapsed completely and did not revive for some years. Not only did demand slump, but production was shattered by rinderpest, the retaliatory scorched earth policy of the settler forces, and the forced resettlement of Africans into larger villages away from the kopjes.[18]

The recovery of African market production coincided with the first serious attempts by Europeans at commercial farming in the area. Also the trading network changed. In 1907 the Native Commissioner of South Mazoe observed that 'the old trading days, where kaffir stores were noticed at most of the large kraals, seem to be an institution of the past'.[19] Thus although the Africans were able to raise their agricultural output again to pre-*Chimurenga* levels, they now had to carry their grain long distances to find a market.

The revival seems to have affected only a limited number of African producers. Tenants on European farms, being near to the markets, 'copied the farmers' and produced far beyond their own consumption requirements. In many cases they were able to sustain a great economic and social independence from their landlords, selling crops and beer and rejecting labour demands. A few sold 100 to 200 bags of maize a season and employed casual wage labour. Thus here the social organisation of production changed. As there was no change in technology, higher outputs depended on additional labour inputs, apart from that provided by the family. These entrepreneurs produced in exactly the same manner as the mass of the cultivators. No plough was in use, and they tried to select the most fertile patches of soil (presumably the rich *vleis* [*dambos*]), as did the rest of the peasantry. Thus they were able to achieve, under a regime of land abundance and shifting cultivation, very high yields per land unit.[20]

But the further expansion of this emergent group of African commercial farmers, as well as the mass of the peasantry, was inhibited by the rapidly growing competition from white farmers, and the disturbance and uncertainty caused by racial land apportionment. When the first white farmers moved into Mazoe Valley in 1901 they had to compete with the Africans for a very limited market: a few mines, the Doctor, the Police Camp, Post Office officials and one store.[21] After a second wave of immigration in 1905-8 and then a further increase in numbers after the railway was built in 1912, the Europeans rapidly pushed most Africans out of the market. In 1910 the Native Commissioner observed:

> The farmers are in too great competition with them [Africans] and grow everything that the mines require. Beans, monkey-nuts, and everything that the Natives used to supply and even kaffir tobacco made up in ball or cone in correct native style.[22]

Apart from white competition, the delimitation of Reserves and the first removals of tenants from 'private' lands created an insecurity among the peasants which reinforced the stagnation in market production. This stagnation is most evident from the relatively constant figures for acreage planted throughout the first decade of the twentieth century (Table 1).

White agricultural capital gained a temporary victory, but the peasantry, instead of being turned into a proletariat, recovered and initiated a second phase of market production. The three preconditions for this revival were: the recovery in the numbers of cattle following the *Chimurenga*, the Rinderpest and East Coast Fever outbreaks which led to a structural shift in livestock holdings from goats to cattle; the increased security in land tenure *within* the boundaries of the Reserve; and the expansion of markets within the capitalist centre of the colony and the growth of a marketing network.

TABLE 1: African agriculture in Mazoe District

Year	Population	No. of male taxpayers	No. of cattle	No. of goats	Acreage under production	Production (in bags)	Yield per acre (bags)	No. of ploughs	Traded maize (in bags)
[a] 1901-05	9,241		723	2,962	4,082	20,178	4.9	0	
[a] 1906-10	10,798		1,766	5,849	5,816	23,267	4.0	2	
[a] 1911-15	11,659		6,242	7,799	11,600	37,400	3.2	14	
[a] 1916-20		4,189	12,656	9,244	21,313	58,785	2.7	41	
1924		3,352	16,199	6,100	43,300	133,300	3.0	498	25,000
1928		4,098	20,359	7,800	61,700	123,750	2.0	1,810	14,000
1932		4,401	16,916	10,020	82,000	165,000	2.0	2,866	48,679
1936		5,636	22,185	14,690	83,400	138,412	1.7	4,875	36,472
1938		5,951	24,267	15,848	98,394	157,460	1.6	5,710	50,426

[a] Average

Source: Mazoe District, Annual Reports 1901-38; CNC, Annual Reports 1901-38; Report of the Native Production and Marketing Branch 1946. On traded maize, additionally: S 622 (1925), NC Mazoe to CNC, 29 December 1925; Maize Control Board, Annual Reports. These last figures tend to underestimate the amount of grain actually traded.

TABLE 2: Productivity in African agriculture in Mazoe District

Year	Yield per capita (bags)	Yield per taxpayer (bags)	Yield per capita (calculated by dividing yield per taxpayer by 3.5	5.0)
1902	1.3			
1911	2.0			
1921		29	8.3	5.8
1925		43	12.3	8.6
1929		38	10.9	7.6
1933		35	10.0	7.0
1937		27	7.7	5.4

Source: See Table 1. The divisions by 3.5 and 5.0 reflect different estimates of family size.

From about 1913 the African peasants increased their acreage under cultivation, a trend which was still evident in the late 1930s. Shifting cultivation was the major land-use technique. Although the Reserve was slowly settled by the trickle of evicted tenants from white farms, it was still sparsely populated in the early 1920s.[23] But the few favourable plots were soon taken up, often by commercially oriented ex-tenants, and most peasants had to farm increasingly marginal lands. This, together with the gradual impoverishment of the soil, contributed to declining yields per acre in the long run.

The widespread adoption of the ox-drawn plough (see Table 1) was the primary means of extending acreage. Consequently the traditional hoe (*chifengu*) declined in importance. Ploughs were first used by tenants on European farms, but from about the late 1910s this innovation spread into the Reserve, the first impulse coming from evicted tenants. The initial suspicion and opposition from older Africans was quickly overcome and the number of ploughs rose from 2 in 1910 to more than 2,000 in 1929.[24] Ploughs are a labour-saving device; they were clearly adopted in order to extend the cultivated acreage with a given supply of labour, rather than being adopted as a reaction to labour shortages due to migration.[25] With the help of the plough, the few heavy red soils came under cultivation and the fields became concentrated near the homesteads.[26] The resulting increase in agricultural output per capita is clearly shown in Table 2. Another aspect of agricultural change was the growing dominance of maize as both a subsistence and a cash crop. Although in pre-colonial times (yellow) maize had had a certain importance, in the first decade of the twentieth century *rukweza* (millet) was still the staple crop. At first maize expanded as a cash crop, but it gradually developed as a dietary staple, having some advantages here over millet.[27] By making the cash crop the staple diet, peasants were able to combine security-oriented subsistence agriculture with market production. Nevertheless, agricultural change was characterised mainly by extension rather than by intensification of production.

By the mid-1920s the peasants in Chiweshe Reserve were on a secure footing. They produced enough food for themselves as well as a substantial surplus to satisfy the demands of the state and of the capitalist economy. As Major Wane put it: 'They are successful according to their own way of thinking',[28] and they displayed great economic independence in the face of colonialism. Their way of life often proved too great an attraction for the foreign workers on the white farms, and caused farmers to write desperate letters to the Native Commissioner:

> They entice our farm boys over there [Kanyemba's village] and now instead of drunken boys over the weekends only (which is quite bed [*sic*] enough) they are now in a muddled state most of the week, coming past the house at 2 or 3 a.m. singing and shouting.[29]

Selling beer to farmworkers was an important source of money income for the peasants, much to the displeasure of nearby farmers. The women especially made money that way.

> I have caught them [women selling beer] once . . . and given them a thrashing, they revenge themselves by setting the veld alight, when they know I am not about.[30]

Beer brewing and selling was not checked by the Native Commissioners and 'became a business throughout the whole Reserve to the extent that the Reserve is nothing more nor less than a brewery'.[31] Apart from selling to outside people, there was also a large trade, especially in cattle, taking place among the Africans within the Reserve.

Reacting to the growing peasant prosperity in Chiweshe Reserve, an increasing number of traders (mostly from European minorities) attempted to open stores in the area. In 1929 there were eight stores in the Reserve, most of them in the southern part, and a further six at the Reserve's boundary, on adjacent farms. The Native Commissioner rejected many such applications because he feared 'overtrading'.[32] In addition, numerous itinerant traders entered the Reserve to trade grain for cash or cattle during harvest time; and many neighbouring farmers acquired their maize supplies from local Africans. The highly competitive trading conditions and the generous credit facilities the traders granted their African customers for purchases of agricultural implements, were an expression of the traders' high expectations for the future of peasant production. Buying ploughs and other implements on credit and on the security of future crops was very common, in particular among rich peasants.[33] It left the traders with an extensive network of debtors throughout the Reserve. In 1929 Mrs Borrer, a farmer and trader, was trying hard to collect debts, all of which should have been paid in grain, in 13 villages. In Kanyemba's village alone, peopled owed her £200. Mr Marufu, the son of the outspoken critic of white traders at the Native Board meeting, recalls that Mrs Borrer supplied an ox-cart 'from England' to his father against future crops. But the story has mellowed in his memory. In truth Mr Marufu senior attempted to avoid settling his debts, and Mrs Borrer filed a court order against him in order to 'frighten the Native into paying his debts'.[34] It was common for Africans to become indebted to more than one trader, which led to a rush for their crops by their various creditors. Mr Marufu, for example, bought ten mules (because the East Coast Fever restrictions prohibited all cattle transport) together with a Mr Gideon for their joint transport business: the mules were bought from another trader, Mr Smith in Avondale, also on credit.[35]

The general peasant prosperity interacted with growing regional and social differentiation. Successful peasant production was concentrated, owing to favourable physical features and accessibility, in the southern part of the Reserve. The vast majority of peasants produced enough for subsistence and state demands, but some individuals accumulated land, cattle, implements and presumably money. Mr Marufu senior was not only heavily in debt, but also one of the richest peasants in the area. The headmen of Gweshe, Nyashuru, Shutu and other villages in the southern part of the Reserve sold substantial amounts of grain each year, often more than 100 bags. At Nyashuru, immigrant Xhosas emerged as rich peasants. Rural accumulators often invested in transport (ox-carts) and sold these services to fellow peasants.[36] Not only the traditional accumulators (headmen, heads of clans) but also the new social group of salaried employees, invested heavily in agriculture and cattle. 'Native Messenger' Marawanyika was able to offer 100 bags of maize at 7s 6d each to a trader in 1927; and Joseph Gusha, before his retirement as Head Messenger in 1928, was busily selling grain to traders. In 1928 the first African opened a butchery in the Reserve.[37] But social differentiation did not radically transform the mode of production: rich peasants did not employ wage labour. They mobilised additional labour through an extensive use of *nhimbe* (the communal work party), called *hoka* in this part of Zimbabwe. Reciprocal communal labour in exchange for beer and food was widespread until the 1940s. It enabled the rich peasants to farm (and particularly to harvest) extensive acreages, simultaneously guaranteeing survival to poor peasants without adequate labour, cattle or implements. Communal work parties concentrated on Fridays, when the Spirit Mediums disallowed all other agricultural work. Thus accumulation took place in a 'spirit of communalism', where the same social institution served both the rich and the poor. An explicit consciousness of antagonistic differentiation did not take root in this period. Rich people had certain, albeit limited, obligations towards their poor neighbours, and 'the poor were ready to help the rich'.[38]

Prosperous peasant production was clearly reflected in the relationship of Africans in the District to the capitalist labour market. During the early phase of colonial rule many men were forced into migrant labour (*Chibaro*). In 1905, 1,725 Africans from Mazoe District applied for 'passes' to leave in search of work.[39] But although chiefs and headmen had to act as recruiting agents, the peasants were substantially able to retreat from the labour market. Only some of the young unmarried men migrated for work, usually for a period of up to three months, which fitted neatly into the agricultural cycle. Even this very selective integration into the capitalist labour market became more rare in the late 1920s. In early 1930 it was observed that 'very few of the natives of this reserve [Chiweshe] appear to go out to work. The kraals are full of young men'.[40] As a result of the local opposition to wage labour, most of the labour on the farms and mines in the District came from Nyasaland and Portuguese East Africa (Mozambique). In 1921, 19,500 *male* African foreigners lived in the District; the total local population was just 12,400.[41]

By the end of the 1920s the peasantry in Chiweshe Reserve had established itself very successfully. But its prosperity and independence came under severe pressure in the 1930s, as the Great Depression hit Southern Rhodesia. The depression occurred there not as a single event but as a series of blows, as demand for the various commodities which linked the colony to the capitalist centres collapsed. In 1928 the short-lived tobacco boom came to an abrupt end. This was followed in late 1929 by a sudden fall in demand and price for Southern Rhodesia's mineral exports, which was accompanied by a drop in the internal and external prices for maize and cattle. The total value of the colony's exports fell by one-third from 1929, and did not reach pre-depression levels again until 1936. The full impact of the depression in Southern Rhodesia was initially delayed by the Northern Rhodesia copper mines construction boom. And after 1931, the impact of declining world markets was weakened when Southern Rhodesia followed Britain off the Gold Standard, causing gold prices to soar. Yet the depression, although its impact was mitigated in Southern Rhodesia, still brought a serious slump in economic activities, falls in commodity prices, unemployment and destitution. But it did not affect everyone alike. Capital, although adversely affected, was in a position to use the depression to create more favourable conditions for accumulation, and it was generally able to overcome the crisis within a short period. Most peasants and workers suffered much longer: real wages were kept below pre-depression levels until the end of the second World War.[42]

For the peasants in Chiweshe, the depression abruptly ended their prosperity. The world market slump was transmitted to them through the agents of a white-dominated, colonial economy which gave the depression in Chiweshe Reserve, as in other rural African areas, its particular political expression. The crisis was first felt as a sudden demonetisation of exchange with the white rural traders. The favourable trade conditions Africans enjoyed during the late 1920s were reversed. Traders collectively turned to barter when they sought African-produced grain. Africans, formerly able to take advantage of competition among traders, now found themselves trapped: 'The Native has had the choice of accepting a few yards of limbo or having his mealies left on his hands'.[43]

The trade value of grain dropped considerably. From the early 1930s goods worth 2s 9d or 3s were offered for a bag of maize, whereas formerly Africans realised around 8s in cash. Cheating and 'profiteering' by traders during these transactions further aggravated African ill-feeling.[44] The Africans in Chiweshe Reserve were acutely conscious of their vulnerable socio-economic position and of the threat the crisis posed to it. 'Natives depend on maize for tax and dip fees; if price reduced he would be compelled to go to seek work on farms as an ordinary worker'.[45]

Demonetisation and adverse exchange hit especially hard those rich peasants who were indebted to the traders. Their room for manoeuvre was suddenly curtailed when all traders turned to barter, yet still insisted on debt repayment in cash. Thus Mr Marufu's harsh attacks on the traders. But not only he was desperate; so was Mrs Borrer:

> If the natives do not pay up by July there is nothing else for me to do but hand over my books to the firm I am indebted to on behalf of the natives. . . Last year we spent £1000 from the farm crops in trying to straighten things up.[46]

Now she was on the verge of bankruptcy, and other traders did not fare better, rather worse, having no farm income on which to draw. When African purchasing power dropped in the 1930s, traders came under pressure not only from the forces of the market and their capitalist superiors (the wholesalers), but also from state manipulations of the economy. Here they suffered along with the Africans.[47]

It was the passage of the Maize Control Act (MCA) in 1931 and the resulting unpredictability of profits from the maize trade which was the traders' main justification for turning to barter in Chiweshe, and in the rest of the country. Some even withdrew from maize transactions completely. Maize control was an attempt by the politically dominant white farmers to off-load the crisis onto the Africans and the consumers of maize. They had been asking the government to control the maize market from 1924, when it had become evident that maize surpluses could be exported only at a price lower than the local one. After the export price for Southern Rhodesian maize dropped from 10s to 4s 3d a bag in 1930, the Rhodesia Agricultural Union committed itself fully to the maize issue and entered politics to press for Maize Control. The outcome was the Maize Control Act of 1931. The Act established a fixed buying and selling price for maize in those parts of the Colony which came under control, with the Maize Control Board (MCB) as the sole agent there for all maize transactions. Within the controlled areas, consumers paid a price above the export price and losses on exports were borne proportionately by all producers. But the Act did not produce the desired results, and much dispute arose. The 1934 Amendment tried to satisfy conflicting interests. It introduced two maize marketing pools (the local pool and the export pool), with a sliding scale for white participation in them. The larger white growers had a progressively smaller percentage of their maize delivered to the more profitable local pool; the smaller farmers were allowed to deliver up to 80 per cent of their maize to the local pool. But the different pools were really only what the Assistant Chief Native Commissioner, Bullock, called a 'system of fictions', a means of allocating different prices to individual growers.[48]

The system became even more clearly fictitious when applied to African growers. Traders in African-grown maize were restricted to the less profitable export pool. But of course most African maize never left its district, let alone going into export. It was resold by the traders on what the Act called 'cross entry plus payment basis'. This meant that the Africans had to sell their maize below the export price, and that the Maize Control Board earned a substantial 'rake-off', roughly the difference between the export price and the local pool price.

Although in theory the 1931 Act put African and white growers on the same footing, its impact on African maize producers was very destructive. The Act gave the traders a sudden monopoly in most areas, at least for a period. The difference between controlled and excluded districts, often adjoining, was marked. While in Rusape, Africans received only 3s for their maize during 1931, in neighbouring Umtali, 7s 6d was paid per bag. Direct delivery to one of the Board's depots, an option which in theory guaranteed the same price as Europeans received, was in practice restricted to a dwindling minority. Most Africans could not afford to buy bags, transport their crop to the depot, cope with the paperwork involved, and wait for payment which would be months later.[49] The 1934 Amendment made the situation even worse, and extended control to the whole colony. It contained openly pro-settler regulations whereas the old Act was discriminatory only in practice. As the traders were now excluded from the local pool, which meant that they could not afford to purchase African maize at or above the export price, the price for African maize was kept low by statute. Only a minority of African growers were able to enjoy the small African quota in the local pool by making direct delivery to one of the Board's depots. This stipulation increased the social and regional differentiation among growers. Remote areas were worst hit: here it was the policy of the Board to eliminate African maize production for the market.[50]

THE MOTIVES

Why did Major Wane so freely concede the demands of the Native Board? What was his interest in keeping alive the Africans' cash crop option during the depression and its aftermath, particularly as African market production contributed to the labour shortage in Mazoe District? More generally; why did interference in maize marketing on behalf of the African peasants become the policy of the Native Department? There are some obvious reasons: the maintenance of the pre-depression level of tax payments is one. As a consequence of the Maize Control Act, Major Wane expected difficulties with tax collections, as did many other NCs.[51] African tax payments were not only a vital source of revenue during the depression but also *the* symbol of state power. When the Africans' ability to pay this tribute declined in the early 1930s due to the combined impact of the depression, demonetisation and Maize Control, the state embarked on a dual strategy. First, the administration developed an elaborate machinery of enforcement to squeeze the last of the cash resources from the African people. This yielded impressive results; but 'Native Tax' revenue still fell in the early 1930s. These coercive measures were mainly, but not exclusively, directed at workers in the capitalist sector.[52] Although many rural families earned money to pay taxes by sending their young men out to work for a limited period, there were large sections of the population, as in Chiweshe, who secured that money in normal circumstances by sales of grain or cattle. Demonetisation eroded the basis for their tax payment, as was impressively demonstrated by the protests at the Native Board meetings throughout the country. Thus the state attempted to restore this basis by intervening in marketing.

In addition, the ruling white ideology displayed a hostile attitude towards the traders in the rural areas, who were often of Jewish or Greek origin. Because some of them had secret African wives or otherwise entertained sexual relations with African women, rural traders *in toto* were blamed for undermining the clear racial divisions and rigid moral standards which the white ruling elite tried to maintain, as part of its ideology. The Native Commissioner of Mazoe District was so disturbed by the traders' 'immoral activities', although he knew that 'real' whites in the District also had affairs with African women, that he suggested criminal legislation on South African lines.[53] But the traders' economic performance also came under heavy criticism. Major Wane was one of the first Native Commissioners to blame the Maize Control Act *and* the traders for the distress. He realised that the Act put the traders in a position of monopsonists, of which they took full advantage, while simultaneously curtailing their profits. In the course of time his dislike of 'kaffir truck traders', in particular if they were non-British or Jewish, increased.[54] This antipathy was shared by many Native Commissioners: it was partly based on racial prejudice, but also on a notion of legitimate and illegitimate forms of exploitation. Trading was considered to be on the borderline, but 'double profit' from barter was clearly unacceptable. In the crisis, and this seems to be a universal truth, both the ruling and the ruled came down on the traders, reflecting their position as intermediaries in commodity production.[55]

As the Native Department failed to relax Maize Control and barter persisted, it increasingly blamed the traders for the deterioration of exchange in the Reserves. The traders' unwillingness to return to cash transactions became the official justification for state marketing, besides being, to some extent, its real cause.[56]

But the Native Department was also opposed to the Maize Control Act out of more long-term considerations. In 1931 the Chief Native Commissioner posed the rhetorical question: 'Are we to advise the Natives to cease production?' He tried hard to convince the Premier that 'the Maize Control Act . . . is detrimental to the interests of the native maize producer'.[57] The Native Department criticised the Act for excluding many Africans (those on the geographical periphery of the colony) from cash cropping altogether, and for worsening the terms of participation for the rest. It was denounced as an instrument to protect the interests of the white farmers. But the criticism of Maize Control by the then acting Chief Native Commissioner, Charles Bullock, was more fundamental. He assumed that the Act 'may . . . place in jeopardy the good relationship between Europeans and Natives'.[58]

This criticism points to a major cause of state involvement in marketing, and to the underlying reason for Major Wane's scheme. The crisis of the 1930s was undermining the emerging system of domination and control in the rural areas which was based on a partial unity of interests between the Native Commissioner and the African elders.

The system of control in the rural areas which evolved as a coherent bureaucratic structure from the mid-1920s saw the Native Commissioner as a single ruler, retaining all aspects of power and authority in his person, with the Chiefs and elders as junior but essential partners. The latter were designed to be the only spokesmen for rural Africans, and the Native Commissioners were to be their mediators with the outside world. The alliance evolved on the basis of a gradual acceptance of the permanence of the Reserves, and of the move towards complete territorial segregation. The consolidation of land apportionment was accompanied by a parallel change of attitude on the part of Europeans towards the remains of 'tribal society'.[59]

Although the 1889 Royal Charter, which made the British South Africa Company the effective ruler over Zimbabwe and Zambia, required the preservation of certain 'tribal' laws and customs, the disintegration of the pre-colonial system of rule was still seen as inevitable, indeed welcome in the early 1920s.[60] But the consolidation of the Reserves changed 'Native Policy'; traditionalists in the Native Department gradually increased their importance, advocating the strengthening of the position of Chiefs and elders, which had been eroded by their loss of control over the land. Tribal disintegration and the decreasing power of the Chiefs, as many Native Commissioners now saw it, were followed not by 'healthy individualism' but by a vacuum in control and increased 'insubordination'. The social equivalent of an economically self-sufficient Reserve was the concept of an 'organic', self-regulated, tribal society, characterised not by internal antagonism and strife but by a social 'equilibrium'.[61] Thus the ideology of 'tradition' and 'traditional rule' was used for domination, to keep the Reserves quiet.

This eclectic utilisation of tradition was pursued not only by the Native Commissioners who wanted to rule through 'tribal' institutions but also by the elders to serve their own ends. One of their main concerns *within* the framework of colonialism was also control: control of women and of the agricultural surplus, in order to regain authority within their polity.

Control of women was an important and persistent issue at the Native Board meetings in Chiweshe, and Wane proved to be outspoken in his support of his male subjects' demands. 'They [the men] have my sympathy, for there is no doubt that the native woman is deteriorating very rapidly in her moral character, in fact it is doubtful whether she has any at all'.[62] This issue, which was one of the central elements in the traditionalists' alliance, also became a major source of conflict between on the one hand the mission churches and on the other the elders and the Native Department.[63] More generally, political control over rural people, the power to enforce the Chief's decisions despite decreasing authority of the elders, was another important element in the traditionalists' alliance. Increased control was in the interests of both the elders and the Native Department officials, for all attributed growing 'disobedience' to a slackening of the authority of 'tribal' rulers.[64]

This traditionalists' alliance, which aimed at conserving structures which were already disintegrating, developed in the 1920s, during a period of growing peasant prosperity. It was based on sustained peasant production, and on the exclusion from the labour market of the elders in African society. In the early 1930s this fragile arrangement came under pressure from various directions. Most importantly, Maize Control and demonetisation directly eroded the economic base of African producers. Many Native Commissioners saw that the very group on which their alliance was based, the elder men, was faced with the disintegration of its economic position. Demonetisation also intensified the struggle between men and women for the surplus family production, and for the production from the women's own gardens. Barter trade made access to this surplus more difficult for the men.[65] The system of migrant labour, from which the elders wished to benefit, was also shaken. They complained about decaying morals, reflected in the reduced payments received from their young family members.[66]

But other developments, which cannot be directly linked to the depression, also threatened the fragile alliance. The growing impact of 'kraal school' teachers on rural communities undermined the elders' control over children and young women. The increasing importance of this rival social group also had an immediate economic dimension, when teachers shifted the labour power of the schoolchildren (and sometimes the community as a whole) from the family estate and from the Chief's holding to their own plots.[67]

In the late 1920s and early 1930s the concept of exclusive African representation by the Chiefs was also threatened by the activities of modern political movements in the rural areas. In the early 1930s the Industrial and Commercial Workers Union (ICU) took up rural Africans' grievances and made them public, thus encroaching on the relationship between the Native Commissioners and the elders.[68] Similarly, the attempt by some 'Native Associations' to extend their activities into the rural areas threatened the alliance between 'tribal' authority and the state by offering alternative spokesmen and channels of communication to rural Africans. Consequently the boundary of their activities was defined: 'Native Associations will receive sympathetic consideration in urban and industrial areas, but have no mandate to speak for the Reserves'.[69] Reacting to the threat from the 'Native Associations', the Chief Native Commissioner pressed for speedy formation of the Native Boards as the channel of communication between the state and rural Africans.

Finally, the rise of the Shona Independent Churches in the 1930s was initially seen by both sides of the alliance as a serious threat to the emerging pattern of control. At first tribal elders viewed these Churches, especially the spirit type, with great suspicion, and were in most cases opposed to their activities. The administration tried to use this initial hostility on the part of many tribal elders in its attempts to control or ban Independent Churches.[70]

But it was not only developments within African society that posed a threat to the emerging alliance. Administration itself created institutions to challenge the exclusive control exercised by the Native Commissioners and the elders. These institutions, the Native Development Department (NDD), the Demonstrators and the Jeanes Teachers, were not under the direction of the Native Department, and were thus seen as detrimental to the principle of unity of control. Through these institutions the state carried out its development efforts, when it realised in the late 1920s that the 'carrying capacity' of the land 'eternally' allocated to Africans had to be increased to make land apportionment viable.[71] Premier Moffat was explicitly against the Native Department controlling African education and development. Thus in 1929 the Demonstrators, whose task it was to teach intensive agricultural methods, came under the newly created NDD. The Native Commissioners were not opposed to the demonstration scheme as such, but they resented the disturbance to the established pattern of authority and the exclusiveness of control. The Africans, it was assumed, would be confused by the dual control of state activities in the Reserves. The Native Commissioners repeatedly urged the Chief Native Commissioner 'to point out to the Agriculturalist of the Natives that the Native Commissioner controls the Native Reserves of his district'.[72]

The main administrative struggle, however, was fought over the control of the Jeanes Teachers, between on the one hand the Native Department and on the other the NDD and the missions. The inspiration behind the introduction of the Jeanes Teachers was a broader definition of education (not restricted to school learning) which evolved in the 1920s.[73] This expansion beyond the school yard and the performance of 'community work' provoked opposition from many Native Commissioners and from the Native Department. Development should be under the control of the Native Commissioner and carried out by 'his instruments, [being] . . . either the Chiefs, headmen and Native Boards . . . or Government servants under his control'.[74] In Chiweshe Reserve, the struggle for control of development and education was clearly evident. When the first Jeanes Teacher for Chiweshe Reserve, Matthew Magorimbo, reported to Wane, the latter felt his authority to be threatened by the former's potential independence. He feared that 'this lack of control, or possibly this dual control [is] not only impossible in practice but gravely dangerous to the interests of both the Native and European population in this Colony'.[75] Consequently he attempted to make life hard for Magorimbo in every way. In 1934 Magorimbo ignored an order to report to Wane's office. The Native Commissioner claimed that this 'act of disobedience' would set a bad example to the whole Reserve:

> The matter is so serious in that if this line of conduct is followed all proper control of the natives in Chiweshe will become impossible. I have always done my utmost to maintain that proper control and discipline and, during the nearly 6 years I have been here have been successful in doing so, only now to find all my efforts rendered abortive.[76]

He demanded that Magorimbo be removed from the Reserve immediately, and in this found a strong ally in the Chief Native Commissioner. Col. Carbutt took this occasion to make clear 'to the Missionaries that they are allowed in the Reserves on sufferance only', and that it was the Native Commissioner who ruled the Reserve.[77]

In this departmental struggle for control of the development and education of the rural Africans, the Native Department won all the major battles, aided by a rightward shift of the white electorate. For the Jeanes Teachers, no satisfactory form of control was achieved by the Native Department; consequently their training by the state was abandoned. Village school teachers came under the control of the Chiefs, as advocated by the Native Department (and strongly opposed by the missions). The centrepiece of the new system of control was the alliance of Chiefs and elders with the state. The attacks upon it were mastered, and the now strengthened alliance secured its legal basis with the passing of the 'Native Law and Courts Act' in 1937. The Act sanctioned a widespread but until then illegal practice: the Chiefs' jurisdiction in the case of civil disputes between Africans in the Reserves. The state-Chief relationship was never without its friction or contradictions, but on the whole the state managed to ensure that the Chiefs depended upon it to safeguard their interests. Most Chiefs did not really fit into the new relationship, but as they were now 'part of our machinery', administration training programmes were started for them at Domboshawa in 1936.[78]

The struggle for the control of women was one area where the elders could utilise the state's wish to reinforce tradition to further their own ends. The minor legal status of women was not undisputed in the colonial period; but in the 1930s official opinion clearly shifted in favour of it. The minor status of women became a part of 'Tribal Law',[79] and recent discussions have shown that the struggle for female equality has not been ended even by the passage of the 'Age of Majority Act' in 1982.

THE CONSEQUENCES

The depression hit the peasants in Chiweshe after a period of growing prosperity. By late 1930 the effects of demonetisation began to be felt. The severe drop occurred in 1931. The problems brought about by the depression were aggravated by severe transport restrictions, due to the outbreak of foot-and-mouth disease. Some traders used lorries to get the grain out of the Reserve, which further depressed the prices paid to Africans. Wane summed up the situation: 'In this district the natives depend on maize for sale . . . They have suffered most severely from the financial point of view'.[80]

But although from 1931 the peasants had to work within a much altered marketing structure which adversely affected their income from grain, their production system did not break down. The peasants continued the trends of the 1920s; they further expanded their acreage, partly to offset the impact of declining prices; and they fought their battle at the Native Board meetings and finally made Wane intervene on their behalf.

When the adverse impact of the Maize Control Act of 1931 became apparent, Wane made urgent representations to the Chief Native Commissioner, who passed on the complaint to the Maize Control Board. Wane did little initially to deal with the repercussions of the Act. In 1932 he put pressure on the traders to buy some grain for cash (at 3s 6d per bag), to which they reluctantly agreed.[81] After the 1934 amendment to the Maize Control Act, Wane, with the persistent pressure from the Native Board at his back, acted swiftly. He applied to the Chief Native Commissioner for a Treasury advance, and for the equipment required for the bulk purchase of maize. He arranged for a maize-receiving depot, with sheds and corrugated iron tanks for storage, to be built at Rosa. In June 1934 he appointed a white buyer at Rosa on 13s a day; and 5,000 new grain bags were bought and distributed to the Africans, for payment either in cash or in maize. The collected maize was then transported by African wagon-owners to Glendale (22 miles), where it was 'surrendered' to the local Maize Control Board agent. Using the Treasury advance, payment of 4s per bag was made.[82] At first some of the peasants were suspicious and refrained from dealing with Wane. In 1933/4, 5,774 bags were channelled through Wane's office; a year later, owing to drought, only 3,379 bags. After 1935 the scheme came into full swing, and the Treasury loan had to be increased to £2,000. From then, the Chiweshe deliveries made up half of all African maize delivered directly to the Board. In the 1935/6 season, the price rose to 5s 9d net per 203 lb bag, and ultimately increased to 9s.[83]

In 1938, the Farmers' Co-op in Salisbury, which had already marketed some non-maize crops from the Reserve, offered to take over Wane's project. Wane, very suspicious of their real motives, forced the Co-op to follow exactly his scheme. While state marketing continued in Shamva and Bindura Sub-districts, in 1939 the Co-op took over in Chiweshe Reserve; but it was able to handle only 1,729 bags, mainly owing to very wet weather.[84]

Wane's marketing scheme took until 1935 to have any real impact. From that year peasant prosperity revived as acreage and output vigorously responded to the new opportunities (see Tables 1 and 3). Mono-cropping of maize became very widespread, such that even the demonstration plots where people were supposed to practise crop rotation, were put purely to maize cultivation. For the African peasants, 'Magomo's maize' was the starting-point for serious cash cropping, marking a qualitative change in their involvement in produce markets. Because of the scheme, many traders had to offer cash again, although most paid a lower price than Wane. The peasants survived the depression without being turned into proletarians. In 1936, again, Wane reported that 'little labour [is supplied] from indigenous natives . . . [They] are far better off working for themselves'.[85]

TABLE 3: Maize sold in Chiweshe Reserve

Year	Total maize sold (bags)	of which: maize sold direct to the MCB through the NC (bags)
1934		5,774
1935		3,379
1936	25,000	11,000
1937	35,723	11,115
1938	37,720	11,957
1939	14,714	
1940	17,584	
1941	14,099	
1942	13,853	

Source: See Table 1.

But the scheme also increased the social differentiation that was evident at the end of the 1920s. It also increased the regional divisions within the Reserve, as it affected only the southern parts. The north, already at a disadvantage before the depression, did not benefit from the better prices and cash markets. Also the very poor peasants had difficulties in participating in the scheme. Deliveries below a full bag were not accepted by Wane; and some peasants were unable to transport their grain to Rosa and consequently had to sell to traders.[86] The rich peasants in the south benefited the most; they extended their acreage, some cultivating up to 200 acres, purely of maize. Mr Dofo, who was able to accumulate big lands in the 1920s, 'was one of the people we saw at the back-pay [final pay-out] collecting a lot of money'.[87] Mr Marufu profited both as a large producer and as a transporter, for Major Wane used his transport business to carry the grain from Rosa to Glendale.

In the late 1930s these accumulators came under increasing attack from some officials. Alvord, the 'Agriculturalist for Instruction of the Natives', argued that some peasants could not find any land because a minority had grabbed so much. He and his deputy, Palmer, saw all their demonstration efforts thus ruined, and they agitated strongly against, in their words, 'a dog in the manger habit of private farming on large acreage in the Reserve'.[88] But Wane defended increased peasant production:

> I do not consider that the increase of 6000 odd acres arable land [under African cultivation] in the course of 9 years can be considered as 'running wild with ploughs'. To my own knowledge the increase in European-owned arable land in the District . . . is considerably more than that in the same period.[89]

But after this harsh reply, Wane started to have second thoughts. In 1938 he came to the conclusion that some provisions of the Maize Control Act did in fact work against white farmers.[90] He was referring to the only change in the Act which the Native Department had been able to push through in its long struggle against Maize Control; that which allowed traders to market 25 per cent of all African-grown maize in the more profitable local pool. Wane's second thoughts clearly demonstrate that, although he had greatly stimulated peasant production, he had not intervened on behalf of the Africans because he was pro-peasant *per se*. His major concern had been to re-establish a social balance between the interests of white farmers and those of black peasants, which he considered essential for the maintenance of colonial rule. He saw himself as a mediator between those competing interests, detached from immediate short-term considerations. In 1938 he moved in the opposite direction because he perceived that the balance he sought was now threatened by increased African cash cropping.

It took him a year to apply this changed perception systematically. In 1939 he supported Alvord's opinion that 'some of the more pushful and advanced natives [in Chiweshe Reserve are] grabbing large areas of land to the detriment of their fellows'.[91] As a remedy he suggested centralisation of the Reserve, in anticipation of Alvord's plans. The Reserve was surveyed in 1939, and centralisation was completed in the mid-1940s.[92]

Centralisation forced the peasants to adopt intensive agricultural methods. It provided for the separation of arable and grazing lands; the limitation of individual landholdings to a certain acreage, depending on ecological conditions and family size (about six acres in Chiweshe); and resettlement in villages along the 'roads'. It implied the most severe direct interference in the social and economic patterns of the people since their removal into the Reserve.

The centralisation programme marked a transition in state development policy from a voluntary to a coercive approach. A certain degree of approval was needed from the Africans, and their opposition had to be reasonably explained. Alvord and later Wane put considerable stress on the acquisitional tendencies of rich peasants and on the rejection of this acquisitiveness by the mass of the people, in order to justify their scheme further. With centralisation, the ideologies of a social equilibrium and of an ecological balance came together. Social differentiation was not part of the African tradition the state intended to preserve. Rather, an 'egalitarian' landowning structure was the socio-economic corollary of subsistence agriculture and of the 'organic coherence' of 'tribal society'.

Alvord's and Wane's justification for centralisation was more a product of ideologies than of reality: nor did the Africans have an explicit consciousness of fundamental socio-economic contradictions within their own society; neither was a land shortage perceived by the peasants before centralisation. Rather, land shortages and the awareness of social contradictions were the result of the government's measure. Centralisation did not take into account the needs of future generations; it created 'reserves within the reserve'.[93] Thus fathers had to carve out plots from their own arable land for their sons. Those who started farming in the 1940s were the first to talk about land shortage; they could not farm the acreage they wanted. Centralisation curtailed the arable acreage and put the accumulators back in line with the majority of the peasants, at least for a limited period.[94] It scaled down elements of unequal land distribution, for some time; but it did not completely halt the process of social differentiation. After centralisation people started to realise their social divisions. With centralisation and the gradual implementation of more intensive agricultural methods, it became increasingly difficult to mobilise additional labour through the *nhimbe*-work party. The rich peasants turned to wage labour instead, thus gradually transforming the social process of production.[95] It was in the 1940s that *nhimbe/hoka* started to die out, and 'communalism' gave way to 'individualism'.

> The young generation did not want to use its time working in *hokas* [communal work parties]. People wanted to work for themselves. This also killed the *dare* [meeting of the elders] held by our fathers. Now every married man had his separate table.[96]

Centralisation, the new Maize Control Act of 1940, and a series of bad rains brought another crisis to the peasants in Chiweshe. But again they were able to overcome adversity and they entered a new phase of gradually more intensive agriculture after the second World War.[97]

CONCLUSION

The experience of the peasants in Chiweshe, as it has been described here, differs greatly from the image of the Zimbabwean peasantry portrayed in general analyses of the political economy of the colony. The Chiweshe peasantry was not a helpless victim of a settler state intent on its destruction and proletarianisation. The people in Chiweshe had an explicit consciousness of their existence as peasants, and successfully fought to maintain their socio-economic position. Their answer to the intrusion of colonial capitalism was increased production for an agricultural market. Agricultural change in the period under review was extensive in character, an enlargement of scale. Increased productivity per person was achieved not by a switch to more intensive agricultural methods but by an extension of acreage, with the help of the ox-drawn plough.[98] The peasantry of Chiweshe was thus able to sustain its agricultural expansion through the crisis of the 1930s.

The Chiweshe experience might be unusual in the context of Southern

Rhodesia, but it was not unique. Many peasants in other parts of Mashonaland shared the Chiweshe experience and struggles. For them, the 1930s also saw a severe assault on their ambition to establish themselves on a secure agricultural footing; but they too were able to respond to the challenge. The outstanding example here is that of the peasantry of Makoni District, who increased their sales of agricultural produce through the 1920s and 1930s, from 10,000 bags in 1926 to 97,000 bags in 1938.[99] The determination of the peasantry to maintain their mode of production was the main driving force behind this increase, but state involvement in marketing also contributed. Though this was less impressive in scope and impact than in Mazoe, Native Commissioners helped Africans to market their produce in about ten Districts during the depression.[100] With these interventions the state assumed major additional functions in African agriculture, as it did in relation to white farming. The state's assumption of responsibility for the marketing of produce was one important long-term result of the *ad hoc* measures taken during the depression; it was a responsibility, much extended, which was institutionalised after the second World War.[101]

For the Africans the state became stronger and was more directly experienced. During the depression the aim of the state was to preserve social structures which were considered to be necessary in the interest of the whole socio-economic system. By the end of the 1920s, the framework of a settler economy, which necessitated some African peasant production, had been firmly established. In the 1930s the state had to preserve this structure, in the face of threats created by the depression. Thus the state changed from being a creative to a conservative force.

As has been shown, the findings of this study of Chiweshe can be applied to other Districts. But they do not apply to all parts of the colony. In the drier south and in some parts of the Midlands, the Africans experienced the depression much more fundamentally. For them, the crisis of the early 1930s came as an economic and environmental breakdown, aggravated by Maize Control and by foot-and-mouth disease restrictions. Drought hit the herds severely; and a shattered cattle market, along with disease restrictions which favoured the settlers, made their struggle desperate. Rapidly declining opportunities in the labour and produce markets prevented Africans in these areas from finding viable alternatives during the crisis. In Shangani Reserve, for example, it was observed that in 1931 'food supplies have been very short and the people in consequence are living in a state of semi-starvation'.[102]

NOTES

1 This paper considers one aspect from a broader research project on the impact of the Great Depression on colonial Zimbabwe. I wish to acknowledge the financial support given by the Stiftung Volkswagenwerk. I also want to thank L. Bessant, H. Bley, B. Davis and the participants in the Henderson Seminar at the History Department, University of Zimbabwe, for their helpful criticism of this paper.

2 C. Coquery-Vidrovitch, 'L'Afrique coloniale française et la crise de 1930: crise structurelle et genèse du sous-développement', L'Afrique et la crise de 1930, *Revue d'Histoire d'Outre-Mer, 63,* Numéro special (1976), p.386.

3 J.C. Scott, *The moral economy of the peasant: rebellion and subsistence in Southeast Asia* (Yale University Press, New Haven, 1976), p.114.

4 G. Arrighi, 'Labour supplies in historical perspective: a study of the proletarianization of the African peasantry in Rhodesia' in G. Arrighi and J.S. Saul, *Essays on the political economy of Africa* (Monthly Review Press, New York, 1973), pp.180-234; R.H. Palmer, 'The agricultural history of Rhodesia' in R.H. Palmer and N. Parsons (eds), *The roots of rural poverty in central and southern Africa* (Heinemann, London, 1977), pp.221-54.

5 Palmer, 'Agricultural history', p.243.

6 For a criticism of Palmer's approach see T.O. Ranger, 'Growing from the roots: reflections on peasant research in central and southern Africa', *Journal of Southern African Studies, 5,* 1 (1978), pp.99-113; P. Mosley, *The settler economies: studies in the economic history of Kenya and Southern Rhodesia, 1900-1963* (Cambridge University Press, Cambridge, 1983).

7 S 1542/N 2, N[ative] C[ommissioner] Mazoe to C[hief] N[ative] C[ommissioner], 12 July 1934. All archival references are from the National Archives of Zimbabwe.

8 Ibid., Minutes of N[ative] B[oard] Meeting, Chiweshe Reserve, 13 and 14 July 1932.

9 Ibid.

10 Ibid.

11 Ibid.

12 Ibid., NB Meeting, Chiweshe Reserve, 17 August 1933.

13 Ibid., NB Meeting, Chiweshe Reserve, 12 June 1934.

14 Ibid., NB Meeting, Chiweshe Reserve, 3 June 1936.

15 'Magomo', meaning 'the mountain', was the name the Africans gave to NC Wane. The scheme is well remembered by all the older Africans I interviewed in Chiweshe Reserve. I wish to express my thanks to Mr E. Muringai, who skilfully conducted the interviews and made the translations.

16 Planning Branch, Dept of Conservation and Extension, *Mazoe Valley agricultural survey* (Government Printer, Salisbury, 1972). Chiweshe Reserve belongs to Region II ('Intensive crop production supported by livestock') in Vincent and Thomas's land classification. Only 25 per cent of this region could be used by Africans in colonial Zimbabwe; the rest was alienated to white farmers; R.C. Riddell, *The land problem in Rhodesia* (Mambo Press, Gwelo, 1978), p.36.

17 Hist[orical] M[anu]s[cript] Collect[ion], RU 3/1/1, Radio interview with Mr Rudland, who prospected in Mazoe District in 1890. For pre-colonial trade see A[frican] O[ral] H[istory]/7, Interview with Mhako, pp.83-4; AOH/13, Interview with Alexander Mapondera.

18 N 9/1/10, Mazoe South District, Annual Report 1907; E.E. Burke, 'Mazoe and the

Mashona Rebellion, 1896-97', ***Rhodesiana***, no.25 (1971), p.23; C.G. Chivanda, 'The Mashona Rebellion in oral tradition: Mazoe District', unpublished BA Honours III Seminar Paper, Dept of History, University College of Rhodesia, 23 June 1966.

19 N 9/1/10, Mazoe South District, Annual Report 1907.

20 N 9/1/8 to N 9/8/12, Mazoe South District, Annual Reports 1903 to 1909.

21 Hist. Ms. Collect., SO 5/2, C.W.R. Southey, Reminiscences.

22 N 9/1/13, Mazoe District, Annual Report 1910.

23 N 9/1/16 to N 9/1/23, NC Mazoe, Annual Reports 1913 to 1920. For relative land-abundance see for example S 622 (1929), Wane to Director for Native Education, 19 December 1929.

24 N 9/1/20, Mazoe District, Annual Report 1917; interview with Mr Chakanyuka at Musarera, 19 May 1985.

25 R.W.M. Johnson, 'The economics of African agriculture in Southern Rhodesia: a study in resource use', unpublished PhD thesis, University of London, 1968, p.87.

26 Interview with Mr Matswetu at Rosa, 19 May 1985; interview with Mr Shamuyarira at Shutu, 5 April 1985.

27 Johnson, 'Economics', p.58; R.C. Smith, 'Maize in Zimbabwe', *Heritage, 1* (1981), pp.42-4; M.P. Miracle, *Maize in tropical Africa* (University of Wisconsin Press, Madison, 1966), p.157; N 9/1/10, Mazoe District, Annual Report 1907; interview with Mr Kanyemba at Kanyemba, 5 April 1985.

28 S 622 (1929), Wane to Jowitt, 19 December 1929; S 235/459, NC Mazoe to Land Commission, 4 March 1925.

29 S 622 (1926), Mrs Borrer, The Birch at Glendale, to NC Mazoe, 17 September 1926.

30 S 622 (1924), C.L. Cowen to NC Mazoe, 15 September 1924.

31 S 235/488, Major Wane at the Salisbury Senior Native Commissioners' Conference, 1935. See also S 622 (1930), Trooper i/c patrol to NCO i/c BSA Police, Amandas, 2 March 1930.

32 S 622 (1929), NC Mazoe to CNC, 30 August 1929, and NC Mazoe to CNC, 26 January 1929.

33 S 235/506, Mazoe District, Annual Report 1928; S 622 (1930), NC Mazoe to CNC, 19 December 1930.

34 S 622 (1929), Wane to NCO i/c BSA Police, Amandas, 10 October 1929. See also S 622 (1929), Mrs Borrer to Wane, 9 September 1929 and 6 October 1929; interview with Mr Marufu at Gweshe, 5 April 1985.

35 S 622 (1930), NC Mazoe to F.J.W. Smith at Avondale, 20 March 1930.

36 Interviews with Mr Marufu at Gweshe, 5 April 1985; Mr Matswetu at Rosa, 18 May 1985; Mr Shamuyarira at Shutu, 5 April 1985; Mr Nyakotyo at Shutu, 19 May 1985. S 235/509, Mazoe District, Annual Report 1931.

37 S 622 (1927), NC Mazoe to C.L. Tennant, 20 December 1927, and NC Mazoe to J.G. Du Preez, 18 May 1927; S 622 (1927), Wane to CNC, 21 August 1927.

38 Interviews with Mr Matswetu at Rosa, 19 May 1985; Mr Nyakotyo at Shutu, 19 May 1985; Mr Marufu at Gweshe, 5 April 1985; Mr Kanyemba at Kanyemba, 5 April 1985; Mr Chakanyuka at Musarera, 19 May 1985; Mr Chiwocha at Mukodjengi, 19 May 1985.

39 N 9/1/9, Mazoe District, Annual Report 1906.

40 S 622 (1930), Tpr i/c patrol to NCO i/c BSA Police, Amandas, 2 March 1930. See also

N 9/1/14, Mazoe District, Annual Report 1911; N 9/1/10, Mazoe District, Annual Report 1907; NSH 3/2/1, NC Mazoe, Monthly Report October 1911; N 9/1/26, Mazoe District, Annual Report 1923.

41 N 9/1/24, Mazoe District, Annual Report 1921.

42 F. Clements and E. Harben, *Leaf of gold: the story of Rhodesian tobacco* (Methuen, London, 1962), p.100. Southern Rhodesia, *Statistical Yearbook, 1938*. For detailed calculations of real wages in this period and further consideration of the impact of the depression in Southern Rhodesia, see my forthcoming thesis.

43 S 235/509, Mazoe District, Annual Report 1931. Demonetisation was first mentioned as a problem in Mazoe District in 1930. See S 622 (1930), Wane to CNC, 26 June 1930.

44 Interview with Mr Marufu at Gweshe, 5 April 1985; ZBJ 1/1/1 to ZBJ 1/1/4, Minutes of the N[ative] P[roduction] [and] T[rade] C[ommission], 1944.

45 S 1542/N 2, NB Meeting, Chiweshe Reserve, 12 June 1934: Statement by Ndzwimbo.

46 S 622 (1930), Mrs Borrer to NC Mazoe, 20 June 1930. See also S 1542/N 2, NC Mazoe to CNC, 2 October 1933.

47 ZBJ 1/2/1, NPTC, Memo[randum] by 'Fort Victoria Small Traders Association'; ZBJ 1/1/2, NPTC, Ev[idence] by Mr Hughes, Trader in Victoria District, p.1492. For traders' opposition to the Maize Control Act, see: S 482/603/39.

48 For a detailed analysis of the Maize Control Act see C.F. Keyter, *Maize Control in Southern Rhodesia, 1931-1941* (Central African Historical Association, Salisbury, 1978); Mosley, *Settler economies*, p.44; D.J. Murray, *The governmental system in Southern Rhodesia* (Oxford University Press, London, 1970); E.R. Jacklin, 'The "Maize Control Amendment Act" No. 17 of 1934', *Rhodesia Agricultural Journal, 31* (1934), pp.487-95. See further S 1542/M 2, Memo by Bullock, 8 August 1934.

49 S 1561/38, CNC to Secr. to the Premier (NA), 24 July 1931 and 7 August 1931.

50 Jacklin, 'Maize Control'; S 1216/SCI/100/5 (1934), Correspondence between A.S. Cripps and the Acting CNC; ibid., Jacklin to Ag CNC, 26 July 1934.

51 S 1561/38, Wane to CNC, 9 July 1931; S 235/488 (1930), ND Advisory Committee, Minutes, p.170; ibid., (1935), Salisbury Senior NCs' Conference 1935, Minutes, p.181.

52 ZAY 2/2/28, Economic Development Commission 1939, Memo by T.C. Ball; S 138/2, Returns and Reports: 1923-35 (Inspection Reports); S 1042, Confidential CNC Circular 3 October 1931; S 235/510 and 511, Bulawayo District, Annual Reports 1932 and 1933. An accurate indication of the depression's impact on rural income is the fact that collections of the tax on dogs, being a 'discretionary' tax (an owner could elect to kill his dog if he was unable to pay the tax), did not resume pre-depression levels until 1946. See Southern Rhodesia, *Statistical Yearbook, 1938* and *1947*.

53 S 622 (1926), NC Mazoe to CNC, 30 October 1926.

54 S 1561/38, Wane to CNC, 9 July 1931 and 27 June 1932; S 235/488, Salisbury Senior NCs' Conference 1935, Minutes, p.161.

55 For detailed study of these rural traders, see B.A. Kosmin, 'Ethnic and commercial relations in Southern Rhodesia: a socio-historical study of the Asian, Hellenic and Jewish populations, 1898-1943', unpublished PhD thesis, University of Rhodesia, 1974.

56 S 1561/38, CNC to Private Secr. to the Premier, 14 September 1931.

57 S 1561/38, Carbutt to Premier, 7 August 1931, and Carbutt to Priv. Secr. to Premier, 9 October 1931.

58 S 1542/M 2, Ag. CNC to Secr. to the Premier, 27 June 1934.

59 For the impact of territorial segregation on 'Native Policy' see M. Steele, 'The foundations of "Native" Policy in Southern Rhodesia, 1923-1933', unpublished PhD thesis, Simon Frazer University, 1972.

60 Chief Native Commissioner, Annual Report 1920, p.1.

61 S 1561/49, Memo by Bullock, 1936; S 1561/59, Posselt to CNC, 14 November 1931.

62 S 1542/N 2, Wane to CNC, 30 April 1931.

63 S 178, CNC to Right Rev. Bishop Chichester, Bishop Vicarate of Salisbury, 12 November 1931; S 1059, Wane to CNC, 7 December 1936.

64 S 235/488, Salisbury Senior NCs' Conference 1935, Minutes, p.11.

65 ZBJ 1/2/1, NPTC, Ev. by Mr Hughes, p.1468.

66 See Minutes of Native Board Meetings in S 1542/N 2.

67 S 138/41, CNC to Director of Native Development, 6 August 1929, and S[uperintendent of] N[atives] , Bulawayo, to CNC, 20 August 1929.

68 S 138/55, NC Ft Rixon to SN, Byo, 20 January 1931; S 1042, CNC Circular, 25 September 1932.

69 S 235/349, CNC to Minister of Native Affairs, 21 July 1930.

70 M. Daneel, *Old and new in southern Shona Independent Churches*, vol.1 (Mouton, The Hague, 1971), p.431; S 138/140, NC Zaka to Rev. J. Roux, 5 June 1931; S 1542/M 8D, NC Chipinga to CNC, 9 September 1935; S 138/140, Ass. NC Buhera to NC The Range, 21 January 1939; S 1042, CNC Confidential Circular Minute, No. 23, 10 May 1934, and CNC Circular, 20 August 1934; S 235/516, Mazoe District, Annual Report 1938.

71 S 235/487, Minutes of the NCs' Conference, 1933; S 1542/C 9, Memo for the Native Affairs Departments' Conference, 1933; G. Passmore, *The national policy of community development in Rhodesia* (Dept of Political Science, University of Rhodesia, Salisbury, 1972).

72 S 138/72, Memo by Moffat, 27 February 1928. See also NC Selukwe to SN, Byo, 11 January 1929, and NC Marandellas to CNC, 8 March 1932, and Ass. NC Goromonzi to CNC, 2 September 1932.

73 S 170/1171, Jowitt to CNC, 21 September 1932.

74 S 1542/J 1, CNC to Minister of Native Affairs, 12 April 1934. See also CNC to Secr. to the Premier (NA), 31 October 1934.

75 S 1542/J 1, Wane to CNC, 1 February 1933.

76 Ibid., Wane to CNC, 6 March 1934.

77 Ibid., CNC to Minister of Native Affairs, 9 March 1934. See also CNC to Stoyle (Salvation Army), 13 April 1934.

78 Steele, 'Foundations of "Native" Policy', p.322; S 235/488, p.17 and p.186; S 1042, CNC Circular, 16 January 1934.

79 S 235/486, Memo by Coghlan (1922) read at the Native Department Advisory Committee Meeting, 1932; H. Child, *The history and extent of recognition of tribal law in Rhodesia* (Ministry of Internal Affairs, Salisbury, [1965]), p.89.

80 S 235/511, Mazoe District, Annual Report 1933. See also S 235/509, Mazoe District, Annual Report 1931. Interview with Mr Chiwocha at Mukodjengi, 19 May 1985.

81 S 1561/38, Wane to CNC, 27 June 1932; CNC to Secr. MCB, 11 July 1931; Wane to CNC, 27 June 1932; S 235/510, Mazoe District, Annual Report for 1932.

82 S 1542/M 2, Wane to CNC, 21 June 1934; ZBJ 1/2/2, NPTC, Memo by Bowles, Ag.

Ass. NC, Umvuma. The white buyer was later replaced by two Africans: S 1542/M 2, Wane to CNC, 14 July 1934 and 31 August 1934.

83 S 1542/J 1, Wane to CNC, 22 March 1935; interview with Mr Matswetu at Rosa, 19 May 1985; S 1542/M 2, Wane to CNC, 9 April 1936; Maize Control Board, Annual Reports; S 1542/N 2, NB Meeting, Chiweshe Reserve, 3 June 1936; S 235/514, Mazoe District, Annual Report 1936; ZBJ 1/2/2, NPTC, Memo by Bowles.

84 S 1542/M 2, CNC to Wane, 25 June 1938; S 1059, General Manager, Farmers' Co-op to CNC, 28 February 1939; S 1542/M 2, General Manager, Farmers' Co-op to Wane, 28 February 1939.

85 S 235/514, Mazoe District, Annual Report 1936. See also S 1542/A 4, Palmer to Alvord, 26 March 1938. Interviews with Mr Matswetu at Rosa, 19 May 1985; Mr Marufu at Gweshe, 5 April 1985; Mr Kanyemba at Kanyemba, 5 April 1985.

86 Interviews with Mr Chiwocha at Mukodjengi, 19 May 1985; Mr Marufu at Gweshe, 5 April 1985.

87 Interview with Mr Shamuyarira at Shutu, 5 April 1985.

88 S 1542/A 4, Palmer to Alvord, 26 March 1938; S 1542/S 10, Minute by Alvord, 7 June 1939.

89 S 1059, Wane to CNC, 29 June 1936.

90 S 482/34/42, Wane to Huggins, 30 June 1938.

91 S 1542/S 10, Wane to CNC, 3 May 1939.

92 S 1542/S 10, Wane to CNC, 11 May 1939 and 15 July 1939; ZBJ 1/1/1, NPTC, Ev. by A. Midzi, p.493.

93 L. Bessant, '"Going into the lines": centralisation and the perception of land shortage in the Chiweshe Reserve, 1940-1944', unpublished Henderson Seminar Paper, Dept of History, University of Zimbabwe, May 1985.

94 By the late 1950s a pattern of unequal landownership had re-emerged to some extent. See P. Hamilton, 'Population pressure and land use in Chiweshe Reserve', *Rhodes-Livingstone Journal*, no.36 (1965), p.40.

95 Interviews with Mr Chiwocha at Mukodjengi, 19 May 1985; Mr Nyakotyo at Shutu, 19 May 1985; Mr Chakanyuka at Musarera, 19 May 1985.

96 Interview with Mr Chakanyuka at Musarera, 19 May 1985.

97 In 1946 for example African peasants in Mazoe District sold no less than 45,344 bags of maize. S 1563, Mazoe District, Annual Report 1946.

98 This contrasts with Mosley's analysis of agricultural change in Zimbabwe in the 1930s. Mosley, *Settler economies*, p.71.

99 Makoni District, Annual Reports. In Salisbury, Darwin, Marandellas, Mrewa, Mtoko Districts too, to name only a few, the peasants were able to increase their maize sales substantially during the 1930s.

100 S 1542/R 6 and S 1542/R 7, Annual Inspection Reports. The Districts were: Gwelo, Mazoe, Bindura, Shamva, Victoria District and Province, Lomagundi, Makoni, Marandellas, Wedza, Gutu, Mtoko.

101 See Annual Report of the Native Production and Marketing Branch (of the Native Department), 1948.

102 London Missionary Society, Shangani Mission, Annual Report 1931. (Deposited in the Library of the School of Oriental and African Studies, London.)

3

THE PEASANT AND THE DEPRESSION: THE CASE OF THE BOMBAY PRESIDENCY, INDIA

NEIL CHARLESWORTH*

The depression of the inter-war period stands as a great crisis amidst British India's otherwise undramatic economic history. As is well known, from 1929 a deep-seated agricultural depression coincided with the world financial collapse, and the primary producing economies like India experienced a large slump in prices, following on the instability of the 1920s.[1] Within the space of five years after 1928/9 the value of India's foreign trade was very nearly halved and recovery thereafter was sluggish and restricted.

The immediate transfer of a major international crisis to the Indian locality, on the scale that occurred in 1929, was a new phenomenon. The previous 'Great Depression', that of 1873-96, had seen a sustained fall in world agricultural prices, but India's internal economy had remained relatively insulated. The only marked decline in crop prices came temporarily in the 1870s and there was never any serious loss of foreign trade values. Partly, internal prices held up because the impact of the depression was counter-balanced by the inflationary effect within India of the steady devaluation of the rupee between the 1870s and the 1890s.[2] Yet the situation also suggests that, at the price level, India was not yet fully incorporated within the Western-centred international economy. With transport imperfections, world prices were still transmitted to many villages in a variable, protracted fashion and could anyway be countermanded by local market influences. By 1929 this cushioning effect was far weaker. The Indian peasant, as much as the bosses of the export houses, was thrust to the forefront as a prominent victim of depression.

In addition, the inter-war depression was more violent than that of 1873-96. Hence the Indian locality had become more fully integrated within the international economy at the very time, after 1914, when the latter had become so much more unstable. This would intensify the disruptive impact on the peasant economy. An optimistic 'diffusionist' view of rural India's economic development down to 1929 would argue that extending commercial agricultural production for world markets had proved stimulatory and generally beneficial and that more rapid growth and change was inhibited only by lack of capital, climatic and ecological difficulties and market imperfections. Yet, if so, the inter-war depression must stand as a devastating blow to this process. The prices of India's major export crops like cotton slumped with particular intensity. Traditional balance of payments relationships were disrupted as India, always regarded as a sink for precious metals, exported gold on a large scale, allegedly because distressed peasants were forced to realise their assets.

Following such features, the existing specialist studies of the depression fully emphasise the profound impact on the Indian agrarian economy and society.[3] All social groups apparently faced distress. The landlords and rich peasants were squeezed by sharply falling cash crop prices, but they found it difficult to retrench quickly and their cultivation costs usually remained high. For the poorer peasant the burden of agrarian indebtedness became more oppressive, and short-term credit was very difficult to obtain. Agrarian protest increased, often, in the circumstances, involving new cross-currents of inter-peasant conflict.[4] The only productive dimension lay in the mobilisation of resources away from the depressed agricultural sector, for capital hitherto heavily committed to the land, rural money-lending and cash crop trade, might now be diverted to business and industry in the market town and the city.[5] However, this was a common feature of the depression in less developed countries and, despite its influence, orthodox views maintain that India's industrial development remained disappointing during the 1930s.[6]

This paper will examine the impact of the depression on the peasant economy and society of Bombay Presidency, and try to test existing interpretations by focusing on the twin themes of cropping patterns and the fortunes of differing peasant social groups. The eventual aim will be to draw some conclusions about the depression's role in shaping the economic and social structure of the Indian countryside.

Firstly, though, what was the nature and condition of Bombay agriculture in 1929? As in most parts of India, cultivation was dominated by the staple food-grains of the peasantry, in this case the millet crops of jowar and bajra. However, the commercial sector was broadly based, both regionally and in range of products. Cotton was widely cultivated, especially in Gujarat and in Dharwar District in the south, and wheat, ground-nuts, tobacco and, on irrigated lands, sugar-cane were all extensively grown for the market. Land under cultivation was expanding, though not now as rapidly as during the nineteenth century. The statistics on land acreage indicate that the Bombay Presidency's gross cultivated area stood at around 24 million acres in the first years of the twentieth century, rising to just over 27 million acres by the early 1920s and about 29 million acres by the mid 1930s.[7] At the same time, however, the population growth rate began to accelerate and the Presidency's total numbers rose by over 13 per cent between 1921 and 1931, from 19.3 millions to 21.9 millions.[8]

Yet there is no marked evidence of any gathering crisis of subsistence in the 1920s. Cultivation of specific fodder crops did expand notably and this was probably a reflection of increasing pressure on pasture. Otherwise, there was no major sign of a switch from commercial to subsistence crops. Indeed, cotton was the boom crop of the 1920s. Total cotton cultivation in the Bombay Presidency, averaging just under 3.5 million acres in the early years of the twentieth century, rose over the 4 million acres level for most of the first World War period and reached a recorded peak of just over 5 million acres in 1925/6. Some more minor cash crops, notably tobacco and ground-nuts, showed similar scales of expansion. At the same time, the threat of serious scarcity and famine, present in many areas in 1918/19 and in some again in 1920/1, receded. Partly this was because the 1920s were a more favourable decade climatically after the marked instabilities of the era between 1895 and 1920. Indeed, the onset of the world depression in the late 1920s was accompanied in western India by a series of extremely favourable seasons. Officials described 1930/1 as one of the best seasons since the war, and the following two years were similar. This relative stability of underlying trends makes it possible to judge the depression and its impact on peasant agriculture in Bombay as a sharp external force.

This force materialised in the Bombay countryside as a dramatic and sustained fall of prices. One official report recorded: the 'slump in prices, which set in by about May 1930, was emphatic by the time the *kharif* [autumn] harvest began to come into the market . . . and became almost crushing by May 1931 when the *rabi* [spring] produce of the previous year [1930] arrived in the market. This sudden permanent . . . fall in the prices of agricultural produce is probably unparalleled in the economic history of the country'.[9] Table 1 provides a general impression of the average annual prices of different crops in appropriate Bombay localities. The overall, immediate picture is that prices plummeted between 1929 and 1932. They then stabilised at a low level, experienced some rally during 1935 and 1936, but fell away again markedly over the late 1930s. The collapse of 1929 came after a period in the mid and late 1920s when prices, particularly those of export crops like cotton, had already moved downwards. As the agricultural price trend had been generally upwards since the middle of the nineteenth century, this appeared a decisive turning-point for commercial agriculture in western India, with major social implications.

The impact was different for different groups in a society where major commercial producers were a minority, and where many poorer peasants worked in agricultural labour to supplement incomes. Official orthodoxy argued that the cash crop producer experienced a massive blow, whilst the subsistence cultivator and, especially, the labourer were much less adversely affected. As early as 1922/3, a downswing in the prices of all the leading crops except cotton was alleged to have produced 'a rise in the prosperity of the labouring classes in the rural areas', whilst most employers of labour 'suffered badly': 'this fact may lead to very marked economic changes in the near future, the exact nature of which it is difficult at present to forecast'.[10] With the onset of the depression the changes were apparently accomplished. By 1930/1 conditions for labourers were 'especially good' because

> while prices have greatly fallen the reduction in the rates of wages has been relatively small . . . The class of the agricultural population which has suffered most is the big cultivator employing hired labour on a large scale in producing his crop . . . especially . . . the Deccan Canal Irrigator and the cultivator of commercial crops like cotton and groundnut.[11]

This seemed logical, at least for the depths of the depression between 1929 and 1931. As prices started to fall and then slumped dramatically in the space of a few years, it does seem unlikely that employers could have forced down wages as rapidly and consistently as the general decline in prices demanded. Real wages for labour, as in the industrial West, therefore rose, in the short term anyway. This was regarded as economically harmful since, with the rise in real wage costs, 'agriculture cannot hope to be as remunerative as it has been for the past twenty years'.[12] Similarly, where tenancy existed, the balance of the relationship between landlord and tenant might have shifted significantly against the landlord. The key influence here was the fact that rents were still very commonly paid in kind in the Bombay Presidency. As Sykes, the Bombay Governor, argued, 'where there is a crop share system, and this prevails to a fairly considerable extent in this Presidency, the tenant class have no great difficulty but the landlords are hard hit':[13] clearly the value of the produce the landlord received was dropping.

In the longer run, commercial agriculture and its adherents may also have been adversely affected by differential price movements. The price collapse, across the deepest trough of the depression, was severe in all crops. Table 1 shows that prices of jowar, the leading millet food-grain, were halved in Sholapur District in the relatively uncommercialised east Deccan famine tract. However, these and the other food crop prices did stabilise during the course of the 1930s. Export crop prices seemed more volatile and, in particular, slumped badly during the downswing of the late 1930s: prices of Broach cotton in fact reached their lowest ebb in 1938/9. The phenomenon is explicable. The depression of 1929-32 was sufficiently traumatic to rule all prices even in the more isolated markets, but in the long run food-grain prices were also shaped by other, local influences. Thus in a relatively poor district like Sholapur, significant numbers of poor peasants and labourers needed to buy food to supplement subsistence needs, and hence levels of local demand, especially with rapidly growing population, acted as some countervailing force to international trends. This would explain why jowar prices at Sholapur and other food-grain prices held up in the late 1930s. Export crops, however, including here Ahmedabad wheat as well as Karad ground-nut and Broach cotton, continued to be dominated by international overproduction and the further dip in world prices in the late 1930s.

TABLE 1: Harvest prices in the depression

[Except for cotton, figures are quantities sold for one rupee, in seers of 80 tolas - that is, higher numbers indicate lower prices. For cotton, the reverse applies, as the figures are prices (in rupees) of a khandi of 784 lb.]

	Food crops			Export crops		
	Jowar at Sholapur	Bajra at Nasik	Rice at Thana	Wheat at Ahmedabad	Ground-nut at Karad	Broach cotton at Bombay
1929/30	10	7	6	7	8	257
1930/1	22	9	8	12	17	197
1931/2	23	16	9	12	15	194
1932/3	21	12	9	9	10	199
1933/4	20	12	9	11	17	207
1934/5	15	11	9	11	18	261
1935/6	21	13	8	8	13	207
1936/7	16	11	7	7	10	234
1937/8	17	11	9	10	14	168
1938/9	16	11	8	11	15	160

Source: *Annual Crop and Season Report of the Bombay Presidency* 1934/5, para 42; 1938/9, para 32.

In addition, commercial farmers were financially squeezed by the land revenue, the main fiscal imposition on peasant landowners. The burden of land revenue charges in the Bombay Presidency must have increased markedly in real terms over the depression. Table 2 gives details on the land revenue demand and actual collections. The Bombay revenue system allowed for 'suspensions' and also total 'remissions' of land revenue in unfavourable circumstances and, as the figures show, these were steadily granted on a moderate scale. Yet, during the depression, the revenue administration firmly set its face against concessions on the grounds of falling prices and demand: the revenue report on the Central Division of the Presidency for 1933/4, for example, boasted that ' no remissions were granted on account of the slump in prices'.[14] Instead, standard practice was followed and suspensions and remissions were given for crop failures linked to climatic and ecological factors, particularly during the poorer years of the late 1930s. Furthermore, political resistance to land revenue payment during the depression was weak, and officialdom itself seemed surprised how 'although the prices have fallen the agriculturists paid the land revenue put down for collection . . . without undue pressure'.[15] The socially divisive impact of the events of 1929-32 was probably the cause. Political unity between peasant groups in western India was fractured during the early 1930s, as the gloomy tone of the Maharashtra Congress's Peasant Enquiry Committee Report of 1936 conceded: ' the peasant cannot spontaneously respond to the call of the Anti-Imperialist struggle'.[16] The consequences are clear from Table 2. Levels of land revenue collection were barely affected by the depression. They held up in absolute terms and the real burden on individual payers must have increased significantly. Since land revenue was levied on formal ownership of land, this hit most those who owned most land, and thus further discriminated against them; tenants and labourers were not affected.

TABLE 2: Land revenue 1926/7-1938/9

(Figures are for the Bombay 'Presidency proper' - i.e. excluding Sind - in rupees)

	Original revenue demand	Suspensions remissions and previous collections	Actual collections realised
1926/7	4,49,39,143	58,08,614	3,90,78,445
1927/8	4,53,45,438	31,67,239	4,20,35,856
1928/9	4,37,90,996	39,27,923	3,94,33,990
1929/30	4,36,26,495	51,15,189	3,76,92,791
1930/1	4,53,25,325	60,74,669	3,90,67,096
1931/2	4,57,82,685	65,52,831	3,94,03,504
1932/3	4,64,42,361	62,27,759	4,05,52,496
1933/4	4,55,39,241	62,72,694	3,94,22,161
1934/5	4,39,96,975	76,59,564	3,54,67,122
1935/6	4,60,24,846	58,13,932	4,10,91,349
1936/7	4,40,11,436	83,09,849	3,60,43,211
1937/8	4,65,39,312	1,02,13,204	3,65,93,997
1938/9	4,63,27,078	88,29,298	3,75,77,797

Source: *Annual Land Revenue Administration Report of the Bombay Presidency*, 1926/7-1938/9, Appendix 1.

All this, then, provides a powerful case that the depression and its legacy proved a great watershed in the history of western Indian agrarian society. The landlords and the rich peasants, so often seen as the beneficiaries of economic change over the British period, were apparently the very groups most adversely affected. The main victim of the depression as portrayed in the Bombay official literature is a stereotype of a big rent-receiving and labour-employing landlord. These certainly did exist in many regions of the Presidency, but the problem is that the typicality of actual tenures by the inter-war period was much less rigid and clear-cut. Many peasants owned some land, rented more and perhaps even engaged in part-time labouring activities. Hence even the major commercial producer may not have been so disadvantaged in some of the roles he played. In particular, those - in regions like south Gujarat and the Deccan canal tracts - who had rented extensive areas of land to expand commercial activities now probably enjoyed declining rent levels, for the evidence suggests that even cash rents fell substantially.

Nevertheless, the onset of much lower prices in 1929-31 undoubtedly did gravely affect commercial farmers. Many growers of cash crops, as might be expected, initially tried to expand production to maintain their incomes, but this of course increased their labour costs and hence the real wages received by labourers, whilst exacerbating the price problem by flooding the market. The phenomenon had already occurred in cotton cultivation. The price boom in the commodity reached its peak in 1924, but then came the first abrupt fall: by 1926 prices in Bardoli taluk of south Gujarat, for example, were under half the level of two years previously.[17] Meanwhile cotton cultivation had continued to extend rapidly, passing, as we have seen, the five million acres mark for the whole Presidency for the first time in 1925/6. There is little doubt that, under these conditions, labourers in the cotton-growing areas had enjoyed a notable improvement in their relative position whilst landowners, with no quick price recovery, had further committed themselves to a now less profitable enterprise. In similar vein, an investigation into sugar-cane cultivation on the Poona canal tract revealed that (in many cases in 1925/6 and 1926/7) the value of the crops fell short of total costs.[18] It seemed that 'the cane-growers on the canals are running their businesses at a loss nowadays. This is because the prices of gul [well-boiled cane-juice, a mixture of sucrose and molasses] have fallen very low, while the costs have remained high on account of the high price of labour'.[19]

This evidence about trends already in progress in the mid 1920s highlights one vital aspect of the depression in the Bombay Presidency. Whilst the major collapse in prices occurred between 1929 and 1932, a difficult period of complex economic and social change was already in process and cultivators were having to make adjustments. Furthermore, the fullest of the official comments about the difficulties of commercial farmers and the relative advance of labourers refer to the period between the mid 1920s and 1931. This raises the possibility that there was a two-stage, short-term and long-term impact of the agrarian depression with a divide around 1931 and 1932. In the short term, cash crop producers undoubtedly suffered severely: but to discuss the continuing effects in the 1930s we need now to widen our focus.

An obvious mechanism is to examine the long-term crop acreage statistics.

One might have expected, with the differential price trends and the social indicators we have noted, a steady movement to the food-grains during the 1930s, especially when population pressure on subsistence added additional motive. In fact, no such overall pattern seems to have occurred: the food-grains did not noticeably increase their share of the land. In 1922/3 all the cereals and pulses combined covered 18.6 million acres out of Bombay's gross cultivated area of 27.7 million acres, or 67 per cent. By 1938/9 they mustered 19.4 out of 29.7 million acres, 65 per cent of the total. Similarly, the commercial crops in overall terms maintained their share of the land. Here, however, there were sharp individual variations. Cotton experienced what might be seen as the natural reaction to its large price falls. Cultivation dropped from the 5 million acres peak of 1925/6 to 4.7 million acres in 1928/9, and then slumped sharply to 3.8 million acres in 1932/3 before tailing away still further to 3.6 million acres in 1938/9. Yet some other cash crops apparently extended their acreage markedly across the depression. Sugar-cane cultivation, a special case admittedly because it benefited from substantial protection, continued to expand with only a short-lived decline in the mid 1920s. Its total acreage in the Bombay Presidency, standing at 58,000 in 1922/3, had risen to 73,000 by 1938/9, an increase of 25 per cent. Tobacco experienced a boom during the 1930s. Its pre-depression peak was the 114,000 acres of 1924/5, but by 1938/9 tobacco cultivation covered 153,000 acres, a rise of over 34 per cent. Ground-nut cultivation extended considerably during the 1920s to around 1 million acres in 1928/9, and maintained this level throughout most of the depression years before experiencing a further expansion during the late 1930s. Individually, these obviously were less important crops than cotton, but their experience does not suggest that a broadly based crisis of commercialisation emerged out of the depression. In this context, too, it is notable that wheat, the food-grain with the most extensive market, expanded its acreage more than the millets. And, on reflection, even the fate of cotton was not as dramatic as might have been expected. The falls in cultivation were large but they came after a great period of expansion after the first World War, so that by 1939 cotton cultivation in the Bombay Presidency had merely returned to the levels of the early years of the twentieth century.

Commercial agriculture, therefore, reacted in a very diffuse way to the depression. What accounted for the variations? At the general level they can be explained in terms of the opportunities available in different markets. Crops like cotton which were highly dependent on international markets were the most severely affected. The boom in cotton cultivation in Gujarat and parts of Maharashtra in the ten years before 1925 depended much on increasing demand from the Japanese cotton industry. This slumped as the Japanese mills experienced first the severe effects of the depression and then an impressive recovery, but one based on more extensive use of the longer staple American cotton. Other commercial crops, though, particularly where linked to local industry, could expand on the basis of home demand in the more autarkic climate of the 1930s. Sugar is a well-known example here. Its linkage effects in the Bombay Presidency were less striking than in the United Provinces but, even so, a number of small new sugar refineries opened in the Deccan during the early 1930s, particularly in Rahuri taluk of Ahmednagar District.[20] In Gujarat, tobacco formed another fine example of a crop sustained by home demand and local refining skills.

However, this explanation dominates only at the broadest Presidency-wide level. Below this, in the districts, the detailed trends in cropping patterns were more complex, and cultivators seemed to be switching between different crops for diverse reasons. A good illustration of the subtlety of reactions comes in the East Khandesh District. This was traditionally a major centre of cotton cultivation but, as Table 3 shows, a series of shifts in cropping patterns occurred during the 1930s. Amidst the trough of the depression between 1929 and 1932 cotton cultivation contracted and land was switched to food-grains or left fallow. Then in 1932/3 acreage under ground-nuts leapt substantially and 'the sowing was extended to deep soil lands' which had traditionally grown cotton.[21] This surge of ground-nut cultivation is the more curious because at around the same time in Satara District, the leading centre for ground-nut production in western India, the acreage under the crop was declining.[22] Yet the shift was short-lived. Cotton cultivation in East Khandesh soon recovered at the expense of ground-nuts, and by 1935/6 the extent of cotton acreage was little lower than pre-depression levels.

How do we explain such patterns? The simple answer is continuous reaction to the vagaries of local price trends. For all the dominating force of the international depression, prices still varied significantly from district to district: thus, for example, jowar prices in July 1932 were 20 per cent lower in Ahmednagar compared with Poona, and more than 4 per cent lower again in Sholapur.[23] Hence ground-nut prices may have remained higher in East Khandesh District than in Satara District, for certainly the main official explanation for the East Khandesh ground-nut boom emphasised that 'though the price of groundnut also was low, the fall was small as compared with that in the price of cotton'.[24]

TABLE 3: Cash crop cultivation in East Khandesh District, 1928/9-1935/6 (Figures are in acres)

	Extent of land under:	
	Cotton	Ground-nuts
1928/9	790,406	350,833
1929/30	736,269	351,603
1930/1	668,076	363,553
1931/2	651,988	361,401
1932/3	589,527	421,929
1933/4	637,660	337,550
1934/5	687,006	227,819
1935/6	744,057	217,325

Source: *Annual Land Revenue Administration Report of the Bombay Presidency* 1931/2, p.39; 1935/6, p.39.

Yet price responsiveness does not entirely explain the East Khandesh phenomenon. The marked recovery of cotton in the mid 1930s took place conspicuously at a time when 'the rate [price] of cotton in East Khandesh remained practically unchanged', whilst ground-nuts still 'fetched a good price'.[25] Indeed cultivators faced intense problems over economic calculations in the depression. Prices were so volatile and unpredictable that organised reaction to them, in terms of choice of crop sown, was very complex and difficult. Prices in the sowing season were no sure guide to harvest prices. Hence in East Khandesh, the agricultural season of 1934/5 saw 'very low' cotton prices over the latter part of 1934, 'a welcome rise by the middle of January 1935', and then 'a sudden drop in March 1935'.[26] Peasants may have been strongly price-responsive in approach, but the frequent mis-match with actual price trends, evident in East Khandesh, may simply reflect the difficulties of being right in the unstable circumstances. The official reports are littered with accounts of failed calculations. In 1934/5 again, ground-nut prices in one taluk of Satara District seemed to be rising markedly, and peasants 'held back their crops in the hope of large profits . . . however, the demand for the article fell with the result that those who harvested their crops late or held them back had to suffer'.[27]

Such episodes pointed to the dangers of too slavish a reaction to short-term prices. The situation suggests that entirely different calculations became paramount during the depression, calculations about the ease and costs of cultivating different crops. Baker, thinking along similar lines, has argued in Madras for 'a transfer of acreage from crops that were relatively cheap to produce, such as groundnut and local cotton, to crops that required more expensive inputs such as good quality cotton, sugar, spices, fruit and vegetables'.[28] Bombay was different. Here, perhaps because of more established industries in sectors like cotton, or because commercial farming was rather less 'under the control of the oligarchy of village leaders',[29] the cheaper crops held up. Indeed, it might well be argued that in western India, economies of cost proved the key mechanism whereby commercial agriculture rode the depression.

The ground-nut story is one clue. Unlike in Madras, ground-nut cultivation did not decline during the depression, and indeed in 1932/3 proved a valuable reserve for many East Khandesh cotton farmers. The special value of ground-nut was that it was cheap and easy to grow: 'it requires less rain than cotton, is not subject to many deteriorating causes which may affect cotton and so is more certain to give a satisfactory return . . . it ripens early and can be sold in October and so brings in money much sooner than cotton'.[30] With these qualities it was a particularly economical crop for commercial farmers at the depths of a severe depression. Before 1929 it can be argued that many Bombay cash-crop producers had acquired comparatively high cultivation costs. It had made sense, as prices had steadily increased, to maximise production without too meticulous an investigation of outlays. Thus, on the Deccan canal-irrigated lands, 'during the boom period when the prices of gul were most alluring, the tendency of sugarcane cultivators was to get the maximum outturn, spending more money on manuring and labour'.[31] This approach had helped to create the improved conditions for labourers about which there is such widespread comment in the Bombay revenue papers even in the early twentieth century. It also ensured that the initial impact of the depression on the big commercial landowner was disastrous, particularly where he reacted by trying to increase production in a still more profligate manner. Costs came down, at best, only 'slightly', whilst the fall in the value of commodities was 'relatively much greater'.[32]

In the long term, though, there was no panic retreat from commercial crops into the food-grains because this was not necessary. Instead, the retreat could be made into cultivation methods and types of commercial agriculture which were cheaper and, in particular, less labour-intensive. This helps to explain the Presidency-wide trends in the cultivation of various crops. Cotton cultivation declined overall because the largest cotton producers in Gujarat and the southern districts of Maharashtra enjoyed limited opportunities for adjustment within cotton cultivation, and therefore switched crops. Jan Breman gives an excellent example of the process in south Gujarat: the agrarian elite in his villages turned to the tending of mango trees, which required relatively little labour.[33] As a result, they were able to strengthen their hold over the village and increase the economic divide between themselves and the *halis*, the farm servants and labourers who traditionally worked for them.

Elsewhere, however, entire shifts in cropping patterns were unnecessary.

Sugar-cane cultivation, for example, had experienced a rapid growth in costs before the depression. These had reached as much as Rs 1,000 per acre per year on some Deccan canal plots by 1925/6,[34] but retrenchment was clearly possible. Most plots on the canal lands were tiny, only one or two acres in size, and more intensive work by the family might diminish cash costs significantly. The same logic would apply to the tobacco-growing smallholders in areas like south-eastern Kaira (Kheda) District in Gujarat. Equally in East Khandesh, the return to cotton cultivation may have followed a shake-out of labour and a retrenchment on costs. In general, where commercial agriculture rested mainly on intensive cultivation of small units of land, as it did in western India with sugar-cane, tobacco and some types of cotton, considerable economies to counteract price falls were possible. Greater use of family labour would also be an option encouraged by demographic trends. Accelerating population growth, created as it was by declining mortality rates, would have increased the availability of adult labour to most peasant farms by the 1930s.

This hypothesis has important social implications. Given the land revenue squeeze, labour costs were everywhere the largest and most obvious expenditure on which economies were available. The inference is that, whilst in the short term the depression severely afflicted the landlord and rich peasant, its more long-term and substantive impact was to weaken the ability of labourers and the poor to earn good wages. By the last years of the early twentieth-century commercial expansion in Bombay Presidency, many of the richer agricultural producers were retreating from day-to-day involvement in cultivation, preferring leisure and social position to maximum efficiency within the family budget. The depression arguably drove them back to greater use of their own and family labour. But if this, for the rich peasant, was a social and cultural loss, the main economic consequences would be lower wages and loss of opportunities for those who sought labouring work. The largest contraction in commercial agriculture occurred in the crop, cotton, where demands for additional labour at times like harvesting were especially great. By December 1931, therefore, the Bombay government was already arguing that a significant change had occurred: 'as compared with two years ago wages in rural areas have now fallen by 22 per cent'.[35] At the same time credit was contracting, making it more difficult for the poor to borrow. As with Baker's Madras, renewed social stratification may well have been the long-term legacy of the depression in Bombay agrarian society.

In reviewing the depression, it is impossible to deny its role as a major crisis for the Indian agrarian economy. It introduced a sharply changed relationship with the external world, identified by officialdom as the general 'lack of purchasing power among the cultivators'.[36] The credit contraction affected all groups adversely. In western India, dislocation was intense in the first stage of the depression down to 1931: commercial agriculture was severely affected and deep-seated social changes seemed in train. However, in the second stage from about 1932 the agricultural theme was adjustment and adaptation. Retrenchment occurred, and there were subtle shifts rather than major reorganisation in cultivation patterns.

During the 1930s, then, the most striking feature in the Bombay Presidency is the relative imperviousness of the agricultural economy to revolutionary change. Given that the depression *did* create large dislocations in some other sectors, notably in India's foreign exchange relationships, this finding reasserts the value of concepts like dualism and the distinction between the formal and informal economy, as well as the view that the long-term impact of the international economy on India was actually to strengthen that divide. Against the vast size, weight and stability of the agricultural economy, external pressures for change, even when in the shape of a massive international depression, *were* weak. The commercial agriculture sector in a province like Bombay was, by the interwar period, too institutionalised to be subject to swift and radical change.

Since, then, commercial agriculture did not experience a fundamental structural decline in the Bombay Presidency, it is hard to see that there was any justification for a decisive inter-sectoral shift of resources. The cotton industry did diversify into a wider range of upcountry centres in western India, but in so far as new capital resources were involved, they were probably the already more mobile funds of moneylenders and traders (the Marwaris and Gujaratis) rather than capital of explicitly agrarian origin. In Bombay, resources remained tied up on the land, underpinned by the continued demand for land as an asset as well as by the adaptability of commercial agriculture. This contrasts with the situation in some other developing economies. In Japan, for example, agriculture was devastated by the dramatic collapse in the international price of silk, hitherto consistently the country's leading single export and buoyed up in the 1920s by the favours of Western fashion designers. Japanese agriculture was further afflicted by intense competition for the home market in rice from the imperial possessions of Taiwan and Korea. Here then was a greater and more long-term agricultural crisis. Capital left agriculture, and the desperate quest of peasants to supplement incomes drove down wages and labour costs. Whatever the massive social problems involved, these processes were at the heart of Japan's successful industrial recovery in the 1930s. The developments we have outlined in Bombay agriculture and its adaptability in the face of the depression, therefore help to explain why in the 1930s industrialisation was not stimulated so strongly in India as it was in some other developing economies.

NOTES

* Neil Charlesworth completed this paper in October 1985. Soon after, his health began to deteriorate (he was unable to attend the London conference) and he died in June 1986. His paper is being published as he left it, with only the very minimum of editorial amendments. I am very grateful to Sarah Charlesworth for giving permission for the paper to be published, and to Peter Robb for his editorial advice. Readers might wish to refer to Neil's *Peasants and imperial rule: agriculture and agrarian society in the Bombay Presidency, 1850-1935* (Cambridge University Press, Cambridge, 1985) which, in a number of important respects, provides the context for the present paper. IB.

1 For a general discussion of the phenomenon, see C.H. Lee, 'The effects of the depression on primary producing countries', *Journal of Contemporary History, 4*, 4 (1969), pp.139-55; C.P. Kindleberger, *The world in depression 1929-1939* (Allen Lane, Penguin Press, London, 1973).

2 For a discussion of price trends in the late nineteenth century, see M.B. McAlpin, 'Price movements and fluctuations in economic activity (1860-1947)' in D. Kumar (ed), *The Cambridge economic history of India*, vol.2 (Cambridge University Press, Cambridge, 1983), ch.11. On the impact of rupee devaluation, see also J. Adams and R.C. West, 'Money, prices and economic development in India 1861-1895', *Journal of Economic History, 39*, 1 (1979), pp.55-68.

3 See, for example, the works of C.J. Baker, particularly 'Debt and the depression in Madras, 1929-1936' in C. Dewey and A.G.Hopkins (eds), *The imperial impact: studies in the economic history of Africa and India* (Athlone Press, London, 1978) pp.233-42 and *An Indian rural economy 1880-1955: the Tamilnad countryside* (Oxford University Press, Delhi, 1984). For an all-India survey, see also D. Rothermund, 'Agrarian distress in India 1930-1935', ch.7 of his *The Indian economy under British rule and other essays* (Manohar, New Delhi, 1983).

4 J. Pouchepadass deals with this aspect well in his 'Peasant classes in twentieth century agrarian movements in India' in E.J. Hobsbawm *et al.* (eds), *Peasants in history: essays in honour of Daniel Thorner* (Oxford University Press, Calcutta, 1980), ch.9.

5 These views are suggested in the cited works of C.J. Baker and in the important study of the Indian economy in the late British period by B.R. Tomlinson, *The political economy of the Raj 1914-1947: the economics of decolonization in India* (Macmillan, London, 1979).

6 See, for example, A.K. Bagchi, *Private investment in India 1900-1939* (Cambridge University Press, Cambridge, 1972).

7 See the *Annual Crop and Season Report of the Bombay Presidency (*henceforth *Crop and Season Report)*, Appendix A. All subsequent references to crop and acreage statistics, where not explicitly stated, come from these reports.

8 *Census of India 1931, vol.8, part 2, Bombay Presidency* (Government Central Press, Bombay, 1932), Table 2.

9 *Crop and Season Report* 1930/1, para 43.

10 *Crop and Season Report* 1922/3, para 24.

11 *Crop and Season Report* 1930/1, para 44.

12 *Annual Land Revenue Administration Report of the Bombay Presidency (*henceforth *Land Revenue Report)* 1930/1, p.45.

13 India Office Records, Papers of Sir Frederick Sykes, Vol 3B, Sykes to Lord Willingdon, 20 December 1931.

14 *Land Revenue Report* 1933/4, p.23.

15 *Land Revenue Report* 1932/3, p.36.

16 *Report of the Peasant Enquiry Committee of the Maharashtra Provincial Congress Committee* (Poona, 1936), p.91.

17 R.S. Broomfield and R.M. Maxwell, *Report of the Special Enquiry into the Second Revision Settlement of the Bardoli and Chorasi Talukas* (Government Central Press, Bombay, 1929), Appendix A.

18 P.C. Patil, 'Studies in the cost of production of crops in the Deccan. No.1. Crops in the neighbourhood of Poona' *(Bombay Agriculture Department Bulletin*, 149, 1928, p.6.)

19 Ibid., p.8.

20 *Land Revenue Report* 1932/3, p.40.

21 Ibid., p.39.

22 *Land Revenue Report* 1931/2, p.39.

23 *Land Revenue Report* 1934/5, p.47.

24 *Land Revenue Report* 1931/2, p.39.

25 *Land Revenue Report* 1935/6, p.39.

26 *Land Revenue Report* 1934/5, p.42.

27 Ibid.

28 C.J. Baker, *An Indian rural economy*, pp.164-5.

29 Ibid., p.166.

30 *Land Revenue Report* 1932/3, p.39.

31 P.C. Patil, 'Studies in the cost of production of crops', p.8.

32 Ibid.

33 J. Breman, *Patronage and exploitation: changing agrarian relations in south Gujarat, India* (University of California Press, Berkeley, 1974).

34 P.C. Patil, 'Studies in the cost of production of crops', p.6.

35 Sykes Papers, Vol 3B, Sykes to Willingdon, 20 December 1931, para 6.

36 *Crop and Season Report* 1938/9, para 35.

4

THE LONG DEPRESSION: WEST AFRICAN EXPORT PRODUCERS AND THE WORLD ECONOMY, 1914-45[1]

S. M. MARTIN

In the wake of the severe and prolonged depression which afflicted Western industrial economies in the 1970s, there has been a renewed interest in the problems and lessons of the 1930s. Among Africanists, this interest was first manifested by French scholars, who in 1976 published a wide-ranging collection of articles on the period.[2] Their detailed research at first sight confirmed the consensus view of Anglophone historians; that the world depression from the end of the 1920s marked the start of a new era in West Africa. In Hopkins's well-known terminology, the slump placed the 'open economy' under a strain from which it was never to recover. Trading links between West Africa and the world economy, weakened by the slump, were further eroded by shipping problems during the second World War. Meanwhile, colonial administrations began to erect systems of direct control over trade and production which were to outlast not only the period of economic 'strain' but the colonial period itself.[3]

The French historians writing in 1976 focused mainly on the Hopkins transition from the 'open' to the 'managed' economy, arguing that the 1930s depression was a major watershed in this process. However, almost as a sideline, they provided statistics which show that the immediate impact of the 1930s depression on the incomes of West African export producers was by no means as severe as the consensus suggests. Instead, the depression formed part of a long series of events which cumulatively eroded rural producers' standard of living, and finally drove many to seek a new life in the towns.[4]

In this essay it will be argued, from statistical evidence relating to the Gold Coast and Nigeria, that a long depression can be identified, extending not, as the French scholars have suggested, from the mid-1920s to the late 1930s, but from the first World War to the second. The causes of decline in West Africa's barter terms of trade varied during this long period, but the underlying decline remained unchecked.[5] In analysing the responses of governments and producers to price changes in the world economy in this period, a distinction therefore needs to be made between immediate strategies designed to cope with the problems posed specifically by the 1930s slump, and long-term investment plans which, it will be argued, were developed from the 1920s onwards in response to the underlying deterioration in the terms of trade.

The main focus of the paper will be on the responses of African producers to the 'long depression'. It will be argued that these responses varied markedly between different areas of West Africa; and that the two main theories which have commonly been applied by economic historians to West Africa as a whole, actually have a limited applicability to the circumstances of different sub-regions. These two approaches are the vent-for-surplus theory as developed by Hla Myint from the views of Adam Smith; and dependency theory, as applied to Africa by for example Samir Amin and the historians working with Professor Coquery-Vidrovitch.[6] Both analyse the implications for primary producers of a growing involvement in the world economy. However, Myint focuses on the early stages of export growth, and highlights the existence of supply-side options at each stage thereafter. In contrast, the dependency approach lays emphasis on the ability of colonial officials or European merchants to close down many such options, and on the shattering impact of price fluctuations in a mature export economy.

It will be argued below that while the history of the 'long depression' bears out the dependency view that reliance on the world economy could be highly dangerous for the producers involved, yet a reliance on dependency theory alone in analysing producer reactions to this crisis could be dangerous for historians. The dependency approach highlights the mechanisms which could 'lock farmers in' to export industries. However, in some areas of West Africa this 'locking in' process had occurred only partially, if at all, by the 1930s. In these areas Myint's vent-for-surplus theory could be more useful for exploring producer responses to world market fluctuations, particularly if extended, as in Smith's original version, to the case of producers who had begun to invest and to undertake productivity-raising innovations following the initial entry into export production. This approach emphasises that within the agricultural export sector, producers could well be 'locked in' to specific specialisms through local resource constraints and past investments. However, producers are assumed to retain freedom of choice over future investment decisions, and over the most basic issue of whether to continue within the agricultural export sector or move into other occupations.[7]

In this paper, the regional applicability within West Africa of these two approaches will be explored with the aid of two main analytical distinctions: between French and British colonies, and between areas producing different cash crops. The three main export crops of West Africa during the 1920s and 1930s were cocoa, palm-oil and ground-nuts. Both the barter and income terms of trade for each crop followed a distinctive trend; and their contrasting patterns of resource use produced similarly distinctive patterns of social differentiation. These contrasts set the scene for markedly different patterns of response to the special stresses of the 1930s slump and to the longer-term real price decline.

Meanwhile, the policies of governments and the strength of rural resistance varied markedly from colony to colony, and overall between British and French West Africa. With this striking and complex regional variation, the need for theoretical flexibility becomes clearly apparent.

THE LONG DEPRESSION: EARLY STAGES, 1914-29

1914 is the conventional end-point for studies of the cash-crop boom in early colonial West Africa. By this year the oil-palm and ground-nut industries of Senegal, Sierra Leone and southern Nigeria were well established. Cocoa production was well under way in the Gold Coast, and rapidly becoming popular in Western Nigeria; and the railway from Lagos to Kano had been opened, stimulating an astonishingly rapid growth of ground-nut production by Hausa farmers, in defiance of all colonial hopes and official plans for cotton.[8] In contrast the decade which followed is conventionally viewed as one of (wartime) disruption, consolidation and then modest prosperity, before the shock of 1929.[9] However, as Hopkins noted in 1973, historians have tended to skim over this decade rather than give it the benefit of detailed research; and this despite the compilation by 1972 of indices for the Gold Coast and Nigeria barter terms of trade, which showed a dramatic fall during the world trade collapse of 1920-1, followed by stabilisation at levels well below those of 1910-14.[10]

The French scholars who participated in the 1976 conference 'L'Afrique et la crise de 1930', reinforced the view suggested by these indices. They found that the slump of 1920-1 had been followed by a very short-lived revival: export prices began to fall again throughout Francophone Africa in 1926-7. From 1929 they began to decline more rapidly, but this fall was muted in real terms by a simultaneous fall in the prices of manufactured imports.[11]

This general view can be supported and refined by a detailed look at the terms of trade for cocoa, ground-nuts and palm produce, exported from the Gold Coast and Nigeria. Tables 1-3 provide a series of five-year averages which make the basic patterns clear. These indices build upon the work of earlier authors, notably Helleiner, and on more recent research on specific crops and on the movement of import prices.

The indices constructed during the 1960s differed in their view of the first World War period. While Helleiner's work on Nigeria suggested a sharp decline in the barter terms of trade from as early as 1914, the work of Kay and Hymer on the Gold Coast suggested only a small decline before 1918, followed by a rapid collapse as import prices soared and then export prices slumped in the violent post-war trading crisis.[12] This divergence was surprising, as fragmented evidence from colonial records suggests that the Gold Coast shared the wartime problems of lost German markets and shipping shortages which caused declining terms of trade elsewhere. More recently compiled indices for Senegal and Dahomey show a similar trend to the Nigerian one.[13] Intrigued by this anomaly and by contradictions between the Kay-Hymer index and an import price index compiled by Ady, Francis Teal has recently constructed a fresh import price index for the Gold Coast, using data taken from these authors' original source, the Gold Coast Blue Books.[14] This index shows marked rises in import prices during the first World War. When combined with the export price index for Gold Coast cocoa, it confirms that the outbreak of the War marked the beginning of the 'long depression'.

While shipping shortages and high import prices eroded the living standards of West African farmers, they provided ample opportunities for European firms to make windfall gains. Despite the concern expressed by local British officials, nothing was done to curb the firms' activities or to regulate prices. However the British government's response was to remove its own surcharge on exports of palm kernels to outside the British Empire.[15] Thus persistently high import prices were allowed to compound the difficulties faced by West African export producers during the slump of 1920-1 and the years of slow export recovery which followed. As can be seen from Table 4, a wide gap opened between UK wholesale prices and British West African import prices during the first World War and the post-war boom. During the later 1920s, this gap failed to close. Throughout the decade, the barter terms of trade for West African cocoa, ground-nuts and palm produce remained below the levels for 1910-14.

During the difficult decade of the 1920s there were major differences between the experience of the three staple cash crops of West Africa. It is clear from Table 1 that the barter terms of trade for ground-nuts remained relatively buoyant throughout the inter-war period, while for cocoa and palm produce there was unsteady decline. In 1920-4 the barter terms of trade for palm produce and for cocoa had sunk to between a third and a fifth of their 1910-14 average, and after a brief recovery these depths were reached again in the 1930s. It may be argued that this decline was related to the very rapid expansion of production in Africa and Asia, which helped to cause a glut on the world market.[16] However, there was no direct relationship between the degree of supply increase and the degree of price decline, as can be seen by comparing Tables 5 and 1. The supply of all three commodities rose rapidly during the period 1910-30; the least rise was in palm produce, which suffered the most severe price decline. The amount of palm-oil entering world trade rose by 112 per cent between 1909-13 and 1926-30; palm kernels and copra (which were close substitutes) by 89 per cent; ground-nuts by 139 per cent; and cocoa by 256 per cent.

Palm producers suffered particularly severely during the 1920s for a number of reasons. Long-established customers in the tin-plating industry and in low-quality soap manufacture were not growing rapidly in the inter-war period. Moreover no new uses for palm-oil were being developed. Although margarine and higher-quality soap production were growing steadily in Europe during the 1920s, West African palm-kernel exporters found it hard to exploit the most important new demand, that from the American food and soap industries. These were switching from home-produced cotton-seed oil to coconut oil, extracted from copra imported from the Philippines. Copra had two important advantages which offset the fact that it was more expensive per ton than palm kernels: a higher proportion of oil could be extracted from copra than from palm kernels; and coconut processing yielded a higher proportion of glycerine as a by-product.[17] In brief, West African kernel producers were at a disadvantage in the new, expanding segments of the market, while palm producers in general were confronted with slow growth in their staple demands.

In contrast, cocoa producers in the Gold Coast and Western Nigeria were expanding their share of a still rapidly growing trade. A combination of light population density and ideal climatic conditions had enabled farmers there to secure 42 per cent of world cocoa exports by 1910-14; this was increased to 72 per cent in 1925-9.[18] The barter terms of trade for cocoa, initially very favourable, fell just as sharply as those for palm produce at the start of the 'long depression', and remained depressed by the high import prices of the 1920s. Yet the market was able to absorb the major increase in exports which occurred during the 1920s, as cocoa trees planted during the boom of the early 1910s came to maturity. This expansion in export volumes ensured that farmers in the Gold Coast and in Western Nigeria experienced the mid-1920s as years of relatively high real agricultural incomes.[19]

Ground-nut producers too were relatively well off during the 1920s. In contrast to palm kernels and copra, ground-nuts yielded a fine-quality oil which could be used in cooking and as a salad oil as well as in the manufacture of high-quality soap and margarine. The 1920s saw a growing demand for salad oil, especially in France, and a growing European taste for the edible nuts themselves; and this helped to sustain the barter terms of trade for West African ground-nuts despite the high cost of imports after the war.[20] In Senegal, production expanded rapidly during the 1920s. Sine and Wolof cultivators needed to obtain money to pay taxes and buy imports, and despite the decline in their barter terms of trade during and after the first World War, ground-nuts still provided the surest way of doing this. Like the palm producers of Eastern Nigeria and Sierra Leone, the ground-nut farmers of Senegal and Northern Nigeria were locked into their export monoculture by local resource constraints. In dry savanna regions like these there were few crops which could be grown profitably, and the main alternative, cotton, posed even heavier labour demands than ground-nuts at peak-season. Nevertheless, in a buoyant market these ecological constraints were not an obvious cause of hardship. Far more striking was the burden of direct taxation in both French Senegal and British Northern Nigeria, for this deprived local farmers of much of the benefit arising from relatively buoyant terms of trade.[21]

At this stage of the 'long depression', to summarise, farmers in specialist palm-producing regions probably had most cause for worry. Ground-nut producers were equally 'locked in' to a single cash crop, but as yet had less cause to worry about their future income. Meanwhile, cocoa producers had become 'locked in' by investment in a tree crop which took seven years to begin substantial yields; however in Western Nigeria they had maintained a steady level of palm production, and both here and in the Gold Coast were enjoying an unprecedented burst of prosperity as cocoa production levels soared. These contrasts between export industries were increasingly becoming regional contrasts, as each region became more closely identified with a specific cash crop. As the 'long depression' advanced into the 1930s, these contrasts became overlain by a further distinction: between those producers who were 'locked in' to the cash crop economy, and were being impoverished by fixed obligations to tax-collectors, landlords and creditors; and those who retained enough wealth and freedom of action to develop investment strategies in response to the slump. This second distinction was partly regional, between colonies where the burden of direct taxation was more and less important, and where European firms held a greater or lesser monopoly power over external trade; and partly social, between African farmers and brokers who controlled land and credit facilities and their poorer neighbours. In either case it was sharpened and entrenched by the events of the 1930s, when the 'long depression' entered a new and distinctive phase.

THE 1930s

The most distinctive features of the slump which took hold from the close of the 1920s were a generalised deflation and contraction of credit.[22] These had extremely uneven effects on the volume and value of trade as between specific commodities, and so as between different regions of the world. In West Africa, the slump intensified the pattern of declining barter terms of trade and growing export volumes which had been characteristic of the 1920s. The accelerated decline in nominal palm-produce prices began as early as 1926. For ground-nuts, the slide began in 1927; and for cocoa, in 1928.[23] The major break with previous West African price trends was a sharp drop in import prices, resulting from the rapid deflation in Europe and America in the early 1930s. The collapse was so severe that it eroded much of the gap which had opened up during the first World War between British and British West African price levels. Between 1925-9 and 1935-9 Nigerian and Gold Coast import prices fell by over 40 per cent, while UK wholesale prices fell by only 20 per cent.[24] This sharp fall in import prices cushioned the impact upon West African producers of declining cocoa, ground-nut and palm-produce prices. Yet the decline in barter terms of trade continued; only for cocoa were these more favourable in the early 1930s than they had been during the slump of the early 1920s. In compensation, and again as in the 1920s, growing export volumes ensured that the total export income from cocoa and ground-nuts continued to grow. Meanwhile, palm produce remained set in a pattern of erratic decline, which increased production volumes could do little to alleviate.[25]

As the volume of production grew, more people became involved in the export economies of West Africa so that those who had long been committed to this sector began to face acute pressures on land and labour resources. Two examples from the Gold Coast and Eastern Nigeria illustrate the varying impact of these pressures.

In Eastern Nigeria, oil palms grew in symbiosis with subsistence food farming, and as export production rose the main pressure was felt on labour rather than land resources. Some groups of producers, for example the Ngwa-Igbo, reacted by taking up labour-saving processing methods or simply by limiting the volume of output; others, for example the Ibibio, reacted by specialising in palm production and importing an increasing volume of staple foodstuffs from outside the main palm belt. The latter strategy led to a closer integration of local food prices with those of palm produce. In 1920 British officials had observed that local food prices fluctuated far less than palm-produce prices; but by 1938 the anthropologist J.S. Harris found that these prices were tending to move together, for the specialised palm producers were now providing the main market for local food crops.[26]

In the cocoa-producing districts of South Asante in the Gold Coast, export expansion was accompanied by a rapid growth in labour migration from the Northern Territory of the colony and from neighbouring French possessions. By the late 1920s many of these labourers were working on annual contracts for payments agreed in advance. Meanwhile, within Asante, pressures on land resources were beginning to emerge. 'Stranger' (immigrant) farmers (including the subjects of neighbouring stool chiefs, the local traditional rulers) were liable for a rent which had been fixed at ld per cocoa tree in 1913, at the time of the major planting boom. A final, important fixed cash demand arose for farmers from the 'advances' which African cocoa brokers and moneylenders had lent them; this was initially on the security of one year's crop, but by the late 1920s and early 1930s increasingly on the security of several harvests or on the farm itself.[27] An advances system also operated in the Eastern Nigeria palm-produce trade, but it applied only to dealings between traders and involved no security; in this area many African traders simply defaulted on their debts to European firms at the beginning of the 1930s slump.[28]

These examples illustrate two different ways in which the 'long depression' was beginning to have more severe effects by the beginning of the 1930s. In Eastern Nigeria the impact of falling export prices was now felt in other areas of the domestic economy, while some producers were reaching the limit of their ability to produce more and so to slow the decline in their cash incomes.

Meanwhile, in South Asante the rapid deflation of the early 1930s sharpened the conflict between those with fixed cash obligations and their creditors. In both regions, the resulting tensions were brought to a head by the actions of outsiders: colonial officials and European traders. In the remainder of this section, these tensions and conflicts will be outlined, and compared with the parallel events occurring in French West Africa. Finally, in the section which follows, the long-term investment strategies of wealthier farmers and of colonial governments will be outlined, and related to the underlying problems revealed by the 'long depression' as a whole.

In French West Africa the 1930s crisis had its greatest impact upon European traders and officials, precisely because they were closely tied in to a credit system severely shaken by the Wall Street crash. The crisis underlined their weaknesses: the narrow colonial revenue base; the absence of local credit sources; and the 'archaic' commercial structure of many firms.[29] While the firms concentrated on mere survival, French officials began to strengthen the administration's position. African farmers were forced to bear fresh financial burdens as taxation shifted from customs duties (which at least were proportional to export incomes) towards fixed capitation taxes. While those who remained on the farm struggled to maintain their incomes by increased export production, many found that the increased tax burden was the last straw and fled in desperation to the towns. Yet there too employment opportunities were shrinking and wages falling. Thus began a gradual transformation of the impoverished peasantry into the urban poor, a process which, Coquery-Vidrovitch argues, continues today.[30]

British officials had less cause for concern in the 1930s over their tax system than had their French counterparts, for they had carried out extensive fiscal reforms following a major crisis during the first World War. Before 1914 British officials had relied heavily upon customs duties levied on imported Dutch and German spirits, but on the outbreak of war this source of revenue suddenly dried up and new ones had to be found. By 1922, customs duties were being supplemented by railway revenues and by income from direct taxation in Northern and Western Nigeria.[31] Meanwhile, in 1916, export duties were introduced; and in a series of changes introduced over the following years both these and the import duties were redefined to relate to the volume rather than the value of trade. This made them relatively impervious to deflation.[32] Between 1926-9 and 1930-3 the nominal value of Nigerian customs revenues fell by 25 per cent: over the same period, import prices fell by 36 per cent.[33]

While the slump thus caused less of a fiscal crisis in British than in French West Africa, none the less the early 1930s saw vigorous tax protest in the British territories. While French historians write of African peasants reduced to the level of bare survival, deprived even of the reflex of revolt, in British West Africa direct taxation so provoked rebellion that officials were ultimately forced

using them to reshape the trading economies of West Africa itself had taken hold. Among contemporary economists, Bauer opposed the idea but Helleiner welcomed it.[45]

Although the prospect of state-sponsored 'modernisation' was implemented on a large scale only after the second World War, enthusiasm for it had begun to grow during the early stages of the 'long depression'. During the first World War, British metropolitan officials had toyed with the idea of taking over the West African produce marketing system; and during the 1920s they gave serious thought to supporting private-sector mill-and-plantation schemes to revitalise the ailing oil-palm industry. William Lever's earlier 'modernisation' schemes for the industry had been rejected because of his demands for monopoly concessions over transport facilities, land and palm trees; but in the 1920s they received support from merchants and officials faced by low world market prices and an emerging Sumatran plantation industry.[46] During the 1930s, limited metropolitan funding became available for West African state investment, especially in the French colonies. Here, historians have found that the inflow of public and private loans established an invidious aid-debt cycle: there was thus a net outflow of funds by the mid-1930s. Within Africa, many of the new loans were used in well-established ways, financing road construction and in other forms of infrastructural investment. Some plantation experiments were carried out in French West Africa, and in France itself ambitious schemes for industrialisation were vigorously debated, although to little effect.[47]

In British West Africa from the 1940s the expansion of government revenues through the Marketing Boards proceeded inexorably. For example, in Nigeria, between 1947 and 1962, export duties, Marketing Board surpluses and produce purchase taxes accounted for between 20 and 32 per cent of the export income from African cocoa, ground-nut, palm produce and cotton production.[48] In the case of the oil-palm industry, part of the government revenue was used to establish large-scale Pioneer oil mills and plantations. As with French development plans, this strategy had two main aims: to lower production costs in response to the real price decline of the 'long depression'; and to improve quality to match the standards achieved by South-East Asian producers. The solution to the 'long depression' was thus seen to lie in overcoming the technical limitations of peasant export production. Post-war policies were designed to do this at a stroke; but the plantations proved to be vulnerable to diseases which were rare among semi-wild palms, and the mills became unprofitable owing to operating inefficiencies, lack of spare parts and a shortage of skilled management. A similar tale could be told for the post-war Gold Coast (Ghanaian) cocoa industry.[49]

These official experiments in 'modernisation' revealed the high initial costs and production difficulties involved in the more radical solutions to the income problems of the 'long depression'. Meanwhile, during the depression itself and later when trade revived during the 1950s, African farmers were seeking their own solutions. For many, there was pitifully little choice. As Coquery-Vidrovitch has emphasised, the hopelessly indebted and the landless - those most tightly caught in the 'dependency' trap - had little choice but to stay on the land and work for ever-diminishing returns, or else to drift to the cities. However, there is evidence from recent research on southern Nigeria of the existence of alternative strategies which could be pursued by those less firmly 'locked in' to a particular form of production. A first example, of Ngwa-Igbo palm producers and traders in Eastern Nigeria, indicates the freedom of action implicit in a 'vent-for-surplus' pattern of export expansion, within which a viable food-producing sector demanding little investment was sustained, thus freeing the wealthy to invest elsewhere. The second case, that of Yoruba cocoa producers in Western Nigeria, shows how a second generation could profit from their parents' investment in farming and from a strong local tradition of diversification when the terms of trade moved against them.

The Ngwa-Igbo people of Eastern Nigeria had been involved in the palm-oil export trade from the early nineteenth century. The poor soils and high population densities of their region prevented them from diversifying into rubber or cocoa during the late nineteenth and early twentieth centuries, so that by the 1920s they appeared firmly locked into the faltering oil and kernel trades. However, partly because of the poor transport facilities in their landlocked region, they had always kept their expanding oil-palm production within the limit compatible with self-sufficiency in staple, starchy foodstuffs. During the 1920s and 1930s they successfully relieved the pressure placed by growing population on their land resources by adopting cassava, which placed extra burdens on women (because of its time-consuming cooking requirements) but which could be grown on previously fallow land and which could be harvested during the previously hungry season. At first the adoption and spread of cassava thus followed a logic internal to the domestic economy, rather than following the impulses of the commercial sector. However, as the 'long depression' in the oil-palm industry wore on, Ngwa women began to prepare *gari* (cassava meal) for sale in local urban markets. During the second World War, a thriving trade grew up, taking *gari* to the urban markets of Northern Nigeria, and so diverting the local economy away from the production of palm-oil and kernels for the war effort. Finally, as the growth of the state and the oil boom during the 1960s and 1970s fuelled the growth of Nigeria's towns, *gari* (for sale in the urban markets) took over from palm produce as the main source of income for many Ngwa farmers.[50]

While the expansion of cassava production provided an alternative to palm production for Ngwa women, Ngwa men found alternatives which took them off the land altogether. Their departure was not always for life. I was able to interview a number of returners in villages near Aba (Eastern Nigeria) in 1980-1. Many had begun with village-based palm production in the 1920s and 1930s, but had then used their savings or their education to go into urban work. Some had been bicycle traders; others, clerks or labourers; one, a domestic servant and one, a herbalist. All saw the period in which they had worked outside the village as a time when they had earned the money essential to marry and to set up an independent household. They had returned to invest their wealth in yam and oil-palm farming: but their sons and daughters were following a different life-cycle, living and working permanently in the cities.[51]

This pattern of migration differs significantly from that described by Coquery-Vidrovitch for French West Africa. The farmers I interviewed in Eastern Nigeria were not driven from their villages by desperation: they went to increase wealth and social status, taking some savings or skills with them to ease their way. Unfettered by mortgages or inescapable debts, they retained enough income from faltering export production to be able to take up more attractive opportunities elsewhere. During the 1920s, while Western Nigerian farmers were still investing in cocoa, the younger generation of palm producers were investing in trade, in education and in new urban skills.

But even in Western Nigeria, enthusiasm for cocoa was waning by the opening of the 1930s. Two recent studies of cocoa-farming communities around Ife and Ilesha have emphasised the contrast between the first generation of cocoa farmers and their educated descendants.[52] Within these highly differentiated Yoruba communities, young Christian and Muslim men used cocoa and trade in their search for social and economic emancipation at the turn of the twentieth century. The rate of cocoa planting rose steadily to reach a peak in 1930, but then declined. There was a further brief revival in the early 1940s during wartime campaigns for increased production. However, by the 1960s planting was falling off; it then collapsed during the oil boom of the 1970s. These more recent trends are directly related to the second-generation farmers' uses of cocoa income, and so to the circumstances of the 'long depression' itself.

The early cocoa pioneers in Western Nigeria spent much of their income on marrying more wives and acquiring slaves and pawns (debtors who discharged their debts in labour services). During the 1920s, however, pawning died out, and an increase in wage labour allowed the pioneers' sons to look beyond their households for help with their expanding cocoa farms. Land remained easily available by comparison with South Asante, and rents charged to 'strangers' were low. Thus the expansion of a cocoa farm did not embroil its owner in substantial rent obligations, although some debts were incurred through the advances system. In short, social differentiation in cocoa-producing areas was only beginning to emerge, and remained less marked than in South Asante. No Yoruba 'gentry' emerged, partly because those who made most money out of cocoa farming preferred to spend it on town houses and on urban politics, rather than in rural investment.[53]

While this taste for town life may have had its roots in Yoruba culture rather than in the circumstances of the 'long depression', it was during the 1920s and 1930s that wealthier cocoa farmers and traders began to invest in education, to enable their sons to pursue careers in commerce, the professions and the bureaucracy. In some cases the educated sons travelled widely, for example as sellers of imported cloth in remoter villages. In others, increasingly so from the 1940s, they pursued a more settled life in the larger administrative centres. Meanwhile, many continued to earn a rentier income from cocoa farms which they rarely visited; and the farms themselves were rarely replanted with fresh cocoa trees. Since 1950, most new cocoa planting has been carried out by migrant farmers from outside the cocoa belt or by farmers on its fringes, who had not shared in the initial growth of the industry.[54] In her study of several migrant communities from the savanna villages of Iree and Eripa, Sara Berry suggests that a failure to re-invest in cocoa may now also be found in these newer cocoa-farming communities.[55] During the late 1930s and 1940s young men from Iree and Eripa went out to plant cocoa in Ife and Ondo Divisions, earning money which paid for their sons' education and for their own entry into trade. They also invested in family ceremonies, houses and community projects back in Iree and Eripa, ensuring their social standing there. Thus cash-crop production was seen as a means to progress within a community whose heart lay elsewhere.

This view of cash cropping and this desire to invest elsewhere can be seen as thoroughly reasonable responses to the circumstances of the 'long depression'. Between 1914 and 1945, producer prices for cocoa and for palm produce were not only low by comparison with those of the early twentieth century; they were also declining, in several painful stages, of which the 1930s slump was just one. While some money could still be made from export production, it brought higher immediate returns if then invested in trade - the point most clearly recalled by informants in interviews; and ultimately it brought higher returns still if invested in the education of the next generation. As Berry has pointed out with reference to the 1970s, as long as the state prospered and the bureaucracy expanded, some educated sons could far outstrip in wealth the fathers who had worked for their future as cocoa farmers.[56]

CONCLUSION

It is often argued that the downturn in West African export production which has occurred since the 1960s has its origins in contemporary government policies, and especially in the inefficiency and high surpluses of Marketing Boards controlled by urban-based African governments.[57] However, the evidence presented in this paper suggests that the decline has deeper roots, not only in the policies of colonial governments and Marketing Boards in their earlier years but also in the investment decisions being pursued by wealthy export producers since the 1920s. Their decision to put money into houses, politics and education arose from the economic circumstances of the 'long depression', from the series of falls in the barter terms of trade. The Marketing Board policies of the recent past are but the latest in a long line of challenges to the prosperity of export producers. Faced with 30 years of price stagnation or decline, it is hardly surprising that producers began to look outside agriculture for prospects of wealth.

Ironically, the onset of the 'long depression' may have short-circuited the very process of cost-cutting, quality-raising innovation with which the planners of the 1950s hoped to end it. Palm producers in Eastern Nigeria and cocoa planters in South Asante, for example, were beginning to feel pressures on land and especially on labour supplies by the eve of the first World War. However, the gradual opening of employment opportunities in commerce and clerical work combined with the export price collapses of the period 1914-45 to divert much of the wealth which remained within rural communities into trade and education. Meanwhile, those who worked for wages, who were heavily mortgaged or seriously in debt, found themselves vulnerable in the face of the rapid changes in money values and credit terms which occurred at the close of the 1920s. For the more heavily taxed producers of Northern Nigeria and French West Africa, there was little escape from either the export economy or the financial problems within it. While those with cash were able to invest elsewhere, many export producers remained trapped within the rural economy, too poor to improve their circumstances within it.

TABLE 1: Barter terms of trade: 1910-14 = 100

	Nigeria Cocoa	Ground-nuts	Palm-oil	Palm kernels	Gold Coast Cocoa
1910-14	100.00	100.00	100.00	100.00	100.00
1915-19	43.09	60.09	50.87	45.07	52.22
1920-24	17.76	58.67	32.15	27.89	28.55
1925-29	40.15	68.97	38.27	34.72	44.82
1930-34	25.01	50.46	20.88	24.81	34.62
1935-39	32.46	58.27	25.47	28.26	41.42
1940-44	14.65	40.15	11.11	12.66	18.93

TABLE 2: Export volumes: 1910-14 = 100

	Nigeria	Eastern Nigeria		West and central Nigeria			Gold Coast
	Ground-nuts	Palm-oil	Palm kernels	Palm-oil	Palm kernels	Cocoa	Cocoa
1910-14	100.00	100.00	100.00	100.00	100.00	100.00	100.00
1915-19	503.96	Not available		Not available		360.07	233.03
1920-24	540.40	132.78	124.33	94.07	113.10	707.34	405.50
1925-29	1452.92	177.08	170.45	131.51	136.19	1179.35	540.37
1930-34	2303.15	198.36	201.84	105.92	138.23	1633.03	546.79
1935-39	2576.45	236.15	244.38	103.92	165.12	2504.07	655.05
1940-44	2218.87	230.22	263.05	102.26	149.43	2136.05	461.47

TABLE 3: Income terms of trade: 1910-14 = 100

	Nigeria	Eastern Nigeria		West and central Nigeria			Gold Coast
	Ground-nuts	Palm-oil	Palm kernels	Palm-oil	Palm kernels	Cocoa	Cocoa
1910-14	100.00	100.00	100.00	100.00	100.00	100.00	100.00
1915-19	171.49	Not available		Not available		164.12	110.81
1920-24	176.23	44.87	35.57	32.73	32.52	135.95	113.51
1925-29	553.15	68.57	58.97	51.51	47.20	465.36	240.54
1930-34	626.47	41.77	49.04	23.65	34.42	413.19	186.49
1935-39	863.15	61.56	69.16	29.17	47.96	809.45	266.22
1940-44	536.82	25.75	32.75	11.52	18.65	318.25	87.84

Sources for Tables 1-3: G.K. Helleiner, *Peasant agriculture, government, and economic growth in Nigeria* (Richard D. Irwin, Inc., Homewood, Illinois, 1966), Tables II-B-2 to II-B-4, IV-A-7 and IV-A-8; E.J. Usoro, *The Nigerian oil palm industry: government policy and export production, 1906-1965* (Ibadan University Press, Ibadan, 1974), Table 2.10; S.S. Berry, *Cocoa, custom and socio-economic change in rural Western Nigeria* (Clarendon Press, Oxford, 1975), Appendix III; T.R. Birnberg and S.A. Resnick, *Colonial development: an econometric study* (Yale University Press, New Haven, 1975), Table A.32; S.M. Martin, 'The history of the oil palm industry in south-eastern Nigeria, 1891-1929', unpublished PhD thesis, University of Birmingham, 1984, Statistical Appendix; on Gold Coast cocoa prices and export volumes, F.J. Teal, 'Growth, comparative advantage and the economic effects of government. A case study of Ghana', unpublished PhD thesis, University of London, 1984, Appendix, Tables 6 and 9; on Gold Coast import prices, F.J. Teal, 'The foreign exchange regime and growth: a comparison of Ghana and the Ivory Coast', *African Affairs, 85*, 339 (1986), p.271.

TABLE 4: Import price indices: 1910-14= 100

	Nigeria	Gold Coast (Teal)	Gold Coast (Kay)	UK wholesale prices
1910-14	100	100	100	100
1915-19	210	229	168	199
1920-24	356	340	199	203
1925-29	273	231	163	148
1930-34	176	158	129	108
1935-39	162	133	131	120
1940-44	293	241	237	188

Sources: As for Tables 1-3, plus G.B. Kay, *The political economy of colonialism in Ghana: a collection of documents and statistics, 1900-1960*, with a statistical abstract prepared in collaboration with S.H. Hymer (Cambridge University Press, Cambridge, 1972), Table 20c; B.R. Mitchell, *Abstract of British historical statistics* (Cambridge University Press, Cambridge, 1962), pp.476-7; B.R. Mitchell and H.G. Jones, *Second abstract of British historical statistics* (Cambridge University Press, Cambridge, 1971), pp.188-9.

TABLE 5: Total quantities of palm produce, copra, coconut oil, ground-nuts and cocoa entering world trade, 1909-13 and 1926-30
(Five-year averages: thousands of tons per annum)

	Palm-oil	Palm kernels	Copra	Coconut oil	Ground-nuts	Cocoa
1909-13	122	317	551	not known	586	226
1926-30	224	546	1,064	208[a]	1,401	493

[a] exports from copra-producing countries

Sources: Empire Marketing Board, Nos. 54 and 61, *Survey of oilseeds and vegetable oils, vol.1. Oil palm products* (HMSO, London, 1932), pp.117 and 123; *vol.2. Coconut palm products* (HMSO, London, 1932), pp.174-5 and 186; Imperial Economic Committee, Intelligence Branch, IEC/S/2, *Survey of oilseeds and vegetable oils, vol.3. Ground nut products* (HMSO, London, 1934), pp.220-1; D.H. Urquhart, *Cocoa* (Longman, London, 1956), p.174.

NOTES

1 I wish to thank Dr Francis Teal of the Bureau of Agricultural Economics, Canberra, for many stimulating discussions, for ideas put forward in an earlier joint version of this paper, and for his valuable statistical material on the Gold Coast (Ghana). Special thanks are also due to Dr Gareth Austin of the Institute of Commonwealth Studies, London, for the use of his unpublished material on Asante social history. I remain responsible for the views put forward in this paper. Dr Teal brings the story up to date, and provides further details on Ghana, in 'The foreign exchange regime and growth: a comparison of Ghana and the Ivory Coast', *African Affairs, 85*, 339 (1986), pp.267-82.

2 C. Coquery-Vidrovitch (ed), 'L'Afrique et la crise de 1930', *Revue Française d'Histoire d'Outre-Mer, 63*, 232-3 (1976).

3 A.G. Hopkins, *An economic history of West Africa* (Longman, London, 1973), ch.7, 'The open economy under strain'; G.K. Helleiner, *Peasant agriculture, government, and economic growth in Nigeria* (Richard D. Irwin, Inc., Homewood, Illinois, 1966), pp.18-19.

4 C. Coquery-Vidrovitch, 'L'Afrique coloniale française et la crise de 1930: crise structurelle et genèse du sous-développement. Rapport d'ensemble', in 'L'Afrique et la crise', pp.386-424. See also J. Marseille, 'Le commerce de l'Algérie de 1924 à 1938: interprétation des termes de l'échange, ibid., pp.529-37. Coquery-Vidrovitch's article has been reprinted, with slight modifications, under the title 'Mutation de l'impérialisme colonial français dans les années 30', *African Economic History, 4* (1977), pp.103-52. All references below are to the 1976 version.

5 'Barter terms of trade' means the price level of exports relative to that of imports. When multiplied by the volume of exports, this gives the 'income terms of trade', that is, the level of import-purchasing power generated by that export industry.

6 H. Myint, 'The "classical theory" of international trade and the underdeveloped countries', *Economic Journal, 68*, 2 (1958), pp.317-37; S. Amin, *Unequal development* (Harvester Press, Hassocks, 1976). For an illustration of the contrasting West Africa-wide application of these theories see J.S. Hogendorn, 'The "vent-for-surplus" model and African cash agriculture to 1914', *Savanna, 5*, 1 (1976), pp.15-28; W.M. Freund and R.W. Shenton, ' "Vent-for-surplus" theory and the economic history of West Africa', *Savanna, 6*, 2 (1977), pp.191-9.

7 A. Smith, *An inquiry into the nature and causes of the wealth of nations*, edited by E. Cannan (The Modern Library, New York, 1937), book 4, ch. 1, esp. p.415.

8 Hopkins, *Economic history*, chs 5 and 6; J.S. Hogendorn, 'Economic initiative and African cash farming: pre-colonial origins and early colonial developments', in P. Duignan and L.H. Gann (eds), *Colonialism in Africa, 1870-1960* (Cambridge University Press, Cambridge, 1975), vol.4, pp.283-328.

9 A.J.H. Latham, *The depression and the developing world, 1914-1939* (Croom Helm, London, 1981), p.175.

10 Hopkins, *Economic history*, pp.180-4.

11 Coquery-Vidrovitch, 'L'Afrique et la crise', p.387; H. d'Almeida-Topor, 'Interpretation graphique', ibid., pp.713-76; J. Marseille, *Empire colonial et capitalisme français: histoire d'un divorce* (Albin Michel, Paris, 1984), pp.165-71.

12 G.B. Kay, *The political economy of colonialism in Ghana: a collection of documents and statistics, 1900-1960,* with a statistical abstract prepared in collaboration with S.H. Hymer (Cambridge University Press, Cambridge, 1972), Table 20c; see graphs in Hopkins, *Economic history*, p.180.

13 D. Killingray, 'Repercussions of World War I in the Gold Coast', *Journal of African*

History, 19, 1 (1978), pp.39-59; M. Mbodj, 'Sénégal et dépendance: le Sine-Saloum et l'arachide, 1887-1940', in C. Coquery-Vidrovitch (ed), *Sociétés paysannes du Tiers-Monde* (Presses Universitaires, Lille, 1984), p.150; P. Manning, *Slavery, colonialism and economic growth in Dahomey, 1640-1960* (Cambridge University Press, Cambridge, 1982), p.245.

14 See Table 4. See also P. Ady, 'Trends in cocoa production', *Bulletin of the Oxford University Institute of Economics and Statistics, 11*, 12 (1949), pp.399-404; F.J. Teal, 'Growth, comparative advantage and the economic effects of government. A case study of Ghana', unpublished PhD thesis, University of London, 1984, Table 8; F.J. Teal, 'Foreign exchange regime', p.271; Gold Coast Colony, Blue Books (Government Printer, Accra, annually 1910-44).

15 *West Africa: Committee on Edible and Oil-Producing Nuts and Seeds: Minutes of evidence* (PP 1916, IV, Cd 8248), pp.35, 51-4, 67-70 and 209-11; *Report of a Committee on Trade and Taxation for British West Africa* (PP 1922, XVI, Cmd 1600).

16 For a similar argument relating to food-grains, see Latham, *Depression*, pp.175-6. On palm produce, ground-nuts and cocoa, see sources for Table 5.

17 In 1921 UK copra prices were 50 per cent higher than those for palm kernels; in 1938 they were only 20 per cent higher. Comparable figures are not available for the US market. C. Wilson, *The history of Unilever: a study in economic growth and social change* (2 vols., Cassell and Co., London, 1954), vol.1, pp.278-80; E.J. Usoro, *The Nigerian oil palm industry: government policy and export production, 1906-1965* (Ibadan University Press, Ibadan, 1974), pp.19, 21 and 28; K. Snodgrass, *Copra and coconut oil* (Stanford University Press, Stanford, California, 1928), ch.1. See also Empire Marketing Board, Nos.54 and 61, *Survey of oilseeds and vegetable oils, vol.1. Oil palm products* (HMSO, London, 1932), pp.117 and 123; *vol.2. Coconut palm products* (HMSO, London, 1932), pp.174-5 and 186; Imperial Economic Committee, Intelligence Branch, IEC/S/2, *Survey of oilseeds and vegetable oils, vol.3. Ground nut products* (HMSO, London, 1934), pp.220-1; D.H. Urquhart, *Cocoa* (Longman, London, 1956), p.174.

18 Empire Marketing Board Nos. 54 and 61, *Survey of oilseeds and vegetable oils, vol.1*, pp.117 and 123; *vol.2*, pp.174-5 and 186; Imperial Economic Committee, *Survey of oilseeds and vegetable oils, vol.3*, pp.220-1; S.S. Berry, *Cocoa, custom and socio-economic change in rural Western Nigeria* (Clarendon Press, Oxford, 1975), pp.40 and 221-2; C. Gunnarsson, *The Gold Coast cocoa industry, 1900-1939* (Swedish Economic History Association, Lund, 1978), p.176; Urquhart, *Cocoa*, pp.25-8 and 181.

19 See Tables 2 and 3.

20 Imperial Economic Committee, *Survey of oilseeds and vegetable oils, vol.3*, pp.219 and 230-1.

21 Mbodj, 'Sénégal et dépendance', pp.139-54; J. Tosh, 'The cash-crop revolution in tropical Africa: an agricultural reappraisal', *African Affairs, 79*, 314 (1980), pp.79-94; M. Watts, *Silent violence: food, famine and peasantry in Northern Nigeria* (California University Press, Berkeley, 1983), pp.305-26; see also Tables 2 and 3 and, on cotton, T.B. Ingawa, 'A study of the rural economic history of Katsina Emirate, *c*.1900-1939', unpublished PhD thesis, University of London, 1984.

22 Coquery-Vidrovitch, 'L'Afrique et la crise', pp.390-401; see also Marseille, *Empire colonial*, pp. 162-5.

23 Berry, *Cocoa, custom and socio-economic change*, p.223; Mbodj, 'Sénégal et dépendance', p.148; Helleiner, *Peasant agriculture*, Tables II-B-2 and II-B-3. On the trends in the barter terms of trade, see Table 1.

24 See Table 4.

25 See Tables 1 and 3.

26 S.M. Martin, 'Gender and innovation: farming, cooking and palm processing in the Ngwa region, south-eastern Nigeria, 1900-1930', *Journal of African History, 25*, 4 (1984), pp.411-27; Martin, 'The history of the oil palm industry in south-eastern Nigeria, 1891-1929', unpublished PhD thesis, University of Birmingham, 1984, p.148; J.S. Harris, 'Some aspects of the economics of sixteen Ibo individuals', *Africa, 14*, 6 (1944), pp.302-35.

27 G.M. Austin, 'The emergence of capitalist relations in South Asante cocoa-farming, *c.* 1916-1933' (forthcoming, *Journal of African History*); N. van Hear, 'Northern labour and the development of capitalist agriculture in Ghana', unpublished PhD thesis, University of Birmingham, 1982; A.B. Holmes IV, 'Economic and political organizations in the Gold Coast, 1920-45', unpublished PhD thesis, University of Chicago, 1972, ch.2; *Report of the Commission on the Marketing of West African Cocoa* (PP 1937-8, IX, 2, Cmd 5845), ch.3.

28 File on'Trust system in the Calabar and Owerri Provinces', 1930-1, Nigerian National Archives, Ibadan, CSO 26/26209.

29 Coquery-Vidrovitch, 'L'Afrique et la crise', pp.388-96; R. Robin, 'La Grande Dépression vue et vécue par une société d'import-export en AOF: Peyrissac (1924-1939)', ibid., pp.544-54; L. Zinsou-Derlin, 'La Banque de l'Afrique occidentale dans la crise', ibid., pp.506-18; J.I. Guyer, 'Head tax, social structure and rural incomes in Cameroun, 1922-1937', *Cahiers d'Etudes Africaines, 20*, 79 (1980), pp.305-29.

30 Coquery-Vidrovitch, 'L'Afrique et la crise', pp.401-22; see also M. Lakroum,'Les salaires dans le port de Dakar', ibid., pp.640-53.

31 *Report of a Committee on Trade and Taxation for British West Africa* (PP 1922, XVI, Cmd 1600), pp.11-12 and 24.

32 Killingray, 'Repercussions of World War I', p.45; data on Nigeria from the Blue Books and annual Customs Department Reports, cited in Martin, 'History of the oil palm industry', Statistical Appendix.

33 Nigeria: Annual Report, Customs Department, 1930, PRO CO 657/27, p.12; Nigeria: Trade Report, 1935, CO 657/40, p.16. See also Table 4 for import price trends.

34 For the French view, see Coquery-Vidrovitch, 'L'Afrique et la crise', pp.411-12.

35 A. Abraham, *Mende government and politics under colonial rule* (Sierra Leone University Press, Freetown and Oxford, 1978), ch. 5; A. Osuntokun, *Nigeria in the first World War* (Longman, London, 1979), pp.126-32.

36 S.M. Martin, *Palm oil and protest: an economic history of the Ngwa region, south-eastern Nigeria, 1800-1980* (Cambridge University Press, Cambridge, 1988), ch.9, and N.E. Mba, *Nigerian women mobilized: women's political activity in southern Nigeria, 1900-1965* (University of California, Institute of International Studies, Berkeley, 1982), ch.3.

37 *Report of the Commission of Inquiry appointed to inquire into the disturbance in the Calabar and Owerri Province, December 1929* (Lagos, 1930), CO 583/176/1002/30, p.102.

38 Assessment Schedules, Owerri Province, 1929-30 and 1930-1, Enugu Archives, Abadist 1/1/7, file C10/1929; Nigeria: Annual Report, Southern Provinces, 1937, CO 657/45, p.61.

39 S. Shaloff, 'The income tax, indirect rule, and the depression: the Gold Coast riots of 1931', *Cahiers d'Etudes Africaines, 14*, 2 (1974), pp.359-75.

40 Coquery-Vidrovitch, 'L'Afrique et la crise', pp.387-422; Abdoul Sow, 'Les Sociétés Indigènes de Prévoyance du Sénégal des origines à 1947', unpublished thèse de 3e cycle, University of Dakar, 1983-4; Marseille, *Empire colonial*, ch.12.

41 F. Pedler, *The Lion and the Unicorn in Africa: a history of the origins of the United Africa Company, 1787-1931* (Heinemann, London, 1974), pp.139-48; documents on the 1929

merger, CO 554/81/4174/29; *Report of the Commission on the Marketing of West African Cocoa*, part 3.

42 G.M. Austin, 'Capitalists and chiefs in the cocoa hold-ups in South Asante, 1927-38', *International Journal of African Historical Studies* (forthcoming, vol.21, 1988); Hopkins, *Economic history*, p.255; J. Miles, 'Rural protest in the Gold Coast: the cocoa hold-ups, 1908-1938' in C. Dewey and A.G. Hopkins (eds), *The imperial impact* (Athlone Press, London, 1978), pp.152-70; S. Rhodie, 'The Gold Coast cocoa hold-up of 1930-31', *Transactions of the Historical Society of Ghana, 9* (1968), pp.105-18; R.J. Southall, 'Farmers, traders and brokers in the Gold Coast cocoa economy', *Canadian Journal of African Studies, 12*, 2 (1978), pp.185-211.

43 See sources in n.40; also *Report of the Commission on the Marketing of West African Cocoa* , part 4; Hopkins, *Economic history*, pp.264-5.

44 On the Marketing Boards and the second World War, see Hopkins, *Economic history*, p.266; Teal, 'Growth, comparative advantage and the economic effects of government'; P.T. Bauer, *West African trade* (Routledge and Kegan Paul, London, 1954).

45 Bauer, *West African trade*; Helleiner, *Peasant agriculture*, pp.160-2.

46 Martin, *Palm oil and protest*, ch.5; D. Killingray, 'The Empire Resources Development Committee and West Africa, 1916-20', *Journal of Imperial and Commonwealth History, 10*, 2 (1982), pp.194-210; Colonial Office, Colonial No.10, *West Africa: palm oil and palm kernels* (HMSO, London, 1925); W.K. Hancock, *Survey of British Commonwealth affairs* (2 vols. in 3, Oxford University Press, London, 1937-42), vol.2, part 2, pp.188-200; Hopkins, *Economic history*, pp.210-16; D. Meredith, 'Government and the decline of the Nigerian oil-palm export industry, 1919-1939', *Journal of African History, 25*, 3 (1984), pp.311-29.

47 Coquery-Vidrovitch, 'L'Afrique et la crise', pp.387-422; on industrialisation, see Marseille, *Empire colonial*, chs. 10 and 11; on British West Africa, see Hopkins, *Economic history*, pp.265-7 and 279-88; D. Meredith, 'The British government and colonial economic policy, 1919-1939', *Economic History Review*, 2nd ser., *28*, 3 (1975), pp.484-99; and A. Adedeji, 'The economic evolution of developing Africa', *Cambridge History of Africa*, vol.8 (Cambridge University Press, Cambridge, 1984), pp.243-7.

48 Helleiner, *Peasant agriculture*, pp.163-4.

49 Usoro, *Nigerian oil palm industry*, pp.88-92 and 104-10; Teal, 'Growth, comparative advantage and the economic effects of government', pp.126-31 and ch.6.

50 Martin, 'Gender and innovation', pp.422-6.

51 For details, see Martin, *Palm oil and protest*, chs 8 and 10.

52 Berry, *Cocoa, custom and socio-economic change*, pp.45-9; J.D.Y. Peel, *Ijeshas and Nigerians: the incorporation of a Yoruba kingdom, 1890s-1970s* (Cambridge University Press, Cambridge, 1983), pp.102-6 and 116.

53 Peel, *Ijeshas and Nigerians*, ch.7.

54 Ibid., chs 7 and 8.

55 Berry, *Fathers work for their sons* (California University Press, Berkeley, 1985), chs 2 and 3.

56 Berry, *Fathers work for their sons*, chs 4 and 5.

57 See, for example, R. Bates, *Markets and states in tropical Africa* (University of California Press, Berkeley, 1981).

5

SUBSISTENCE IN THE SLUMP: AGRICULTURAL ADJUSTMENT IN THE PROVINCIAL PHILIPPINES

NORMAN G. OWEN[1]

At the end of the first World War the economy of the Bikol region of south-eastern Luzon started a roller-coaster dive that would reduce it, over the next two decades, to its lowest state in a century. The region's economy was overwhelmingly agricultural, with three crops - abaca (Manila hemp), rice and coconuts - accounting for well over 90 per cent of total cultivated land and crop values. When the prices of these commodities collapsed, and the production of abaca, the region's dominant industry since the mid-nineteenth century, fell by half, an unprecedented economic disaster ensued. While precise statistics are difficult to compile, the trend in market value of regional production of these three commodities is unmistakable.[2] From a pre-war annual average of around 25 million pesos the roller-coaster climbed to a peak of nearly 49 million pesos in 1917/18, then plummeted to under 18 million pesos in 1921/2 before rising to a secondary peak of just over 40 million pesos in the middle of the decade. Starting down slowly over the next few years, it plunged toward a new low after 1929, falling below 10 million pesos per year in the early 1930s, with a slight rise after 1935 merely adding a final fillip as it coasted toward its terminus, virtual disintegration of the Bikol cash economy during the second World War.

On a per capita basis the drop was even more pronounced, from 35 pesos before the first World War to under 10 pesos at the heart of the depression, with intervening plateaux averaging 49 pesos in 1915/16-1919/20 and 42.50 pesos in 1924/5-1927/8. One visible consequence of this decline in the value of agricultural production was a parallel fall in internal revenue collections per capita - primarily excises, licences (incorporating a percentage tax on retail sales), and the *cedula* (head tax) - in the region. During the 1910s annual collections per capita rose steadily from just over 1 peso to well over 2 pesos; they then fell in the early 1920s to around 1.25 pesos, rose anew to average over 2 pesos between 1925 and 1929, and plummeted to an average of just 0.75 peso between 1932 and 1935, before a slight upturn in the latter half of the decade.[3] The trend in Bikol wages is harder to compute, as some sources purport to provide minimum and maximum figures, while others offer only some kind of 'average' or random observation. Nevertheless, there was a clear drop from the 1920s, when male agricultural labourers earned wages generally quoted at 0.50-1.00 peso or more per day, and the 1930s, when the range was more often 0.20-0.50 peso, with some men working for 0.10 peso a day or even less.[4]

For purposes of analysis it would be highly desirable to turn these nominal rates into 'real' pesos, since the purchasing power of the currency varied enormously in the Philippines (as elsewhere) during the inter-war years. Unfortunately we lack the data to construct price series specific to the Bikol region throughout this period; the best we can do is adjust Bikol crop values using the wholesale price of rice in Manila or an index of Philippine imports.[5] Inasmuch as a substantial proportion of Bikolano rice consumption was of grain shipped from Manila, and as most of the textiles and manufactured goods consumed in the region would have been imports, the use of these indices is not entirely arbitrary.

Such adjustments certainly flatten out the first World War boom; the per capita value of regional production of the three major agricultural commodities remained almost constant relative to the price of rice, 1912/13-1917/18, and increased only 25 per cent relative to that of imports over the same period. But price adjustments do not explain away the inter-war depression. If we express the per capita value of regional abaca, copra and rice production in terms of Manila prices and set an index of 100 for the 1912/13-1917/18 average, we find the index dropping to an average of 50 over the next six years, rising to 77 between 1925/6 and 1927/8, and after a gap in the records of three years, reappearing to average just 31 between 1931/2 and 1938. An index expressed in terms of Philippine import prices shows a similar, but less precipitous, decline, from 100 down to 60 for the period 1918/19-1923/4, then up to 102 before tumbling to 38 in the 1930s. However calculated, a 60-70 per cent decline in real per capita cash income from agricultural production is hardly insignificant.

There are a number of questions that might be asked about this inter-war depression in the Philippines, including whether it is most usefully seen as a single downward movement temporarily interrupted by the resurgence of the late 1920s, as two consecutive but distinct slumps, or simply as a phenomenon of the 1930s preceded by a decade of more-or-less normal fluctuations in the export economy. Unfortunately we lack many empirical data pertinent to this question, including reliable statistical series for the period of 'normality' before the first World War and year-to-year (or even decade-to-decade) data on migration, tenantry, irrigation, and double-cropping. Yet this question is essentially one of perspective and perception; even the assumption that the period 1900-13 constitutes a valid base for measuring 'normality' in the Bikol region is dubious, as there was a sustained food-production and mortality crisis there between 1900 and 1905 (during and after the Philippine-American War).

We could also enquire further into the reasons for the collapse of the Bikol economy between the wars, though the broad outlines are clear. Essentially the collapse was caused by forces external to the region. Since the 1840s the price of abaca had been dictated by the economic cycles of the industrial West, and as abaca went, so went the rest of the regional economy. 'A chart of abaca prices in Manila', I have observed elsewhere, 'would be almost instantly familiar to anyone who had studied the economic history of the United States or England'.[6] In the twentieth century the American market came to be dominant; Doeppers has demonstrated a high (.90) correlation between the total value of Philippine exports and the gross national product of the United States, 1905-38.[7] Most of the major trends in Bikol abaca and copra are easily explicable in terms of US-dominated international markets for hard fibres and lauric oils.[8] One exception may be the inter-war decline in abaca production which, though triggered by and responsive to price declines, may also reflect soil exhaustion and the comparative inefficiency of the region's pattern of fragmented smallholder plots, as against the 'industrial' agriculture practised on Japanese-owned abaca plantations on the island of Mindanao.[9]

The central question addressed by this essay, however, has to do not with the causes of the inter-war depression in the Bikol region but with its effects. How did the Bikolanos respond to such a precipitous decline in cash income? How did they survive, and do so without rebellion or even visible unrest?

One way in which they coped with this fall in cash income was simply to reduce unnecessary expenditures, a choice most clearly demonstrated in the decline in government revenues from cock-fights, always a major leisure activity (and expense) within the Philippines. Per capita collections from the annual licence for cockpits and from the tariff paid by the proprietor for each fight fell from almost eight centavos, 1923-9, to just over two centavos, 1931-8, a net drop of around 70 per cent.[10] Accounts of the bankruptcies of shops suggest that the Bikolanos were also curtailing expenditure on non-perishable goods; the fact that the region's principal bus company had to put many of its vehicles into storage indicates a reduction in travel.[11] From missionary accounts we learn that Bible 'portions' could no longer be sold in the region, as 'pasetas [*sic*] are harder to find now than pesos used to be', and that local Protestants were contributing less to their churches - a 75 per cent decline, 1929-34.[12] Not all unnecessary consumption vanished, however; by 1933 at least two theatres showing the new 'talkies' had opened in Naga City.[13]

The Bikolanos also reduced expenditure by defaulting in large numbers on the payment of their *cedulas*, apparently without dire consequences. It is not entirely clear how they were able to get away with this, only that they did.[14] Throughout the 1930s there was always one or other important sector of the Philippine economy that remained buoyant while the rest was sinking, particularly sugar prior to 1934 and gold after that date; from 1937 onward the Philippine treasury also benefited from the 'windfall' rebate of the excise tax on coconut oil collected in the United States, which accounted for approximately one-third of all insular revenues over the next five years.[15] Thus it was not difficult for the government to maintain a balanced budget or, at worst (in 1930-2), to limit deficits to manageable proportions, particularly since governmental expenditures were substantially lower, on a per capita basis, than in most other countries in South-East Asia.[16]

The United States had also, by its early decisions to 'Filipinize' the insular bureaucracy and legislature,[17] decreased administrative pressure in the Philippines, as compared with other colonies. The gradual devolution of political authority to the Filipinos - from the creation of the Assembly in 1907 to the establishment of the Commonwealth in 1935 - had placed much of the executive power in the colony into the hands of an indigenous elite that had no desire to undercut its own wealth or that of its electoral constituents, many of whom did not pay their *cedulas* in 1935 because they thought it was unnecessary under the new Constitution.[18] American governors-general tried to 'spread the gospel of fiscal responsibility' and vetoed various attempts to remit or abolish taxes, but they were not in a position to demonstrate the 'blind rigor' James C. Scott attributed to the colonial state, its power to '*stabilize its income at the expense of its rural subjects*'.[19]

The other major strategy for the Bikolanos during the depression was diversification of economic activity, a conscious and rational reallocation of their labour. For a few it meant leaving agriculture entirely, though in the absence of rural industry this would commonly have implied migration to the towns for service and construction work, to enclaves on the northern coast of the Bikol region for mining and lumbering, to the nearby island of Masbate for cattle-ranching or gold mining, even to Manila for whatever livelihood the urban sector might provide. The building trade in the Bikol region itself seems to have been counter-cyclical, like that of Manila; in 1932, at any rate, it was reported that unemployment in Naga and Legazpi was alleviated by an increase in construction work due to 'the moneyed people . . . taking advantage of the low price of materials and low rate of wages prevailing at present'.[20] There was also a local mining boom in the 1930s, after the price of gold rose nearly 75 per cent with the devaluation of the American dollar in 1933. By the end of the decade mining employed, at above-average wages, nearly 14,000 men in the Bikol region, the majority in the Paracale district of Camarines Norte. This represented only about 3 per cent of the potential male work force of the Bikol provinces, however, and many of the workers were not in fact Bikolanos, but immigrants from elsewhere in the Philippines. About commercial lumbering we know less, but it seems to have followed the same pattern, with continued growth through the 1930s, concentration in a few enclaves away from the major population centres, and a disproportionate number of outsiders amongst its

3,500 workers.[21]

Due to the absence of ethnic or linguistic identification in the 1918 census, we cannot measure with any precision the pattern of Bikolano out-migration during the American period, except to observe that in 1903 only 1 per cent of the Bikol 'tribe' lived outside the region, while in 1939 nearly one in eight Bikol speakers lived elsewhere - two-thirds in Masbate, the rest mostly in Manila and the Tagalog provinces.[22] Much of this out-migration would have been agricultural; despite the fame of its cattle and gold, Masbate had more farmers (growing coconuts and maize) than ranch hands and miners. Though far less mobile than the Ilokanos who emigrated to Hawaii and California, or even than the Bisayans who populated northern Mindanao, the Bikolanos demonstrated that they were willing to transplant themselves when conditions looked better elsewhere.[23]

Most Bikolanos, however, stayed where they were and continued farming during the depression, 'turn[ing] their attention to the production of other agricultural products in which they were assured a greater return for their labour'.[24] During the first two decades of the twentieth century there had been a considerable boom in coconut cultivation; in the immediate post-war period there was a sudden and substantial swing from abaca to rice production, as the price of abaca fell 50 per cent in 1920-1 and that of rice stayed high. This would not have been a conversion of fields, since abaca grows best on well-drained slopes while irrigated rice prefers the plains, but essentially a reallocation of labour, as 'small abaca farmers and strippers [were] deserting the hemp fields and flocking to the rice fields'.[25]

The shift was permanent, nevertheless, though abaca production rallied somewhat when prices later improved. Between 1912/13-1919/20 and 1920/1-1927/8, the average area planted to rice increased 62 per cent, from 69,000 to 112,000 hectares, and average production expanded 120 per cent, from 1.2 million to 2.6 million cavans of paddy.[26] The improved productivity of rice-growing presumably reflected a greater intensity of labour in cultivation, as well as an increased use of draught animals (the number of water buffaloes in the region doubled over approximately the same period).[27] At the same time the average area of abaca cultivation declined 22 per cent, from 253,000 to 196,000 hectares, and production dropped 32 per cent (in fact 53 per cent in the first two years).[28] Coconuts were also 'gradually replacing abaca' in the early 1920s;[29] the data indicate a surge during the first World War, followed by a slow and steady expansion of coconut cultivation - from an average of just over 50,000 hectares, 1919/1920-1924/5, to nearly 60,000 hectares, 1932/3-1935/6 - and production throughout the inter-war period.[30]

In the 1930s the reallocation of agricultural labour continued, but much less dramatically, as there was now less flat terrain available for conversion into paddy fields. Instead there seems to have been an intensification of wet-rice agriculture and a simultaneous expansion of the cultivation of maize, camotes (sweet potatoes) and other secondary staples. The double-cropping of rice was a technique known to the Bikolanos from at least the turn of the century, and perhaps from long before.[31] As late as the 1960s, on the other hand, the majority of the rice fields were still single cropped;[32] only with the development of 'miracle rice' did double-cropping become commonplace. Nevertheless, a number of sources suggest that in various different Bikol localities this procedure was introduced during the 1930s as a specific response to the depression.[33] By 1938, at any rate, about 15 per cent of the lowland rice fields in the region were double-cropped. The spread of irrigation, a prerequisite for double-cropping, must have accompanied this innovation; by 1938 the total irrigated area in the region was equivalent to about 36 per cent of the area planted to lowland rice.[34]

Maize, camotes and other secondary staples were well known before the depression, and are commonly listed among the products of the region as far back as the eighteenth century. They were an important source of food during subsistence crises in 1845-6 and 1900-3, as they grew more rapidly than rice and could occupy less favourable terrain. So far as we can calculate, however, in non-crisis years they rarely accounted for more than 1.5-2 per cent of the area, production or value of rice during the nineteenth century. Encouraged by a government-sponsored 'Food Campaign' during the first World War, maize and camote production expanded until by the end of the war the two crops accounted for about 11 per cent of the total area planted in staple crops and probably supplied about 3 per cent of total regional carbohydrate consumption. Over the next 20 years, recorded production of the two crops grew by more than 250 per cent (over twice the rate of growth of rice production). We lack even remotely plausible production figures for other secondary staples, but the area planted in other root crops (*gabe, ubi* and *tugue*) also doubled between 1918 and 1938, while recorded cassava hectarage increased a hundredfold.[35] Much of this expansion must have occurred on abandoned abaca fields, which are frequently mentioned in the 1930s.[36] By 1938 secondary staples accounted for around 17 per cent of the area planted in staple crops and about 10 per cent of average Bikol carbohydrate consumption - a sign of poverty, as well as ingenuity, for Bikolanos, like most Filipinos, will eat these crops only if rice is not available or affordable.[37]

It is also likely that production per capita of fruits and vegetables increased during the inter-war years, though we do not have the evidence to substantiate this. One historiographical problem with depression, in fact, is that the reversion to subsistence tends to imply the disappearance of production from the standard sources of economic data.[38] Colonial statistics are undoubtedly best on international trade and government revenue, considerably less reliable on provincial prices and production of export crops, and virtually non-existent for gardening, gathering, fishing, hunting, home crafts,[39] and barter or unofficial (contraband) trade - areas in which Bikol activity was expanding during the depression. Field agents of the Bureau of Commerce and Industry reported in November 1931 that many of the unemployed were 'successfully tiding over the situation by resorting to gardening and the production of short term crops'; in August of the following year they noted that 'the tightness of money has given rise to barter in many places'.[40] A soil technologist who visited the region in May 1934 commented on the typical slash-and-burn squatter who produced 'a few sacks of upland rice or corn, and a few vegetables'; in the same year more operators of illegal stills were apprehended in Albay than in any other province in the Philippines.[41] The 1936 'fact-finding survey' in Albay province found that in the 'off-season' farm labourers either 'switch[ed] to wage earning elsewhere or stay[ed] at home doing odd jobs'; it was calculated that the families surveyed received 'other resources' during the year equivalent to nearly 90 per cent of their wages from agricultural labour.[42]

One way or another, the Bikolanos survived and, as far as we can tell, did so with no increase in mortality. Though detailed data are missing for some of the worst depression years, the demographic reaction to the slump in the Bikol region appears to have resembled that in the United States or Europe.[43] Nuptiality was highly responsive to economic fluctuations: the crude marriage rate rose from under 6 per thousand in 1920-2 to 9 in 1925-7 before tumbling to less than 4.8, 1931-3, and then rebounding to around 6, 1936-8.[44] The crude birth rate showed corresponding (time-lagged) fluctuations, rising from 36.0 per thousand, 1921-5, to 38.8, 1926-9, then falling to around 35.2 in the 1930s. In mortality, however, there was a continuing long-term decline, presumably due to improvements in medicine and public health; the crude death rate slid steadily from 20.6 per thousand to 18.2 to 17.0 over the same period, and infant mortality fell from roughly 130 (per 1,000 births) in the 1920s to around 105 in the 1930s.[45] The data are too unreliable for us to be completely certain of these trends, but we can at least be sure of what did not occur: famine and epidemics. Indeed it appears that the 20 years following the influenza epidemic of 1918-19 were in some respects the healthiest in the history of the region to that date, over the century and a half for which we have records.

This is not in any way to suggest that these were not hard times for ordinary Bikolanos, whose living standard was low even at the best of times. It simply indicates that the hardships they suffered should be assessed primarily, like those of workers in the West, in terms of the loss of comfort, the loss of security, the loss of opportunity, the loss of dignity, perhaps even the loss of health - but not in terms of the loss of life. Malnutrition, still a major problem in the Bikol region today, may have worsened during the depression, as apparently it did elsewhere in the Philippines.[46] Morbidity may actually have increased.[47] Nevertheless, it is clear that the Bikolanos were *not* archetypical Asian peasants, perpetually tottering on the brink of starvation. If they had been, in Tawney's metaphor, 'standing permanently up to the neck in water',[48] then the inter-war depression, no mere 'ripple', would have drowned many more of them.

But if all survived, not all thrived. There were clearly sectoral and geographical variations, most notably due to the mining boom of the later 1930s, which made Camarines Norte far more prosperous than any other district in the region.[49] The 1930s might also have been good years in some smaller enclaves, such as villages near the newly opened lumbering areas or barrios newly reached by the road or railway.[50] The most significant (and elusive) differential impact of the depression would have been in terms of economic strata, however. Very few actually prospered during the slump, but some lost less than others, either because they had the resources to cushion the blow or because they had nothing to lose. What is suggested here is that neither the wealthier landlords nor tenants and the landless poor lost as much from the depression as the class in between: the Bikol smallholder.

The wealthy undoubtedly suffered a considerable curtailment of profits on their investments. One large abaca plantation reported a drop in profits from 42,000 pesos in 1917 to just 8,000 pesos in 1919. A dozen years later it was calculated that the gross return per hectare on abaca land had fallen in one year (1930-1) from 88 to 30 pesos.[51] But such losses were more easily borne by large landowners than by smallholders. It might, of course, have been harder for the wealthy to pay for some imported luxuries, to travel, or to send their children abroad to university, but there seems to have been little risk of actually losing property.[52] Instead, those who had wealth were able to employ it to improve their relative position within the faltering economy by loaning money to those less fortunate, by taking advantage of low construction wages to build, or by investing in mining or other profitable ventures. Wealth might also be employed in running for electoral office or financing the education of children, thus reinforcing the hold this class had on government employment; we may assume that, as in Manila, the real income of civil servants improved considerably during deflationary times, making the bureaucracy, in spite of occasional retrenchment and pay cuts, an even more desirable career.[53] Above all, rich landowners could use their wealth to buy land from those who could no longer keep up debt payments or taxes. Though the Bikol region never developed a plantation system like that which characterised the sugar-growing island of Negros, observers in the 1930s often remarked on 'extensive estates growing abaca'.[54]

The counterpart of this improved opportunity for the wealthy was, of course, a decline in the position of the poorer classes. Certainly there was an increase in indebtedness, often at exorbitant rates of interest.[55] There was also a high degree of 'unemployment', though in such an economy this term might in fact imply considerable and diverse activity in the subsistence sector.[56] Population growth and the collapse of other avenues of employment seem to have led to deterioration in the terms of tenantry in some districts; tenants in the rice-growing areas of Albay province were said to have been forced into unfavourable contracts, vulnerable to dismissal at will, and otherwise subject to what some observers called 'unjust practices tantamount to oppression'.[57] Yet the Bikol region saw no rebellion or significant organised protest in these years, so perhaps conditions were not so unbearable as they might seem to us at first.

To put the depression into perspective, it is useful to remember that a condition of permanent indebtedness is an ancient one in the Philippines, dating back to pre-Hispanic times, when it formed the basis for what the Spaniards called 'slavery'. Over the centuries a substantial proportion - perhaps a majority - of Filipinos remained in some form of perpetual debt dependency to their *datu*, landlord or other creditor.[58] In such circumstances the rate of interest and the size of the debt matter little, since it is widely assumed that the debt will never be entirely repaid.[59] What concerns the debtor is assurance of livelihood (being left enough to live on), implied security of tenure and some measure of respect from his or her creditor and peers. It is when these conditions start to disintegrate, as Kerkvliet has shown for Central Luzon, that rural unrest really takes hold.[60]

So far as we can tell, the deterioration of Bikol agrarian relations during the depression was by no means as advanced as it was in Central Luzon at the same time - or as it would become in the Bikol region in the 1960s, when the once-peaceful peninsula became a hotbed of the New People's Army. Most tenant contracts continued on old terms, retaining traditional mechanisms of equity even in the depths of the depression: in the early 1930s it was reported that when the price of abaca went down, the labourers' share of the harvested fibre went up, thus assuring them a more stable income.[61] Even the 'fact-finding' survey of Albay in 1936, so hostile to the tenantry system in general, admitted that crops were normally divided 'share and share alike' and that most tenants continued to maintain complete confidence in their landlords.[62] It may be that Bikolano landlords in the depression were less prone than their counterparts in Central Luzon both to physical absenteeism and to that 'moral absenteeism' which repudiates traditional reciprocal responsibilities, perhaps because they were farther removed, geographically and culturally, from Manila.

If tenantry in the depression was not in fact much worse than usual for the majority of tenants, it would nevertheless have represented a distinct loss for those new to it. Traditionally the Bikol region was a stronghold of what is often referred to as 'smallholder' agriculture, though we should not understand by this term the sturdily independent yeomen farmers cherished in Western mythology, but petty landlords or 'large peasants', members of an ill-defined local gentry (up to one-third of all householders) working holdings of less than 20 hectares by themselves or with a few tenants or hired labourers.[63] They hardly constituted a 'middle class' in any but the most literal sense - as falling somewhere between the large landowners and the peasant majority - yet in the early twentieth century they might well have been a middle class in the making. The years between 1905 and 1918 offered generally high commodity prices (especially for coconuts), abundant and inexpensive public land, improvements in transportation and education under the new American regime, and considerable scope for advancement in an expanding civil service that was being 'Filipinized'. Probably at no other juncture in Bikol history was there such an opportunity for smallholders and their families to consolidate or improve their position.

In the inter-war depression all this changed, and it is among smallholders that we would expect to find most of the 'bankruptcies' mentioned in the Manila press,[64] those who defaulted on loans taken simply to stay in production. Seven out of every eight of the landowners surveyed in the 1936 'fact-finding' report were said to be unable to 'live decently' on their income, so that after they paid their taxes they would be in 'a critical condition'.[65] These smallholders must have played a central role in one of the most striking developments of the inter-war years, a four to fivefold increase in the proportion of cultivated land under tenantry, from 8 per cent (26,000 hectares) to around 38 per cent (160,000 hectares) between 1918 and 1938.[66]

Meanwhile, other doors that had opened during the first two decades of American rule were starting to swing shut. As Doeppers has shown, by the early 1920s the great wave of 'Filipinization', when even a rudimentary education might provide entry to a good job with chances for promotion, had passed. Now the civil service was no longer expanding, and university degrees, essentially the prerogative of the wealthy, came to be prerequisites for upper-level posts or even for good entry-level positions. Much the same was probably true in the world of business, where employment opportunities were always dictated by the volume of international trade.[67] At the same time the educational system itself was stagnating, with fiscal problems preventing the opening of new schools and forcing occasional reductions in the activities of existing ones.[68] Such developments would not have impoverished Bikol smallholders directly, but they would have restricted opportunities for upward or lateral mobility. As agricultural prices plummeted and the pressure on credit increased, there was no place to go but down.

To confirm this admittedly speculative interpretation of the structural implications of the depression in the Bikol region would require either far better statistical evidence than we possess or more information on Bikolano perceptions of the period. Only scattered issues of local newspapers seem to have survived, and there are no collections known to me of the kinds of personal documents (letters, diaries, etc.) that might throw light on everyday life in the depression. Nor has anyone yet undertaken a systematic oral history of the region. As a result, most of our impressions of how the depression was experienced in the Bikol region are derived either indirectly, from the observations of outsiders (missionaries, officials, etc.), or retrospectively, from local histories recorded after the second World War.

The outside observers agree on one general conclusion: there were no visible signs of unrest in the region. It is hardly surprising that the *American Chamber of Commerce Journal* described the Bikolanos in 1927, when there was 'certainly no lack of employment', as 'contented and happy'.[69] But it may be more significant that the field agent of the Bureau of Commerce and Industry reported in 1931 'no actual suffering or disturbances . . . among the unemployed workers', or two years later observed that 'with all the adversities the people are facing at the present time, peace and contentment generally prevail'.[70] Even the 'fact-finding' report of 1936, though explicit about the bitterness felt by some oppressed tenants, admitted that there were 'no agrarian conflicts', a fact attributed to 'the good nature and extraordinary patience of the Bicol farmer'.[71] Such accounts cannot refute - and the last may even confirm - the possibility of discontent falling short of rebellion or overt protest, limiting itself to the kinds of 'everyday resistance' described by Scott, Kerkvliet and others.[72] Yet the absence in the Bikol region of the active peasant movements found elsewhere in the Philippines during this period is quite striking. There were no leftist peasant unions, such as those that would later form the core of the 'Huk' movement in Central Luzon, no Sakdalistas revolting in 1935, and no 'colorum' or other millenarian rebellions between the wars; their absence would appear to set some upper limit on the levels of distress within the region.

In local histories recorded in the early 1950s the inter-war depression is generally most conspicuous by its absence. To some extent this can be explained by the circumstances in which these histories were written; they were a response to a presidential directive that was accompanied by a set of questions and suggested topics that included the Philippine Revolution and the second World War, but not the depression.[73] Yet the terms of the directive were broad enough, and the responses sufficiently lengthy, to incorporate all manner of other non-specified materials; what is remarkable is how few of the authors considered the depression worth mentioning. It seems likely that, as Doeppers found in his Manila interviews, whatever hardship the Bikolanos had endured in the depression was overshadowed in their memories by the far greater suffering imposed by the Japanese occupation and the American liberation of the Philippines during the second World War.[74] Frequently the whole American era, in fact, is portrayed as 'the age of prosperity and contentment' when 'liberty and freedom were given to the people [and] ways of living were improved'.[75]

When the depression is mentioned, it seems to be restricted to the 1930s and associated with changes in agricultural production, such as the planting of abaca fields in upland rice or camotes, or the opening of new areas to irrigation or double-cropping.[76] On rare occasions the populist rhetoric of the Commonwealth is echoed in reports of the government's concern for 'the social upliftment [*sic*] of the masses'.[77] Absent, however, is any mention of hunger or other real hardship in the inter-war period, though there are references to food shortages in the first World War,[78] as well as to those caused by the

Japanese occupation and more recent typhoons. Most references to the 1920s and 1930s, beyond those to the elections of mayors and other local officials, are to signs of progress: schools, roads, new settlements, mines, newly opened fields, improved agricultural techniques. Again, we certainly cannot assume that life in the Bikol region during the inter-war years was as idyllic as these documents imply, but it does seem reasonable to conclude that by local standards the times had not been unduly hard.

In this context it must be remembered that the inter-war depression was not so very different from earlier experiences of the Bikolanos during a century of involvement in the capitalist world system. Ever since they had started to grow abaca for the international market they had been exposed to major crises in that market - in 1842-7, 1858-65, 1874-80, 1884-7, 1893-7, and 1908-12.[79] And when crises came, wages fell, taxes went unpaid, cock-fight revenues declined, weddings were postponed and people reverted to subsistence agriculture.[80] The inter-war depression was both deeper and more prolonged than any which had gone before, but the Bikolanos seem to have responded to it much as they had to crises of the past, with only a few hints of the kind of 'modern' behaviour - tenant expulsion, increasing absentee landlordism, trade unionism - that would eventually come to break down the traditional order.[81] It would have been for most of them just another illustration of the timeless cyclical nature of reality rather than, as for so many people in the West, a shattering of the dream of progress.

APPENDIX

In attempting to construct statistical series from the official publications covering the inter-war period in the Philippines, several anomalies must be borne in mind.

(1) The two relevant censuses, taken on 31 December 1918 and 1 January 1939, contain many data which differ extraordinarily from those provided on an annual basis by the Bureau of Agriculture and published in *SB, SHPI,* and *PSR*. The census figure for Bikol abaca production in 1918, for example, is 25 per cent higher than the highest annual figure ever recorded by the Bureau, and 50 per cent higher than the average of Bureau figures for 1917/18 and 1918/19, though the recorded area in cultivation is 20 per cent smaller. Similarly, the *Census of 1939* records an area planted to coconuts 150 per cent higher than any Bureau data for the 1930s. Such discrepancies have generally been resolved in favour of the Bureau figures, not because they are necessarily more valid, but because they provide a more consistent basis for measuring change within the inter-war period. Change in certain other indicators - e.g. population, tenantry and area planted in root crops - can be estimated only by

intercensal comparison, however, as these are not regularly covered in the annual statistical publications.

(2) It is difficult to locate provincial agricultural data for the years between 1927/8 and 1931/2, due to the gap between the last issue of the *Statistical Bulletin* (1929) and the sole issue of the *Statistical handbook* (1933), which preceded the *Philippine Statistical Review.* Various individual series have even longer gaps, as not all of the same information was recorded for each year.

(3) Population figures in all official publications between 1920 and 1939 were based on extrapolations from the 1918 census at rates that turned out to be lower than the actual rates achieved in the inter-war period. Thus all published calculations of per capita tax collections, mortality rates, etc., are too high, especially for the 1930s. In this essay annual population figures for the Bikol region have been obtained by interpolation between the 1918 and 1939 census figures, at an annual growth rate of 2.07 per cent.

(4) In most sources (except the *Census of 1918*), prior to 1920/1 the province of Sorsogon included the island of Masbate, which is not part of the Bikol region as defined here. To create rough comparability with later data, the following downward adjustments (based on 1918 and 1920/1-1922/3 averages) have been made to these early figures: total area (of Bikol region) 23 per cent; population and cultivated area 8 per cent; abaca area and production 1 per cent; rice area and production 3 per cent; coconut area and production 11 per cent (copra 15 per cent; coconut oil 2 per cent); maize area and production 36 per cent; water buffaloes 15 per cent. It should also be noted that after about 1918-20 data for the old province of Ambos Camarines are listed under the two new provinces into which it was split (Camarines Norte and Camarines Sur); and that in some - but not all - tables the 'sub-province' of Catanduanes is recorded separately from the province of Albay, in which it is otherwise included.

(5) Various conversions and adjustments need to be made to many of the published data. Some statistics are recorded for calendar years, others for a fiscal year running 1 July-30 June; for purposes of comparison the fiscal year has been treated as equivalent to the latter calendar year (e.g., 1917/18=1918). The magnitude of coconut cultivation is indicated in some years by the number of hectares planted, in others by the number of trees; conversions have been made on the basis of 190 trees to the hectare. Production volumes may be recorded in kilograms, in piculs (for abaca and copra) or in litres (for coconut oil); these have been converted at 63.25 kg to the picul, and 0.925 kg per litre of coconut oil. Proportions of area under cultivation that are actually harvested or of coconut trees actually bearing fruit have been calculated for some years from data on average yield per harvested hectare or per bearing tree.

(6) Provincial prices for agricultural commodities are available only for the 1930s, so calculations of crop values in this essay have generally been based on average 'municipal market' prices throughout the Philippines, as recorded in *SB, SHPI* and *PSR*. Bikol prices, where available, tend to be slightly lower than these national averages, particularly for rice. It is assumed, however, that movements in these national prices accurately mirror the rise and fall of local prices.

(7) The value of coconut production, unlike that of rice and abaca, cannot be calculated on the basis of a single commodity. Beside copra and coconut oil, for which reasonably good data are available, there were sales of the unprocessed nuts (for food) and of *tuba* (coconut wine), made from the sap of buds tapped before they could bear fruit; as these were sold in the domestic, rather than the export market, they are much less well documented. From such broad calculations as do appear, however, it would seem that copra and oil generally accounted for around 80 per cent of total market value, and they have thus been taken as a proxy for the value of all coconut products. Coconut oil was distinctly subordinate to copra, accounting for only about 8 per cent of their combined value in the boom that began in the first World War and just 3 per cent in the 1930s.

NOTES

1 This essay was written when the author was Senior Research Fellow in Pacific and Southeast Asian History, Australian National University. I am grateful to Daniel F. Doeppers, Leonor F. Dy-Liacco, Benedict J. Tria Kerkvliet, Morton J. Netzorg, James J. O'Brien, S.J., and Godofredo Rueda for comments on an earlier draft.

2 Most agricultural data for this paper are derived from: Philippine Islands, Census Office, *Census of the Philippine Islands . . . in the year 1918* (Bureau of Printing, Manila, 1920-1; hereafter cited as *Census of 1918*); Philippine Islands, Dept of Commerce and Communications, Bureau of Commerce and Industry, *Statistical Bulletin*, annual, 1918-29 (hereafter cited as *SB*); Philippine Islands, Dept of Agriculture and Commerce, Division of Statistics, *Statistical handbook of the Philippine Islands: 1932* (Bureau of Printing, Manila, 1933; hereafter cited as *SHPI*); Philippine Islands, later Philippines (Commonwealth), Dept of Agriculture and Commerce, Division of Statistics, *Philippine Statistical Review*, quarterly, 1934-7 (hereafter cited as *PSR*; later *Bulletin of Philippine Statistics*, 1938-9, cited as *BPS*); Philippines (Commonwealth), Commission of the Census, *Census of the Philippines: 1939* (Bureau of Printing, Manila, 1940-3; hereafter cited as *Census of 1939*); and Philippines (Commonwealth), Bureau of the Census and Statistics, *Yearbook of Philippine Statistics: 1940* (Bureau of Printing, Manila, 1941). See appendix for a discussion of the assumptions required to derive economic series from these sources.

3 Philippine Islands, later Philippines (Commonwealth), Dept of Finance and Justice, Bureau of Internal Revenue, *Annual Report of the Collector of Internal Revenue*, 1910/11-

1937 (hereafter cited as *ARCIR*), *passim.*

4 *Census of 1918*; Philippine Islands, Dept of Commerce and Communications, Bureau of Labor, *Labor: Quarterly Bulletin of the Bureau of Labor*, 1923-9; H.T. Edwards, 'Conditions in the Bicol abaca industry' [1932?], United States National Archives (hereafter cited as USNA), Record Group (RG) 350, 845-904A; O.P.D. LaPorte and M.R. LaPorte, 'After furlough, back to work', *Philippine Presbyterian, 24* (December 1932), p.10; R.L. Pendleton, 'The Bicol region: from the notebook of a soil technologist', *Philippine Agriculturist, 23* (September 1934), p.248; D. Ponce and T.P. Perez, 'Albay' [1936?] in Philippines (Commonwealth), Dept of Labor, 'Fact-finding survey report', 21 January 1937, pp.108-9, American Historical Collection, Manila; J.T. Valbuena, *Sociological aspects of poverty in the Philippine Islands* (University of Santo Tomas Press, Manila, 1939); E.J. Frei, 'Survey of the Bicol region', in 'Report of the Survey Committee of the Presbyterian Mission 1938', p.49, Presbyterian Historical Society, Philadelphia; *BPS*, 1939; *Census of 1939*. Female agricultural labourers, when reported, received average wages varying from 45 per cent to 65 per cent of those of male labourers; no clear trend in these ratios is apparent through this period.

5 D.F. Doeppers, *Manila, 1900-1941: social change in a late colonial metropolis* (Yale University Southeast Asia Studies, New Haven, and Ateneo de Manila University Press, Quezon City, 1984), pp.145-6; T.B. Birnberg and S.A. Resnick, *Colonial development: an econometric study* (Yale University Press, New Haven, 1975), pp.305-8.

6 N.G. Owen, *Prosperity without progress: Manila hemp and material life in the colonial Philippines* (University of California Press, Berkeley, and Ateneo de Manila University Press, Quezon City, 1984), pp.49-50.

7 Doeppers, *Manila, 1900-1941*, pp.37, 150n.

8 On the fibre market see Owen, *Prosperity*, pp.42-56; on copra see A.J. Nyberg, 'The Philippine coconut industry', unpublished PhD thesis, Cornell University, 1968.

9 Owen, *Prosperity*, pp.80-1; H.T. Edwards, 'A survey of abaca culture in Luzon's "Bikol region"', *Cord Age Magazine* (New York), *13*, 3 (1928), pp.26, 28; Edwards, 'Abaca production in Luzon's "Bicol area" provinces', *Cord Age Magazine, 13*, 4 (1928), pp.14, 16.

10 *ARCIR*, 1923-39/40. Adjusted by the price of Manila rice or of imports, the decline in real cock-fight revenues per capita was 49-55 per cent.

11 'Review of business conditions for the first quarter of 1932' in Philippine Islands, later Philippines (Commonwealth), Bureau of Commerce and Industry, *Philippine Commerce and Industry Journal* (hereafter cited as *PCIJ*; later *Philippine Journal of Commerce*, cited as *PJC*), *8* (April 1932), p.5; 'Provincial trade notes', *PCIJ*, *9* (March 1933), p.18.

12 'Report of the Philippine Agency of the American Bible Society to the Presbyterian Mission 1931', and 'Annual Report of the Philippine Mission to the Presbyterian Church in the USA' (1933-4), Presbyterian Historical Society, Philadelphia.

13 'Provincial trade notes', *PJC*, *9* (May 1933), p.24.

14 *ARCIR*, 1923-38. These reports do not include statistics on tax delinquency as such, but in the absence of any significant change in the regulations governing the head tax, the 57 per cent decline in average Bikol *cedula* collections between 1923-9 and 1932-6 - while the population increased by about 18 per cent - is clearly indicative of extensive non-payment. In 1937, when the economy was enjoying a slight upturn, the authorities offered remission of past delinquencies to those who paid their *cedulas* on time; Bikol collections that year were 150 per cent higher than the average for the previous five years.

15 J.R. Hayden, *The Philippines: a study in national development* (Macmillan, New York,

1942), p.158.

16 S. Fine, *Frank Murphy: the New Deal years* (University of Chicago Press, Chicago, 1979), pp.66-9; F.H. Golay, 'The search for revenues' in P.W. Stanley (ed), *Reappraising an empire: new perspectives on Philippine-American history* (Harvard University, Committee on American-East Asian Relations and Council on East Asian Studies, Cambridge, Mass., 1984), pp.259-60.

17 The reduction in the number of high-salaried expatriate officials was also an important factor in keeping total government expenditures low.

18 *ARCIR*, 1935, p.9; cf. Golay, 'The search for revenues', pp.231-60.

19 Fine, *Frank Murphy*, pp.66-9, 183-4; J.C. Scott, *The moral economy of the peasant: rebellion and subsistence in Southeast Asia* (Yale University Press, New Haven, 1976), pp.92-4 (emphasis in original). Though such an interpretation is still speculative, it might be argued that by the 1930s the Philippines was on its way to becoming a post-colonial 'soft state', of the type later described by Gunnar Myrdal, *Asian drama: an inquiry into the poverty of nations* (Random House, New York, 1968), pp.66, 894-900, 911-12 and *passim.*

20 'Review of Philippine business', *PCIJ*, *8* (April 1932), p.5; cf. Doeppers, *Manila, 1900-1941*, pp.44-50.

21 *Census of 1939*; Owen, *Prosperity*, pp.164-5, 169-70.

22 US Bureau of the Census, *Census of the Philippine Islands . . . in the year 1903* (Government Printing Office, Washington, DC, 1905); *Census of 1939.*

23 The assertion of Ponce and Perez, 'Albay', p.110, that the Bikolanos were 'not willing to leave their homes for other places, much less Mindanao' is obviously inaccurate; such plausibility as it has derives from an implied comparison with other Filipinos, who were even more mobile; cf. S. Low, 'The effect of colonial rule on population distribution in the Philippines: 1898-1941', unpublished PhD dissertation, Fletcher School of Law and Diplomacy, 1956, pp.68-72, 254-5 and *passim.*

24 Adn. Hernandez to Wigglesworth and Co., 9 December 1920, USNA, RG 350, 845-696.

25 Ibid.; cf. Owen, *Prosperity*, pp.73, 120-9, 178.

26 One cavan=75 litres. Paddy is unhusked rice (called *palay* in the Philippines); two cavans of paddy normally produce one cavan of clean rice.

27 *SB*, 1918-29.

28 The sharp drop in abaca production in 1920/1-1921/2 was due in part to a temporary abandonment of fields, reflected in a decline in the proportion of cultivated area harvested from 71 per cent, 1913/14-1918/19, to just 51 per cent in those two years; *SB*, 1918-22; USNA, RG 350, 845-241.

29 [H.T. Edwards], 'Report on investigation of the abaca industry in the provinces of Albay, Sorsogon, South Camarines, and North Camarines', 14-27 January 1925, USNA, RG 350, 845-808A.

30 The paradox of continued, if slow, growth in coconut production in an epoch of falling prices requires some explanation. Much of the planting appears to have occurred in brief boom periods, such as the first World War and the mid-1920s, but these trees would have been available for harvest only 6-8 years later, during the ensuing slumps. As the collection of nuts and their processing into sun-dried copra is not overly laborious (particularly in comparison with rice-growing or gathering and stripping abaca), these tasks would have remained worth the effort even when coconut prices were too low to justify further planting. Such an interpretation is corroborated by a steady increase in the proportion of bearing trees to all trees under cultivation - from less than 60 per cent in the early 1920s to over 70 per cent

by the mid 1930s - which suggests that planting was not keeping pace with utilisation. Another factor in the expansion of production as prices fell would have been the multitude of domestic uses (for food and drink, for construction, and for handicrafts) to which coconut products may be put, making it a subsistence as well as a market crop.

31 See Journal of E. Winifred Mitchell, 1901, fol.10, Wisconsin State Historical Society, File 1901 (copy provided to me by Daniel F. Doeppers). In the Tagalog region, double and even triple-cropping of rice date back to at least the sixteenth century.

32 F.L. Wernstedt and J.E. Spencer, *The Philippine Island world: a physical, cultural and regional geography* (University of California Press, Berkeley, 1967), pp.195, 416; cf. Pendleton, 'The Bicol region', p.249.

33 'Provincial trade notes', *PJC*, *9* (November 1933), p.21; Ponce and Perez,'Albay', p.111; Historical Data Papers (hereafter HDP), Albay, Bacacay (town) and Guinobatan, Barrio Malipo, National Library, Manila.

34 *Census of 1939.* Unfortunately the 1918 census provides no information on double-cropping, and gives only the total area of farms having some irrigation, so we cannot measure the increase in either factor. As the basic technology of gravity-flow irrigation had been known to the Bikolanos for centuries, it presumably would not have been regarded as worthy of mention in most accounts of the period; HDP, Albay, Guinobatan, Barrio Malipo, is the only reference I have seen to expansion of irrigation in the region between the wars.

35 *Census of 1918*; *Census of 1939;* Owen, *Prosperity*, pp.137-40. *Gabe* is a form of taro (*Colocasia antiquorum* or *C. esculenta*); *ubi* is the greater yam (*Dioscorea alata*); *tugue* is the lesser yam (*Dioscorea sativa* or *D. esculenta*).

36 Edwards, 'Conditions'; 'Review of Philippine business', *PCIJ*, *8* (April 1932), p.5; 'Business conditions in the provinces', *PCIJ*, *8* (August 1932), p.21; cf. HDP, Albay, Bacacay (town) and Guinobatan, Barrio Malipo.

37 *Census of 1939*; Owen, *Prosperity*, pp.139-40. If fields double-cropped in rice are counted twice, it reduces the secondary staples to 15 per cent of total staple-crop area.

38 Ironically, it is likely that the gaps that exist in published agricultural and health statistics for the Philippines were also due to the depression, through resultant constraints on government expenditures.

39 Curiously, though domestic weaving is mentioned as a renewed subsistence activity in 'Business conditions in the provinces', *PCIJ*, *7* (November 1931), p.11, most later sources imply that the long-term trend toward the replacement of home-woven abaca textiles by imported cotton goods continued through the depression; M. Goyena del Prado, *Ibalon: ethnohistory of the Bikol region,* trans. M.L.F. Realubit (AMS Press, Legazpi City, 1981), p.94; HDP, Albay, Bacacay (town) and Guinobatan, Barrio Maoraro; cf. Owen, *Prosperity*, pp.149-51; N.G. Owen, *Textile displacement and the status of women in Southeast Asia* (University of Michigan, Women's Studies Program, [Ann Arbor], 1981), pp.6-7.

40 'Business conditions in the provinces', *PCIJ*, *7* (November 1931), p.11; 'Business conditions in the provinces', *PCIJ*, *8* (August 1932), p.21; cf. Edwards, 'Conditions'.

41 Pendleton, 'The Bicol region', p.251; *ARCIR*, 1935, pp.40-1. A substantial (55 per cent) decline in the number of illegal distillers apprehended in Albay in 1935 was attributed to improvements in the price of abaca and coconuts in that year, implying an inverse relationship between official and 'black' economies.

42 Ponce and Perez, 'Albay', pp.108-10.

43 Cf. A.J. Coale, 'Introduction', and D. Kirk, 'The influence of business cycles on marriage and birth rates', in National Bureau of Economic Research, *Demographic and economic change*

in developed countries (Princeton University Press, Princeton, NJ,1960), pp.8-9, 241-57.

44 The correlation of marriages with economic cycles, like that of tax payments and cock-fight revenues, can be traced back in Bikol history to at least the 1840s; Owen, *Prosperity*, pp.107-12.

45 Philippine Islands, Dept of Public Instruction, Philippine Health Service, *Report of the Philippine Health Service*, 1920-29; *SHPI*, pp.19-22; Philippines (Commonwealth), Dept of Public Instruction, Bureau of Health, *Annual Report of the Bureau of Health*, 1936-June 1939 (hereafter cited as *ARBH*). Data for 1933 were obtained by extrapolation from incomplete provincial figures in the Manuscript Reports of the Bureau of Health (in USNA, RG 350), provided to me by Bruce Cruikshank. (Incomplete figures for 1932 are also available, but are so low as to suggest considerable under-registration.) Average provincial death and infant mortality rates for the years 1934-5, not available elsewhere, have been calculated from monthly data provided in Philippines (Commonwealth), Dept of Public Instruction, Bureau of Health, *Monthly Bulletin of the Philippine Health Service, 19* (1939). No provincial birth or marriage data from any source have been found for 1930, 1934-5, or 1939-40.

46 Valbuena, *Sociological aspects of poverty*, p.21; cf. Memorandum of G.C. Dunham to the Governor-General, 26 October 1935, Joseph Ralston Hayden Papers, Michigan Historical Collections, Ann Arbor, Box 11, File 28.

47 The national data (no data are available on a provincial or regional basis) indicate that morbidity rates for several of the most prevalent Philippine diseases - tuberculosis, influenza, infantile beriberi, dysentery, measles, and whooping cough - rose significantly between 1924-8 and 1929-33 before falling again in the next quinquennium (1934-8); *ARBH*, 1938, pp.64-5. The rise may simply reflect improved reporting rather than increasing morbidity. But we cannot reject out of hand the possibility that the expansion of modern medicine, better at preventing death than at improving everyday health, reduced case fatality rates to the point where mortality could decline in the heart of the depression even while sickness was increasing, particularly as there is a firm correlation between malnutrition and the incidence of most of the above diseases.

48 As quoted in Scott, *Moral economy*, p.vii.

49 Pendleton, 'The Bicol region', p.251; Frei, 'Survey', p.45; cf. also wage rates from *PSR*, *BPS*, and the *Census of 1939*.

50 J. Eleazer, 'Tandoc' in J.J. O'Brien (ed), *The historical and cultural heritage of the Bicol people* (2nd edn, [Ateneo de Naga, Naga], 1968), pp.144-5; HDP, Albay, Polangui, Barrio Santicon, and Guinobatan, Barrio Malipo. The Manila-Legazpi railway was not completed until 1938, but for a decade earlier was in use within the Bikol region.

51 Hernandez to Wigglesworth; Edwards, 'Conditions'. Hernandez does not specify that this plantation was in the Bikol region. In *Prosperity*, p.111, I mistakenly described the 1930-1 decline as from 35 to 12 pesos per hectare.

52 Curiously absent from most of the sources is any reference to banks foreclosing on mortgages, property confiscated in lieu of delinquent taxes, or land passing into the hands of alien (i.e. Chinese) moneylenders or shopkeepers. To the extent that land did change hands as a consequence of the depression it would seem to have passed from Bikolano smallholders to wealthier indigenous proprietors. The major American agricultural properties in the region, such as the San Miguel Estate and the extensive coconut landholdings of Judge Robert E. Manly, were acquired by the mid-1920s.

53 Doeppers, *Manila, 1900-1941*, pp.78-9; cf. Frei, 'Survey', pp.50-3. Hayden, *The Philippines*, p.491, implies that the real wages of elementary school teachers in the

Philippines declined between 1925 and 1938. In fact, when adjusted by rice or import prices, they *increased* greatly between 1925 and 1932 before falling back to levels still substantially higher than those at the beginning of the period.

54 Pendleton, 'The Bicol region', p.248; cf. Edwards, ' Conditions'. Ponce and Perez, 'Albay', pp.108-9, assert that 'no single landowner possesse[d] a farm or plantation extensive enough to be considered an hacienda', but 6 per cent of the landowners in their sample owned more than 100 hectares - mostly in scattered 'parcels' of land - and collectively would have owned well over half of all the land surveyed. The 1939 census is of little use in assessing concentration of land ownership, as it enumerates individual 'farms' (whether tenant or owner-operated) rather than total landholdings.

55 Valbuena, *Sociological aspects of poverty*, pp.39-41, refers to 'usury' in the Bikol region of around 10 per cent a month, or 50-100 per cent for six months; Ponce and Perez, 'Albay', p.111, mention 'exorbitant' rates of 20-25 per cent, but for an unspecified period.

56 *PCIJ/PJC*, 1931-3 *passim*. Ponce and Perez, 'Albay', p.111, claim that 37 per cent of the population of Albay were unemployed in the mid-1930s.

57 Ponce and Perez, 'Albay', p.112.

58 W.H. Scott, '*Oripun* and *Alipin* in the sixteenth century Philippines' in A. Reid (ed), *Slavery, bondage and dependency in Southeast Asia* (University of Queensland Press, St Lucia, 1983), pp.138-55; N.G. Owen, '"Without slaves there are no datus": social change and continuity in the Hispanized Philippines', paper prepared for the ninth conference of the International Association of Historians of Asia, Manila, 21-5 November 1983.

59 Owen, *Prosperity*, pp.89-93. W. Robb, 'Demigods of Bikolandia' in his *Filipinos: pre-war Philippines essays* (Araneta University Press, Victoneta Park, 1963), pp.91-2, refers to the 'ghost of any peasant dying with a debt over his head' returning to haunt surviving relatives until the debt is repaid; but he concludes that this ultimate sanction tends in practice to remove urgency about repayment: 'As debts are certain to be paid eventually, why all this fuss and impatience about paying on stipulated due dates . . . ?'

60 B.J. Kerkvliet, *The Huk rebellion: a study of peasant protest in the Philippines* (University of California Press, Berkeley, 1977); cf. Scott, *Moral economy*, pp.1-12, 157-240; V.T. King, 'Moral economy and peasant uprisings in South-East Asia', *Cultures et Dévéloppement, 10*, 1 (1978), pp.123-49, esp. pp.147-9, where his adaptation of Aberle's 'relative deprivation' theory seems apposite.

61 Philippine Islands, Dept of Commerce and Communications, *Quarterly Labor Bulletin*, 14 (December 1922), pp.11-20; *Labor*, 27 (1929), pp.107-20; Republic of the Philippines, Dept of Commerce and Industry, Bureau of Census and Statistics, *Census of the Philippines: 1948* (Bureau of Printing, Manila, 1956), vol.3, pp.2558-62; H.H. Miller, *Principles of economics applied to the Philippines* (Ginn and Co., Boston, 1932), p.392; Pendleton, 'The Bicol region', p.248. Ponce and Perez, 'Albay', p.112, however, describe some rice landowners collecting rent in full even if that meant that tenants would be left 'completely empty handed'.

62 Ponce and Perez, 'Albay', p.112. See also HDP, Albay, Bacacay, Barrio Gubat, and Polangui, Barrio Santicon, for later assertions of general agrarian harmony in the depression, attributed to the 'spirit of cooperation' and 'just and peaceful . . . crop shares'. The HDP for Central Luzon municipalities, by contrast, contain numerous references to agrarian discontent, peasant organisation and violence during the depression: Benedict J. Tria Kerkvliet, personal communication, 1 October 1985.

63 Owen, *Prosperity*, pp.83-7. It is generally assumed that a peasant family cannot till

more than 3-5 hectares of rice land with only their own labour.

64 E.g., 'Economic depression exists in Bicol provinces', *Tribune*, 16 May 1930.

65 Ponce and Perez, 'Albay', p.113.

66 *Census of 1918, Census of 1939*. In making these comparisons, it is assumed that: (1) farms listed in 1918 as paying 'no rental' were not operated by tenants; (2) the area cultivated by those listed in 1939 as 'part-tenants', who worked some lands of their own and rented other fields, can be considered half tenant- and half owner-operated; and (3) tenants worked the small number of large farms listed in 1939 as being operated by farm-managers. In an earlier study I pointed out the impossibility, due to changes in census definitions, of direct comparisons between censuses of number of tenants or number of tenant farms; Stephen Rosskamm Shalom later showed how the cultivated area could serve as a surrogate for these missing indicators. Owen, 'Philippine economic development and American policy: a reappraisal' in N.G. Owen (ed), *Compadre colonialism: studies on the Philippines under American rule* (University of Michigan, Center for South and Southeast Asian Studies, Ann Arbor, 1971), pp.116-18; S.R. Shalom, 'U.S.-Philippine relations: a study of neo-colonialism', unpublished PhD thesis, Boston University, 1976, pp.95-101.

67 Doeppers, *Manila, 1900-1941*, pp.51-84.

68 Hayden, *The Philippines*, pp.463-511; cf. HDP, Albay, Bacacay (town), on the virtual hiatus in the opening of new barrio schools between 1927 and 1933.

69 'Population and resources of Bikol provinces', *ACCJ, 7* (June 1927), p.8.

70 'Business conditions in the provinces', *PCIJ, 7* (November 1931), p.11; 'Provincial trade notes', *PCIJ, 9* (March 1933), p.18.

71 Ponce and Perez, 'Albay', pp.112-13.

72 See *Journal of Peasant Studies, 13* (January 1986), special issue on 'Everyday forms of peasant resistance in South-East Asia', edited by J.C. Scott and B.J.T. Kerkvliet.

73 B. Cruikshank, 'The Historical Data Papers as a source of Filipiniana', *Bulletin of the American Historical Collection* (Manila), *1* (March 1973), pp.14-23.

74 D.F. Doeppers, 'Filipino careers in metropolitan Manila during the 1930s and 1940s', seminar presentation in Dept of Pacific and Southeast Asian History, Australian National University, 10 July 1985.

75 HDP, Albay, Polangui, Barrio Matacon, and Bacacay, Barrio Manait. Cf. N. Ezequiel and N. Simbahan, 'Tabaco' in O'Brien, *The historical and cultural heritage*, p.108, for a later assertion that the administration of a municipal mayor who served from 1927 to 1941 was 'considered to be the best period in Tabaco's history'.

76 HDP, Albay, Bacacay (town) and Guinobatan, Barrio Malipo.

77 HDP, Albay, Bacacay (town).

78 HDP, Albay (province), Ligao (town) and Bacacay (town); cf. Ezequiel and Simbahan, 'Tabaco', p.107. Annual crop reports (in *SB*) indicate significant shortfalls in Bikol rice production during 1915/16 and 1919/20.

79 Owen, *Prosperity*, pp.49-56.

80 Ibid., pp.107-13, 134-6.

81 E.g. *Labor, passim*; Ponce and Perez,'Albay', p.112; Pendleton,'The Bicol region', p.248.

6

JAPAN'S RURAL ECONOMY IN CRISIS

ANN WASWO

Raw silk, which for a period of some 60 years from the 1870s to the early 1930s was Japan's single most important export item, is still produced in some of the same districts in which agriculture and silk-reeling flourished over a century ago. But the raw silk industry that once was heralded as 'the foundation of the Empire' for its ability to supply annually about 30 per cent by value of the nation's expanding exports, and hence to pay for a significant share of imports of raw materials and technology during the crucial early decades of Japan's economic transformation, now exists in relative obscurity, supplying not quite all the needs of silk fabric manufacturers who cater almost exclusively for the home market.

In its passage from key export item to ordinary domestic product, raw silk can be compared to more recent commodities such as cotton and synthetic textiles which, having lost their comparative advantage in world trade in the late 1960s, faded from centre stage of the Japanese economy, ceding the limelight to the products of new growth industries but still finding buyers within Japan. Raw silk differed from these other commodities, however, in that it was an export based on primary production, not on processing trade. The raw silk industry of the past relied totally on domestically produced mulberry and domestically produced silkworm cocoons. Those cocoons were raised, literally 'at home' by Japanese farm households and then unravelled into silk thread (i.e. raw silk) by the young women, most of them farmers' daughters, who were employed in filatures.[1]

Raw silk's 'fading' as a key export became apparent suddenly and dramatically in the late spring of 1930 with the collapse of the American market on which it had come to depend for more than 90 per cent of its foreign sales. By the time the depression that had caused that collapse had eased, synthetic fibres such as rayon and nylon had captured a large share of both US and world demand for silk and - not insignificantly - Japan was on the verge of war with the country that formerly had been her best customer. Japan possessed other industries, notably cotton textiles, that had been developing for some time and that were able in the early 1930s to compensate for the fall in export earnings occasioned by the decline in silk prices. Indeed owing to the rationalisation of many manufacturing industries during the 1920s and to the devaluation of the yen after abandonment of the gold standard in 1931, Japan's exports grew in real and nominal value from 1931 even though nominal world trade was falling and real world trade was stagnating. For exports, then, and in many respects for Japanese industrial development as a whole, the decline of the raw silk industry was of relatively minor importance in a continuing process of structural transformation.[2] But for those involved in raw silk production - including the large number of farm households who were engaged in sericulture and who are the focus of this paper - the decline was anything but minor.

More than two million farm households, or roughly 40 per cent of Japan's still large agricultural population of some five and a half million households, raised silkworms in 1930.[3] A sizeable minority of these households did so as their major agricultural activity, while for the majority it was an adjunct to the cultivation of rice and other crops. For both groups the decline in raw silk prices on the Yokohama Exchange in the spring of 1930 and the immediate decline that resulted in cocoon prices from the previous year's level of 7.58 yen per *kan* (3.75 kg) to 4.03 yen - a decrease of almost 47 per cent - proved devastating. Not only did they suffer a reduction in income; that reduced income was some 29 per cent below the estimated cost of producing cocoons that year.

Nor was this the full extent of the disruption to their livelihoods. On 2 October, after a summer in which vegetable, livestock and poultry prices had declined steeply, the Minister of Agriculture announced that the current year's rice harvest would amount to a record-breaking 66,870,000 *koku* (1 *koku* = 4.96 imperial bushels), a 12.5 per cent increase over average annual rice production during the previous years. This announcement sent rice prices plummeting the next day on the major exchanges, to around 19 yen per *koku* from 30.5 yen in August and 28.7 yen in September.[4] As this new price was, like the price of cocoons, below the estimated cost of production, and as rice remained the nation's most widely cultivated crop, virtually no farm household was left unscathed.

What became known as 'the bumper crop famine' for the hardships it imposed was followed in 1931 by severe crop failures for rice and other cereals in Hokkaido and in the Tohoku region of northern Honshu and then by a second wave of crop failures in the Tohoku in 1934. The cumulative result was an agricultural depression of unprecedented seriousness. As shown in Table 1, farmers' incomes declined, but their operating costs and tax burdens did not decline proportionately. Rural indebtedness, which had been increasing during the 1920s, rose in 1932 to an average of 846 yen per household, a figure roughly equivalent to the annual income of many farmers.[5] In districts heavily dependent on rice (e.g. the Tohoku) or on sericulture (e.g. Yamagata and Fukushima prefectures in the Tohoku and most of the mountainous Chubu region of central Honshu), rates of indebtedness were higher than the national average, and loans that earlier had been used, at least in part, to finance agricultural improvements were now increasingly used to sustain consumption. In some parts of the Tohoku farmers were reduced to foraging for edible nuts and weeds, and when those were exhausted, to gathering tree bark in order to eat its inner phloem. There was a significant increase in the number of young girls sold by their parents to brothels, geisha houses and cafes, for cash payments of about 100 yen, in order to meet debt payments or to assure food and shelter for the remaining family members.[6]

TABLE 1: The financial status of farm households, 1929-30

	Owner-cultivators (of *c.* 1.7 *chō*)		Tenant farmers (of *c.*1.5 *chō*)	
	1929	1930	1929	1930
Agricultural income				
gross income	2,131	1,440	1,769	1,285
farming costs	1,020	752	1,120	879
[tenant rents in above]	[19	15	372	279]
net income (A)	1,111	688	649	406
Non-agricultural income (B)	398	273	252	195
Total income (A+B)	1,509	961	901	601
Consumption (C)	1,245	901	867	654
Taxes (D)	170	142	35	29
Balance (A+B-C-D)	94	-82	-1	-82

Note: The above data are drawn from surveys of the household finances of a relatively small number of farmers with holdings that were above average size. 1 *chō* = 0.992 hectares.

Source: Sumiya Mikio (ed), *Shōwa kyōkō* (Yuhikaku, Tokyo, 1974), p.293.

Although the non-agricultural sector of the economy showed signs of recovery by 1932 or 1933, as indicated in Tables 2 and 3 agricultural output per hectare remained stagnant and agricultural prices did not recover their pre-depression levels until 1936 or 1937. A notable exception to this latter recovery was, of course, the price of cocoons.

TABLE 2 Agricultural indicators

	Absolute levels				Average annual rates of growth (%)		
					1907-	1917-	1927-
	1907	1917	1927	1937	1917	1927	1937
A. Amount produced	2,304	2,880	3,090	3,360	2.2	0.7	0.8
B. Gross value added	1,953	2,411	2,498	2,646	2.1	0.4	0.6
C. Agricultural productivity	81.66	97.24	101.52	104.46	1.7	0.4	0.3

Notes: Absolute levels are 7-year moving averages. A and B (¥ million) at 1934-36 prices; C as index with 1934-46 = 100.
Source: Takafusa Nakamura, *Economic growth in prewar Japan* (Yale University Press, New Haven and London, 1983), p.214.

TABLE 3: Agricultural prices (1934-6 = 100)

	All farm goods	Cultivated crops	Livestock & poultry	Cocoons
1911	68.0	64.3	80.1	93.2
1912	79.3	76.2	82.0	93.2
1913	78.8	74.9	84.8	104.6
1914	56.5	51.7	83.7	102.3
1915	53.3	49.3	82.2	84.1
1916	60.5	54.8	86.1	122.8
1917	85.5	77.7	96.5	178.4
1918	132.7	124.7	129.6	205.5
1919	182.0	170.9	170.6	284.1
1920	145.6	140.5	201.3	153.5
1921	143.3	136.3	191.4	171.9
1922	127.8	109.2	183.5	251.6
1923	138.5	122.4	176.6	252.6
1924	148.5	140.8	173.5	198.8
1925	148.8	134.3	170.2	258.5
1926	134.1	123.3	171.9	202.9
1927	117.3	110.4	165.5	145.5
1928	115.6	107.9	156.1	156.3
1929	114.3	105.7	142.2	170.6
1930	75.3	71.8	122.3	76.0
1931	69.3	66.4	98.7	75.5
1932	77.8	76.4	80.5	88.1
1933	75.6	79.8	91.6	131.5
1934	92.2	95.4	95.8	62.2
1935	101.0	97.7	98.8	113.7
1936	106.8	104.9	105.4	124.1
1937	118.0	117.0	114.1	129.8
1938	126.8	126.5	138.4	122.3

Source: Takafusa Nakamura, *Economic growth in prewar Japan* (Yale University Press, New Haven and London, 1983), p.215.

Tables 2 and 3 also indicate that the problem of stagnation and declining prices had not begun in 1930. On the contrary, Japan's agricultural sector as a whole had been in difficulty throughout the preceding decade, with relatively slow growth in output and productivity, and with prices for all crops falling from the peak levels they had reached during or immediately after the first World War. Until the mid 1920s, however, the decline in cocoon prices was relatively modest in comparison with the decline in prices for cultivated crops and, as we shall see, a significant number of farm households took up sericulture in these years. Indeed, their number and their total output continued to increase through to 1930, even though cocoon prices began to fall more rapidly after 1925. What an economist might describe as yet another example of the inelasticity of agricultural supply in response to falling prices was, in less abstract terms, a reflection of an increasingly desperate struggle on the part of millions of farmers. The sector on which they depended for their livelihoods was faltering, its potential for growth within the existing structure of land tenure and small-scale, labour-intensive farming, almost exhausted. Unable to obtain enough cash income from raising staple crops or from part-time non-agricultural employment, they devoted more and more of their energy to rearing silkworms.[7] And yet, as we shall also see, the income they sought proved elusive, not only because of slackening American demand for raw silk but also because of the character of the domestic market for the cocoons they wanted to sell.

THE DEVELOPMENT OF SERICULTURE, 1859-1929

Before July 1859 and Japan's sudden entry, after more than two centuries of national seclusion, into world trade under the 'unequal' commercial treaties with the Western powers, cotton rather than silk had been the leading fibre in what was basically a foodstuffs agriculture. Grown principally in western Japan, cotton was the fibre that clothed the overwhelming majority of the population. Its weaving and trading, once monopolised by urban guilds, had developed during the latter half of the eighteenth and early nineteenth centuries into the leading sector of rural cottage industry and commerce. Silk, as had been the case since its introduction from China in about A.D. 200, remained the fibre for the aristocracy. Although cocoon production had increased during the long and peaceful Tokugawa period, and although silk weaving and trading also had developed in the countryside to challenge established urban guilds, silk remained less important than cotton.

After July 1859, however, a swift reversal occurred. Japan's homespun cotton yarn and hand-loomed cotton cloth proved no match in either quality or cost to machine-made products from the West, and imports - principally from England - increased rapidly, penetrating not only urban markets (as elsewhere in

Asia) but rural markets as well. Nor could domestically produced raw cotton compete in either quality or cost with foreign fibre. Although Japan exported some raw cotton during the world-wide cotton shortage brought about by the American Civil War, the acreage planted to cotton declined thereafter. The mechanised cotton yarn and textile industry that Japan began to develop in the 1870s to compete with Western imports would be based on imported raw materials.

Silk, on the other hand, encountered not foreign competition but timely surges in foreign demand. In the 1860s, owing to the silkworm blight that had curtailed cocoon production in Europe, European silk textile manufacturers were desperately in need of raw silk. At the same time, cocoon production in China, to which they might have turned, was disrupted by the Taiping Rebellion. By 1863 Japan's production of raw silk had doubled, and more than half of that production was exported, primarily to Europe. For the next 15 years or so, most of Japan's silk exports continued to go to Europe; then, in the early 1880s, just as European demand slackened, American demand developed. Abandoning long-standing efforts to promote domestic sericulture and silk-reeling, the United States government decided that raw silk should be imported for the American silk textile industry. Thereafter, reflecting the growth of per capita real income and the high income elasticity of demand for silk, imports increased dramatically from a few million pounds per year in the mid-1880s to more than 25 million pounds in 1914.[8]

In the early 1880s Japan was only one of four major suppliers for this burgeoning market, the others being China, Italy and France. But among the four, Japan occupied a middling position in terms of the quality and price of her raw silk - it was inferior in quality to European raw silk but cheaper, superior in quality to Chinese silk but dearer - that proved advantageous. Japan's share of the American raw silk market reached 47 per cent in the late 1890s and rose again to 66 per cent during the five years from 1910 to 1914. This amounted to roughly 60 to 70 per cent of total Japanese raw silk exports. As shown in Table 4, the volume of the latter had increased dramatically since the 1880s, as had total domestic production. In 1900 Japan's output surpassed Italy's; in 1909 her share of the world market (though not of world-wide production) surpassed China's.[9]

TABLE 4: Production and export of raw silk (in metric tons)

	Production	Export
1880	1,999	877
1890	3,458	1,266
1900	7,102	2,778
1910	11,904	8,908
1920	21,877	10,481

Source: Gen Itasaka and others, *Kodansha encyclopedia of Japan* (Kodansha, Tokyo and New York, 1983), vol.7, p.194.

Of course, just as foreign demand alone did not create markets for Japanese textiles or consumer electrical goods in the 1950s and 1960s, so too in the nineteenth century other, essentially domestic factors played an important role in enabling raw silk production to expand and secure export markets. The most prominent of these, as far as much of the general literature on Japan's economic development is concerned, were private entrepreneurship in the development and spread of machine reeling, which, in contrast to hand reeling, produced filament of a uniform quality suitable for use on power looms and knitting frames; and the willingness and ability of the government to regulate the quality of exports by such means as its Raw Silk Inspection Office.[10] Less prominently featured in the literature, but no less important in securing the increase in cocoon output on which expanding exports depended, were (1) the need among Japanese farm households for additional sources of cash income to meet new obligations and, in not a few cases, to offset the loss of cash income occasioned by the decline of previous cash crops and cottage industries; (2) the relatively easy 'fit' of sericulture into Japanese family farming; and (3) a number of mostly small but cumulatively important improvements in silkworm rearing and mulberry culture, that were devised by silkworm raisers, silk-reeling firms, and government scientists.

The growth of commercial farming and rural handicraft production during the latter half of the Tokugawa period had led to greater divisions of wealth among rural households, but not to the division of the agricultural population into a small number of large capitalist landowners on the one hand and a substantial number of landless agricultural workers on the other. Nor had such reforms of the early Meiji era as the elimination of seignorial control over arable land, the formal recognition of private property rights, or the imposition of a new nation-wide land tax in cash, done much to upset the existing pattern of small-scale, labour-intensive family farming. Not all farm households owned all the land they cultivated in the 1870s - it has been estimated that some 30 per cent of all arable land was tenanted at that time[11] - but virtually all the agricultural land in Japan was cultivated by family units.

Tenant rents remained payable in kind in most cases, but all farmers who owned land, including the numerous category of those who were part tenants and part owner-cultivators, needed cash for tax payments. Given the decline in farm self-sufficiency that had occurred - at varying rates in differing localities - over the past century, they had further needs for cash: e.g. for the purchase of fertiliser, clothing, soy sauce and other food items that were no longer produced at home. At the same time, some of the sources of cash income - not just cotton and cotton weaving, but sugar-cane and sugar manufacture, rapeseed and pressed oil manufacture - had lost ground to foreign imports. One solution to these straitened circumstances was to leave agriculture, as in fact some people did. But employment opportunities in the non-agricultural sector remained limited, roughly adequate to siphon off the younger, non-inheriting sons of farm families but not sufficient to bring about a rural exodus. Most families had no choice but to remain on the land and try to adjust to the new situation in which they found themselves.

An attractive form of adjustment, at least in some parts of the country, was sericulture, a familiar activity for which, in contrast to several other equally familiar activities, there *was* a market. Not only did those already involved in raising silkworms expand their operations, but others became involved as well, either by working as occasional day labourers in those expanded operations or, provided they had access to an upland field on which to raise mulberry, by adding silkworm rearing to their own farming cycle. It is true that even a modest involvement required a great deal of labour - there could be as many as 35,000 worms in each ounce of worms at hatching, and from that instant until they reached full maturity (at a weight of some 500 pounds) and began spinning cocoons about five weeks later, this multitude would require hand-feeding at frequent intervals a total of some 1,200 pounds of carefully chopped mulberry leaves - but labour was precisely what farm families had to excess at the time. Moreover, it needed to be mobilised, as did the cramped floorspace in farmers' homes, only for a fairly brief period. In the early Meiji era just one crop of cocoons a year, a 'spring rearing' that was ready for market in June, was possible. Although this was a busy time for farmers, when fields needed preparation for the planting of rice and other staple grains, it was also a time when stores of food from the previous year's harvest were running low and when an infusion of cash income was welcome. The prospect of that income and the food it would buy or the debts it would settle helped sustain the family's efforts. Then, with the rearing behind them, they could once again focus on their field crops.

Finally, a number of improvements in silkworm raising and mulberry culture helped make these farmers even more productive. These included the diffusion of improved domestic and foreign silkworm varieties and, eventually, the preparation of silkworm eggs by specialist firms; the invention of a combined cool and warm method of rearing worms that reduced the risks of disease; and the development of new techniques for gathering and feeding mulberry leaves. Perhaps the most significant development was the invention, in 1875, of 'summer-fall rearing', which made two, and subsequently three, cocoon crops a year possible. With the perfection of methods to induce the timely hatching of eggs, 'summer-fall rearing' became steadily more widespread. As shown in Table 5, it had accounted for less than a quarter of total cocoon production in the late 1890s, but by the 1920s it was accounting for half.

Table 5 also shows the increases over time in the number of farm households engaged in sericulture, the area planted to mulberry, the output of cocoons, and the yield of cocoons per 10 *ares* of land and per box of eggs. From 1889 to 1929 the output of cocoons increased eightfold, with roughly one-half of the increase resulting from more intensive cropping per mulberry field (that is, two or more rearings per year). From 1895 to 1929 the output of cocoons per household more than doubled.

There had probably been about 300,000 farm households engaged in sericulture in the 1860s, and by the late 1880s their number had increased to roughly one million.[12] From 1895, when fairly accurate statistics become available, to 1929, their number rose again, by more than 950,000, with the greatest rates of increase occurring at the turn of the century, between 1915 and 1918, and in the mid 1920s.[13] Perhaps 6 per cent of the total number of farm households in the early Meiji era, they constituted 40 per cent in the late 1920s.

This was, of course, a national average. In the mountainous districts of central Honshu, where paddy was relatively scarce and commercial rice production difficult, upwards of 80 per cent of local farm households raised silkworms and had been doing so since the 1890s if not earlier. For many it was their major, or sole, cash crop, although they continued to raise a small amount of rice and vegetables for their own use and to engage in a variety of side employments to make ends meet. Their number included all strata of rural society, except those with the very smallest holdings who needed all the land they cultivated to raise food. It was members of this latter group in particular who provided day labour for their more substantial neighbours during the peak week or so of each rearing season, and who sent their daughters off to work in filatures as an additional source of cash income.[14]

TABLE 5: The development of sericulture

Year	Number of sericulture households	Mulberry field area (hectares)	Cocoon output (metric tons)	Cocoon output per 10 *ares* (kg)	Cocoon output per box of eggs (kg)	Output by rearing spring	summer & fall
1889		216,110	44,426	20.5		33,744	10,682
1892		254,810	55,526	21.8		42,158	13,368
1895	1,256,430	263,950	84,682	32.1		63,668	21,014
1898	1,311,940	301,770	76,015	25.2		56,408	19,607
1901	1,475,190	300,930	94,725	31.5	8.6	67,445	27,280
1904	1,473,900	322,220	105,951	32.9	9.0	69,398	36,553
1907	1,420,550	387,555	129,632	33.5	10.2	84,055	45,577
1910	1,462,150	438,790	146,279	33.3	10.6	90,896	55,383
1912	1,499,540	449,800	166,949	37.1	11.4	96,358	70,592
1915	1,671,300	449,940	174,263	38.7	11.4	97,063	77,200
1918	1,907,530	504,650	256,176	50.8	14.5	133.264	122,912
1921	1,799,470	530,520	237,442	44.8	17.0	120,267	117,175
1924	1,885,880	532,730	276,771	52.0	20.5	148,000	128,772
1926	2,054,560	566,550	325,124	57.4	22.6	165,510	159,614
1929	2,209,320	619,840	382,735	61.8	25.0	189,663	193,072
1932	2,057,310	646,440	335,612	51.9	23.6	173,860	161,752
1935	1,886,840	576,620	307,434	53.3	23.8	165,508	141,926
1938	1,688,020	543,820	281,843	51.8	25.8	153,047	128,795
1941	1,581,490	489,230	261,563	53.5	26.4	140,768	120,795
1944	1,138,770	302,160	151,170	50.0	24.1	87,117	64,053

Note: The number of households through to 1912 is for spring rearing only; for 1915 and thereafter, it represents the number of households that were engaged in rearing either in spring, summer or autumn, or in all three seasons.

Source: Takekazu Ogura (ed), *Agricultural development in modern Japan* (Japan FAO Association, Tokyo, 1963), pp.550, 559.

Elsewhere in the country sericulture appears to have been confined to those farmers whose holdings, whether owned or tenanted, were larger than the average prevailing in their region. Most of them owned the upland fields they had planted to mulberry and raised silkworms as a secondary cash crop. Some had begun doing so in the late nineteenth century to replace cotton, rape and other upland crops they had raised in the past but for which there was no longer much demand. Others - that is, most if not all of the increase of roughly

400,000 households engaged in sericulture in the years from 1921 to 1929 - had taken up silkworm rearing because cocoon prices had not fallen as much as the prices for other field crops (including rice) in the years after the first World War. While rice remained the principal crop for many of these farmers - one did not demolish paddy fields casually, no matter what was happening to rice prices - their reliance on income from sericulture increased.

With the perfecting of summer-fall rearing, farmers had the option of raising silkworms at a time of year that did not conflict with the labour needs of spring planting. Some of them may have exercised this option in the early 1900s - that is, have raised a single crop of silkworms in the summer or fall, whichever was more convenient - but by the late 1920s significant numbers were raising two crops a year, despite the burden this imposed on family labour. Those who specialised in sericulture raised a third crop of worms, usually in late spring.

Regardless of the frequency of rearing - or, for that matter, the degree of reliance on sericulture as a source of cash income - the scale of cocoon production per household was relatively small. Table 6 shows that in 1934 (the only year for which I have been able to obtain data) some 58 per cent of sericultural households raised between 20 and 70 *kan* (75.0 to 262.5 kg) of cocoons.

TABLE 6: Scale of cocoon production per household, 1934

Weight of cocoons (*kan*)	Number of households	% of total
less than 5	43,308	2.2
5 to 10	127,964	6.4
10 to 20	290,108	14.5
20 to 30	364,614	18.3
30 to 50	429,209	21.5
50 to 70	339,386	17.9
70 to 100	224,489	11.2
100 to 150	116,865	5.9
150 or more	59,200	3.0
Total	1,995,143	100.0

Source: Sumiya Mikio (ed), *Shōwa kyōkō* (Yuhikaku, Tokyo, 1974), p.171.

In 1929 some 60 per cent of the total output of 382,735 metric tons of cocoons was sold by farmers to silk-reeling establishments. Of the 40 per cent not sold, one portion consisted of second-rate cocoons - those that were off-colour or out of shape - which would be reeled at home by the women of the household and then hand-loomed by them during the slack season. A second and larger portion, consisting mostly of higher-quality cocoons, was kept by farm households who were involved in the traditional silk-reeling industry that catered primarily for the domestic textile market. With the exception of these latter households, who numbered roughly 62,000 in the late 1920s,[15] farmers generally sought to sell as high a proportion of their cocoon output as possible. Provided they had obtained good-quality eggs, were skilled in rearing techniques, and fortunate in weather conditions, they were able to minimise the number of inferior cocoons they produced. Their next step was selling their output, and in this they entered a buyers' market.

THE MARKET-PLACE FOR COCOONS

Perhaps the easiest way of explaining the workings of the cocoon market in the mid to late 1920s is to begin by describing what farmers, as sellers within it, were unable to do. In the first place, they could not defer their sales. Usually this is attributed to their pressing need for cash - that is, that they were engaged in distress selling. This may have been true in some cases, but a far more basic reason for the rapidity with which they sold their crops was that there was a market only for raw cocoons - that is, for cocoons with live pupae inside them. There was no market for 'dried' cocoons in which the pupae had been killed. Secondly, although there were more than 3,500 filatures in the nation, farmers could not benefit from any competitive bidding among them. In some cases, farmers had a commitment to sell to a particular buyer, from whom they had obtained eggs on credit. More typically, the filatures in a particular region had formed an association, one of whose functions was to determine the prices that would be offered by all member firms each harvest season. In determining those prices a rather strict formula was applied that took into consideration only the market price for raw silk and raw silk by-products, the costs of reeling the raw silk and transporting it to market, and the other liabilities (e.g. interest payments) of the reeling firms. Some allowance was made for the quality of the cocoons purchased (shape, colour, silk layer percentage), but in contrast to the procedures followed in the commercial sale of rice, grading was carried out by the reeling firms or their agents, not by prefectural authorities. Thirdly, although reeling firms encountered few obstacles in organising associations, cocoon raisers did. Under the terms of the Industrial Association Law of 1900, they could, in concert with other landowners in their communities, establish credit co-operatives and co-operatives for the purchase of fertilisers and other farming inputs. They were not permitted, however, to set up production or marketing co-operatives whose membership was confined to silkworm raisers only.[16] In other words, what farmers *could* do was to sell their cocoons as isolated individuals, each with a small volume of a highly perishable crop, at whatever price they were offered.

The marginal position they occupied as sellers was not simply a reflection of rural poverty and the lack of alternative forms of employment. Nor was it simply a reflection of their involvement in producing a crop that was destined, once semi-manufactured, for export, and hence subject to fluctuations in world prices. To a significant degree their marginality had been engineered during the late nineteenth and early twentieth centuries by the domestic raw silk industry, aided and abetted by government policies, in order to keep export prices relatively low and, by doing so, maintain the advantageous position Japan occupied *vis-à-vis* her competitors in world silk trade.

During the first decade or so following the opening of Japan, there had been no cocoon market as such, for farm households themselves had hand-reeled raw silk from the cocoons they raised. Roughly half of what they reeled was purchased by rural merchants, who in turn sold the raw silk to foreign trading companies in the treaty ports of Yokohama and Kobe. These foreign companies monopolised every aspect of Japan's trade at the time, from the handling of exports and imports to the provision of shipping, insurance and banking facilities, and they used their position to acquire raw silk at only one-third to one-half prevailing world prices. Although barred by the treaties from engaging in trade outside the treaty ports, they were able to circumvent this restriction to a degree by employing Japanese agents whom they sent out to purchase raw silk (and other commodities) directly from producers. They also began to concern themselves with machine silk-reeling, either indirectly by means of loans to Japanese entrepreneurs or directly by establishing filatures within the treaty ports.[17]

Their attempts to penetrate the interior (as well as the unfair trading practices they were perceived, often correctly, to engage in) helped fuel a 'trading rights recovery' movement in the 1880s that merged with a more general national rights recovery movement and resulted, at the end of the nineteenth century, in revision of the unequal treaties and the abolition of treaty port trade. Thereafter foreign companies remained participants in the raw silk trade, but they no longer enjoyed a monopoly over it or, for that matter, over the shipping and exchange banking that it and other trade required. Dockside prices for raw silk came to approximate world prices (less freight and handling charges), and real influence over the raw silk market devolved upon Japanese brokers (*urikomidonya*) and upon Mitsui, Mitsubishi and a few other Japanese trading companies.

While rebuffing the efforts of foreign trading companies to extend their dominion over the raw silk trade to raw silk production itself, the Japanese did, however, pay heed to foreign criticisms of the uneven quality of their hand-reeled raw silk, and a slow but fairly steady development of machine reeling was undertaken. By the mid 1890s, slightly more than half of the nation's total raw silk output was filature silk, although most filatures remained very small (with fewer than ten basins each) and employed only the simplest machinery:

wood was used wherever possible in place of metal, and although steam might be used to boil the cocoons, human hands were relied upon to unravel the 2,000 to 3,000 feet of silk filament in each cocoon.[18] By 1911 filature silk accounted for over 74 per cent of total raw silk output, and an increasing number of larger filatures were being established. In 1913, for example, there were 546 filatures with over 100 basins, out of a total of some 4,700 filatures, compared with only 124 filatures with over 100 basins in 1894.[19]

The development of filature silk had two consequences of relevance to this discussion. The first, stemming from the separation of cocoon raising and reeling, was the creation of a distinct market for cocoons.[20] The second was the steadily increasing, and ultimately institutionalised, dependence of machine reeling establishments on borrowed working capital. Initially, in the 1870s and 1880s, the scale of investment per filature had been rather small, averaging roughly 1,500 yen (about £270), and funds for both equipment and operating costs had been drawn for the most part from the rural districts in which the filatures were located, either from local banks or directly from wealthy individuals. The subsequent expansion of raw silk production to meet foreign demand was, however, more than local sources of capital could accommodate. Other than setting-up costs, machine reeling establishments faced two major and recurring expenditures - the purchase of cocoons at harvest time and the payment of wages to their operatives - that together accounted for roughly 90 per cent of production costs. To provide for these expenditures they came to rely, from the late 1880s onwards, on loans from state banks (which in turn relied on loans from the Bank of Japan) or on advance payments from the *urikomidonya* (who in turn relied on loans from the Yokohama branches of the 2nd and 74th State Banks, the Yokohama Specie Bank, and Japanese foreign trading firms).[21]

Faced with the necessity of repaying both the principal and interest on these loans, and unable to exert any significant influence over world raw silk prices,[22] the managers of filatures devoted their energies to keeping their production costs down. On the one hand, this meant attention to wages. Although a detailed description of how this attention manifested itself (and resulted in wages at the turn of the century that appear to have been lower than the wages paid to cotton textile workers in British India) is beyond the scope of this paper, three basic points should be noted. The first is that when the development of filatures outstripped local supplies of nimble-fingered young women, managers established elaborate recruitment networks to tap into the supply of young female labour in remote mountain villages throughout the country, where off-season work was scarce and where even the low wages they offered (80 to 90 per cent of which went to the girls' families) looked attractive. Second, they required each operative's father to sign a contract in which he agreed to return the advance money he had received and/or pay a penalty, if his daughter left the filature to work in another; and they agreed with nearby filatures not to hire away each other's workers. Third, managers devised a system of 'ranked wages' that put operatives in competition with one another to surpass daily output and quality targets in order to secure a higher share of a fixed total of daily wage payments.[23]

On the other hand, the effort to keep production costs down meant attention to cocoon prices. As already noted in passing, some filatures supplied eggs to farmers, ostensibly as a means of guaranteeing cocoons of the standardised quality they required, but also as a means of insuring that those farmers would sell cocoons only to them. This practice, however, was confined to the larger filatures and did not develop until after about 1915. Before that time the most common means of controlling cocoon prices was, as also noted previously, joint action by local filatures. This began on a fairly informal basis in the early 1890s with a number of small firms in a given locality joining together to purchase cocoons in bulk and, if prices were on the upswing, threatening to boycott local producers unless prices were lowered. Eventually the firms formed associations, agreed among themselves on the price they were willing to pay at a given harvest season, and posted a notice of the agreed price on their office doors. Even if there were hand-reeling establishments in the same area, these tended to be essentially self-sufficient in cocoons or to buy them only in very small quantities, so farmers had no alternative outlet and were forced to accept the reelers' agreed price.

It would also seem that some filatures took steps to divide the farmers in a given village into rival groups, thereby reducing the possibility that the farmers might organise against them. As John Embree noted in his study of a village in Kyushu, two of the largest filatures in Japan, Katakura and Kanebo, supplied eggs to and bought cocoons from local farmers. Each had organised the farmers it dealt with into a sericultural association that received advice from company agents and, from time to time, a banquet at company expense. After commenting that 'the silkworm raisers have certain privileges in addition to the rather small cash payments for the cocoons', Embree went on to observe:

> The two companies . . . have as heads of their respective village silk associations the village headman and a village councillor, both rich and influential men in village affairs. These men receive many special favors from the companies in the way of gifts and, on their part explain the company's aim to the farmers and offer explanations when the company hands out a poor batch of eggs or happens to pay a lower price for cocoons than usual. One of the few examples of rivalry in village affairs is that between these two company associations. They always hold their meetings separately and attempt to outshine each other in production and in parties after the sale of cocoons and even in the type of priest hired to thank the gods for a good year.[24]

Owing to these and other measures, filatures generally were able to impose the full extent of decreases in dockside raw silk prices on farmers and, when prices rose again, to determine the increase that would be permitted in cocoon prices.[25] Although they were unable to insulate themselves totally from the vicissitudes of the world raw silk trade - for example, not a few small reeling establishments went out of business during the depression that accompanied the American crisis of 1908 - they were able in most years to garner substantial profits for themselves (and for their creditors); and the portion of those profits that was not spent on consumption or on expanded reeling operations was, as officials of the government in the Meiji era had hoped, made available for other commercial and industrial investment.

THE RETREAT FROM SERICULTURE

To assume that farmers had fatalistically accepted their marginal position in raw silk production, or that any discontent they felt had been mollified by an occasional banquet, would be to underrate them and the changes that had occurred over time in their attitudes toward farming. By the early 1920s certainly, if not earlier, most farmers were not only basically literate but basically numerate as well.[26] Many of them kept accounts of their farming costs, yields and revenues, and while they paid closest attention to such cash expenditures as fertiliser, silkworm eggs and day labour, they had more than a rough idea of the value of their own family labour and of crops other than mulberry they might grow on their upland fields.[27]

Moreover, although the majority of farmers who engaged in sericulture owned the fields they had planted to mulberry, significant numbers of them rented at least a portion of the remaining land they cultivated and had become involved to one degree or another in the tenant union movement that developed after the first World War.[28] Having themselves participated in a successful rent strike to bring about rent reductions on rice paddy (the immediate goal of most tenant agitation in the 1920s), and, in some cases, in a longer-term effort to establish 'rational' rents that took the tenants' costs of production into account, these farmers quite naturally became more aware that the *status quo* was malleable and that all sorts of 'traditional' arrangements could be changed. Except for a few instances in the Chubu district, however, where farmers rented mulberry fields to an extent not found elsewhere in the country, and where tenant-sericulturalists had been able to secure modest improvements in the local cocoon market,[29] most of their efforts to overcome the disadvantages they faced in selling cocoons came to naught.

Nor could the reform-minded officials who assumed positions of responsibility in the Ministry of Agriculture in the late 1920s achieve much at the outset, for silk reelers and their urban backers enjoyed too much political influence at the national level for any significant changes in market structure to win approval in the Diet. Only after the American silk market had collapsed and efforts by reelers and exporters to maintain revenues by selling increased quantities of raw silk at substantially lower prices had failed - and even then with difficulty - were officials able to secure passage of a Cocoon Disposition Control Law (1936) that abolished transactions in raw cocoons in favour of dried; established prefectural grading of cocoons in place of private grading by buyers; and permitted farmers to organise cocoon-raising associations in which they were able to co-operate in all aspects of rearing silkworms and selling cocoons.[30]

Officials in the same ministry had enjoyed more immediate success in implementing other, less controversial, measures to aid sericulturalists (and Japan's foreign exchange position) during the initial years of the depression. On the one hand, the existing tariff on wheat imports was raised in 1932, and a five-year plan for increasing domestic wheat production at the expense of mulberry was launched; those farmers whose mulberry fields were not suited to wheat were encouraged to grow other commercial crops such as vegetables or fruits, or to begin raising poultry or pigs.[31] On the other hand, to protect farmers in regions where, owing to climate and terrain, few alternatives to sericulture were feasible, government officials sought to maintain raw silk prices by controlling production and exports; in addition, the National Sericulture Experiment Station began a search for new end-uses for raw silk, mulberry and cocoons.[32]

These policies served to quicken the pace of a retreat from sericulture that depressed prices had initiated. As shown in Table 5, more than 320,000 households abandoned silkworm raising in the first half of the 1930s. To be sure, this retreat did not occur at a uniform rate throughout the country. Only some 7 per cent of the households that had raised silkworms in 1930 in Fukushima, Yamanashi and Nagano prefectures, all three part of the mountainous heartland of Japanese sericulture, had ceased doing so in 1935. Elsewhere in the country, and especially in south-western Japan where sericulture had been a less important activity for farmers, the percentages generally were much greater. In Shiga and Hiroshima prefectures, for example, 34 per cent of the households that had raised silkworms in 1930 had ceased doing so by 1935; in Osaka prefecture, where less than 2 per cent of farm households had raised silkworms in 1930, over 53 per cent had withdrawn by 1935.[33]

Even those households that remained in sericulture tended to reduce the intensity of their operations. As also shown in Table 5, the cocoon yield per 10 *ares* of mulberry fell by 16 per cent between 1929 and 1932, and, except for a slight increase in 1935, continued to fall thereafter. Part of this decrease was brought about by the abandonment of summer/fall rearing by some households, but a larger part of the decrease was caused by a reduction in fertiliser and labour inputs on mulberry fields themselves. Fertiliser costs money, after all, and farmers had little if any cash to spare. At the same time, labour that formerly had been devoted to the pruning of mulberry trees and the careful picking of leaves or shootlets could now be employed with greater expectation of net gain in attending to other crops or in paid work for other farmers. Even though agricultural wages had fallen by 1932 to roughly 60 per cent of their 1929 level, this fall was not as great as the decline in cocoon prices.[34]

Non-agricultural employment was not a viable alternative for farmers in the early 1930s, when there were far more seekers of such work than work itself; indeed the number of part-time farm households (those in which one or more members were employed in the non-agricultural sector), actually decreased slightly between 1929 and 1938.[35] Nor did any significant changes occur during the early 1930s in land ownership, rates of tenancy, or the scale of farming. On the contrary, roughly the same number of households continued to farm the same plots as before, and in the same capacity as owners or tenants.[36] In contrast to the immediate pre-depression years, however, they were slightly more dependent on agricultural income; and those who had once relied on sericulture to make ends meet found it increasingly difficult to do so.

As a direct result of the collapse of world silk prices, the only notable structural change in Japanese agriculture was the beginning of a shift in cropping patterns. The area planted to mulberry, which had reached a peak of some 714,000 hectares in 1930, fell by 19 per cent to 576,620 hectares in 1935. In the same period the area planted to wheat (excluding wheat grown as a second crop on drained rice paddies) increased by 32 per cent from 269,000 to 350,400 hectares; and the area planted to potatoes rose by 28 per cent from 366,000 to 468,000 hectares.[37]

Especially in the early 1930s, when the impact of losses of income from sericulture was most keenly felt, many farmers were in a bitter frame of mind, and their bitterness was not necessarily directed, as some members of the Japanese establishment would have had it, at the reckless behaviour of Wall Street financiers or the fickle buying habits of Yankee women, but at the Japanese establishment itself. As one leader of a farmers' organisation in Nagano prefecture, whose population was highly dependent on sericulture, put it in an article published in 1932:

> It is a well known fact that the countryside has been made subordinate to the city in Japan's industrialisation to date. All laws have protected commerce and manufacturing and exploited rural villages; the burden of taxes, too, has been made heavy in rural areas and light in cities. Although elected by the votes of farmers, members of the House of Representatives have become the tools of city financial cliques, and like the city-based newspapers, they have ignored the countryside. [Meanwhile] the high interest rates paid by farmers have filled the coffers of finance capitalists; merchants have robbed

> the countryside by means of their commissions and handling charges; and for manufacturers the countryside has become a place where raw materials can be bought cheaply and finished goods sold dear. Their most able young men siphoned off by the cities and many of their young women taken away [to work in urban factories and shops], rural villages have found their [natural] balance between male and females destroyed.[38]

In its content, though not in its tone, this statement bears a striking similarity to the assessment made some three decades later by the economists Kazushi Ohkawa and Henry Rosovsky about the role of the agricultural sector in Japan's industrial transformation during a 'crucial interval' from the mid nineteenth century to the early twentieth. But whereas these later observers placed stress on the ability of the non-agricultural sector to finance its own growth after the crucial interval came to an end and noted that the agricultural sector, having supplied the nation with food, tax revenues, foreign exchange and industrial labour, was left faltering, the rural leader above was passionately concerned with conditions within that faltering sector. His article was written to encourage farmers to submit petitions demanding debt relief and other aid from the government, and its thinly disguised contempt for cities, capitalism, liberalism and parliamentary process was not unrelated to the shifts that occurred in Japanese politics and foreign policy later in the 1930s.

NOTES

1 As William Lockwood has observed, 'cocoons . . . cannot be regarded strictly as the product of an "extractive" industry. Nor were they exported in quantity until converted into yarn by the silk filatures. But it seems best to treat them as a farm export crop, since cocoon growing normally comprised 70 per cent of the cost of raw silk, and was a farm occupation directly associated with the growing of mulberry leaves for silkworm feeding'. *The economic development of Japan* (Princeton University Press, Princeton, NJ, 1968), pp.356-7.

2 See, for example, Takafusa Nakamura, *Economic growth in prewar Japan* (Yale University Press, New Haven and London, 1983) pp.244, 254-61. Nakamura thinks the devaluation of the yen was of greater importance than the rationalisation of cotton and other domestic manufacturing industries in enabling exports to grow during the 1930s.

3 At an average of 5.5 individuals per farm household, they numbered some 11 million persons out of a total population of some 65 million. Children under the age of 14 and the very elderly generally did not play an active role in farming, but in sericulture even their labour might be needed at peak times during the rearing cycle.

4 Some scholars have suggested that the Hamaguchi government deliberately timed this announcement to bring about the sharp fall in rice prices and hence to contribute to the rationalisation of agriculture. See, for example, Nakamura Masanori, *Shōwa no kyōkō* (Shogakkan, Tokyo, 1982), p.254. I think these scholars confuse effect with intention.

5 At the time the average annual income of owner-cultivators was 961 yen; of tenant farmers, 601 yen.

6 For further details, see Mikiso Hane, *Peasants, rebels, and outcasts* (Pantheon Books,

New York, 1982), pp.114-36.

7 It should be noted that as time was required before newly planted mulberry trees could provide an adequate supply of leaves, the households who took up sericulture in the late 1920s had been motivated to do so at least a few years previously, before cocoon prices began to fall.

8 After the first World War rayon production in the United States increased steadily; by 1927 it amounted to 75.5 million pounds, slightly more than raw silk imports in that year. Owing to competition from rayon, the rate of increase in raw silk imports had become lower after 1920. Kenzo Hemmi, 'Primary product exports and economic development: the case of silk' in Kazushi Ohkawa, Bruce Johnston and Hiromitsu Kaneda (eds), *Agriculture and economic growth: Japan's experience* (Princeton University Press, Princeton, NJ, and Tokyo University Press, Tokyo, 1970), p.313.

9 In 1897 Japan had provided 24 per cent of the world's raw silk, ranking after China (at 39 per cent) and Italy (at 27 per cent). In 1909 Japan's share of the world market was 34 per cent while China's was 30.5 per cent and Italy's 17.3 per cent.

10 See, for example, G.C. Allen, *A short economic history of modern Japan*, 2nd revised edn (Allen and Unwin, London, 1962), pp.68-70.

11 The proportion of tenanted land rose to about 37 per cent in the mid 1880s and to 45 per cent in 1908.

12 These are very crude estimates, derived from production data, not from enumeration of sericultural households.

13 The apparently high rate of increase between 1912 and 1915 is attributable to a change in the method of counting sericultural households. See note following Table 5.

14 Concerning the family background of girls at work in the filatures of the Suwa district in Nagano prefecture, see Nakamura Masanori, *Rōdōsha to nōmin* (Shokakkan, Tokyo, 1977), pp.90-3.

15 The traditional (i.e. hand) reeling industry (*zaguri*) produced thread whose very imperfections appealed to Japanese consumers. *Zaguri* households had numbered 285,000, with 350,000 basins, in 1913; by 1924 their number had declined to 142,000, with 175,000 basins.

16 Substantial landowners, who often functioned as moneylenders or fertiliser merchants as well, were frequently in a position to block the formation of any kind of co-operative in their communities.

17 Only a few such filatures were established, however. Foreign trading companies were far more active in establishing tea processing plants within the treaty ports.

18 On the adaptation of borrowed technology to Japanese conditions, see Nakamura, *Economic growth in prewar Japan*, pp.70-1.

19 The total number of filatures declined to 3,509 in 1928, of which 3,215 had ten or more basins. Allen, *Short economic history* , p.118.

20 This became a market for raw cocoons because the owners of filatures feared that farmers new to sericulture might damage the silk filament in attempting to kill pupae themselves. Subsequently, owners perceived that it was easier to keep cocoon prices low when only raw cocoons were traded; thereafter until the mid-1930s they resisted almost all attempts by sericulturalists to sell dried cocoons.

21 Ōishi Kaichirō and Miyamoto Ken'ichi (eds), *Nihon shihonshugi hattatsushi no kiso chishiki* (Yuhaikaku, Tokyo, 1975), pp.155-6; Hemmi, 'Primary product exports', pp.314-16.

22 Especially before the early 1910s they were concerned that if they tried to influence world prices by curtailing production, other silk-producing countries would make inroads into their markets.

23 Nakamura, *Rōdōsha to nōmin*, pp.96-8.

24 J. Embree, *Suye Mura: a Japanese village* (University of Chicago Press, Chicago, 1972), p.40.

25 For a detailed analysis of the movement of raw silk and cocoon prices, see Sumiya Mikio (ed), *Shōwa kyōkō* (Yuhaikaku, Tokyo, 1974), pp.172-5.

26 As a result of the universal elementary education system established by the government from the 1870s. After the turn of the century most children of statutory age were attending school for a period of six years.

27 Keeping accounts had indeed been encouraged by government agricultural advisers since the early 1900s.

28 For a detailed discussion of the tenant union movement, see A. Waswo, 'In search of equity: Japanese tenant unions in the 1920s' in Tetsuo Najita and Victor Koschmann (eds), *Conflict in modern Japanese history* (Princeton University Press, Princeton, NJ, 1982), pp.366-411.

29 In particular, the rudiments of a 'neutral' grading system for cocoons, and of joint sales of dried cocoons.

30 Takekazu Ogura (ed), *Agricultural development in modern Japan* (Japan FAO Association, Tokyo, 1963), pp.215-17.

31 Ibid., p.488.

32 Ibid., pp.213-15, 557.

33 Naikaku Tōkeikyoku, *Nihon Teikoku tōkei nenkan 1930* and *1935*.

34 Sumiya, *Shōwa kyōkō*, p.293 (Table 4.12) for the fall in wages 1929 to 1933.

35 Institute of Economic Research, Hitotsubashi University, *Annotated economic statistics of Japan* (Tokyo, 1961), p.48 (Table 3.3).

36 Ibid.

37 Ogura, *Agricultural development*, p.488 (Tables 25.7 and 25.8). This shift in cropping patterns was accelerated by the imposition of wartime controls over agriculture in the late 1930s; in addition after 1937 (owing to the recruitment of rural labour by industry) a marked decline in the number of full-time farm households began. From the early 1940s, too, in order to promote the production of food and the delivery of food crops to official distribution centres, various measures were implemented that benefited tenant farmers at the expense of landlords. In short, far more significant structural changes occurred as a result of the outbreak of war than in the immediate aftermath of the depression.

38 Nagano Akira, quoted in Nakamura, *Rōdōsha to nōmin*, pp.333-4.

7

EGYPT IN THE WORLD DEPRESSION: AGRICULTURAL RECESSION AND INDUSTRIAL EXPANSION

ROGER OWEN

INTRODUCTION

The onset of the world depression created an immediate crisis in Egypt by threatening its income from raw cotton, its most valuable crop and its major export. Prices, which had been falling through the 1920s, dropped precipitously, from £E4.072 a cantar in 1929 (1 cantar = 99.05 lb) to £E2.410 in 1930, to a low of £E2.016 in 1931 (Table 1A). A comparatively sharp fall in yields (most probably due to a decreased use of fertiliser, waterlogging of the soil after the high Nile flood of 1932, and continued deterioration of the major cotton strain, Sakellarides) and the government's misguided attempt to force prices up by limiting cotton acreage, only made matters worse. By 1932 total output was down to just under 5,000,000 cantars (as opposed to 8,500,000 in 1929) while its value had fallen to £E14,750,000 compared to the £E44,000,000 which had been the annual average for the years 1925-9. Production then revived, together with that of most other crops, before another sharp fall in price in 1937 and 1938 delayed the full recovery of the agricultural sector until after the second World War (Table 1C).

However, by happy historical accident, it was just at the beginning of the depression that Egypt regained tariff autonomy, as the last of the international commercial treaties to which it was subject ran out in February 1930. And the protection which could now be given to industries producing textiles, sugar, shoes, spirits was enough to allow a steady increase in manufacturing output. The result, according to Hansen and Marzouk's 'guesstimate', was that Gross Domestic Product grew by some 1.5 per cent per annum between 1928 and 1939 (a slight improvement on the period 1913-28), or some 0.25 per cent per annum per head of population.[1] Against this, however, there was a fall of at least 10 per cent in real per capita income in the period 1929-37, due to an overall decline in the income terms of trade.[2] In what follows I will attempt to flesh out this story, looking first at the performance of the agricultural and industrial sectors and then at the role of government.

THE AGRICULTURAL SECTOR IN THE 1930s

In spite of the initial alarm, the period in which the collapse of world commodity prices played an important role in disturbing or re-directing Egyptian agricultural effort was remarkably short. As soon as the government abandoned its attempt to arrest the decline in prices by limiting cotton acreage (1931-3), land usage quickly returned to its pre-depression pattern. As Table 1D shows, this pattern remained remarkably stable for the rest of the decade, showing only a tiny drop in the cotton area, and also in the area under wheat, beans and barley, compensated by a small increase in the area under rice and sugar, made possible by the greater availability of summer water in the irrigation system.[3] Such behaviour would tend to support Hansen and Marzouk's argument that, as cotton is so much more profitable than most of the other Egyptian crops (like cereals), the price elasticity of its supply is very low, and that cultivators have little incentive to search for substitutes.[4] Government efforts to protect local wheat and sugar production by imposing near prohibitive tariffs on imports also may have played a small role in preserving existing patterns of land usage.

A second important feature of the 1930s was the continuation of the steady growth in the yields of the major crops which had begun in the mid-1920s (Table lB). This allowed total agricultural output to increase by over 15 per cent during the 1930s, just ahead of population, doing much to limit the damage caused by the fall in agricultural prices. The reasons for this growth in yields were partly historical, partly the result of a determined effort by the Egyptian government to improve the supply of summer water by building new dams and barrages and to extend the system of drainage. This represented a clear resolve to avoid a repetition of the mistakes made by the British irrigation engineers in the late nineteenth century, whose relative neglect of drainage had produced a sharp decline in soil fertility from which it had taken at least two decades to recover.[5] Because of the Egyptian government's efforts, the supply of summer water was doubled between 1934 and 1938, while the area of Lower Egypt (the main cotton-growing region) provided with proper drainage also doubled between 1930 and 1938.[6] Such investments were still relatively cheap and could generally be financed out of ordinary revenues without recourse to the reserves.

Two other factors must also have been important in increasing agricultural output. One was the growth in the use of chemical fertilisers, consumption of which more than doubled between 1925 and 1935-9.[7] The other was the establishment of the government's Cotton Research Board which, among other things, created the new, prolific strain, Giza 7, to replace the lower yielding Sakellarides which had been the dominant long-staple strain in the 1920s.[8] Finally, it is important to note that the increase in output was not the result of a growth in the agricultural work force, which remained more or less constant during the period. This suggests a considerable improvement in the productivity of labour, albeit from quite a low level.

Nevertheless, in spite of these improvements, the fall in agricultural prices meant a drop in real per capita income of perhaps as much as 9 per cent, 1929-37, and a concomitant reduction in the consumption of a whole host of basic necessities.[9] According to Hansen's calculations, the amount of sugar consumed per head declined by 24 per cent between 1929 and 1937, that of tobacco by 30 per cent, and that of coffee by 23 per cent, although the latter was to some extent replaced by the cheaper beverage, tea.[10] In the agricultural sector gross money income per feddan fell sharply (Table 1C). The situation was undoubtedly made worse by the extreme inequality in property holdings, with nearly 40 per cent of the land being owned in large estates (50 feddans and over: 1 feddan = 1.04 acres), and 30 per cent in medium estates (5-50 feddans), the remainder being divided up into over 2 million small, often highly fragmented plots, most of which could not generate sufficient income to sustain a family even at minimal levels of subsistence.[11] As a result, since the late nineteenth century, the majority of peasants had been forced either to rent land or to work as wage labourers or service tenants on the big estates. Their conditions certainly deteriorated greatly during the early 1930s. For those who owned their own land, the proportion of their income from cotton taken in tax rose sharply, perhaps by as much as two and a half times between 1929/30 and 1932/3. And though this proportion then began to fall, it remained on average much higher in the rest of the 1930s than it had been in the 1920s.[12] The situation for those who worked land belonging to other people is less clear. There was certainly downward pressure on agricultural wages. But for those who rented land for cash payment there may have been some protection from the fact that rents were customarily tied to the price of cotton. Against this, there is some evidence that between 1931 and 1936 landlords responded to the crisis by switching back to some form of share-cropping, so as to give themselves much greater freedom to keep payments from their tenants as high as possible.[13]

Government efforts to assist the agricultural sector were quite extensive. On the one hand, there was an intensification of a whole series of programmes designed to increase agricultural ouput and agricultural exports, in spite of the fact that state revenues decreased by 11 per cent in money terms between 1928/9 and 1934/5. On the other, there was a series of short-term palliatives aimed at easing the financial pressures on those in the rural sector. These included a temporary payment of £E1,000,000 to the mortgage companies on behalf of landowners unable to meet the instalments on their debt for 1929, and a reduction of £E2,000,000 on the total land tax assessment in 1933 and 1934 - equivalent to a reduction of nearly 40 per cent.[14] Another initiative involved efforts to prevent mortgage repayments becoming so burdensome that they threatened wholescale bankruptcies, the large-scale seizure of agricultural estates by their creditors, and the possible collapse of the entire market in rural land. To this end in 1933 the government devised a scheme in conjunction with the three principal mortgage banks, by which, in exchange for government financial support, the latter agreed to extend their outstanding loans and to reduce the rate of interest on them. This led to a reduction of nearly one-half in the average borrower's annual repayment of capital and interest.[15] However, it should also be noted that such schemes were generally more of benefit to the larger landowners than to the smaller ones and that, as was usually the case in the Middle East, the few attempts to target assistance on the poorer strata were not very successful. Apart from the legal reduction of rents by a third between 1929 and 1931, the major effort was the creation of the Agricultural Credit Bank, established in 1931 with a combination of government and private capital. Part of its original intention was to offer short-term cash loans to poor cultivators on the security of land or crops. But as such loans were largely channelled through co-operative societies, and as these societies covered only one-eighth of the rural area and tended to be dominated by larger landowners, the impact on the poorer farmer cannot have been very great.[16]

THE MANUFACTURING SECTOR

According to the Industrial Census of 1927, nearly 85,000 Egyptians were then employed in manufacturing, out of a total labour force of nearly 5 million (Table 2A). But of these, the vast majority worked in one-man workshops which used no mechanical power, while modern industry was confined to a very small group of firms: a textile mill (the Filature Nationale at Alexandria); a sugar refinery (at Hawamdieh near Cairo); the cigarette factories of the American-owned Eastern Tobacco Co. and its main Egyptian rival, Coutarelli; three cement works and a few others. Before 1930 Egyptian industrial activity had had to develop within the context of an 'open' economy, with no more protection than the low tariff of 8 per cent and, with the exception of sugar refining, very little support from the government. In these circumstances some of the early factory industries (e.g. those engaged in sugar pressing or in the manufacture of 'Egyptian' cigarettes) had begun by directing most of their sales abroad. But from the 1890s they had been taken over by foreign interests like the French sugar-refining giant owned by Henri Say, or the Eastern Tobacco Co., whose main aim was to exploit the Egyptian internal market. By the late 1920s Egyptian manufactured exports were confined largely to cotton-seed oil and cattle cake.

The event which allowed a major expansion of Egypt's manufacturing output was the achievement of tariff autonomy in February 1930. The government prepared for this event by inviting foreign advisers to help it construct a more rational tariff structure. Preparations were also laid by the important Egyptian Bank Misr group, which began to build a cotton spinning and weaving mill at

Mehalla in the Delta (Misr Spinning and Weaving) in the late 1920s, on the assumption that it would soon receive all the tariff protection it needed. In the event the government came up with a three-tier tariff structure, with relatively low rates on raw materials (around 4 per cent), somewhat higher rates on semi-manufactured goods (between 6 and 10 per cent), and a high rate for most finished manufactures (15 per cent). However, as the new rates were expressed in specific terms, based on the import prices prevailing in 1928/9, the effective level of protection was higher than originally intended, so long as international prices remained depressed through the early 1930s.[17] Meanwhile, many of the rates were changed in a piecemeal way as the government was forced to respond to pressures from various local industrial interests as well as from foreign governments like the British, the Italian and the Japanese, before a comprehensive reform of the whole tariff structure was undertaken in two stages in 1936 and 1939.

The most important Egyptian industry to benefit from the new tariff regime was that producing coarse cotton textiles and yarn. The Filature Nationale immediately increased its capacity; and in 1931 it was joined by the new Misr Spinning and Weaving Factory, which had 12,000 spindles and nearly 500 looms. By 1932 the two enterprises were producing some 25 million square metres of cloth (as opposed to 7 million square metres in 1930), at a time when imports were about 175 million square metres.[18] It was soon discovered, however, that the industry suffered from a number of disadvantages, notably over-manning leading to low labour productivity, and the government's requirement that the industry use Egyptian medium-to-long staple cotton, when its finished products designed for the local market really required the cheaper, shorter staples imported, notably, from India.[19] This placed the industry at a great disadvantage when it came to competition with cheap textiles from Japan (Table 2B); and it was only after a number of inadequate upward adjustments in the tariff that the imposition in 1935 of a huge 40 per cent depreciated currency tax on Japanese cloth meant that the products of its Eastern rival could be more or less excluded.[20]

Britain's Lancashire cotton industry was another rival which made strenuous efforts to preserve its share of the Egyptian textile market in the face of both local and Japanese competition. Initially its strategy was to use diplomatic efforts to persuade the Egyptian government to devise a tariff structure which would place barriers in the way of cheap Japanese cloth yet keep the door open for higher-quality British products. But while it was generally successful with the first element in this strategy it made much less headway with the second, and it was probably this failure which persuaded two large British firms to jump the tariff barrier by developing joint ventures with Egyptian partners. The first firm to follow this path was British Calico Printers, which joined forces with the Filature Nationale in 1934; the second was Bradford Byers, which in 1937 co-operated with the Bank Misr to establish the Société Misr de la Filature et de

Tissage Fin, with a factory at Kafr al-Dawwar near Alexandria. As a result of this influx of British capital and technical expertise, Egyptian textile output increased enormously towards the end of the 1930s, cloth production expanding from 54.5 million square metres in 1936 to some 100 million square metres in 1939, approaching half of local demand in that year.[21] This expansion provided an important stimulus to associated activities, notably chemical dyeing and the manufacture of ribbons and embroideries.

The new tariff structure provided the basis for a general expansion of Egyptian industry, with employment in manufacturing increasing from 85,000 in 1927 to 140,000 in 1937 (Table 2A). Much of this expansion was in very small-scale enterprises, particularly in food processing and in textiles (where there was a boom in hand-loom weaving).[22] But the tariff also gave an important stimulus to a number of larger factory enterprises, notably those making cement, cigarettes, sugar (and a host of sugar derivatives like alcohol and beer), and cotton-seed oil (and some of its derivatives, for example soap). As a result, by 1939 Egypt was able to meet most, if not all, local demand for a number of simple manufactures like refined sugar, alcohol, cigarettes, soap, shoes, cement and matches (Table 2D). To set against these examples of successful import substitution is the fact that, as with other newly industrialising nations, Egyptian manufactures were almost invariably more expensive than the products of their foreign rivals, due to higher local costs and the fact that most domestic industry was dominated by one or two large firms which usually came to price-fixing and market-sharing agreements between themselves.[23] The manufacture of refined sugar and of cotton-seed oil were dominated by a single firm; cigarette production had two main producers; cement and textiles each had three.

THE ROLE OF GOVERNMENT

When we consider the economic role of government in Egypt in the 1930s, we have to remember that we are examining a constitutional monarchy with the major political parties and political institutions dominated by large landowners. There was some room for bureaucratic initiative by long-serving and well-placed technocrats, particularly in areas involving a high degree of expertise like irrigation engineering. But for the most part, economic policy initiatives were taken by weak cabinets which were as likely to owe their position to support from the Palace (and sometimes the British) as to a majority in Parliament, and which were, almost inevitably, constantly driven to try to win the allegiance of the landowners who controlled the Senate and, just as important, the predominantly rural electorate. In these circumstances it was well understood by both politicians and those who spoke for Egypt's weak manufacturing interests that industrialisation (and the introduction of the tariff structure thought necessary to underpin it) could be achieved only in co-operation with the large landowners who, anyway, constituted the only class with sufficient capital to invest in new manufacturing enterprises.[24] A similar conclusion was drawn by the managers of the Bank Misr, who were deeply conscious of the fact that the Bank, as well as most of its major industrial enterprises, could not have been founded without financial support from agricultural interests.[25]

Thus when it came to policy it is not surprising that successive governments found it expedient not only to stress the complementarity between industry and agriculture but also to work hardest for those industries which relied most heavily on domestic agricultural products, notably cotton and sugar. It was for this reason, too, that whenever there was a conflict between agricultural and industrial interests it was the former which were allowed to win. An obvious example here was the government's decision to prohibit the import of raw cotton, in spite of strong complaints from the Bank Misr that this penalised the domestic textile industry.[26] Another case, which excited less hostile comment from urban industrial interests, was the government's protection of the domestic market for wheat and flour, although this must inevitably have raised the price of food and hence the level of urban wages - except, perhaps, where factories were sited in rural areas and drew their labour force from the surrounding villages (e.g. the sugar refinery and Misr Spinning and Weaving).

It was not until the second World War, as industry developed further and agriculture stagnated, that a number of attacks on land-owning interests were launched, on the grounds that the low land tax meant that landowners did not pay their fair share of government revenue, and that the existence of large estates was a primary cause of rural poverty and thus a major factor inhibiting the growth of the market for domestically produced industrial goods.[27] Thinking of this kind had a major influence on the decision by the Free Officer regime to introduce the first Land Reform Law of 1952.

CONCLUSION

The main conclusion of this brief analysis must be that the effects of the world depression on the Egyptian economy were serious, but that they could have been very much worse. Initially, the fall in real incomes resulting from the collapse in the price of cotton, the country's major export, was exacerbated by the concomitant decline in cotton yields and by the government's misguided policy of seeking to maintain prices by restricting cotton acreage. In addition, Egypt's income terms of trade continued the deterioration which had begun in the 1920s, until at least 1932. However, from 1932 the fall in cotton output was arrested, as restrictions on the area planted were lifted and as yields began to revive, due largely to government investment in irrigation and drainage and to the creation of more prolific strains. These developments were accompanied by steadily rising cotton prices until 1936, and by an increase in the output of other agricultural products to 1937. As a result, anyone taking stock of the Egyptian economy in 1936-7 might well have concluded that the depression was over. But there was a second sharp decline in the price of cotton in 1937-8, accompanied by an adverse movement in the income terms of trade, sufficient to leave agricultural incomes well below the level they had reached in the late 1920s.

An important factor underlying Egypt's economic vulnerability to the effects of the world depression was clearly its major reliance on foreign trade. Thus when the value of imports and exports declined in the early 1930s, there was a significant contraction in domestic economic activity, which shows up most clearly in reduced consumption, a small decline in government revenues and a sharp reduction in the money supply. Nevertheless, both the government and local and foreign entrepreneurs were able to take advantage of the crisis to begin to industrialise. This proceeded along the usual lines of easy import substitution, and was sufficiently successful to have met local demand for a number of basic products by 1939. Even though the contribution of industry to GNP could not have been more than 10 per cent in 1939, sufficient industrial progress had been made to allow Gross Domestic Product to grow at a slightly higher rate in the 1930s than in the 1920s.

Government efforts to assist the new industries were largely confined to providing them with significant tariff protection, although there were also attempts to encourage state organisations to purchase local manufactures as well as assistance to specific industries (like the sale of government stockpiled cotton to the textile mills at a reduced price). Given the fact that Egyptian politics was dominated by large landowners, it is difficult to see how the government could have done more. And it may well be that future research will show that this dominant concern for the country's agricultural interests in the 1930s had basically beneficial results, in that it very rapidly encouraged the administration to learn from the mistakes made in the 1920s and at the start of the depression. Thus the administration allowed cotton production to expand again as well as devoting resources to infrastructural development, at the same time encouraging a small measure of diversification towards rice, fruit and vegetables, for which there was an expanding local and Middle Eastern market. There is, however, another side to the story: as in Latin America and elsewhere in Africa and Asia, whatever economic progress (in terms of industrial development and agricultural diversification) could be made during the world depression, it was much too slow to satisfy the demands of an increasingly radicalised urban population, which in the 1930s was already beginning to respond to political programmes promising a heady combination of greater economic equality and greater national wealth. This was to produce a complete change in the whole climate of economic thinking once Egyptian politics began to return to peace-time conditions at the end of the second World War.

AGRICULTURE

TABLE 1A: Area planted, harvest size, yield, price and value of Egyptian cotton, 1925-39

	Area planted ,000 feds [a]	Harvest ,000 cantars [b]	Yield cantar/fed	Av.price £E/ cantar	Value (incl. cotton seed) £E,000
1925	1,924	7,965	4.14	6.093	54,508
1926	1,786	7,652	4.29	4.306	38,041
1927	1,516	6,087	4.01	5.936	41,357
1928	1,738	8,068	4.64	5.176	47,718
1929	1,841	8,531	4.63	4.072	40,025
Average 1925-9	1,761	7,661	4.34	5.117	44,329
1930	2,082	8,276	3.97	2.410	23,323
1931	1,683	6,357	3.78	2.016	15,753
1932	1,094	4,956	4.53	2.456	14,756
1933	1,804	8,575	4.75	2.278	22,072
1934	1,732	7,555	4.36	2.650	23,413
Average 1930-4	1,679	7,144	4.28	2.362	19,860
1935	1,669	8,535	5.11	2.726	27,349
1936	1,716	9,107	5.32	2.870	31,393
1937	1,978	11,009	5.57	2.154	27,610
1938	1,784	8,340	4.67	2.136	21,220
1939	1,625	8,692	5.35	2.896	28,675
Average 1935-9	1,754	9,137	5.20	2.556	27,249

[a] 1 feddan = 1.04 acres = 0.42 hectares.

[b] 1 cantar = 99.05 lb

Source: *Annuaire Statistique, 1939-40,* p.412.

TABLE 1B: Index of yields of major Egyptian crops, 1925-9 and 1930-9 (1913=100)

	Cotton	Wheat	Maize	Barley	Beans	Rice	Sugar
Average 1925-9	97.8	92.4	109.7	98.7	77.2	86.0	108.7
1930	89.4	93.7	109.6	97.9	78.0	86.6	109.8
1931	85.1	100.2	106.0	101.9	75.4	73.6	110.7
1932	102.0	107.0	110.7	106.0	88.1	77.5	109.6
1933	107.0	100.6	105.5	101.5	90.8	84.1	110.5
1934	96.2	92.8	112.8	102.0	74.0	86.5	120.2
1935	115.1	105.9	120.0	119.6	82.3	99.6	117.7
1936	116.9	112.0	118.3	123.2	88.4	97.7	112.5
1937	125.5	114.3	119.4	125.4	89.3	93.8	119.4
1938	105.2	112.0	118.3	125.4	86.4	101.0	114.7
1939	120.5	117.1	111.1	128.8	92.9	107.8	115.9

Source: *Annuaire Statistique, 1939-40*, p.387.

TABLE 1C: Index of agricultural production, average price of agricultural products, and average gross revenue per feddan, 1925-9 and 1930-9 (1913 = 100)

	Agricultural production	Average price of agricultural product	Average gross revenue per feddan
Average 1925-9	93.7	125.5	126.0
1930	92.3	101.3	84.0
1931	91.5	110.2	72.3
1932	97.3	72.4	66.1
1933	95.9	70.1	75.2
1934	94.1	106.4	94.4
1935	104.9	96.7	92.3
1936	105.5	92.0	96.3
1937	108.1	88.5	95.3
1938	103.0	95.8	87.9
1939	110.3	90.8	100.5

Source: *Annuaire Statistique, 1939-40,* p.387.

TABLE 1D: Area planted with 7 major Egyptian crops, 1925-9 and 1930-9 (thousands of feddans)

	Cotton	Wheat	Maize	Barley	Beans	Rice	Sugar
Average 1925-9	1,761	1,497	1,497	355	464	271	52
1930	2,082	1,465	1,827		427	346	54
1931	1,683						
1932	1,094	1,697	1,968		492	472	70
1933	1,804						
1934	1,732	1,389	1,572		432	392	60
1935	1,669						
1936	1,716	1,410	1,520	272	395	471	64
1937	1,978	1,369	1,559	261	386	363	68
1938	1,784	1,416	1,497	264	385	476	68
1939	1,625	1,446	1,549	263	385	547	72

Source: *Annuaire Statistique*, various.

INDUSTRY

TABLE 2A: Employment in manufacturing industry by sector, 1927, 1937 and 1947 (thousands)

Sector	1927	1937	1947
Food processing	14.3	32.5	59.9
Beverages and tobacco	9.1	10.3	13.1
Textiles	21.3	40.5	134.4
Clothing and footwear	4.7	9.6	3.3
Wood and products	9.2	4.2	3.8
Paper and products	0.6	2.5	4.5
Printing and publishing	5.2	6.9	5.4
Leather and products	1.5	1.4	2.7
Rubber products	-	-	1.0
Chemicals	2.9	6.4	15.8
Petroleum and products	-	0.2	3.6
Non-metallic mineral products	4.5	7.7	13.0
Metals and products	10.5	11.5	13.5
Transport equipment	-	-	2.3
Miscellaneous	0.4	5.9	1.1
Total	84.2	139.6	277.7

Source: P.K.O'Brien, *The revolution in Egypt's economic system: from private enterprise to socialism, 1952-1965* (Oxford University Press for the Royal Institute of International Affairs, London, etc., 1966), p.16.

TABLE 2B: Imports of cotton piece goods from Egypt's major suppliers, 1925-9 and 1930-9 (millions of sq. metres)

	UK	Italy	Japan	Others	Total
Average 1925-9	129.4	35.6	29.44	16.6	209.1
1930	92.0	34.1	46.1	18.7	190.9
1931	61.7	29.0	44.9	11.4	147.0
1932	68.7	30.0	67.8	7.9	174.4
1933	53.8	21.7	116.8	4.5	196.8
1934	36.3	18.2	123.9	82.1	260.5
1935	30.3	15.9	142.1	5.1	193.4
1936	51.2	20.2	71.3	26.9	169.6
1937	43.4	66.6	20.3	39.2	169.5
1938	35.0	69.6	10.4	22.4	137.4
1939	28.4	30.1	12.9	11.1	82.5

Source: H. Shimizu, *Anglo-Japanese trade rivalry in the Middle East in the inter-war period,* St. Antony's Middle East Monographs, 17 (Ithaca Press, London, 1986), p.99.

TABLE 2C: Consumption of Egyptian cotton by local mills, 1925/6 - 1929/30 and 1930/1 - 1937/8 (cantars) [a]

	Mills in Alexandria	Others	Total
Average 1925/6-1929/30	56,580	-	56,580
1930/1	52,509	-	52,509
1931/2	86,060	15,250	101,310
1932/3	158,466	81,822	240,288
1933/4	121,278	118,880	240,158
1934/5	115,487	119,582	235,069
1935/6	127,847	267,357	395,204
1936/7	145,804	290,840	436,644
1937/8	153,793	356,942	510,735

[a] 1 cantar = 99.05 lb.

Source: H.K. Selim, *Twenty years of agricultural development in Egypt (1919-1939)* (Government Press, Cairo, 1940), p.135.

TABLE 2D: Estimates of Egyptian local demand supplied by Egyptian industry, 1939

Sugar	100%
Alcohol	100%
Cigarettes	100%
Salt	100%
Cereal milling	99%
Lamps, glass	99%
Boots, shoes	90%
Cement	90%
Soap	90%
Tarbushes	90%
Furniture	90%
Matches	80%
Beer	65%
Vegetable oils	60%
Cotton cloth	40%

Source: Egypt, Ministry of Commerce and Industry, quoted in UK Dept. of Overseas Trade, *Egypt: review of commercial conditions* (HMSO, London, 1945), pp.21-2.

NOTES

1 B. Hansen and G.A. Marzouk, *Development and economic policy in the UAR (Egypt)* (North Holland, Amsterdam, 1965), pp.4-5.

2 B. Hansen, 'Income and consumption in Egypt, 1886/1887 to 1937', *International Journal of Middle East Studies, 10,* 1 (1979), p.29.

3 Summer water was required to allow high-value crops like cotton, rice and sugar to be irrigated during the period of the year April to August, when the level of the Nile was at its lowest.

4 Hansen and Marzouk, *Development and economic policy*, pp.56-7.

5 R.Owen, 'Agricultural production in historical perspective: a case study of the period 1890-1939' in P.J. Vatikiotis (ed), *Egypt since the Revolution* (George Allen and Unwin, London, 1968), pp.55-60; A. Richards, *Egypt's agricultural development 1800-1980: technical and social change* (Westview, Boulder, 1982), pp.69-80.

6 H.K. Selim, *Twenty years of agricultural development in Egypt (1919-1939)* (Government Press, Cairo, 1940), pp.36, 56n.

7 Hansen and Marzouk, *Development and economic policy,* p.68.

8 Selim, *Twenty years of agricultural development,* p.119.

9 Hansen, 'Income and consumption', p.46.

10 Ibid., pp.34-41.

11 G. Baer, *A history of landownership in modern Egypt 1800-1950* (Oxford University

Press, London, 1962), ch.3.

12 R.L. Tignor, *State, private enterprise and economic change in Egypt, 1918-1952* (Princeton University Press, Princeton, NJ, 1984), p.116.

13 Le Groupe d'Etudes de l'Islam, *L'Egypte indépendente* (Paul Hartmann, Paris, 1938), p.191.

14 Selim, *Twenty years of agricultural development*, p.74; Tignor, *State, private enterprise and economic change*, p.116.

15 Selim, *Twenty years of agricultural development*, pp.74-5.

16 E. Eshag and M.A. Kamal, 'A note on the reform of the rural credit system in U.A.R. (Egypt)', *Bulletin of the Oxford University Institute of Economics and Statistics*, *29*, 2 (1967) pp.99-100.

17 R. Mabro and S. Radwan, *The industrialization of Egypt 1939-73: policy and performance* (Clarendon, Oxford, 1976), pp.50-1.

18 A. Eman, *L'industrie du coton en Egypte: étude d'économie politique* (Imprimerie de l'Institut Français, Cairo, 1943), p.91; L. Gadd and I.G. Levi, 'Observations générales sur le nouveau tarif douanier', *L'Egypte Contemporaine*, *23*, 133-4 (1932), p.219; Tignor, *State, private enterprise and economic change*, p.131.

19 Eman, *L'industrie du coton*, pp.64, 67, 76-7.

20 Mabro and Radwan, *Industrialization*, p.51; H. Shimizu, *Anglo-Japanese trade rivalry in the Middle East in the inter-war period*, St Antony's Middle East Monographs, 17 (Ithaca Press, London, 1986), pp.110-12.

21 Eman, *L'industrie du coton*, p.91.

22 Ibid, pp.88-9.

23 A.A.I. el-Gritly, 'The structure of modern industry in Egypt', *L'Egypte Contemporaine*, *38*, 241-2 (1947), pp.502-28.

24 Tignor, *State, private enterprise and economic change*, p.110-11.

25 E. Davis, *Challenging colonialism: Bank Misr and Egyptian industrialisation 1920-1941* (Princeton University Press, Princeton, NJ, 1983), pp.108, 131.

26 Eman, *L'industrie du coton*, p.65.

27 M. Ghali, 'Un programme de réforme agraire pour l'Egypte', *L'Egypte Contemporaine*, *38*, 236-7 (1947), p.6.

8

JAPAN'S INDUSTRIAL RECOVERY, 1931-6

KAORU SUGIHARA

The Great Depression reached the Japanese economy in more or less the same way as it reached other primary producers, through a drastic fall in exports to the West from the late 1920s. The most important channel of transmission was the decline in raw silk exports, primarily to the United States. Between 1929 and 1931 their total value more than halved, never to regain its pre-depression level (Table 1).[1] This affected two other sectors of the economy in particular.

TABLE 1: Main exports 1929-36 (¥ million)

	Raw silk	Silk cloth	Artificial silk cloth	Cotton cloth	Machinery	Total
1929	781 (36)	122 (6)	28 (1)	413 (19)	39 (2)	2,149 (100)
1930	417 (28)	66 (4)	35 (2)	272 (19)	35 (2)	1,470 (100)
1931	355 (31)	43 (4)	40 (3)	199 (17)	30 (3)	1,147 (100)
1932	382 (27)	50 (4)	61 (4)	289 (20)	35 (2)	1,410 (100)
1933	391 (21)	64 (3)	77 (4)	383 (21)	68 (4)	1,861 (100)
1934	287 (13)	77 (4)	113 (5)	492 (23)	58 (3)	2,172 (100)
1935	387 (15)	77 (3)	128 (5)	496 (20)	64 (3)	2,499 (100)
1936	393 (15)	68 (3)	149 (6)	484 (18)	82 (3)	2,693 (100)

Source: Yokohamashi, *Yokohamashi-shi shiryō-hen 2* [History of Yokohama City, reference volume 2] (Yokohamashi, Yokohama, 1962), pp.27-9, 37, 40. Figures in brackets are percentages.

First, the decline in cocoon rearing contributed greatly to the rural depression which had begun in the early 1920s. Between 1929 and 1931 the cocoon price dropped 56 per cent; cocoon production declined by 5 per cent, with the result that the farmers' income from cocoons fell by 58 per cent. Coupled with the fall in the price of rice, the total value of agricultural production fell by 42 per cent.[2] The debts of farm households increased enormously in 1930 and 1931. According to the Farm Household Budgets Survey, 59 per cent of owner-cultivator households and 74 per cent of tenant households recorded budget deficits in 1930.[3] As 47 per cent of the working population was engaged in agriculture at that time,[4] this would have seriously reduced domestic purchasing power.

Second, as a result of the drastic decline in raw silk exports, Japan experienced increasingly severe balance of trade deficits, and, having returned to the gold standard in January 1930 at the pre-war parity, she was forced to abandon it in December 1931 and to devalue the yen sharply. Between December 1931 and November 1932 the dollar price of 100 yen dropped from 49.4 to 19.8; after a modest recovery, from 1934 it stayed at 28-29. The government made no attempt to prevent the devaluation, although (in the interests of trade) it did seek to avoid too violent shifts in the rate.[5]

It was in these conditions, the severe rural depression and the drastic devaluation of the yen, that industrial recovery took place. After 1931, Japan's industrial production and exports recovered perhaps more rapidly than those of any other industrial nation. The value of industrial production increased from 7,877 million yen in 1931 to 16,280 million yen in 1936.[6] Table 1 shows a rapid increase in the exports of light industrial goods, cotton textiles and artificial silk cloth. Table 2 shows a comparably important contribution from government expenditure to the creation of demand. However, that table also indicates that it was the expansion of the private domestic market which contributed most in absolute terms to the increase in aggregate demand.

The purpose of this paper is to sketch the process of this recovery, citing primarily more recent Japanese research. Most of the contemporary literature on this subject emphasised the importance of the devaluation of the yen, the availability of cheap labour and the government's deficit financing, within which framework a new industrial structure was created and the domestic market expanded.[7] The more recent literature has explored the ways in which linkages between large and small firms within each industry as well as those between industries rapidly developed, and drawn attention to certain aspects of business strategy, such as overseas marketing, choice of technology and labour management practices, which were instrumental in securing industrial recovery.

I shall now discuss respectively the development of light industries, such as cotton textiles, and that of heavy and chemical industries. Finally I attempt to demonstrate the importance of my conclusions here in developing a fuller understanding of the experience of the Japanese economy as a whole in the 1930s.

TABLE 2: Trends in aggregate demand (¥ million)

	Total aggregate demand	Domestic market		
	(1) = (2) + (3) + (4)	(2) Private	(3) Government	(4) Exports
1929	18,828 (100)	13,402 (71)	2,822 (15)	2,604 (14)
1930	16,512 (100)	12,179 (74)	2,462 (15)	1,871 (11)
1931	14,879 (100)	10,812 (73)	2,587 (17)	1,480 (10)
1932	15,509 (100)	10,775 (69)	2,932 (19)	1,802 (12)
1933	17,751 (100)	12,160 (69)	3,240 (18)	2,351 (13)
1934	19,843 (100)	13,812 (70)	3,242 (16)	2,789 (14)
1935	21,421 (100)	14,674 (69)	3,471 (16)	3,276 (15)
1936	22,732 (100)	15,537 (68)	3,610 (16)	3,585 (16)

Note: (2) personal consumption expenditure + private gross domestic fixed capital formation; (3) government consumption expenditure + government gross domestic fixed capital formation.

Source: Ryōichi Miwa, 'Takahashi zaisei-ki no keizai seisaku' [Economic policy during the period of [Finance Minister] Takahashi's administration] in Tokyo Daigaku Shakai Kagaku Kenkyūsho (ed), *Fashizumu-ki no kokka to shakai 2. Senji Nihon keizai* [State and society in the period of Fascism 2. The wartime economy in Japan] (Tōdai Shuppankai, Tokyo, 1979), p.137.

I

The principal driving force behind the development of the light industries during this period was clearly the increase in exports. In terms of the value of production, textile and textile-related industries still comprised the largest single sector in Japanese industry, though its share was declining. The cotton industry occupied the dominant position within textiles. Although nearly half the cotton textiles produced in Japan were consumed domestically, the rate of increase of exports was much higher than that of domestic consumption. The production of rayon, the fastest-growing element in the textile sector, was also mainly for exports, in the form of artificial silk cloth.

Let us first look at the nature of export demand. Table 3 shows dramatic changes in the geographical distribution of Japanese cotton textile exports in the first half of the 1930s. The growing dispersal of markets is also evident, reflected in the sharp decline in the relative importance of the top three and the top ten markets between 1929 and 1935. The standard explanations for these changes are as follows. For China, Japanese investment there increased after 1920, and the Japanese mills in China were able to produce more competitive goods for the local market than the Japanese mills in Japan. The sharp rise in China's tariffs in the early 1930s almost completely extinguished cotton textile imports from Japan by 1936. The Chinese civil war also disrupted trade.[8] For other markets, the Western powers, notably Britain, Holland and the United States, reacted strongly to the rapid increase in Japanese cotton textile exports to their colonies from the early 1930s, imposing tariffs and quotas against Japan. In the Indian market there was fierce competition between local and Japanese cotton goods, but the political representation of the interests of the Indian cotton textile industry was somewhat confused by the fact that India remained a major supplier of raw cotton to Japan and by British intervention in Indian negotiations with Japan.[9]

TABLE 3: Destination of cotton textile exports, 1929, 1931, 1935 (¥ million)

1929		1931		1935	
(1) China	150 (36)	(1) India	50 (25)	(1) India	85 (43)
(2) India	109 (26)	(2) China	43 (22)	(2) DEI	67 (34)
(3) Dutch East Indies	42 (10)	(3) DEI	28 (14)	(3) Manchuria	36 (18)
(4) Egypt	24 (6)	(4) Egypt	15 (8)	(4) Egypt	32 (16)
(5) Hong Kong	21 (5)	(5) HK	10 (5)	(5) Argentina	20 (10)
(6) Kwantung Province	15 (4)	(6) KP	6 (3)	(6) Australia	17 (9)
(7) Straits Settlements	6 (1)	(7) South Africa	5 (3)	(7) East Africa	16 (8)
(8) The Philippines	6 (1)	(8) SS	5 (3)	(8) KP	15 (8)
(9) Argentina	4 (1)	(9) Phil.	4 (2)	(9) Phil.	14 (7)
(10) Siam	4 (1)	(10) Turkey	4 (2)	10) Iraq	14 (7)
(1)-(3) total	301 (73)	(1)-(3)	121 (61)	(1)-(3)	188 (38)
(1)-(10) total	381 (92)	(1)-(10)	170 (85)	(1)-(10)	316 (64)
Grand total	413 (100)	Total	199 (100)	Total	496 (100)

Source: Yokahamashi, *Yokohamashi-shi*, pp.168-70.

But Japanese cotton goods continued to find new markets in Asia, Africa and Latin America each year. The immediate reason for this was clear; they had a considerable price advantage as a result of the devaluation of the yen. It must be remembered, however, that more than 60 per cent of the cost of cloth production went in the purchase of raw cotton; this was entirely imported, mainly from the USA and India, and its price rose as the yen fell. Therefore, the yen devaluation did not necessarily provide such a major advantage to the industry. Indeed the export drive was partly a response to the difficulties it faced in the domestic market, as the domestic price of textiles was pushed up by the rise in the yen price of raw cotton.

In order to take advantage of the devaluation, the industry sought to exploit new markets abroad, and to concentrate on relatively high value-added products. Moreover, a reduction in domestic manufacturing costs was to be particularly effective in enhancing international competitiveness. In both spinning and weaving sectors, efforts were made to reduce total wage costs and to increase labour productivity. The nominal average wage rate fell by 30 per cent between 1930 and 1936; converted to sterling, this implied a fall in wage costs of 60 per cent. And labour productivity in the spinning sector increased by more than 40 per cent between 1929 and 1934, mainly as a result of the introduction of the High Draft spinning system. The feasibility of this labour-saving foreign technology had been extensively studied in Japan in the 1920s. Its diffusion represented the industry's first major shift towards a capital-intensive technology, and it began to make an important impact in the first half of the 1930s. A comparable increase in productivity was achieved in the weaving sector, with the wider use of automatic looms (including notably the Toyoda) and iron-frame power-looms, most of which had been developed in Japan. Sakichi Toyoda's original automatic power-loom dated from 1903, and mass production of a refined model had begun in 1926. The automatic looms increased per capita productivity in large-scale operations; other innovations raised productivity in small- and medium-sized plants. By the 1930s looms themselves had become a significant Japanese export.[10]

The expansion of production was led by the weaving sector, which at that time was divided into two forms of organisation: large factories operated by a small number of cotton-spinning firms, and numerous small- and medium-scale concerns situated in local weaving centres. Between 1931 and 1936 the latter's production rose from 1,277 million yards to 2,578 million yards, and its share of total cloth production increased from 49 per cent to 59 per cent. It was therefore the small- and medium-scale weavers in particular that actively exploited the new technology and markets. Some local weaving centres produced a wide variety of textiles from a considerable number of small-scale workshops; others specialised in a small range of products from relatively few medium-scale concerns. Because of severe competition between weavers, for the majority of local weaving centres production declined. But I shall briefly sketch three different successful examples.

First, the weavers in Banshū District, Hyōgo Prefecture, specialised almost entirely in exports by the 1930s; they developed a variety of new products from relatively small workshops, the number of looms most weavers possessed ranging from 10 to 50.[11] In 1929 and 1930 Tarō Yoshida, the head of the Nishiwaki Industrial Experimental Station (which was sponsored by the local government) visited Singapore and the Dutch East Indies to carry out market research. On his return he advised the Banshū weavers to shift their production from the woven-in coloured textiles which at that time were still popular in South-East Asia to high value-added textiles, such as sarongs, artificial silk cloth and cloth made of a mixture of cotton and artificial silk. By 1931, partly as a result of the now depressed market for woven-in coloured goods, many weavers had responded to his suggestion. Yoshida distributed to each weaver a sample sarong which he had produced at the Experimental Station, and the Station held exhibitions and public lectures to promote the use of artificial silk. A similar effort was made in the Enshū District of Shizuoka Prefecture from the middle of the 1920s,[12] so that the two districts dominated the expansion of sarong production in Japan in the early 1930s. The unit price of Japanese sarong imports into the Dutch East Indies dropped from 0.345 guilder in 1931 to 0.142 guilder in 1932; Japan's share of the Javanese striped sarong import market (by value) rose from 14 per cent to 75 per cent between the same years.[13] Other examples of new textile exports developed in Banshū included zephyrs (production started in 1932), which was originally an Italian product used as underwear in Egypt and Turkey, and kikoi (started in 1933),[14] which was a loin-cloth for males in Mombasa, Kenya, until then produced by a local handicraft industry. In the case of kikoi, the market information came from Fujimoto Shōten, an Osaka-based merchant, and it was passed by a local weaver to the Nishiwaki Experimental Station.

Second, the Sennan District in Osaka Prefecture was the principal export-oriented local weaving centre in this period, around 80 per cent of its production being exported after 1933.[15] Four big local concerns there each had more than 1,000 looms in 1936. By that time Sennan weavers were able to sell their production directly to the Osaka merchants who handled most textile exports; and they received market information from them in turn. In the second half of the 1920s Yagi Shōten, one of the major Osaka merchants, had identified the market potential for satin in China. Yagi organised production in co-operation with Kanebō, one of the principal spinning firms, and with Obitani Shōten, among the largest Sennan weavers. Obitani wove the yarn supplied by Kanebō; the cloth was then passed back to Kanebō for finishing; and it was exported to China by Yagi. Although the main focus of production shifted from satin to drill in the 1930s, Sennan continued to specialise in the mass production of a small range of medium-quality cloth. The introduction of improved iron-frame looms counteracted the relatively high level of wages in the district.

Third, large cotton-spinning firms, which also had weaving and finishing departments, carried out their own market research and maintained offices in the main overseas markets. They had close contacts with the major merchants such as Mitsui and Tōyō Menka through the latter's purchase of raw cotton, and sometimes co-operated with them to open up new markets. They still concentrated on the production of plain cloth, but introduced a higher-quality range for the European, South American and Australian markets.[16]

In response to the growing demand for yarn arising from the expansion of weaving, right up to 1935 the large cotton-spinning firms partially abandoned their earlier agreements to restrict production, although the smaller spinning firms tended to resist this. On the whole, the spinning sector absorbed the rise in the yen price of raw cotton by reducing the unit price of yarn; it preferred to expand production with a smaller profit margin per unit. This was consistent with the industry's emphasis on increasing labour productivity through heavy replacement investment. As was often noted, the very high rates of profit which large cotton-spinning firms had enjoyed in the 1920s had now disappeared, and the firms managed to remain profitable partly by diversifying into rayon, and partly by making high-return investments in China.[17]

Finally, the spread of industrial paternalism and a wider adoption of length-of-service related wage structures, played an important part in successfully reducing the total wage bill, without increasing international criticism of Japanese working conditions. Unlike the heavy industries, cotton employed a large number of female workers who generally were poorly organised. The industry had been strongly criticised by the ILO, which had long advised the Japanese government to abolish the night-shift system, reduce working hours, and in general improve working conditions.[18] This pressure had considerable economic implications; for example, the Indian Tariff Board's proposal in 1927 to raise the import duty against Japanese cotton textiles was largely prompted by accusations of 'unfair' competition, arising from very poor working conditions in Japan.[19]

In the 1930s most large spinning firms still had dormitories where their young female workers from the rural districts stayed. By that time, however, many firms also had various incentive schemes and welfare facilities, such as schools, cooking and sewing classes and hospitals, for their workers. Although the starting wage was very low, and became even lower during this period, a wage structure was created which provided for sharply increasing increments in accordance with length of service. For the first five years the incremental increases were greater for female workers, reducing their differentials with male workers; after that, wage differentials with males widened. As a result, it was common for girls to stay in a firm for the full period they had intended.[20]

At the same time, the rapid expansion of local weaving centres meant that the proportion of poorly paid workers, and of those who did not benefit from welfare facilities, increased. Many local weaving centres started to recruit workers from distant areas, including Korea, during this period. In some weaving centres the proportion of small weavers who received very low wages under the putting-out system increased.[21] Thus, while large cotton-spinning firms were offering comparatively better wages and working conditions, as laid down by the Greater Japan Cotton Spinners' Federation, the total wage bill of the industry as a whole tended to fall in this period.

II

Although the light industries still dominated the industrial sector in the first half of the 1930s, it was the heavy industries, particularly iron and steel, that played the leading role in developing a new industrial structure. Table 4 shows the new trend of the time: chemical and heavy industrialisation.[22] If we include private-sector arms production, the proportion of heavy and chemical industry production to total industrial production exceeded 50 per cent for the first time in 1936 (see Table 4).

TABLE 4: Production of heavy and chemical industries, 1929-36 (¥ million)

	Chemical	Metal	Machinery	Total	Arms
1929	1,044 (14)	739 (10)	711 (9)	2,495 (32)	
1930	909 (15)	568 (10)	629 (9)	2,105 (36)	
1931	822 (16)	479 (9)	456 (9)	1,757 (34)	58
1932	946 (16)	639 (11)	534 (9)	2,183 (36)	162
1933	1,293 (17)	950 (12)	821 (10)	3,163 (39)	90
1934	1,483 (16)	1,580 (17)	1,081 (12)	4,145 (44)	151
1935	1,815 (17)	1,991 (18)	1,359 (13)	5,165 (48)	213
1936	2,112 (17)	2,331 (19)	1,600 (13)	6,043 (49)	262

Note: Figures in brackets are for percentage of total industrial production. Figures for 'arms' refer only to production in the private sector, which was excluded from the total for chemical, metal and machinery production. They are taken from, Akira Hara, 'Senji tōsei keizai no kaishi' [The beginning of the wartime controlled economy] in *Iwanami kōza Nihon rekishi* [Iwanami lectures on Japanese history], vol.20 (Iwanami Shoten, Tokyo, 1976), p.249.
Source: Research and Statistics Division, Minister's Secretariat, Ministry of International Trade and Industry (ed), *History of the Census of Manufactures for 1909-1958* (Japanese language publication with all tables in Japanese and English, vol.1, reprinted) (Ryūkei Shosha, Tokyo, 1979), pp.9, 11, 13.

Recent research has tended to play down the importance of military demand and of the civilian demand generated by military spending, in accounting for the recovery. In the first place, government expenditure was not particularly high during the period 1931 to 1936. Its share of aggregate demand fluctuated between 16 and 18 per cent throughout these years, being only slightly higher than that of exports. The proportion of military spending in total government expenditure did rise, but its share of aggregate demand increased only from 3 per cent in 1931 to 4.7 per cent in 1936. It was government policy to minimise the increase in military expenditure in the period 1933-6. Second, while military spending generated demand for the shipbuilding, arms and machinery sectors, government spending on relief works seems to have been comparably important for expanding aggregate demand, through its impact on the civil engineering and construction sectors. Both were responsible for the initial recovery of the heavy and chemical industries; but expansion after 1933 was based primarily on the growth of the private domestic market.[23]

The iron and steel industry played a central role in this development. Military and other government demand for steel accounted for not much more than 10 per cent of the total in the first half of the 1930s.[24] Only towards the end of this period did the industrialisation of Manchuria begin to provide a significant government-led demand for Japanese steel. The principal demand for iron and steel came from the civil engineering and construction sectors, the machinery and shipbuilding industries and from the steel industry itself. The expansion of these sectors, mostly private, created a large self-generating demand. The machinery industry also played a key role in the development of the private domestic market. The contribution of military spending to demand for machinery was crucial in 1932, but it remained relatively small for the rest of the period. The production of machinery for the heavy and chemical industries and for the textile industries expanded notably rapidly; that of printing machinery, agricultural machinery and consumer durables (such as electric fans) less so. The electric machinery, textile machinery, machine tool and crane and motor industries created a rapidly increasing demand for the iron and steel industry: at the same time, industrial expansion created a growing and diversifying domestic market for the machinery industry. For example, in electrical machinery, the largest component of the machinery industry in 1936, demand for small motors (less than 10 h.p.) came from the rayon, cotton-spinning and machinery sectors; demand for large motors (more than 100 h.p.) came from the metal, machinery and chemical sectors.[25]

Both devaluation and tariff protection contributed greatly to product price increases in the heavy and chemical industries. The rise from the end of 1931 to early 1932 clearly reflected the increase in import prices following the devaluation of the yen. Another rise from August 1932 to early 1933 reflected the increase in tariff rates. These two factors were effective for the remainder of the period; as a result the heavy and chemical industries were in general in a far more advantageous position against foreign competition in this period than they had been in the 1920s. For example, after 1933 the domestic price of Japanese steel bars and steel sheets became extremely competitive to the (after duty) price of steel imports, despite the fact that the Japanese iron and steel industry was still not cost competitive in international terms.[26]

In addition, those segments of the heavy and chemical industries which faced little or no direct foreign competition were helped indirectly by devaluation and tariff protection. The machine-tool industry illustrates this point well. The industry was particularly sensitive to technological progress in the heavy and chemical industries as a whole. On the one hand, the technologically most advanced machine tools were largely imported. These were in heavy demand particularly in the arsenals and in the aircraft and automobile industries, although even those industries depended for their less sophisticated machines on domestic producers. At the same time, import substitution in other sectors of the machinery industry, such as textile machinery and electrical machinery, created a large demand for these less advanced machine tools, where the domestic manufacturers had a comparative advantage. As the prices of these machine tools remained high, their manufacturers saw little reason to invest in the production of the most advanced machinery. Their plant and equipment investment was generally small-scale, and targeted towards gradual increases in productivity. The growth of medium-scale firms here was particularly rapid; the share of manufacturers with 50 to 100 employees in total machine-tool production (by value) increased from 6 per cent in 1931 to 25 per cent in 1936. The result was that total production of machine tools increased nearly eightfold between 1931 and 1936; and the ratio of imports (by value) to domestic consumption of machine tools decreased from 45 per cent to 34 per cent in the same period.[27]

Within their domestic market, the heavy and chemical industries rarely had protection to maintain high prices; in the same way as the large cotton-spinning firms had responded, the iron and steel industry kept its prices relatively low, and expanded production to maintain profits. In 1934 a number of private iron and steel producers merged with the government-owned Yahata ironworks to form a new giant, Nihon Seitetsu. The Ministry of Commerce and Industry and Nihon Seitetsu pursued rationalisation measures in an attempt to keep iron and steel prices low, in order to generate further demand in the private sector.[28]

The large-scale fixed investment in the heavy and chemical industries was made possible by the high rate of profit that prevailed during this period. Indeed despite the heavy investment in fixed assets, long-term borrowing from financial institutions fell, and internal reserve funds increased. Many new *zaibatsu* such as Nissan, Nitchitsu and Nihon Soda emerged, while the existing *zaibatsu* such as Mitsui, Mitsubishi and Sumitomo became more deeply involved in the chemical and heavy industries (especially the coal- and copper-related sectors) and continued to dominate shipbuilding, cables and railway locomotives, carriages and wagons.[29]

Wages in the heavy and chemical industries were related to length of service. This seniority structure became more widespread, partly because these industries needed skilled workers with many years of experience, partly because of pressure from the labour movement, but also because a large pool of cheap labour was available outside the system if they needed extra hands. There were important changes in the wage structure during this period.[30]

First, wage differentials (according to length of service) in heavy industries seem to have widened between 1930 and 1936. Generally speaking, the daily wage for those with longer service rose, while starting wages remained much the same. Thus workers with permanent status could not experience a fall in wages. The prospect for them of a steady rise in wages played an important part in securing their commitment to work and training. At the same time, the composition of the work-force according to length of service changed dramatically, with the result that the total wage bill might well have been smaller in 1936 than in 1930. Table 5 shows that, between 1930 and 1936, the proportion of workers whose length of service was less than five years rose from 37 per cent to 52 per cent in the metal industries, and from 23 per cent to 49 per cent in the machinery industries.

TABLE 5: Composition of work-force according to length of service (1,000 persons)

	All industries		Metal		Machinery	
	1930	1936	1930	1936	1930	1936
up to 5 years	230 (35)	515 (51)	34 (37)	87 (52)	41 (23)	182 (49)
5 to 15 years	271 (41)	290 (29)	39 (42)	48 (29)	83 (46)	91 (25)
more than 15 years	124 (19)	202 (20)	18 (20)	33 (20)	57 (31)	95 (26)
Total	627	1,010	93	169	182	370

Note: 'Total' includes workers whose length of service is unknown.

Source: Naikaku Tōkeikyoku, *Rōdō Tōkei Jitchi Chōsa Hōkoku* [Report on the Labour Statistics Field Survey] (Naikaku Tōkeikyoku, Tokyo, 1930, 1936).

Second, the number of temporary workers who were outside the seniority system increased during this period. Most temporary workers were male, and were employed by large-scale firms in the heavy industries. One survey reported in 1934 that the proportion of temporary workers to total workers in the heavy industries was about 19 per cent. Their wage level was thought to be between 10 and 20 per cent below that of permanent workers.

Third, subcontracting became more widespread, especially in the machinery industries, between 1931 and 1934. In 1934, 78 per cent of factories with more than 30 operatives used subcontractors; the latter contributed 12 per cent to the total production of the industry. As the wage level in subcontractors' factories tended to be low, this was another way of reducing industry's total wage bill.

III

It has been shown that Japan's industrial recovery in the first half of the 1930s involved a number of new developments within the industrial sector. Certain factors which were specific to this period played a crucial role in these developments. Thus the devaluation of the yen provided the essential condition for the export-oriented growth of the light industries; government spending, especially on civil engineering and construction programmes as well as on the military, generated demand in the heavy and chemical industries. Driven by these stimuli, a new industrial structure was created, which eventually began to fuel its own expansion.

This development has often been contrasted with the continued rural depression and the stagnation of the domestic consumer market. As was noted earlier, industrial wages were kept low throughout the period. Indeed the contrast between industrial expansion and rural depression was a prime concern in the Marxist debate on the nature of Japanese capitalism which took place in the late 1920s and the early 1930s. To Marxists the contrast was firm evidence of the vulnerability of Japanese capitalism.[31] Many argued that the very high levels of agrarian rent (accounting for about 30 per cent of total income in the tenant household) was depressing domestic purchasing power; and that, while industry benefited from the availability of cheap labour (which was essentially the result of a low standard of living in the rural areas), the absence of an expanding domestic market would eventually set a limit to industrial expansion. Agrarian rent (and the nature of the landlords' power base) thus became a central concern in this debate.

Recent case studies have confirmed the serious economic plight of rural households, both the owner-cultivator and tenant, even after the collapse of 1930 and 1931 had passed. Rural households were unable to reconstruct their pre-1930 economic strength until much later. In the cocoon-rearing districts where the depression was particularly severe, employment in silk reeling also declined. Attempts to shift production from cocoons to rice and other cash crops were often hampered by weakened local credit facilities; and the opportunities to invest in long-term technological improvement of agriculture shrank.[32] The bad weather in north-eastern Japan in 1934 also delayed the recovery. And yet, taking the country as a whole, there was a firm recovery in farm household income during this period, as is shown in Table 6.[33] Despite its limited nature, this recovery played a vital role in sustaining the industrial expansion.

The main reason for the recovery in farm household incomes seems to have been the relatively rapid recovery in prices of agricultural products. The price index here (1934-6=100: prices received by farmers) rose from 69.3 in 1931 to 106.8 in 1936. This rise has rarely been noted by scholars, as it barely compensated for the fall prior to 1931 (from 148.8 in 1925). In addition, despite the fall in cocoon rearing, agricultural production as a whole rose from 1931 to 1936, primarily as the result of a 22 per cent increase (in volume) in rice production. In southern Japan (Shikoku, Kyūshū and Okinawa) rice production increased by 22 per cent; slightly slower growth in the remaining regions was offset by a 147 per cent increase in the most northern part of the country (Hokkaidō and Aomori).[34] The increase in the total value of agricultural production was also due to a shift towards wheat, potatoes, fruit and vegetables, rapeseed, and livestock and poultry. Thus the total value of agricultural production in current prices rose from 2,070 million yen in 1931 to 3,660 million yen in 1936. Although this was far from the 1925 figure of 4,544 million yen, there had been a 77 per cent increase in value during the period from 1931.[35]

This rise in the prices of agricultural products had two implications. First, it meant a modest but definite improvement in the terms of exchange for the farm household. Table 6 shows a 33 (owner-cultivator) and 44 (tenant) per cent increase in household expenditure between 1931 and 1936, at a time when the consumer price index for farm households rose by only 15 per cent. As the number of persons per farm household remained the same, this meant an increase in per capita consumption. For example, the amount spent on clothes rose by 60 (owner-cultivator) and 94 (tenant) per cent, when the price of textiles rose by only 27 per cent. The increase in real farm consumption was not confined to household expenditure. Farm running costs (seed, silk-worm eggs, feed, green manure and forage crops, fertilisers, sprays) rose by 72 (owner-cultivator) and 57 (tenant) per cent, when the price index of farm inputs rose by only 48 per cent. The amount spent on manure and fertiliser, the largest single item here, rose by 56 (owner-cultivator) and 71 (tenant) per cent. Most of the increase represented an increased use of fertiliser, one of the most important products of the chemical industry. The price of fertiliser rose by 34 per cent during the period 1931-6.[36]

Second, the recovery in farm household incomes was accompanied by relatively stagnant manufacturing wages. The wage index for manufacturing industries rose only from 98.5 in 1931 to 100 in 1936.[37] At the same time, according to the Farm Household Budgets Survey, the average annual income per household from wage work (largely but not exclusively from the manufacturing sector) increased from 72.92 (owner-cultivator) and 85.47 (tenant) yen in 1931 to 90.74 (owner-cultivator) and 129.31 (tenant) yen in 1936. A tentative calculation suggests that these increases were mainly achieved through longer working hours.[38] In other words, while it is true that wage rates were kept relatively low, the industrial and other non-agricultural sectors were providing the farm households with more employment.

In sum: the farm household economy was providing the industrial sector with both a modestly expanding market and cheap labour; while the industrial sector was absorbing the declining terms of exchange by raising productivity. With respect to farm household incomes, stagnant manufacturing wages were compensated by the rise in agricultural prices. The incomes of the rural population were slowly increasing; and through this, the rural economy was able to provide a solid base for Japan's industrial recovery.

TABLE 6: Farm household budgets
(¥ current prices)

		(1) Gross income from agriculture	(2) Agricultural costs	(3) Net income from agriculture	(4) Non-agricultural income	(5) Total net income	(6) Household expenditure	(7) (5)-(6)
	1931	790	311	478	163	641	631	10
	1932	851	307	544	159	703	632	71
Owner	1933	1,012	345	667	171	838	694	144
culti-	1934	1,047	373	673	164	837	680	158
vator	1935	1,147	382	765	188	954	794	160
	1936	1,250	402	849	181	1,030	841	188
	1931	719	407	312	137	449	470	-21
	1932	850	452	398	140	538	487	51
Tenant	1933	941	485	455	161	617	526	90
	1934	975	525	450	163	612	561	51
	1935	1,087	584	503	180	683	627	56
	1936	1,178	604	574	203	777	676	102

Source: Taizō Inaba (ed), ***Fukkokuban** Nōka Keizai Chōsa Hōkoku* [The Farm Household Budgets Survey: reprinted edition] (Nōgyō Sōgō Kenkyū Kankōkai, Tokyo,1953), pp.81, 85, 91.

NOTES

1 The decline was also due to the increasing use of rayon in the United States weaving industry. Kōzō Uno (ed), *Kōza teikokushugi no kenkyū 6: Nihon shihonshugi* [Studies in imperialism, vol.6. Japanese capitalism] (Aoki Shoten, Tokyo, 1973), pp.257-8. (This section was written by Hiroaki Yamazaki.)

2 Kazushi Ohkawa, Miyohei Shinohara and Mataji Umemura (eds), *Estimates of long-term economic statistics of Japan since 1868* (Japanese-language publication with English summary of text and all tables in Japanese and English: hereafter *LTES*), vol.9 (Tōyōkeizai Shinpōsha, Tokyo, 1966), pp.147, 161, 181.

3 Taizō Inaba (ed), *Fukkokuban Nōka Keizai Chōsa Hōkoku* [The Farm Household Budgets Survey: reprinted edition] (Nōgyō Sōgō Kenkyū Kankōkai, Tokyo, 1953), p.57.

4 Katsuma Ohsato, *Hundred-year statistics of the Japanese economy* (Japanese-language publication with all tables in Japanese and English) (Statistics Department, Bank of Japan, Tokyo, 1966), p.53.

5 Masanao Itoh, 'Taigai keizai kankei' [External economic relations] in Shakai Keizaishi Gakkai (ed), *1930-nendai no Nihon keizai* [The Japanese economy in the 1930s] (Tōdai Shuppankai, Tokyo, 1982), pp.42-52.

6 *LTES*, vol.10 (1972), p.145.

7 See G.C. Allen, 'Japanese industry: its organization and development to 1937' in E.B. Shumpeter (ed), *The industrialization of Japan and Manchukuo* (MacMillan, New York, 1940), pp.475-786; W.W. Lockwood, *The economic development of Japan* (Princeton University Press, Princeton, 1954), pp.64-77.

8 Naosuke Takamura, *Kindai Nihon mengyō to Chūgoku* [The modern Japanese cotton industry and China] (Tōdai Shuppankai, Tokyo, 1982), pp.204-5.

9 For example, one of the reasons why it took until April 1934 for India and Japan to reach a new agreement, after India's abrogation of the 1904 Indo-Japanese Trade Convention in April 1933, was because Lancashire insisted on a more severe limitation on the import of Japanese bleached cloth into India: this was important for Britain, but not vital for the Indian industry. Haruka Yanagisawa, 'Daiichiji Nichiin kaishō o meguru Ei-in kankei' [Anglo-Indian relations in the course of the first Indo-Japanese trade negotiations], *Keizai to Bōeki, 129* (1980), pp.30-47.

10 Hiroaki Yamasaki, 'Nihon mengyō kōzō-ron josetsu' [An introduction to a structural analysis of the Japanese cotton industry], *Keiei Shirin, 5*, 3 (1968), pp.39-41; Yukihiko Kiyokawa, 'Menkōgyō gijutsu no teichaku to kokusanka ni tsuite: Nihon, Chūgoku oyobi Indo no menkōgyō hikaku kenkyū 1. Senzen Nihon' [On the adaptation of foreign technology and domestic innovation in the cotton industry: a comparative study between Japan, China and India 1. Prewar Japan], *Keizai Kenkyū, 24*, 2 (1973), pp.117-37.

11 Takeshi Abe, 'Senkanki ni okeru Banshū Menorimonogyō no hatten' [The development of the cotton-weaving industry in Banshū District during the inter-war period], *Shakai Kagaku Kenkyū, 36*, 3 (1984), pp.1-94, and 4 (1984), pp.1-83. This paragraph is based on this study, unless otherwise stated.

12 Hiroaki Yamazaki, 'Ryōtaisenkanki ni okeru Enshū Menorimonogyō no kōzō to undō' [Structure and change in the cotton-weaving industry of Enshū District in the inter-war period], *Keiei Shirin, 6*, 1-2 (1969), pp.119-24, 145-8.

13 *Kaigai Shoshijō ni okeru Honpō Seni Kōgyōhin* [Japanese Textile Goods in Overseas Markets], 4 (Shōkōshō Bōekikyoku, Tokyo, 1933), pp.54-5.

14 I am indebted to David Anderson for information on this cloth.

15 Takeshi Abe, 'Ryōtaisenkanki Sennan Menorimonogyō no hatten' [The development of the cotton-weaving industry in Sennan District in the inter-war period], *Tochi Seido Shigaku, 22*, 4 (1980), pp.1-19. This paragraph is based on this study.

16 Jurō Hashimoto, *Daikyōkōki no Nihon shihonshugi* [Japanese capitalism in the era of the Great Depression] (Tōdai Shuppankai, Tokyo, 1984), pp.222-3.

17 Uno, *Kōza teikokushugi no kenkyū 6*, pp.266-70.

18 Hiroshi Hazama, *Nihon rōmu kanrishi kenkyū* [Studies in the history of Japanese labour management] (Daiamondosha, Tokyo, 1964), pp.326-9.

19 A.K. Bagchi, *Private investment in India, 1900-1939* (Cambridge University Press, Cambridge, 1972), p.240.

20 Naikaku Tōkeikyoku, *Rōdō Tōkei Jitchi Chōsa Hōkoku* [Report on the Labour Statistics Field Survey] (Naikaku Tōkeikyoku, Tokyo, 1930, 1933, 1936); Hazama, *Nihon rōmu kanrishi kenkyū*, pp.322-92.

21 Abe, 'Banshū (2)', pp.41-2; Abe, 'Ryōtaisenkanki Sennan', pp.8-9; Abe, 'Senzenki Sennan Menorimonogyō ni okeru "sanchi daikeiei"' ['Big local cotton weavers' in prewar Sennan District], *Shakai Kagaku Kenkyū, 35*, 1 (1983), pp.69-70; Yamazaki, 'Ryōtaisenkanki ni okeru Enshū', p.134; Yamazaki, 'Chita Menorimonogyō no hatten kōzō' [Patterns of development in the cotton-weaving industry of Chita District], *Keiei Shirin, 7*, 2 (1970), pp.52-62, 67-9, 78-9.

22 Takafusa Nakamura, *Economic growth in prewar Japan* (Yale University Press, New Haven and London, 1983), pp.173-93.

23 Ryōichi Miwa, 'Takahashi zaisei-ki no keizai seisaku' [Economic policy during the period of [Finance Minister] Takahashi's administration] in Tokyo Daigaku Shakai Kagaku Kenkyūsho (ed), *Fashizumu-ki no kokka to shakai 2. Senji Nihon keizai* [State and society in the period of Fascism 2. The wartime economy in Japan] (Tōdai Shuppankai, Tokyo, 1979), pp.138-9, 146-68, 169-70.

24 Nakamura, *Economic growth*, pp.245-8.

25 Hashimoto, *Daikyōkōki no Nihon shihonshugi*, pp.277-83.

26 Ibid., pp.237-8.

27 Minoru Sawai, '1930-nendai no kōsaku kikai kōgyō [The machine tool industry of the 1930s], *Tochi Seido Shigaku, 97* (1982), pp.32-50.

28 Hashimoto, *Daikyōkōki no Nihon shihonshugi*, pp.307-21.

29 Uno, *Kōza teikokushugi no kenkyū* 6, pp.271-92.

30 Hashimoto, *Daikyōkōki no Nihon shihonshugi*, pp.255-73. The remainder of this section is based on Hashimoto's cited work.

31 Hirotake Koyama, *Nihon shihonshugi ronsōshi* [The history of the Japanese capitalism debate] part 1 (Aoki Shoten, Tokyo, 1953); Shinkichi Nagaoka, *Nihon shihonshugi ronsō no gunzō* [Vocal participants in the Japanese capitalism debate] (Mineruba Shobou, Kyoto, 1984). A detailed account of the debate can also be found in G.A. Hoston, *Marxism and the crisis of development in prewar Japan* (Princeton University Press, Princeton, NJ, 1986).

32 Yoshiaki Nishida (ed), *Shōwa kyōkōka no nōson shakai undō* [Rural social movements during the Shōwa economic crisis] (Ochanomizu Shobou, Tokyo, 1978), pp.744-70. References to other case studies can be found in Takemaro Mori, 'Nōgyō kōzō' [The structure of agriculture] in 1920-nendaishi Kenkyūkai (ed), *1920-nendai no Nihon shihonshugi* [Japanese capitalism in the 1920s] (Tōdai Shuppankai, Tokyo, 1983), pp.258-66.

33 A similar line of interpretation can be found in R.J. Smethurst, *Agricultural development and tenancy disputes in Japan, 1870-1940* (Princeton University Press, Princeton, NJ, 1986), pp.95-101.

34 *Nōgyō Nenkan* [Almanac of Agriculture], (Teikoku Nōkai, Tokyo). Figures were taken from the editions for 1933, pp.141-3; and for 1937, pp.197-9.

35 *LTES*, vol.9 (1966), pp.146-7, 160-1, 166-81.

36 Inaba, *Fukkokuban Nōka Keizai Chōsa Hōkoku*, pp.84, 88; *LTES*, vol.8 (1967), pp.136, 193, 205. For a discussion of the reliability of the Farm Household Budgets Survey, see Inaba, op.cit., pp.19-23, and Nōrinshō Tōkei Jōhōbu and Nōrin Tōkei Kyōkai (eds), *Nōgyō Keizai Ruinen Tōkei* [Annual Series of Statistics of the Agricultural Economy], vol.3 (Nōrin Tōkei Kyōkai, Tokyo, 1980), pp.165-76.

37 *LTES*, vol.8 (1967), p.243.

38 Inaba, *Fukkokuban Nōka Keizai Chōsa Hōkoku*, pp.61, 86. For example, the number of working hours per tenant household in non-agricultural employment (mostly wage work) increased from 904 in 1931 to 1,271 in 1936.

9

THE EFFECTS OF THE GREAT DEPRESSION ON INDUSTRIALISATION IN EQUATORIAL AND CENTRAL AFRICA

GERVASE CLARENCE-SMITH

The World Wars, especially the second one, are usually taken to be the key events which led to modest industrial development in equatorial and central Africa,[1] whereas the recession of the 1930s is not considered to have had much impact. This is as true of case studies of industrialisation[2] as it is of case studies of the recession.[3] It is certain that the level of industrialisation was low and did not rise dramatically in the 1930s. In 1939, only 15.3 per cent of the national income of Southern Rhodesia (now Zimbabwe) came from manufacturing, and employment was limited to around 15,000 people.[4] And yet this was the most developed territory in the region, and the one which probably had done best in terms of industrial growth in the 1930s.

The statistics covering changes in overall industrial output during the 1930s either do not exist or are hard to interpret. In Southern Rhodesia, industrial statistics began to be collected only in 1938. The figures always quoted for earlier years are estimates, computed according to a quite inadmissible method.[5] One is thus forced back onto the figures for industrial exports, and onto a set of indirect indicators. The best general industrial statistics are those for the second most industrialised territory, the Belgian Congo (now Zaïre), but it is not always clear what is being counted as industry and what is not.[6] The focus of this study is on all factory production, including export processing, but excluding construction, transport and most forms of public utilities.

One thing is certain: that private investment from overseas melted away, especially after 1932 when the magnitude of the recession finally sank into investors' consciousness. This penury of investment was in clear contrast to the 1920s.[7] However, this did not in itself preclude industrial growth, for, as in Latin America,[8] there was often plenty of spare capacity to be brought into operation. There had been a speculative investment boom in the late 1920s, which in some areas carried on into the first two or three years of the 1930s; and there were many examples of industrial output rising because of an earlier influx of capital. Moreover, large corporations were sometimes obliged to put in fresh money or face losing their earlier investments altogether. Nor were local investors always as timid as those overseas, especially if one counts South African firms as being local. The state, at times, provided new investments, whether directly or in the form of infrastructural projects which stimulated industrial production. And finally, industrialists adapted to a spectacular turn-around in the relative prices of labour and capital by substituting labour for capital whenever possible.[9]

The central argument of this study is that slow overall industrial growth hid some sharp contrasts, both regional and sectoral. Regional contrasts were affected by the balance of class forces, both in Africa and in the colonial metropoles. Locally, the size, composition, ideology and political power of the settler population formed the key variable. Settlers usually desired at least some forms of industry; and the more powerful they were, the more chance they had of obtaining aid from the state in pursuit of those ambitions. In the metropoles, large and efficient firms were often in favour of colonial industrialisation, either because they saw opportunities to export capital goods or because they could make savings by relocating their production to Africa. In contrast, small and declining firms allied themselves with their workers to prevent colonial industrialisation, thus retaining markets and jobs.[10]

Caught between these divergent class forces, the state also had some general interests to keep in mind. For the colonial authorities, which enjoyed differing levels of autonomy in the various empires, the key economic and financial considerations were revenue and the balance of payments. As a considerable part of revenue still came from import duties, import substitution could be seen as a threat at a time when colonial budgets were under tremendous strain. However, industry provided employment, and ensured the payment of hut or poll taxes, the other pillar of colonial finances. Moreover, balance of payments problems became more acute in the 1930s than at any previous time in the history of modern colonialism. This could make the colonial authorities favourable to import substitution. However it must be remembered that some forms of import substitution involved considerable imports, not just of machinery but also of raw materials and semi-finished goods. In addition international trade agreements sometimes stood in the way of a vigorous policy of import substitution. Thus colonial authorities were often more keen to stimulate export processing of a labour-intensive kind, in order to earn more foreign exchange with minimal foreign exchange losses.

Colonial authorities were also obsessed with law and order, which impinged on industrial policy through the twin problems of unemployment and the cost of living. Although officials welcomed the initial easing of pressure on the over-stretched labour market of the late 1920s, too much unemployment was potentially dangerous. Industry had the advantage of providing better-paid jobs for the greatest potential trouble-makers, the poor whites and proletarianised blacks. At the same time it was a way of saving small settler entrepreneurs faced with ruin, who often caused political trouble quite out of proportion to their numbers. Industrial development which lowered the cost of living, such as flour-milling, was approved of, though this clearly excluded any 'over-protected' activities.[11]

Metropolitan governments in Europe had yet other preoccupations. The first World War had shown how vulnerable undeveloped colonies could be in times of naval blockade, and how important colonial produce could be to the war effort. Some degree of colonial self-sufficiency was thus seen as desirable; in addition the more raw materials were processed in the colonies for export, the less they threatened to take up valuable shipping space. Metropolitan governments also faced balance of payments problems in the 1930s, as autarky and barter trade mounted. They were thus sometimes prepared to pay more than world market prices for processed goods from their colonies, simply to save foreign exchange. Alternatively, they might use exchange control to siphon hard currency from their colonies. Here they were concerned to increase the value added in colonial industries which sold to foreign markets. The ways in which the resource base of a particular colony meshed with these strategic and economic concerns further influenced state policies towards industry.[12]

Turning to sectoral differences, import substituting industry divided into three main branches. Industries producing intermediate goods experienced a multiplier effect coming from the sectors which they supplied. If government expenditure fell or major exports contracted, the intermediate goods sector felt the blow even more harshly. Import substitution of consumer goods for the settler market tended to move in tandem with the intermediate goods sector inasmuch as settler incomes were affected by much the same factors (although the multiplier effect did not come into play in the same way). Finally, companies manufacturing mainly for the African mass market did significantly better, suggesting that African incomes were less sensitive to the effects of recession than those of the settlers.

Export processing was more fragmented. The 'commodities lottery', as it has been called in reference to Latin America, boosted some sectors, such as gold, and depressed others. But this does not in itself explain the changes in the degree of processing for any particular commodity. One might have expected a higher proportion of raw materials to leave Africa unprocessed in times of crisis, in order to afford protection to metropolitan processing industries. However, the reverse was usually the case. More processing in the colonies was stimulated by reduced profit margins. Costs of energy, land and labour were usually lower in Africa than in Europe, and processing could significantly reduce transport costs; these considerations were particularly important in the mineral ore and timber sectors. There was also a need to provide high quality in a fiercely competitive international market, and the quality of goods made from perishable raw materials benefited from rapid processing on the spot; this was notably important in the production of palm-oil. Export processing was further encouraged by the intervention of the state, for all the reasons noted above.[13]

In order to make some sense of these multiple and contradictory factors pulling industrialisation in different directions, this essay begins by considering the political economy of each of the five imperial groups in the region. This is followed by a detailed examination of the main industrial sectors, with an attempt to show how government policies meshed with the particular conditions in different industries.

THE POSITION OF INDUSTRY IN THE DIFFERENT COLONIAL EMPIRES

Southern Rhodesia occupied a peculiar position in British Central Africa, for the white settler population enjoyed virtually dominion status. For most purposes, this was an independent country of the same kind as South Africa, able to pursue industrialisation at the expense of British interests if it so desired. This said, both British and South African connections remained extremely strong. The Southern Rhodesian government was always afraid that protectionist measures could result in retaliatory moves against its exports by these two major trading partners.[14] At the same time, the Southern Rhodesians were keen to stress their membership of the British empire, in order to secure as large a share as possible of the market for industrial and other goods in British East and Central Africa. Here, their main industrial rivals, apart from Britain itself, were South Africa and Kenya.[15]

The Salisbury authorities not only had to juggle with these imperial complications, but they also had to contend with divisions within the settler population. Some of those most committed to industrialisation were the white workers, represented by the Labour Party in the 1920s, for whom more industry meant more jobs. This preoccupation reached a new intensity as the effects of the recession began to hit the country in the early 1930s. However, the white working class was also sensitive to any increases in the cost of living, a view shared by all whites of modest means. Farmers, who held a disproportionate share of parliamentary seats, were keen to avoid increased costs in agricultural inputs and tariff retaliation in foreign markets. But they were simultaneously clamouring for processing factories to buy up commodities which they could not sell abroad. Small miners also wanted state aid for processing, whereas the great specialised Anglo-Saxon mining houses were hostile to government interference. Commercial interests were wary of any moves which would disrupt the lucrative import business. In the early 1930s, industrialists decided to leave the Chambers of Commerce in Salisbury and Bulawayo to found their own Chambers of Industry, as the interests of commerce and industry had become too antagonistic.[16] A new and aggressive manufacturing ideology emerged in some settler publications in these years, a sign of changing times.[17]

The onset of the recession strengthened the protectionist lobby, and in 1933 the Reform Party won parliamentary elections on a platform which included government aid to secondary industry. Within a year, the Reform Party had split, and the radical rump had been defeated in new elections. However, state support for industry did not cease, even if it was not so strong and so coherent as in South Africa. One can best characterise the attitude of the settler government in the 1930s as one which was favourable to the growth of industry, as long as this did not threaten more vital interests in mining and agriculture.[18]

South African industries were those competing most directly with those of Southern Rhodesia. This competition took the form not only of South African sales in central Africa but was also complicated by the fact that Southern Rhodesian companies in the clothing and food sectors sold to South Africa. Up to 1930, Southern Rhodesia was included in a general Southern African Customs Area dominated by Pretoria, and it was only in that year that Salisbury gained the right to frame its own tariffs.[19] However, protection against South African competition was initially gained not by tariffs but by monetary policy. In October 1931, Salisbury followed London's lead in going off the gold standard, while Pretoria clung to gold until early in 1933. The Southern Rhodesian finance minister claimed that one of the reasons for the government's action had been to help secondary industry.[20] Whatever the truth of this assertion, there can be no doubt that industry in Southern Rhodesia was boosted by this measure, and that some South African manufacturing firms were tempted north of the border.[21]

Tariff measures were needed to cope with the other countries which had left the gold standard in 1931, and with South Africa from early 1933. Negotiations with South Africa proceeded cautiously, owing to the economic dangers of alienating Pretoria, but in 1935 import duties were placed on South African manufactures. Although these were very modest, they had some effect in persuading firms based in South Africa to establish subsidiaries in Southern Rhodesia.[22] In 1931, temporary restrictions on imports of British manufactures were imposed.[23] However, at the Imperial Conference in Ottawa in 1932, Salisbury was obliged to go softly. Concessions to certain British manufactures were granted, in return for British guarantees of imports of asbestos.[24] With Japan, Salisbury could be more brutal, and in 1937 the authorities were empowered to place immediate duties on goods dumped in Southern Rhodesia. However, Japanese goods continued to enter the country.[25] In general, it would seem that tariffs did little to encourage industry and that other measures were probably of greater significance.

Throughout the recession, public spending stimulated industry, both directly and indirectly, as state revenues were buoyed up by the counter-cyclical behaviour of gold prices. Gold accounted for just over a third of exports in 1929, but for fully two-thirds in 1933 at the depth of the recession.[26] The gold premium tax imposed in 1932 enabled the Salisbury authorities to do two things. Firstly, public works projects were kept up, both lowering overhead costs for industry and maintaining the level of effective demand in the economy. Two notable examples were the construction of Salisbury airport and that of the Victoria Falls bridge.[27] Secondly, the government intervened directly to set up processing plants for particular agricultural and mineral raw materials, a point which will be considered in more detail when looking at the different branches of industrial production.[28]

London was content to leave the two other territories in British Central Africa, Northern Rhodesia (Zambia) and Nyasaland (Malawi), as privileged markets for many Southern Rhodesian industrial products. These were the Cinderellas of the British empire, with London interested only in the recently developed copper mines in Northern Rhodesia. In late 1930, the Salisbury authorities persuaded Britain to alter the system of imperial trade commissioners, removing Southern Rhodesia from the sphere of the South African commissioner and transferring Northern Rhodesia and Nyasaland from the Kenyan commissioner to one based in Southern Rhodesia. The sterling exchange system also favoured exports from Southern Rhodesia to the north.[29] At the Ottawa conference in 1932, an agreement was reached for the free movement of goods between the two Rhodesias. Only that part of north-eastern Northern Rhodesia included in the Congo Free Trade Zone was excluded, as well as the trade in alcohol.[30] Already in 1930, three-quarters of Southern Rhodesia's manufactured exports went to her neighbours; these exports grew at a faster rate than national income in the 1930s, with Northern Rhodesia as the largest market.[31] Mozambique was also a significant market. The area ruled by the Mozambique Chartered Company had considerable commercial autonomy, and contained Rhodesia's lifeline to the sea. It was treated by white Rhodesians virtually as part of the British empire.[32]

In spite of the lack of statistical data, it would seem that Southern Rhodesian industry grew during the recession. Numerous scraps of evidence painstakingly collated by Wolfgang Döpcke show that even in the most difficult years of the early 1930s, there were clear indications of industrial growth.[33] Although there was no concerted industrial policy, the 1930s witnessed a broadening and deepening of an industrialisation process which had begun timidly in the very first years of colonial rule in the 1890s. A supportive government and the lucky chance of high gold prices were probably the two main factors responsible. It is harder to determine whether industrial expansion in Salisbury and Bulawayo was at the expense of Northern Rhodesia and Nyasaland. Access to these northern markets undoubtedly aided the expansion of Southern Rhodesian industry, and Northern Rhodesia and Nyasaland had virtually no import substitution industries. However, some forms of export processing developed quite markedly in the two northern territories in the 1930s.

The constellation of forces was quite different in the Belgian empire, including the Congo and the mandated territory of Ruanda-Urundi (Rwanda and Burundi). The 'big four' banking groups, foremost among them the Société Générale de Belgique, exerted a stranglehold over the economy of the empire, and acted in close political unison with the authorities and the powerful Catholic church. The white settler population was not very large, about half that of Southern Rhodesia, and its aspirations to political influence and trade union autonomy had been broken in the 1920s. Moreover, it was, strictly, less of a settler population than that of Southern Rhodesia, as many Belgians in the colonies were short-term contracted employees.[34] In the first years of the recession, about a third of the European population left the country. In 1933, political centralisation was strengthened to the disadvantage of the main concentration of settlers in mineral-rich Katanga (Shaba).[35]

Although the banking conglomerates manufactured consumer goods in Belgium, this was a very minor part of their numerous activities, and they had no strong interest in keeping a captive colonial market for such products. On the contrary, they tended to be more interested in producing in Africa or in exporting capital goods to new industries there.[36] This in part explains why the shrill clamour of small businesses and working-class organisations in Belgium for a bigger share of the Congolese market in the recession went largely unheeded.[37]

The big banks could shelter behind the defence that protection was rendered difficult by the existence of the Congo Free Trade Zone. Set up in 1885, and confirmed by the peace treaty of 1919, it covered the entire Belgian empire as well as part of neighbouring empires. The existence of the free trade zone prevented the Belgians from discriminating against imports from any country which was a member of the League of Nations. However, it was possible for the Congolese government to give modest protection to local industries against imports from all sources; and there was nothing to stop Léopoldville favouring Belgian over foreign firms producing within the Congo, through selective authorisations, concessions and government contracts. Moreover, the fact that the free trade zone covered neighbouring economies enlarged the potential market for companies manufacturing goods in the Congo. The free trade zone had already encouraged a precocious process of industrial development in the Belgian empire, and it continued to do so in the 1930s, although at this time Japanese imports became particularly worrying.[38] These grew from almost nothing at the beginning of the decade to 18 per cent of total imports by 1936, and Japan became the Congo's second supplier of manufactures after Belgium.[39] This proportion would have been even higher without the policy of encouraging import substitution by Belgian firms in the colonies.

However, the state was less effective here than in Southern Rhodesia. The main reason was not a lack of willingness but rather a lesser ability to help. Firstly, Belgium clung to the gold standard until 1935, creating problems for both import substituting and export processing industry in the empire.[40] Secondly, although government revenue was kept up by a great expansion of gold production (which roughly quintupled over the decade), gold still made up only about a quarter of the Congo's exports in 1934, compared to some two-thirds in Southern Rhodesia.[41] Fiscal deficits were eased by loans from Brussels, and the state granted generous concessions to help industry, especially export processing in agriculture. Nevertheless, government expenditure was more restricted than in Southern Rhodesia, and there was no systematic policy of reflating the local economy. In particular, there were no major public works projects of the kind found in Southern Rhodesia.[42] And, finally, the state was unable to use the tariff weapon with the same freedom as the Salisbury authorities, because of the Congo Free Trade Zone. Industry suffered particularly during the first half of the 1930s but recovered and expanded at the end of the decade, as is shown in Table 1.

TABLE 1: Industrial output of the Belgian Congo in millions of constant 1950 francs

1929	335.9
1930	310.1
1931	255.8
1932	215.1
1933	203.5
1934	246.4
1935	252.7
1936	296.5
1937	345.3
1938	416.0
1939	422.7

Source: G. Vandewalle, *De conjuncturele evolutie in Kongo en Ruanda-Urundi, van 1920 tot 1939 en van 1949 tot 1958* (Rijksuniversiteit te Gent, Ghent, 1966), p.39.

The Portuguese colonies of Angola, Mozambique and São Tomé might at first sight appear to have been the territories least likely to experience industrial growth in this period. Since the Portuguese military coup of 1926, the settlers had progressively been stripped of formal political power, and the centralisation of colonial decision-making in Lisbon was far greater than in Brussels. Portuguese capitalism was also quite different from that of Belgium. Most Portuguese entrepreneurs were small-scale capitalists, who clung to colonial markets as their salvation during the storm of the 1930s. Salazar, the economics professor whom the military installed as dictator of Portugal, declared that the colonial pact was to be restored after the liberal experiments of the early part of that decade, experiments which had resulted in modest industrial growth in the colonies. Henceforth, the colonies were to exchange raw materials for the manufactures of the metropolis. In addition, Salazar was a firm believer in balanced budgets and sound money, and he pursued resolutely deflationist policies. It would be difficult to envisage a political situation apparently less favourable to industrial development in the colonies.

And yet, all was not what it seemed in Salazar's dictatorship. The richer settlers had excellent informal and family connections in the small world of the Portuguese elite, and the military coup of 1926 reinforced their influence even if it diminished their formal political rights. Moreover, in the early 1930s the regime was shaken by violent risings of indigent poor whites in the overseas territories, and was thus prepared to be conciliatory by stimulating employment prospects. Within Portugal itself, the most dynamic capitalists were a handful of banking groups, not too dissimilar in structure from the Belgian conglomerates, even if much smaller in size. These banking groups profited most from Salazar's regime, and they were not opposed to relocating activities in the colonies if greater profits could be made there.[43]

The ambition for a renewed colonial pact also came to be tempered by Fascist ideas of the state's role in resolving social conflict and reducing economic competition. Existing industries in the colonies with a market in Portugal were to be protected from 'unfair' competition in that market, a policy which was enshrined in a 1936 decree on colonial industries.[44] That this was not just rhetoric was demonstrated in the case of the colonial sugar industry. The military regime prohibited the manufacture of sugar from beet grown in continental Portugal, in order to give satisfaction to the powerful 'sugar barons' of the colonies.[45]

The regime was not only subjected to political pressures but also suffered from an acute shortage of foreign exchange. The Portuguese balance of payments was traditionally dependent on remittances from Brazil, but these dried up in the depression. Stringent exchange control was introduced in Angola in 1931 and in Mozambique a year later, to prevent any embarrassing foreign exchange deficits in the colonies which might have to be met from Lisbon. Both colonies were encouraged to become self-sufficient in certain industrial products then imported from abroad and which could not be obtained from Portugal; tariffs were added to exchange control to achieve this objective.[46] The 1936 decree on colonial industries confirmed this policy and spelt out another preoccupation of the regime: that as much foreign exchange as possible be earned by the colonies through increasing the processing of their exports sent to foreign countries.[47]

Salazar's fiscal and monetary policies were also tempered by considerable pragmatism. In spite of his fervent belief in the gold standard, he was much too canny not to grasp Portugal's financial dependence on Britain, and thus immediately followed Britain off gold in 1931, sparing the Portuguese colonies the problems faced by the Belgian Congo.[48] Similarly, although balanced colonial budgets were written into the new constitution as a legal requirement, Angola's external debt continued to rise in the 1930s, as a result of special dispensations.[49] Moreover, Salazar followed Mussolini in believing that the state should construct public works both at home and in the empire. In 1937 the first modest colonial development plans were launched, in advance of most democratic colonial powers.[50]

Although we have no global figures for industrial performance, it seems clear that Mozambique suffered less in the recession than Angola. The East African colony had never been so tightly integrated into the protectionist web of Portuguese colonial control, and its industries had grown faster in the 1920s. Mozambique's finances were also more buoyant, not because of its own (meagre) gold resources but because it benefited from the gold-induced boom in South Africa and the relative prosperity brought by gold to Southern Rhodesia. Mozambique's economy rested largely on providing transport and labour for its neighbours, and it thus shared indirectly in the counter-cyclical expansion arising from high gold prices. Mozambique therefore enjoyed more industrial growth in the 1930s than Angola, which was more severely affected by the recession, by a fall in government revenues and by the renewal of the colonial pact.[51]

French Equatorial Africa and Cameroun were even greater industrial laggards in these years than Angola. Their industrial base was much smaller, for there had never been a large settler population with a vocal interest in industry. The African population was also very sparse. In theory, both territories should have benefited from the same international considerations that stimulated industrial development in the Belgian Congo, for most of French Equatorial Africa was *de jure* or *de facto* included in the Congo Free Trade Zone, while Cameroun was a League of Nations mandated territory, open to the trade of all League members. But the chances of competing effectively against the great Belgian conglomerates in the free trade zone were slim. Moreover, the French tradition of colonial pact was strong, and the French colonial authorities tended to concentrate on evading the free trade zone regulations in order to favour imports from France. Matters were not helped by the French refusal to leave the gold standard until 1936 and by hefty budgetary cuts.[52]

Thus the fierce debates which raged in France in the 1930s over whether to industrialise the empire hardly mentioned Equatorial Africa. And yet, distant echoes of Parisian passions did reach these Cinderella colonies. Local governments were particularly preoccupied with the military situation (given the French navy's weakness), and in the late 1930s also became concerned at Equatorial Africa's dependence on manufactured imports. Moreover, autarkic trends in French foreign trade led to an interest in saving foreign exchange by intensifying metropolitan imports of certain processed raw materials from the colonies.[53] Nevertheless, this large stretch of territory must have been one of the least industrialised places in the non-European world when the second World War broke out.[54]

Much the same could be said of the little colony of Spanish Guinea, although some of the features found in the Portuguese territories were reproduced here. The settler population was larger in relation to the total than in neighbouring French colonies, although it did not have the power in Madrid which Portuguese settlers enjoyed in Lisbon. The Spanish suffered from severe foreign exchange problems in the 1930s, for much the same reasons as the Portuguese, and support for increased export processing in Africa was directly related to this problem. The outbreak of civil war in Spain in 1936 gave a new urgency to export processing, as the Franco rebels who seized the colony were desperately short of shipping space. But Franco had no resources to spare for investment in colonial industry, and Spanish Guinea remained at much the same depressed level as the surrounding French territories.[55]

EXPORT PROCESSING - MINERALS

Manufacturing for the domestic market is often considered to be synonymous with industry, but figures for the Belgian Congo in 1931 indicate that by far the greatest concentration of installed industrial horsepower capacity was in metallurgy for export markets. Copper processing alone accounted for more than 20 times the figure for cement.[56] There can be no doubt that the most industrial landscapes in the region were to be found on the Copperbelt, split between the Belgian Congo and Northern Rhodesia, a mining zone reminiscent of the South African Witwatersrand.

Copper was initially hard hit by the recession, but it did relatively well in the latter half of the 1930s, given its use in the new electrical industries and its strategic value as the clouds of war darkened over Europe. World copper consumption declined to about half of its 1929 level by 1933, but recovered quite strongly thereafter. Moreover, the American ore producers did worse in the 1930s than those in the rest of the world. The Copperbelt's comparative advantage lay in its high-grade ores, its new equipment, and the low cost of energy and labour. In the 1930s, production costs were between 3 and 5 cents (US) a pound in Northern Rhodesia, at a time when 7 to 8 cents was considered satisfactory in other parts of the world.[57] Northern Rhodesia also benefited from Britain's willingness to purchase more copper from empire sources, essentially Canada and Northern Rhodesia, which resulted in a duty of 2d per pound being imposed on non-empire suppliers in 1932.[58]

However, the Northern Rhodesian mines had only just come on stream when the recession broke, so that the appearance of an uninterrupted increase in output in the 1930s is deceptive. In reality, the industry was producing well below capacity (with all but two mines closed down in the early 1930s) and it had to find markets outside Britain for about half of its output in this period.[59]

The copper mines of the Belgian Congo fared rather worse, for they were even more dependent on a fluctuating world market. Congolese copper production did not again reach the peak level of 1930 until 1937, and then it dropped slightly, not to recover until the war.[60]

This said, progress in the copper-processing industry was remarkable, especially in Northern Rhodesia. At the bottom of the slump, an electrolytic refinery, producing cathode copper, and two smelters making blister copper were built, with the refinery alone costing £35,000 to erect. This was one of the best examples in the region of a pre-depression investment sucking in new money to avoid a loss. Sites, electric power, coal and labour were much cheaper in Africa than in Britain, and there were considerable savings to be made by integrating mining, smelting and refining operations. Transport costs to the distant coast were greatly reduced, an important consideration with copper ores, which have a very low metallic content. Although blister copper sometimes required further refining, the purity of the Northern Rhodesian product was high in world terms, 99.27 per cent copper in the case of the Rhokana Company's output. Electrolytic copper was over 99.9 per cent pure, and could be used directly in many production processes.[61] By 1938 about a seventh of the colony's exports by value was electrolytic copper.[62] A powerful new industry had been born in the worst years of the slump.

In the Belgian Congo, copper processing both progressed and regressed. A modern electrolytic refinery had just come on stream in 1929, with its own hydro-electric installations. Oxide ores were thus refined to a higher standard, and electrolytic copper gradually began to replace blister copper in the Congo's exports. This factory was equipped with the facilities to refine electrolytic cathodes into pure copper, something which was not available in Northern Rhodesia. However, this final refining was abandoned in 1932, and only began again in an experimental way in 1937. Furthermore, the copper company increasingly concentrated its attention on the rich sulphide ores of the Kipushi mine, opened in 1926. The antiquated coal-fired smelter in Elizabethville transformed these sulphide ores into a copper-iron-sulphur matte, with about 72 per cent copper content, high in world terms, but much lower than blister or electrolytic copper. Transport costs to Europe were around 50 per cent higher for matte than for electrolytic copper, and its refining costs were greater in Belgium than in Africa. Yet, the proportion of copper exported in the form of matte increased from 39.2 per cent in 1932 to 49.5 per cent in 1936.[63]

The official company history explains this regression by stressing the risk and the costs of further investment in smelting and refining during the difficult conditions of the recession. The abandonment of final refining is justified by the poor quality and small number of skilled workers.[64] But the Société Générale, which dominated the monopolistic copper company, also owned the railway to the north, and this was desperate for freight in the recession. Moreover the Société Générale had a heavy stake in metallurgy in Belgium, and needed to keep its smelter and refinery there going.[65] Unlike the specialised Anglo-Saxon mining houses of southern Africa, the Belgian banking conglomerates had to balance their varied interests in both continents.

Notable advances in processing were also made in the booming gold mines. All over central and equatorial Africa, old gold workings re-activated as prices rose. These were often small ramshackle affairs, using large amounts of labour to pan for gold. But whenever gold was mined in reefs, the ore was locally processed. Thus, the Kilo-Moto mines, the largest in the Congo, embarked from 1926 on a major programme of electrification, based on hydro-electric resources. This allowed for more intensive recovery of gold during the 1930s, with crushing mills, Chilean tube mills, and a new flotation process.[66] The number of gold smelters in the Congo increased from three to nine between 1931 and 1939, although final refining was still carried out in Belgium.[67] In Southern Rhodesia, many mines bought processing machinery in the euphoria of the boom.[68] In 1938, the government built a roasting plant, to extract gold from sulphide ores, and also provided the hydro-electricity for it, largely to help the small workers who were predominant in the gold sector.[69]

Tin was another mineral which witnessed advances in processing. Small tin deposits were scattered around the eastern Belgian Congo and Ruanda-Urundi, but by 1931 prices were so low that mining was unprofitable. Prices picked up in the second half of 1932, and in 1934 the Congo and Ruanda-Urundi entered the international tin cartel. With guaranteed prices and an unfilled quota, production grew fast. As with gold, most mines were very labour-intensive, and most exports took the form of tin ore roughly concentrated by washing. However, the Géomines firm in Katanga had begun to build a hydro-electrically powered tin smelter in 1927, which came into operation in 1934. From 1935, about a third of the tin exports of the Belgian empire, calculated in metal content, took the form of smelted tin. The savings in transport costs were very considerable, but the Belgian mines outside Katanga had neither the capital nor the energy sources to engage in smelting.[70]

Processing developments in other mineral sectors were less marked, concerned small quantities, and were often by-products of progress in copper technology. Cobalt was the most significant by-product of electrolytically treated copper in this region, and although production in the Congo was temporarily suspended in the early 1930s, it grew again as new uses were found for this metal. Cobalt was exported from the Congo as a cobalt-iron-copper alloy, and further separation was done in Belgium. Zinc and silver were the other two metals which could be electrolytically recovered from copper ores.[71] New plant for the production of vanadium oxide was brought into production in 1931 in Northern Rhodesia, in the Broken Hill mine; this plant also produced zinc electrolytically. Southern Rhodesia's two main minerals after gold were chrome and asbestos. One of the asbestos mines brought new plant into operation in 1934, for the separation of fibre from the ore.[72] By the end of the

1930s a small proportion of chrome ore was being locally smelted for the first time.[73] None of these developments was very spectacular, but they all pointed in the same direction, that of greater processing of mineral ores.

EXPORT PROCESSING - AGRICULTURAL, FORESTRY, FISHING AND LIVESTOCK

Export processing outside the mineral sector was more scattered and diverse, less capital-intensive, more closely linked to import substitution, and a greater recipient of state aid during the recession. In agricultural processing, international companies were less common than in mining. The struggling settler entrepreneurs and small local companies usually obtained official help, sometimes at the expense of African peasants. In the Belgian Congo, the state gave considerable support in the form of reduced transport costs and fiscal exemptions, arguing that an improvement in quality was essential to compete on a depressed world market. The need to slow down the outflow of settlers may also have been important, as rumours were circulating among the African population that the whites were leaving and that black Americans were coming to free the country.[74]

In the forest zone, stretching from southern Cameroun to eastern Zaïre, there were two dominant export processing industries, palm-oil and timber. Both depended on backward gathering techniques for their raw materials. Forestry operations were in great part limited to coastal areas close to rivers and railways. Gangs of labourers hacked down trees with axes, and no attempt was made at re-planting. In contrast, sawmills were large enterprises using a substantial amount of power and machinery. Timber prices were less badly affected than those of many commodities in the recession, especially for the more valuable woods. Unrolling or sawing the wood allowed companies to use misshapen logs, eliminate the worthless segments, and make substantial savings on freight costs. The number of sawmills and export of sawn wood rose steadily throughout the 1930s.[75] Indeed, in the early 1930s it was found that the industrial zone of Pointe-Noire, at the end of the newly completed Congo Océan railway, was too small to accommodate all the forestry companies wishing to locate there.[76] Although the proportion of processed to unprocessed wood exports remained quite modest, there was none the less a steady expansion of sawn wood exports, contrasting with the fluctuations in exports of logs, as is shown in Table 2.

TABLE 2:

	Exports: processed wood Metric tons			Exports: unprocessed wood Metric tons		
	Cameroun	Gabon	Belg. Congo	Cameroun	Gabon	Belg. Congo
1930			3,862	51,746		9,452
1931	4,885		3,732	31,689		4,691
1932	4,295		3,986	27,126		3,770
1933	8,824	1,428	6,230		290,637	6,230
1934			8,472			16,048
1935	8,540		10,928	27,969		25,820
1936	8,926			21,028		
1937	11,767			39,575		
1938	11,457	13,213		29,360	262,539	
1939	10,239		12,143	19,986		37,859

Sources: For Cameroun, France, *Rapport Annuel au Conseil de la Société des Nations sur l'Administration sous Mandat du Territoire du Cameroun*, and France, *Annuaire statistique du Cameroun, 1938-1945* (Ministère de la France d'Outre-Mer, Paris, 1947); for Gabon, C.F. Pambo-Loueya, 'La colonie du Gabon de 1914 à 1939, étude économique et sociale', unpublished thèse de 3e cycle, Université de Paris-VII, 1980, p.644; for Belgian Congo, Belgium, *Volume jubilaire du Bulletin Agricole du Congo Belge et du Ruanda-Urundi, 1910-1960* (Ministère du Congo-Belge et du Ruanda-Urundi, Brussels, 1960), pp.89-90 and 97; G. Batta, 'Chimie de quelques matériaux congolais', *Revue Universelle des Mines, 13*, 3 (1937), p.146.

Palm fruit has to be processed rapidly, to avoid deterioration and high acidity. But in the 1930s plantations on South-East Asian lines, which achieved this, were only in their infancy in this part of Africa. In the Belgian Congo, peasant extraction of oil, using methods prevalent in Nigeria, had been discouraged; rather, monopsonistic companies bought the fruit from African collectors for industrial processing. By 1934 prices had fallen to a third of 1929 levels, and the producers were clamouring for state aid. The Belgian government responded by reducing fiscal, transport and customs burdens, and by favouring colonial produce in the home market. At the same time, monopsony and constraint on gatherers were made more rigorous, resulting in widespread African resentment. In 1931, in the Kikwit zone of the Unilever operations, a major rebellion broke out and was ruthlessly crushed by the Belgian forces.

Palm-oil production recovered quickly from the early 1930s, with improved quality. The Belgian Congo emerged from the recession with the most efficient industry in Africa, producing high-quality palm-oil by steam sterilisation and increasing yields by the use of centrifuges. The number of mechanised palm-oil factories rose from 66 in 1933 to 118 in 1939. In part, this increase reflected a change in colonial strategy, away from large company factories and toward medium or small plants owned by individual settlers; for the latter did not impose long transportation to the factory for collectors. African artisanal production was not eliminated but two-thirds of output was already from the mechanised processing sector in 1930, and this proportion increased during the recession. The volume of exports doubled over the decade to over 70,000 tons, and their real value rose by half. New regional markets were found in British Central Africa and South Africa, and new internal uses emerged with the employment of low-grade palm-oil for the flotation process in copper refining.[77]

Growth was less marked in the other territories. Exports from French Equatorial Africa and Cameroun increased as a result of measures taken from 1931 to protect imperially produced vegetable oils in the metropolitan market, and to subsidise producers overseas. However, French industrialists preferred copra to palm-oil, and French consumption of the latter was small.[78] Moreover, here the ratio of mechanically processed oil to peasant-processed oil remained low. In 1938, the industrial census revealed only about 1,000 tons of industrially processed palm-oil in Cameroun, compared to total exports of some 9,000 tons.[79] In French Equatorial Africa there were 500 to 600 tons of industrial palm-oil produced, compared to total exports of 6,500 tons.[80]

The experience of the Iberian producers was also a chequered one. Angolan exports stagnated at 3,000 to 4,000 tons per year, partly because the home market in Portugal was small and already saturated. Some firms producing industrial palm-oil went bankrupt.[81] However, others prospered. The Companhia do Açúcar de Angola, buoyed up by profits from sugar, doubled its palm plantations and raised oil production from 240 tons in 1930 to 1,200 tons a decade later.[82] The planters of São Tomé also did well on the Portuguese market, diversifying out of cocoa and expanding exports of palm-oil from a mere 300 tons in 1926 to an average of 900 tons a year in the 1930s.[83] Neighbouring Spanish Guinea exported only 15 tons in 1935 but 455 in 1941, after protection in Spain had led to new processing factories being set up in the colony. At the same time Spanish Guinea continued to import cheaper Nigerian palm-oil to meet local African needs.[84]

The recession jolted the large palm-oil producers into a more rational form of production. Between 1931 and 1934, Unilever made losses of nearly half a million pounds on its operations in the Belgian Congo. A company report of 1933 revealed that it cost over twice as much to produce a ton of oil in the Belgian Congo as in the plantations of the British Cameroons. The blame was placed on the low oil content of wild palm fruit, irregular delivery to the factory, the costs of transport, and the large number of employees, black and white, needed to make a system based on wild palms function properly. The Kikwit rebellion of 1931 also showed how dangerous it could be to push African collectors too far. By 1935, Unilever had taken the decision to shift to plantation production.[85] This decision was followed a year later by the main producer in the French Congo, the CFHC.[85] The shift towards integrated plantations and factories took many years to be fully implemented, but its roots lay in the experience of the recession.

The integration of plantation and factory had always been high in sugar, probably the most capital-intensive form of agriculture in the region. Like palm fruit, cane had to be processed quickly to avoid deterioration, but unlike palms, sugar-cane was a carefully cultivated crop. In the 1930s, sliding-scale tariffs were adopted by Portugal to reserve the home market entirely for colonial production. Only semi-refined yellow sugar imports were permitted, to reinforce the final processes of sugar refining in Portugal, although the colonial sugar companies owned most of the refineries in the metropolis. By 1939, Portugal was importing some 70,000 tons of raw sugar a year from Angola and Mozambique.

However, not all the sugar producers shared in the prosperity which allowed the Companhia do Açúcar de Angola to distribute dividends of between 12 and 25 per cent throughout the 1930s. The allocation of quotas for the home market favoured steadily expanding output by the three Portuguese companies in Angola. In contrast, the British-owned Sena Sugar Estates in Mozambique, which in the 1920s was by far the largest producer, was forced to reduce its output. The company did its best to increase sales in the local market; but this was only some 7,000 tons per year in total, and the Incomati Estates in the south was better placed to supply the largest market concentration in Lourenço Marques. Sena Sugar exploited the lack of a sugar industry in British Central Africa to increase its regional sales, and continued to place some of its output on the very depressed world market. But for all these efforts, the company was obliged to close two of its four factories during the recession.[86]

Another significant sugar exporter was the Belgian Congo, its industry a product of the euphoria of the late 1920s. The sole factory came into full production in the depths of the depression. The Congolese authorities exempted the company from export duties in 1930, and the home government gave it preferential access to the Belgian market. Beet sugar producers in the metropolis then protested, and had a quota imposed on imports from the Congo; but even so exports rose steadily from just over 1,000 tons in 1930 to 14,700 tons in 1939. This was still modest compared to total Belgian consumption of around 250,000 tons, and was well below the exports from Angola and Mozambique. The local market in the Congo was scarcely an alternative at this stage, falling from around 2,000 tons in 1930 to under 1,000 tons in the worst years of the slump; it was still only 2,800 tons at the end of the decade.[87] In Southern Rhodesia, in contrast to the export-oriented Portuguese and Belgian industries, the sugar industry took off in 1935 refining for the local market. It was situated in Bulawayo and imported raw sugar from Mozambique.[88]

An example of the importance which settler self-government could have for export processing industries was Southern Rhodesia's encouragement of meat plants. The combined effects of the recession and of a foot-and-mouth epizootic in 1932-3 brought disaster to ranchers. The Salisbury authorities then negotiated with the large Liebig company, which had major ranching interests, and persuaded it to set up a meat extract factory. At the same time, the government granted favourable terms to the Imperial Cold Storage Company of South Africa to invest in meat chilling works in Bulawayo. But as Rhodesian chilled beef continued to be exported at a loss, the company showed little enthusiasm, though it did proceed with the project; the ranchers then pushed the government into nationalising the chilling works (for over a quarter of a million pounds) at the end of the decade.[90] It is unlikely that non-settler governments in the region would ever have shown such financial commitment to a loss-making industrial plant.

A related form of export processing which became increasingly industrialised was the fishing industry of southern Angola. The recession hit hard at the traditional and rather simple methods of drying and salting of fish, which served an African market stretching from Cameroun to Mozambique. Exports of dried and salted fish had still not recovered the levels of the late 1920s by the end of the recession years. However, the industry went up-market. Fish-oil exports to the West grew, and the canning of fish for the Italian market, which had begun in the mid-1920s, proved extremely lucrative until in 1936 severe foreign exchange problems (after the Ethiopian and Albanian adventures) forced Mussolini to impose drastic exchange controls. The flexible entrepreneurs of southern Angola responded to this crisis by a rapid increase in fish-meal production for the German market, laying the basis for a tremendous expansion in the post-war years.[91]

Other forms of agricultural export processing were less industrial in nature, although the degree of mechanisation can easily be underestimated. There was an increase in mechanical processing across a wide range of crops during the 1930s, at least in the Belgian Congo.[92] Extraction of oil from coconuts, ground-nuts, palm kernels and cotton-seed; cotton ginning and sisal leaf stripping; rubber processing; tobacco curing; the preparation of tea, coffee and cocoa; and the tanning of hides were the chief examples of this kind of processing. To be sure, many companies and settlers went bankrupt, and plant was often producing far below capacity; but the general trend was upwards.

Two groups of industries in this category did particularly well. Firstly, there were those with a protected home market, such as cotton ginning for Belgian, Portuguese and French textile mills. This is an excellent example of countries seeking major foreign exchange savings in the 1930s, even though the ginned cotton was of poor quality and, in the Portuguese case at least, more expensive than that available on the depressed world market.[93] Secondly, there were those who benefited from an effective international commodity agreement, such as the tea industries of Nyasaland and Mozambique. In order to ensure a wide measure of international co-operation in the tea scheme, the great producers were prepared to grant relatively generous quotas to small and struggling African producers.[94]

In general terms, the recession had a dual impact on agricultural exports. It favoured both the extremely cheap producers, in this case the African peasant with low overheads; and the producers of high-quality goods, which in Africa meant the settlers or the companies able to intensify their processing activities. The greatest loser was usually the inefficient poor white farmer.

IMPORT SUBSTITUTION - INTERMEDIATE GOODS

In Africa, import substitution frequently began with the production of simple intermediate goods rather than with light consumer articles. In part this was due to pressure from metropolitan interests to prevent the creation of consumer-goods industries in the colonies, a point to which I will return shortly. But it was also a consequence of extraverted export-led growth in economies with limited internal markets. It often made most sense to produce basic manufactures needed in large quantities for mining, agriculture and construction, goods which because of their bulk were expensive to import. Export processing further stimulated demand for intermediate goods, thus creating a backward linkage. Whereas export processing plants could be found scattered over this huge region, the large capital-intensive units producing many intermediate goods tended to be concentrated in a few limited areas. One thus encountered industrial growth poles along the railway from Stanley Pool to the Atlantic Ocean, in the Copperbelt, in the Rhodesian highlands, and around Lourenço Marques, the gateway to the booming Witwatersrand of South Africa.

Building materials, especially cement, were the most significant part of this branch of industry, servicing almost every sector of the modern economy. Production of cement went back to before the first World War in Southern Rhodesia, and to the years just after the conflict in the Belgian Congo and Mozambique. All companies were hard hit by the onset of recession, as the slowing down in economic activity was brutally multiplied into a calamitous decline in demand for cement. Much the same was true for other building materials, especially bricks, tiles, stone, lime and sawn wood, although here production tended to be scattered in smaller units, many of them artisanal workshops rather than factories proper.

The Belgian Congo's building materials industry suffered most, in part because of the dumping of South African and Southern Rhodesian cement in 1930-2.[95] Output from the plants located near Léopoldville and Elizabethville plummeted from 64,000 metric tons in 1929 to zero in 1935. Recovery was slow and partial, with production reaching only 35,000 tons in 1939. However, the colony did achieve almost total self-sufficiency in cement, whereas in 1929-30 about a third of consumption had been imported.[96]

Mozambique was hit in much the same way, although starting from a lower base-line and recovering rather better. Production stood at some 14,000 metric tons in 1928, and had risen to just over 25,000 tons by 1932, with imports kept low by high duties. The decline was then catastrophic, with production ceasing almost completely in 1935.[97] The South African company defaulted on its loans from the Banco Nacional Ultramarino, which was obliged to take over its factory.[98] By 1939, output had risen once again to 28,000 tons.[99] Bricks did badly too. The Lourenço Marques factory produced 4.5 million bricks in 1932, below its capacity of around 6 million, and its output was only 1.4 million in 1936.[100]

In Southern Rhodesia, the situation was less bleak, reflecting the maintenance of public works expenditure and a generally more mild recession; but nevertheless cement appears to have done worse than many other industrial products. The onset of the economic troubles coincided with the ending of major construction work on the Northern Rhodesian Copperbelt; and the value of cement exports fell from a little over £60,000 in 1930 to a low of just under £20,000 in 1933. One cement company was liquidated in 1932, and another a year later. However, cement exports recovered, averaging over £60,000 a year in the late 1930s.[101] Total production of cement and other building materials was valued at nearly £223,000 in 1938, with imports at a mere £20,000.[102]

Metal goods and machinery were closely allied to building materials, and shared much the same fate. The Southern Rhodesian iron and steel industry had profited greatly from the development of the Northern Rhodesian copper mines. And like the cement industry, it was hard hit by the ending of major construction works there and the parlous state of the mines, although exports picked up in the late 1930s. The booming gold-mining sector provided an internal market for a wide range of simple products, such as pipes, pumps, steel ladders, smoke stacks and miscellaneous tools and machinery. South African firms specialising in steel and mining machinery jumped the tariff barrier to set up in Southern Rhodesia in these years.[103] A shipbuilding and repairing company, which serviced the Belgian Congo's extensive internal waterway system, did worse. An index of its turnover at constant prices fell from 32 in 1929 to only 8 in 1934. Although it rallied somewhat in the latter part of the decade, the index remained below the 1929 level.[104]

Chemicals were closely tied to the fortunes of mining and the urban sector, as these were by far their largest markets. The chemical works in Katanga, which came on stream in 1929 to provide the copper-refining plant with sulphuric acid, saw its production dwindle to almost nothing by 1933. However, it recovered after that date, and by 1940 had reached 1930 levels of output. Costs were substantially lowered in 1938 when it was found that expensive imported sulphur could be replaced by one of the by-products of copper refining. Moreover, new chemicals used in the mining industry began to appear in the production statistics from the mid-1930s, indicating a broadening of the industrial process.[105] In Southern Rhodesia, South African firms producing explosives established themselves in the 1930s. However, in 1938 imports of chemicals and paint were running at four times the level of internal production.[106] In Angola and Mozambique, one factory in each colony was given a monopoly in 1932 for the production of industrial alcohol from molasses. The alcohol was mixed with petrol to keep down foreign exchange losses. Production from the two factories expanded steadily during the decade, although the new fuel for internal combustion engines never dominated the market.[107]

The chemical industry also served the farmers. Southern Rhodesia produced a variety of insecticides, cattle dipping fluid and so forth, but the main product was fertiliser, production of which went back to the first World War.[108] The African Explosives and Chemical Industries Ltd, which opened a Rhodesian subsidiary in Salisbury in 1932, produced fertiliser. However, there are no production figures prior to 1938. Exports of fertiliser dropped to a quarter of the 1930 level by 1933 but then expanded rapidly to the end of the decade; but the sums involved were so small that it is hard to read anything into them.[109] In 1938, imports were running at about two-thirds the level of local production.[110] In the Belgian Congo, the small output of 340 tons of fertiliser recorded in 1930 disappeared entirely in the statistics for later years.[111]

If the picture for intermediate goods was generally gloomy, especially in the Belgian Congo, there was a major exception in the production of electricity. The most dramatic increase in output occurred in Katanga, from a mere 3,200 kwh in 1931 to 226,662 kwh in 1938.[112] This surge in production was repeated all over the region, even in the French territories.[113] In equatorial Africa, this was due almost entirely to the exploitation of the new technology of hydro-electricity, which represented the region's greatest comparative advantage in the industrial field. Nowhere in the world is it possible to produce so much hydro-electricity so cheaply as in equatorial Africa.[114] Central Africa also benefited from cheap coal, and there was an emphasis in this period on thermal stations. Not only was electricity a major new industry in its own right but it also made possible a whole range of other industries, from electrolytic refining of copper in Katanga to the cotton textile mills of Léopoldville.

IMPORT SUBSTITUTION - CONSUMER GOODS

Industries producing wholly or mainly for the settler consumer market were affected not only by the decline in settler purchasing power but also, in some cases, by a decline in settler numbers. The white population of the Belgian Congo fell from 25,000 in 1930 to 17,000 by 1935, and recovered the 1930 level at the end of the decade. A similar pattern could be seen in Northern Rhodesia and Nyasaland. The European population of Angola numbered 59,000 in 1931 but only 44,000 in 1940. However, the settler population of

Mozambique increased from 18,000 in 1928 to 27,000 in 1940; and the figures for Southern Rhodesia were 48,000 in 1930 and 65,000 in 1940.[115] Not surprisingly, industry based on the settler market performed better in these two latter territories, where in addition incomes held up because of the gold boom.

Industries producing wholly or mainly for the African market did well throughout the region, even in the hardest years of the early 1930s. Indeed, a number of industries which had been founded on settler demand went down-market during the recession, producing cheaper goods aimed at the African masses. In general Africans were not highly indebted like the settlers, so their purchasing power remained steadier as prices fell. In addition African numbers rose. Workers' wages were initially quite sticky; thus it was not easy to push them down faster than the rapidly falling cost of living. While barter terms of trade frequently moved against African cultivators, they could compensate by stepping up the volume of cash-crop production. Moreover, the departing settlers sometimes left new economic niches into which Africans could move.[116]

Soap generally did well in this period, as can be seen from Table 3. It was perfectly adapted to the needs of the 1930s, for it had a mass African market and could easily substitute for imports. The low capital intensity of soap works enabled entrepreneurs to take advantage of the cheapness of labour in the 1930s. Soap production required very little imported machinery, and its raw material was produced locally by the export processing firms turning out palm-oil, copra and other vegetable oils. It thus consumed almost no foreign exchange. There were few barriers to entry into this sector. Very large companies, such as Unilever and the Société Générale, owned soap works, but often they belonged to small entrepreneurs such as the Greek traders of Cameroun.[117] Soap works were the most geographically dispersed form of consumer industry in the region, to be found even in territories which had no other form of manufacturing for the consumer market.

TABLE 3: Soap production: metric tons

	Cameroun	AEF	B.Congo	Angola	Mozambique	S.Rhodesia
1928					388	
1929	(*c*.0)		1,369			
1930			1,708	888		
1931			1,325			
1932			1,825			
1933					370	
1934					558	
1935			2,860	1,374	1,140	
1936			3,388		894	
1937			4,386			
1938	*c*.1,000	36	4,989	1,036		3,086
1939			7,448		1,600	

Sources: Belgium, Chambre des Représentants, *Rapport Annuel sur l'Administration de la Colonie du Congo Belge*; France, *Rapport Annuel au Conseil de la Société des Nations sur l'Administration sous Mandat du Territoire du Cameroun*; Archives Nationales, Section Outre-Mer, Paris, Affaires Politiques, Carton 2695(7) and Carton 2853(3); C. Serra (ed), *História de Moçambique* (Tempo, Maputo, 1983), vol.2, p.259; J. Tristão de Bettencourt, *Relatório do governador geral de Moçambique, 1940-1942* (Agencia Geral do Ultramar, Lisbon, 1945), vol.2, pp.126-7; E. de Souza Ferreira, 'La transformacion y consolidacion de la economia en Angola, 1930-1974', *Estudios de Asia y Africa, 15*, 3 (1980), p.581; G. Lefebvre, *L'Angola, son histoire, son économie* (G. Thone, Liège, 1947), p.152; *Economic and Statistical Bulletin of Southern Rhodesia, 7*, 2 (1939), p.6 (my thanks go to Ian Phimister for sending me a photocopy).

Textiles were the greatest gap in the industrial structure of the region, a gap explained essentially by vociferous lobbying on the part of the declining textile firms in the European metropoles. Cotton goods were by far the most valuable single consumer item imported throughout Black Africa, and European firms had no intention of losing this market. This is seen most clearly in the weaker and more backward colonial metropoles. In Portugal, a decree of 1932 prohibited the creation of cotton textile mills in the empire, in return for a guarantee of high prices for colonial raw cotton, a measure exhibiting the Portuguese colonial pact in its purest form.[118] However, in 1933, a cotton-wool factory was authorised for Angola, which did fairly well; and there was also a factory making fishing nets.[119] The French were similarly opposed to textile mills, even though equatorial Africa was supplying a growing proportion of ginned cotton for French mills.[120]

This condition was also found in the British empire. Southern Rhodesia was in the anomalous position of having a dynamic garments industry but no textile mills. New clothing manufactures sprang up in the early 1930s, but British pressure prevented the emergence of a cotton textile industry at this stage. The Ottawa Conference bargaining in 1932 resulted in a trade-off, whereby Rhodesian tariffs on British cottons were kept low in return for guarantees of British purchases of Rhodesian asbestos.[121]

The Congolese textile factory was thus an isolated example in the region, and it owed its existence in large part to the inability of the Belgians to give their metropolitan industry protection, owing to the provisions of the Congo Free Trade Zone. It was a very modern integrated spinning and weaving plant, which came into full production only in 1929, and which acquired its own source of hydro-electric power a year later. There was a brief crisis in 1931 but from then production expanded; exports within the region developed after 1936. However, imports of cotton textiles, essentially extremely cheap Japanese goods, rose much faster than local production, as can be seen in Table 4. Prices were reduced by 20 per cent in 1931-4 to meet competition from imports, and they fell to their lowest point in 1938. Almost no new equipment was purchased during the 1930s, and the company substituted labour for capital whenever possible. The firm's financial situation was difficult in the early 1930s, and in 1934 an unnamed bank took control from the original promoters, a local trader and two Belgian textile companies.[122]

In the related footwear industry, protection intended to benefit metropolitan producers in the Angolan market backfired, creating a space for local industry. In 1936 the Portuguese authorities placed prohibitively high tariffs on foreign footwear entering Angola, with the intention of stimulating imports of Portuguese boots and shoes. However, the results were somewhat different from official expectations. Initially, there was a sudden expansion of artisanal production using local leather: at the same time plans were laid to create a factory producing cheap rubber footwear of the kind imported from Japan. The factory came on stream only in 1941, but its origins lay in the 1936 tariff.[123]

TABLE 4: Cotton textiles in the Belgian Congo
(metric tons)

	Production	Imports	Exports
1931	930	2,113	
1932	940	2,310	
1933	1,114	2,837	
1934	1,109	4,253	
1935	1,430	5,774	
1936	1,430	8,189	
1937	1,570	8,445	98
1938	1,640	6,033	133
1939	1,640	6,858	95

Source: Belgium, Ministère des Colonies, *Plan décennal pour le développement économique et social du Congo Belge* (De Visscher, Brussels, 1949), vol.2, p.576.

The food, beverage and tobacco industries were more closely tied to the settler market, and they often fared rather badly. The two breweries in the Belgian Congo managed to stay afloat and indeed increase their market share relative to imports; but only in 1939 did they regain 1931 levels of production. And that was achieved partly by going down-market and producing cheaper beer for Africans.[124] The brewery planned for Lobito in Angola was abandoned.[125] In contrast, with stiff tariff protection, beer production in Mozambique rose from 93,000 litres in 1929 to over 600,000 litres in 1934, remaining at that level for the rest of the decade. Imports fell away to almost nothing. The beer production monopoly granted in the early 1920s expired in 1935, and a new factory was set up, but the two companies fused in 1938.[126]

The experience of the tobacco and matches industries was similar. The Léopoldville tobacco factory went bankrupt, and a company optimistically set up in Ruanda-Urundi in 1931 also collapsed. It was not until the war that this branch of Belgian colonial industry was revived.[127] The tobacco industry of Angola survived, with the help of stiff protection and a special government fund. However, a number of small tobacco firms went out of business, and total production fell from 154 tons in 1929 to 120 in 1935.[128] The related match factory in Angola also ceased operation in the early 1930s, to the benefit of imports from Portugal.[129] In Mozambique, the tobacco industry stagnated, after output had fallen to a low in 1934 and two factories in Lourenço Marques had closed down. As in Angola, and indeed in Portugal itself, consumption was hampered by a high level of taxation.[130] Southern Rhodesian exports of cigarettes to neighbouring territories fell markedly in the early 1930s, but had regained the 1930 level by the end of the decade. There are no figures for production, but one company set up in 1929 to manufacture cigarettes was liquidated two years later. However, a company producing matches was founded in 1935 and lasted till the outbreak of war.[131]

The food-processing industries were particularly strong in Angola and Southern Rhodesia. In Angola, the government increased tariffs and withheld foreign exchange in order to stimulate this production and save scarce foreign currency.[132] But this policy ran into unforeseen obstacles. The authorities were particularly keen to put an end to the ridiculous situation whereby Angola exported wheat to Portugal for very low profits while importing wheat flour from distant Australia. A new flour mill was set up in Lobito, but for years it was unable to operate because of an obscure legal dispute between the owners and their creditors, the Banco Nacional Ultramarino.[133] Other forms of food processing for the local market were spin-offs from export industries, most notably dried and canned fish.

Southern Rhodesia had the largest food-processing industry in the region, and a sizeable part of its manufactured exports to neighbouring territories consisted of dairy products, processed meat, jams and pickles, sugar, confectionery, and different types of flour. Exports followed the trend noted above, falling away to around 1933 and then recovering. This was an extremely diverse industry, split up into many small units, and it is therefore particularly difficult to gauge its progress in the absence of general statistics. All that one can say is that the steady formation of new companies in this sector through the 1930s is probably a sign of its vitality.[134]

CONCLUSION

Much work remains to be done on the process of industrialisation in this part of Africa, avoiding the deformed perceptions of both yesterday and today. Observers in the 1930s tended to see only mining and agriculture. The lack of industrial statistics for Southern Rhodesia is the most obvious expression of this strangely inadequate understanding of what was happening. And it has been reinforced in contemporary writings by the force of underdevelopment theory, which sees it as axiomatic that Europeans did not industrialise Africa.[135] I hope that this study has shown that industrialisation, whatever its many defects and omissions, was in fact in progress in this region.

The main contribution here of the 1930s recession lay in the indication it provided of the kinds of industry which were most suitable for this poor and undeveloped region. Industrialists came to appreciate the African mass market for consumer goods, although there has been a tenacious nationalist legend that consumer industries up to independence were limited to the settler market.[136] In fact entrepreneurs learned their lesson, and it is significant that the spurt of industrial growth which took place in Angola in the 1940s was concentrated on cheap cotton textiles and simple metal tools, major staple consumption items for rural Africans.[137]

The need to expand and deepen export processing was also revealed by the recession. Export substitution had many advantages over import substitution. Raw materials were local, economies of scale could easily be achieved, and the technology was often quite simple and well adapted to undeveloped economies. Backward linkages were more frequent than has been assumed. The production of intermediate goods was stimulated, crops found more secure markets, and opportunities to learn industrial skills were increased. Even forward linkages were present, in the sense that the economies of scale involved in export processing occasionally allowed the diversion of some output to the internal market at lower prices. A fine example of this was sawn wood, which was widely used in the construction sector of the economy.

A final lesson to be learned from the recession was the significance of the state in fostering industrialisation, with the Southern Rhodesian settler state clearly more committed to industry than non-settler colonial governments, and, amongst the latter, the Belgians more attuned to the needs of industry than other colonial powers. In the long run the African nationalist movements were the most ardent advocates of state-propelled industrialisation. And yet the resounding failure of so many of the nationalists' industrial programmes has prompted a critical reappraisal of the role of the state. The kind of state, the type of industrial programme, the natural and human resource base, and conditions in the international market cannot be ignored in a bid to achieve rapid industrialisation.[138] Governments in Africa struggling with the problems created for industry by the 1980s recession could do worse than consult the record of the 1930s, to ponder both the mistakes and the successes of states confronted with an earlier world depression.

NOTES

1 For an introduction to the region, see D. Birmingham and P. Martin (eds), *History of central Africa* (2 vols., Longman, London, 1983). Equatorial Africa is used here to refer to the Belgian empire, French Equatorial Africa, Cameroun, Angola, São Tomé and Spanish Guinea, while central Africa is restricted to British Central Africa and Mozambique.

2 J.-L. Vellut, 'Originalités et limites de l'industrie manufacturière au Congo Belge [*c.* 1920-1960]' in the catalogue of an exhibition organised by l'Union Royale Belge pour les Pays d'Outre-Mer, *Les Belges à l'étranger, exposition cinquantenaire, Bruxelles, 1985* (no publisher [Brussels, 1985]), pp.121-9 (I am grateful to J.-L. Vellut for letting me see a longer unpublished version of this study, and more generally for help with the economic history of Zaïre); J.-L. Lacroix, *Industrialisation au Congo* (Mouton, Paris, 1967); I.R.Phimister, 'Industrialisation in the periphery: Southern Rhodesia and South African trade relations between the wars', unpublished paper, African Studies Institute, Johannesburg, 28 July 1986. (I am grateful to Ian Phimister for allowing me to see this paper and for encouraging me in my venture into Zimbabwean waters.)

3 A. Wirz, 'Die Entwicklung der kolonialen Zwangswirtschaft in Belgisch-Kongo' in D. Rothermund (ed), *Die Peripherie in der Weltwirtschaftskrise: Afrika, Asien und Lateinamerika, 1929-1939* (G. Schoningh, Paderborn, 1983), pp.59-79; B. Jewsiewicki, 'The Great Depression and the making of the colonial economic system in the Belgian Congo', *African Economic History, 4* (1977), pp.153-76; K. Tshibangu, 'L'impact socio-économique de la grande crise économique dans les années 1929-1935 sur l'ancien Haut-Katanga industriel', unpublished PhD thesis, University of Lubumbashi, 1980; D. Hulec, 'Some aspects of the 1930s depression in Rhodesia', *Journal of Modern African Studies, 7*, 1 (1969), pp.95-105; J.A. Edwards, 'Southern Rhodesia: the response to adversity, 1935-1939', unpublished PhD thesis, University of London, 1978; F. Kouo, 'Les répercussions de la crise économique de 1929 au Cameroun', *Afrika Zamani*, 10-11 (1979), pp.100-31.

4 Southern Rhodesia, *Report of the Committee of Enquiry into the Protection of Secondary Industries in Southern Rhodesia* (Government Printer, Salisbury, 1946), pp.14 and 149.

5 I am very grateful to Wolfgang Döpcke for this information, and for a great deal of material which he has gathered for his doctoral thesis on Southern Rhodesia in the 1930s, and made available to me. The figures for industrial output are in Southern Rhodesia, *Report*, p.14.

6 G. Vandewalle, *De conjuncturele evolutie in Kongo en Ruanda-Urundi, van 1920 tot 1939 en van 1949 tot 1958* (Rijksuniversiteit te Gent, Ghent, 1966), p.39.

7 D.G. Clarke, *Foreign companies and international investment in Zimbabwe* (Mambo Press, Gwelo, 1980), p.21; Vandewalle, *De conjuncturele evolutie*, ch. 6; A.S. Gonçalves, 'O crédito de fomento em Angola', *Boletim da Associação Industrial de Angola, 4*, 15-16 (1953), pp.8-9.

8 R. Thorp (ed), *Latin America in the 1930s* (Macmillan, London, 1984), *passim.*

9 J. Gouverneur, *Productivity and factor proportions in less developed countries: the case of industrial firms in the Congo* (Clarendon Press, Oxford, 1971), *passim.*

10 J. Marseille, 'L'industrialisation des colonies: affaiblissement ou renforcement de la puissance française?', *Revue Française d'Histoire d'Outremer, 69*, 254 (1982), pp.23-34; or see his *Empire colonial et capitalisme français, histoire d'un divorce* (Albin Michel, Paris, 1984), ch.10.

11 Wirz, 'Die Entwicklung', and Phimister, 'Industrialisation', *passim.*

12 G. Clarence-Smith, *The third Portuguese empire, 1825-1975, a study in economic imperialism* (Manchester University Press, Manchester, 1985), ch.6; Marseille, *Empire colonial*, ch.10.

13 Different branches of industry are dealt with in detail later in this study.

14 Phimister, 'Industrialisation', pp.4-13.

15 Hulec, 'Some aspects', pp.100-1.

16 D.J. Murray, *The governmental system in Southern Rhodesia* (Clarendon Press, Oxford, 1970), pp.165 and 174-6.

17 Phimister, 'Industrialisation', p.9; quoting *New Rhodesia*, advertisement for the 'Buy Rhodesian' League (my thanks go to W. Döpcke for letting me have a photocopy of this).

18 I.R. Phimister, 'Zimbabwe: the path of capitalist development' in Birmingham and Martin, *History of central Africa*, vol.2, pp.267-80; and his 'Industrialisation', p.13.

19 Southern Rhodesia, *Report of the Committee of Enquiry into the Protection of Secondary Industries in Southern Rhodesia*, (Government Printer, Salisbury, 1946), pp.82-3.

20 Hulec, 'Some aspects', pp.100-1.

21 Phimister, 'Industrialisation', pp.8-9.

22 P. Mosley, *The settler economies: studies in the economic history of Kenya and Southern Rhodesia, 1900-1963* (Cambridge University Press, Cambridge, 1983), p.211.

23 Hulec, 'Some aspects', p.101.

24 R.L. Cole, 'The tariff policy of Rhodesia', *Rhodesian Journal of Economics*, 2, 2 (1968), p.29.

25 Southern Rhodesia, *Report*, p.52.

26 Southern Rhodesia, *Report of the Commission of Enquiry into the Mining Industry of Southern Rhodesia* (Government Printer, Salisbury, 1945).

27 Hulec, 'Some aspects', pp.95-6.

28 For one example of such government initiative, see Murray, *The governmental system*, pp.135-6.

29 Hulec, 'Some aspects', p.100.

30 Cole, 'The tariff policy', p.29.

31 Mosley, *The settler economies*, pp.208 and 211.

32 *Rhodesian Manual on Mining, Industry and Agriculture*, 1927-38, sections on Portuguese East Africa.

33 I am grateful to Wolfgang Döpcke for sending me numerous photocopies of his data on industry in the 1930s.

34 J.-L. Vellut, 'Hégémonies en construction: articulations entre état et entreprises dans le bloc colonial belge, 1908-1960', *Canadian Journal of African Studies*, *16*, 2 (1982), pp.313-30.

35 Wirz, 'Die Entwicklung', pp.62 and 68; Tshibangu, 'L'impact socio-économique', pp.193, 199, 204 and 459.

36 Lacroix, *Industrialisation*, pp.20 and 101-6.

37 Wirz, 'Die Entwicklung', p.63.

38 Lacroix, *Industrialisation*, pp.19-20.

39 Belgium, Chambre des Représentants, *Rapport Annuel sur l'Administration de la Colonie du Congo Belge*, 1929-39; Tshibangu, 'L'impact socio-économique', pp.119, 129-31, 192 and 342-6.

40 Wirz, 'Die Entwicklung', pp.59-61 and 64.

41 Vandewalle, *De conjuncturele evolutie*, p.306.

42 Wirz, 'Die Entwicklung', pp.62, 66-8.

43 Clarence-Smith, *The third Portuguese empire*, ch.6.

44 G. Lefebvre, *L'Angola, son histoire, son économie* (G. Thone, Liège, 1947), p.115.

45 A. Castro, *O sistema colonial português em Africa* (Editorial Caminho, Lisbon, 1978), p.132, n.

46 A. Monteiro, *O problema das transferencias de Angola* (Imprensa Nacional, Lisbon, 1931); H. Ford, *Economic conditions in Portuguese East Africa* (Dept of Overseas Trade, London, 1933), pp.13-16 and 45; C. Rocha Dilolwa, *Contribuição à historia económica de Angola* (no publisher, Luanda, 1978), pp.38-9.

47 Lefebvre, *L'Angola*, p.115.

48 H. Kay, *Salazar and modern Portugal* (Eyre and Spottiswoode, London, 1970), p.45.

49 F.O. Meara, *Report on economic and commercial conditions in Angola* (Dept of Overseas Trade, London, 1937), pp.2-3 and 7.

50 D.O. Fynes-Clinton, *Portuguese West Africa: economic and commercial conditions in Portuguese West Africa* (Dept of Overseas Trade, London, 1949), p.5.

51 S. Kay and C. Ezard, *Report on economic and commercial conditions in Portuguese East Africa* (Dept of Overseas Trade, London, 1938); Lefebvre, *L'Angola, passim.*

52 France, *Rapport Annuel au Conseil de la Société des Nations sur l'Administration sous Mandat du Territoire du Cameroun*; D. Bouesse, 'L'évolution du commerce extérieur du Congo-Brazzaville entre les deux guerres mondiales, 1920-1937', unpublished MA thesis, Université de Paris-I, 1971.

53 Archives Nationales, Section Outre-Mer (ANSOM), Paris, Affaires Economiques, Défense Nationale, Carton 13, Rapport (mobilisation commerciale et industrielle) Afrique Equatoriale Française, 24 February 1939.

54 ANSOM, Affaires Politiques, Carton 2853, Dossier 3, Industrial Census 1938 (AEF); Carton 2695, Dossier 7, Industrial Census 1938 (Cameroun).

55 D. Ndongo Bidyogo, *Historia y tragedia de Guinea Ecuatorial* (Editorial Cambio, Madrid, 1977), pp.44 and 47-50; R. Perpiña Grau, *De colonización y conomía en la Guinea Española* (Editorial Labor, Barcelona, 1945).

56 Belgium, *Rapport Annuel*, 1931, pp.61-2.

57 P.L. Yates, *Commodity control, a study of primary products* (Jonathan Cape, London, 1943), pp.162 and 166-7.

58 F. Coleman, *The Northern Rhodesian Copperbelt, 1899-1962* (Manchester University Press, Manchester, 1971), p.76.

59 Ibid., pp.66 and 75-6; S. Cunningham, *The copper industry in Zambia* (Praeger, New York, 1981), pp.174-6.

60 Tshibangu, 'L'impact socio-économique', pp.222, 236, 246-59 and *passim*; Vandewalle, *De conjuncturele evolutie*, pp.249-50 and 306-7.

61 Coleman, *The Northern Rhodesian Copperbelt*, pp.xviii-xx, 50, 58, 77 and 142; C.C. Luchembe, 'Finance capital and mine labour, a comparative study of copperminers in Zambia and Peru', unpublished PhD thesis, University of California at Los Angeles, 1982, pp.214 and 217-20.

62 C. Thompson and H. Woodruff, *Economic development in Rhodesia and Nyasaland* (Dennis Dobson, London, 1953), p.159.

63 M. Rey, 'La métallurgie des minerais congolais', *Revue Universelle des Mines, 13*, 3 (1937), pp.115-21; *Union Minière du Haut-Katanga, 1906-1956, évolution des techniques et des activités sociales* (UMHK, Brussels, 1957); Vandewalle, *De conjuncturele evolutie*, pp.247-53.

64 *Union Minière du Haut-Katanga*, pp.134 and 200.

65 For the complex activities of the SGB, see P. Joye and R. Lewin, *Les trusts au Congo* (Société Populaire d'Editions, Brussels, 1961); see also J.-L. Vellut, 'Les bassins miniers de l'ancien Congo Belge, essai d'histoire économique et sociale, 1900-1960', *Les Cahiers du CEDAF*, Cahier 7 (1981), pp.2-18.

66 A. Bakonzi, 'The gold mines of Kilo-Moto in north-eastern Zaïre, 1905-1960', unpublished PhD thesis, University of Wisconsin, 1982, vol.1, pp.274-94.

67 Belgium, *Rapport Annuel*, 1931-9; Rey, 'La métallurgie', p.120.

68 For details and photographs, see *Rhodesian Manual on Mining, Industry and Agriculture*, 1935-6, section on companies.

69 I.R. Phimister, 'Gold mining in Southern Rhodesia, 1919-1953', *Rhodesian Journal of Economics, 10,* 1 (1976), p.36.

70 Vandewalle, *De conjuncturele evolutie*, pp.37-8, 243-6 and 305-7; Vellut, 'Les bassins miniers', pp.31-5.

71 *Union Minière du Haut-Katanga*, pp.146-9; Rey, 'La métallurgie', p.120.

72 *Rhodesian Manual on Mining, Industry and Agriculture,* 1935-6, pp.297 and 363.

73 R. Dumett, 'Africa's strategic minerals during the second World War', *Journal of African History, 26,* 4 (1985), p.398.

74 Jewsiewicki, 'The Great Depression', p.158 and *passim.*

75 For French Equatorial Africa, D. Bouesse, 'L'histoire de l'exploitation forestière au Congo, des origines à la veille de la seconde guerre mondiale', thèse de 3e cycle, Université de Paris-VII, 1980; G. Lasserre, *Libreville, la ville et sa région* (A. Colin, Paris, 1958), pp.147-50; C.F. Pambo-Loueya, 'La colonie du Gabon de 1914 à 1939, étude économique et sociale', unpublished thèse de 3e cycle, Université de Paris-VII, 1980, pp.253-5 and 381; for Spanish Guinea, Ndongo Bidyogo, *Historia,* pp.43-6; for Cameroun, France, *Rapport Annuel*; for Northern Rhodesia, J. Brigden, *Economic conditions in Southern Rhodesia, Northern Rhodesia and Nyasaland, 1935* (Dept of Overseas Trade, London, 1936), pp.39 and 47.

76 Bouesse, 'L'histoire', pp.215-53.

77 D.K. Fieldhouse, *Unilever overseas* (Croom Helm, London, 1978), pp.514-16; E. Leplae, *Le palmier à huile en Afrique: son exploitation au Congo Belge et en Extrême-Orient* (IRCB, Brussels, 1939); B. Mumbanza, 'Les ambiguïtés d'un "développement économique": petite entreprise industrielle, état et économie locale: l'huilerie d'Ebeka, 1929-1980' in B. Jewsiewicki and J.-P. Chrétien (eds), *Sociétés rurales et technologies en Afrique Centrale et Occidentale au XIXe siècle* (Ed. SAFI, Québec, 1984), pp.161-232; Vandewalle, *De conjuncturele evolutie*, p.39; Belgium, *Rapport Annuel.*

78 Bouesse, 'L'évolution du commerce', pp.83-8; Kouo, 'Les répercussions', p.112.

79 ANSOM, Affaires Politiques, C2695 (7); France, *Rapport Annuel,* 1938.

80 V. Thompson and R. Adloff, *The emerging states of French Equatorial Africa* (Stanford University Press, Stanford, 1960), p.186; ANSOM, Affaires Politiques, C2853 (3).

81 J.M. Cerqueira d'Azevedo, *Angola, exemplo de trabalho* (no publisher, Luanda, 1958), p.389; J. do C. Rosado, *Angola, notas ligeiras* (A. Ramos, Lisbon, 1937), pp.47 and 108.

82 Companhia do Açúcar de Angola, *Companhia do Açúcar de Angola* (privately printed, Lisbon, 1940), tables.

83 Agencia Geral do Ultramar, *São Tomé e Príncipe, pequena monografia* (AGC, Lisbon, 1964), p.65.

84 J. Nosti, *Agricultura de Guinea, promesa para España* (IEA, Madrid, 1948), pp.59-62 and 86; M. Liniger-Goumaz, *La Guinée Equatoriale, un pays méconnu* (L'Harmattan, Paris, 1979), pp.390-1; Perpiña Grau, *De colonización*, pp.210-11 and 334.

85 Fieldhouse, *Unilever*, pp.521-6.

86 C. Coquery-Vidrovitch, *Le Congo au temps des grandes compagnies concessionnaires* (Mouton, Paris, 1972), pp.359-62.

87 Sena Sugar Estates, *Moçambique e o problema açucareiro* (privately printed, Lisbon, 1945); L. Vail and L. White, *Capitalism and colonialism in Mozambique* (Heinemann, London, 1980), ch.6; Companhia do Açúcar de Angola, *Companhia*, tables; G. Clarence-Smith, 'Protectionism and sugar production in central and equatorial Africa, 1910-1945', unpublished paper, conference on 'Crisis and Change in the International Sugar Economy, 1914-1945', University of East Anglia, 10-14 September 1986.

88 Vellut, 'Originalités'; Wirz, 'Die Entwicklung', p.66. Figures in annexes of Belgium, Ministère des Colonies, *Plan décennal pour le développement économique et social du Congo Belge* (De Visscher, Brussels, 1949), vol.2, p.575.

89 Federation of Rhodesia and Nyasaland, *Report of the Commission of Enquiry into the Sugar Industry* (Government Printer, Salisbury, 1962).

90 I.R. Phimister, 'Meat and monopolies: beef cattle in Southern Rhodesia, 1890-1938', *Journal of African History, 19*, 3 (1978), pp.391-414.

91 Azevedo, *Angola*, pp.398-425; C. Carneiro, *Conservas de peixe* (Primeira Exposição Colonial Portuguesa, Luanda, 1934).

92 See statistics on mechanised installations in: Belgium, *Rapport Annuel*, from 1933 onwards.

93 For Belgian Congo, Wirz, 'Die Entwicklung', pp.65 and 75; for Chad, U. Sturzinger, *Der Baumwollanbau im Tschad* (Atlantis, Zurich, 1980), ch.2; for Portuguese territories, Clarence-Smith, *The third Portuguese empire*, pp.149-50.

94 R. Palmer, 'The Nyasaland tea industry in the era of international tea restrictions, 1933-1950', *Journal of African History, 26*, 2-3 (1985), pp.215-39; Vail and White, *Capitalism*, pp.265-72.

95 Tshibangu, 'L'impact socio-économique', vol.1, p.132.

96 Gouverneur, *Productivity*, pp.59, 158, 162 and 166.

97 C. Serra (ed), *História de Moçambique* (Tempo, Maputo, 1983), vol.2, p.259; S. Kay, *Economic conditions in Portuguese East Africa* (Dept of Overseas Trade, London, 1935), pp.16, 23 and 26; Kay and Ezard, *Report*, pp.23 and 56.

98 R. von Gersdorff, *Moçambique* (K. Schroeder, Bonn, 1958), p.69. The date of this foreclosure is nowhere given, but it was probably in the early 1930s.

99 J. Tristão de Bettencourt, *Relatório do governador geral de Moçambique, 1940-1942* (Agencia Geral do Ultramar, Lisbon, 1945), vol.2, pp.126-7.

100 H. Ford, *Economic conditions in Portuguese East Africa* (Dept of Overseas Trade, London, 1933), p.36; Kay, *Economic conditions*, p.17; Kay and Ezard, *Report*, p.25.

101 Figures and information kindly supplied by Wolfgang Döpcke.

102 Southern Rhodesia, *Report* (secondary industries), pp.63-5.

103 Mosley, *The settler economies*, pp.211-12; Phimister, 'Industrialisation', p.3.

104 Gouverneur, *Productivity*, p.162.

105 Ibid., pp.43, 47, 60 and 154; Belgium, *Plan décennal*, p.577.

106 Mosley, *The settler economies*, p.211; Southern Rhodesia, *Report* (secondary industries), pp.63-5.

107 Sena Sugar, *Moçambique*, pp.160-2.

108 Phimister, 'Industrialisation', p.3.

109 Figures and information kindly supplied by Wolfgang Döpcke.

110 Southern Rhodesia, *Report* (secondary industries), pp.63-5.

111 Belgium, *Rapport Annuel*.

112 Ibid.

113 M. Soret, *Histoire du Congo-Brazzaville* (Berger-Levrault, Paris, 1978), p.161.

114 C. Young and T. Turner, *The rise and decline of the Zaïrean state* (University of Wisconsin Press, Madison, 1985), pp.298-300.

115 A.J. Wills, *An introduction to the history of central Africa* (Oxford University Press, London, 1967), p.371; Belgium, *Plan décennal*, p.86; Clarence-Smith, *The third Portuguese empire*, p.178.

116 For case studies, see E. Tshund'olela, 'Politique coloniale, économie capitaliste et développement au Congo Belge, cas du Kasai', unpublished PhD thesis, University of Lubumbashi, 1980; Tshibangu, 'L'impact socio-économique'.

117 Fieldhouse, *Unilever*, pp.381-3; ANSOM, Affaires Politiques, C2697 (7), for Greeks in Cameroun.

118 A. de Almeida Teixeira, *Angola intangível* (Primeira Exposição Colonial Portuguesa, Oporto, 1934), p.644.

119 Lefebvre, *L'Angola*, p.143; O'Meara, *Report*, p.28.

120 Marseille, *Empire colonial*, pp.188-97.

121 Cole, 'The tariff policy', p.29. Information on the new garments companies kindly supplied by Wolfgang Döpcke.

122 J. van Ypersele de Strihou, 'Variations des coéfficients de fabrication dans une entreprise congolaise, et équilibre économique', *Recherches Economiques de Louvain*, *27*, 2 (1961), pp.47-96; Vellut, 'Originalités', *passim*.

123 Azevedo, *Angola*, pp.343-5 and 360-1.

124 Lacroix, *Industrialisation*, pp.259-60; Vellut, 'Originalités'; Belgium, *Rapport Annuel*, 1934, p.80.

125 Teixeira, *Angola*, p.446.

126 Kay, *Economic conditions*, p.16; Kay and Ezard, *Report*, p.23; Bettencourt, *Relatório*, vol.2, pp.126-7.

127 Lacroix, *Industrialisation*, p.313; E. van der Straeten, *L'agriculture et les industries agricoles au Congo Belge* (CCCI, Brussels, 1945), p.313.

128 Teixeira, *Angola*, pp.688-9; O'Meara, *Report*, p.29.

129 Lefebvre, *L'Angola*, p.158.

130 Kay, *Economic conditions*, pp.16-17; Kay and Ezard, *Report*, p.24.

131 Information kindly supplied by Wolfgang Döpcke.

132 Dilolwa, *Contribuição*, pp.38-9.

133 Rosado, *Angola*, pp.41 and 51.

134 Information kindly supplied by Wolfgang Döpcke.

135 See for example, W. Rodney, *How Europe underdeveloped Africa* (Bogle-L'Ouverture, London, 1972), pp.237-9.

136 One example among many is provided by A. and B. Isaacman, *Mozambique, from colonialism to revolution, 1900-1982* (Westview Press, Boulder, 1983), p.161.

137 Clarence-Smith, *The third Portuguese empire*, p.164.

138 For general discussions, see P. Kilby, 'Manufacturing in colonial Africa' in P. Duignan and L. Gann (eds), *Colonialism in Africa, 1870-1960* (Cambridge University Press, Cambridge, 1975), vol.4, pp.470-520; M. Fransman (ed) *Industry and accumulation in Africa* (Heinemann, London, 1982).

10

SOME COMMENTS ON INDUSTRIALISATION IN THE PHILIPPINES DURING THE 1930s

IAN BROWN[1]

It is commonly observed that the sharp contraction in world trading activity from the end of the1920s provided a major stimulus for the expansion of industrial production in a number of non-European primary exporting economies. The observation appears perhaps most frequently with respect to the economies of Latin America. Thus in an introductory essay in *Latin America in the 1930s: the role of the periphery in world crisis,* the editor sees the depression as being of 'enormous significance' in building on and pushing further trends in industrialisation established in the preceding decades,[2] while later contributors to that volume present in formidable detail evidence of notably impressive rates of growth in manufacturing output in Latin America over the depression decade. The precise course of industrial expansion inevitably differed in the individual states of the region, but a broad common experience is clearly discernible. In essence, the sharp fall in export earnings from the late 1920s, frequently in alliance with a major contraction in capital inflows, dramatically reduced the capacity of Latin American economies to import.[3] Thus faced with threatening exchange shortages, governments adopted major defensive measures, notably devaluation, exchange control and tariffs. It was behind this protective wall that the expansion in manufacturing output was secured, most prominently and typically in the production of textiles, refined petroleum, tyres, pharmaceuticals, toiletries, processed food for the domestic market (for example vegetable oils), chemicals and cement. In a number of economies the growth in industrial output was sustained in part by expansionary macroeconomic policy; and it was facilitated (notably in Brazil) by the existence of substantial spare capacity in the industrial sector on the eve of the depression.

This paper will offer some comments on industrialisation in the Philippines during the 1930s, drawing comparisons and contrasts from the experience of Latin America outlined too briefly above.

I

At the opening of the twentieth century the Philippine Islands was firmly established as an important producer of primary commodities for the world market, export production being concentrated in sugar, abaca (Manila hemp), coconuts and tobacco. However the cession of the Islands to the United States in early 1899 (following the brief Spanish-American War the previous year) and, in particular, the institution of virtual free trade between the colony and the new imperial power secured under the Payne-Aldrich Tariff Act of 1909 and the Underwood-Simmons Tariff Act of 1913, provided a particularly marked stimulus to export production and, of greater importance in the context of this paper, directed Philippine exports overwhelmingly towards the American market. Thus while the United States had absorbed only some 19 per cent of the total value of Philippine exports in the years 1899-1901, on the eve of the 1930s depression that figure was approaching 80 per cent.[4] For a number of the individual export trades the dependence on the American market was even greater. This was notably the case with sugar, by far the single most important Philippine export in the inter-war period, accounting for 30 per cent of the total annual income of the Islands in the mid-1930s, contributing (directly and indirectly) 43 per cent of government revenue, and providing (directly and indirectly) a livelihood for 6 million Filipinos out of a total population of some 14.5 million.[5] Afforded privileged access to the American market from 1909,[6] the Islands' sugar producers had thereafter experienced only a limited pressure to improve productivity either in the cultivation of the crop or in the crushing of the cane, at a time when other major sugar producers, notably Java, were pursuing substantial innovations. Consequently, in the early 1930s production per hectare in Java (on the European sugar plantations) was some 3.6 times that in the Philippines; and it was estimated that the Philippine cost of production in that decade was more than twice that of the Dutch island.[7] In the period 1925-8 the United States absorbed on average 93.2 per cent of the total value of Philippine sugar exports; in the years 1931-41 that figure never fell below 99.8 per cent.[8] There was every reason to fear that this critically important export trade would not survive outside the protected American market.

The close of Spanish rule and the opening three decades of American administration also saw a growth in production of finished manufactures in the Islands (as distinct from the partial processing of raw materials or small-scale craft production in households and workshops) which, although modest when measured by its contribution to national product or to the absorption of labour, was notably substantial in absolute terms. Four such initiatives from this pre-depression period stand out. Two concerned the manufacture of finished articles (principally for export) from locally cultivated raw materials - cigars and cordage. The factory production of cigars had been an important element in a government monopoly (which also embraced the cultivation of tobacco, the collection of the harvested leaf and the retail sale of tobacco products) established by the Spanish administration towards the end of the eighteenth century. With the dismantling of that monopoly at the beginning of the 1880s cigar production was taken over by a number of private concerns of which by far the most important was La Compañia General de Tabacos de Filipinas, founded in Spain in 1881.[9] In the opening decades of the twentieth century cigar production and exports soared, reaching their peak in 1920. In that year exports stood at 415 million cigars (the annual average for 1902-8 had been around 110 million) and employment (in both cigar and cigarette factories) in Greater Manila (where production was concentrated) exceeded 15,000.[10] Exports then fell very sharply, partially recovered during 1922-3, and then declined for the remainder of the decade, levelling out in the early 1930s at less than half the 1920 peak. This contraction was due primarily to increasingly powerful competition in the crucial United States market from machine-made American brands, promoted by national advertising, and to a major shift in consumer preference in all markets away from cigars and towards cigarettes. Although the manufacture of cordage in modern steam-powered mills was established in the Philippines from the 1840s, local concerns absorbed only a small fraction of the Islands' abaca production during the subsequent decades of rapid expansion, manufacture being concentrated overseas, notably in the United States and Britain.[11] However, in the early 1920s, one of the major American manufacturers, Tubbs Cordage Company of San Francisco, for long an important buyer of abaca, purchased a small, failed rope mill in Manila and recapitalised it as the Manila Cordage Company.[12] Tubbs's decision to establish manufacturing in the Islands was prompted by rising production costs in the United States (which had caused it to lose markets) and by the prospect of appreciably lower costs in Manila where abaca supplies were at hand and labour cheap. Within a few years Manila Cordage's expanding production was finding markets throughout Asia and beyond; at the end of the 1930s the company had a work-force of some 200.

The remaining two industrial initiatives to be noted from this earlier period concerned the manufacture of finished articles for the domestic market in competition with imports - beer and cement. The production of beer rested with one company, San Miguel, founded in 1890 by Don Enrique María Barretto y de Ycaza, a Spanish businessman long resident in Manila.[13] During the company's early years there were a number of major changes in ownership and management, but by the late 1910s San Miguel was under the administration of Don Andrés Soriano, who was to remain the dominant influence within the company throughout the inter-war years. In its competition with imported beers, San Miguel was disadvantaged by a need to import (primarily from central and eastern Europe) its basic raw materials (malt and hops). But it also enjoyed an important measure of natural protection in that beer loses its full characteristics within a few weeks of being brewed: with the establishment of a fine natural local beer (and in this period San Miguel engaged only German brewmasters in its plant), the discerning drinkers of Manila were quick to reject imported beers which, of necessity, contained artificial preservatives to sustain them during the long sea voyage to the Islands.[14] San Miguel also benefited, fortuitously, from Prohibition in the United States, which removed American beers from the Philippine market between 1919 and 1933.[15] In these circumstances San Miguel rapidly dominated local sales. As early as 1908 it outsold imported beers by over five to one.[16] Twenty years later, on the eve of the depression, it accounted for approximately 90 per cent of domestic beer consumption.[17] During the 1920s San Miguel also began a substantial diversification of its interests, undertaking the manufacture of soft drinks and dairy products and securing (in 1927) exclusive rights for bottling and distributing Coca-Cola in the Philippines.[18] In the following decade it began the manufacture of yeast and glass bottles, and acquired interests in Cold Storage Creameries of Singapore and in the George Muehlebach Brewing Company of Kansas City.

The second prominent import-substituting industry of the pre-depression decades, cement, provides a marked contrast to the beer-San Miguel initiative. It was considerably less successful in commercial terms, at least in its early years, and it was held largely in government ownership. Portland cement became widely used in the Philippines only from the early 1900s, demand at first being met through imports, primarily from Hong Kong.[19] A local cement company was then established in 1912, financed by the Recollect friar order in alliance with a number of prominent Manila businessmen.[20] The factory was located at Binangonan, on the northern shore of Laguna de Bay. It was equipped by Krupps of Germany and operated by German technicians. Production began in 1914, but in spite of a war-induced boom in cement prices the company failed to establish a secure position in the Philippine market. It was seriously hindered by technical weaknesses in its plant, the near-impossibility of securing spare parts from Germany once that country was at war and eventually by the internment of its German technical staff when the United States entered the hostilities in 1917. In 1918 the company ceased production.[21] Eventually, in 1928, the concern was acquired by Vicente Madrigal, a prominent local industrialist.[22] Renamed the Rizal Cement Company, it rapidly resumed operation.

A few years prior to this restoration, the government itself had entered the cement industry. Its instrument in this respect was the National Development Company (NDC), created in 1919 to 'engage in commercial, industrial, and other enterprises which may be necessary or contributory to the economic development of the country or important in the public interest'.[23] In 1921 the NDC put up the capital for the establishment of the Cebu Portland Cement Company, whose plant was to be located at Naga on the island of Cebu.[24] The actual founding and initial operation of the enterprise was contracted to a private American businessman, C.F. Massey, but in 1924 the NDC assumed management of the concern. In its first two years of production the Cebu Portland Cement Company apparently suffered heavy losses as imported cement undercut it. But then the government intervened with two major measures of protection - the introduction of a law which required that only cement from the Cebu Portland Cement Company be used in government construction work, and the imposition of a tariff on imported cement.[25] In the four years 1926-9 the company produced on average almost 67 million kilograms of cement per annum:[26] in the same period the average annual import was a little over 44 million kilograms.[27]

Finally in this introduction, brief reference must be made to the political circumstances of the Philippines in this period for, as the following section will establish, those circumstances were to have a major influence on industrial developments in the Islands during the 1930s. From the establishment of American rule at the close of the nineteenth century, the imperial government had moved to transfer political and administrative authority to the indigenous population at a speed and on a scale almost certainly unparalleled in the colonial world of the time. There was a progressive extension of political power to Filipinos from the institution of municipal elections in 1901 to the establishment of an elected Senate in 1916, and a progressive transfer of bureaucratic positions from Americans to the local population such that by the end of the 1920s 'virtually the entire colonial government, from cabinet ministers down to postal clerks, was manned by Filipinos'.[28] The rapidly gathering electoral and bureaucratic authority of Filipinos during this period was accompanied by the emergence of a vociferous, if primarily elite-orientated, nationalist movement which demanded immediate and full independence. In fact the prospect of independence for the Philippines 'as soon as a stable government can be established therein' was formally admitted by the United States, never entirely at ease with its imperial responsibilities, as early as 1916.

That prospect moved decisively towards reality as the United States was plunged into severe depression in the early 1930s. The important influence here was pressure from powerful metropolitan interests - notably beet-sugar farmers, dairymen, bankers with over-extended investments in Cuban sugar and some labour unions - which in crisis sought an end to the unrestricted access of Philippine trade and labour to the American market.[29] The negotiation and passage of independence legislation, temporarily slowed by rivalries within the nationalist elite, was completed in May 1934 when the Philippine Senate ratified the Tydings-McDuffie Act, passed by the United States Senate the previous March. That act provided for the establishment of an autonomous Philippine Commonwealth (in fact inaugurated on 15 November 1935) as the transitional prelude to the complete surrender of American sovereignty on 4 July 1946. On independence, Philippine exports to the United States would attract the full American tariff. To prepare the Islands' dominant economic interests for this major reversal, from 1941 exports enjoying preferential treatment in the metropolitan market were to be subject to an export tax, initially of 5 per cent but increasing annually to 25 per cent in 1946.[30]

II

The prospect of the termination of tariff preference in the American market in July 1946 caused profound alarm to the Commonwealth administration in the second half of the 1930s, for it was widely held that it would bring economic ruin to the Islands. The response was twofold: to seek a renegotiation with the United States of the trade provisions of the independence settlement and to attempt a substantial restructuring of the Philippine economy. In large measure the latter implied industrialisation.[31]

The broad strategy was clear. The administration was to initiate or expand the manufacture (usually from local raw materials) of articles of domestic consumption which hitherto had been largely imported, and in this way compensate for the fall in export earnings that would occur as the Philippines lost its tariff advantages in the United States market; a secondary aim, frequently argued, was to establish manufacturing (again drawing on local raw materials) for export. But the detail was not adequately resolved. Most notably, there appears to have been no precise consideration as to how far the industrialisation initiative was to proceed, nor clear agreement as to the particular manufacturing concerns it would encompass. Thus although the administration quickly identified a number of relatively modest industrial opportunities (the manufacture of cotton yarn, soap, processed foods, furniture, shoes, paper),[32] within a short time far more ambitious projects were being proposed (the establishment of fertiliser, caustic soda, steel and pig iron plants).[33] On occasions the call was heard (notably from the administration's scientific officers) for 'the complete industrialization of the country'.[34]

Neither can it be said that the Commonwealth administration gave adequate consideration to the economic costs and commercial viability of even a modest programme of import-substituting industrialisation. Most notably there appears to have been no coherent response to the argument that import-substituting industries would face fierce competition from an increasingly powerful Japanese industrial sector as well as from American manufacturing interests, continuing to enjoy free entry to the Philippine market until 1946. Certainly this was an argument frequently rehearsed in the business press. For example, the *American Chamber of Commerce Journal*, in its issue for January 1938, scathingly noted the commitment of substantial public funds to the construction of a textile mill that would have to compete against immeasurably more efficient and productive Japanese factories: 'to fight Japanese industry here with competing [local] industry financed by taxpayers is a losing game'.[35] In an editorial in June 1937, *Business and Finance* referred to the government 'throwing away millions of pesos into an ambitious program of industrialization of doubtful success', and noted that even the government initiative most prominently fêted by the proponents of industrialisation, the Cebu Portland Cement Company, owed its survival to substantial tariff protection (which raised domestic prices) and to legislation which gave the company a monopoly in the supply of cement for public construction projects.[36]

It should be added that *Business and Finance* proposed, as an alternative, that the government concentrate on raising the efficiency of existing agricultural export production, in order that the Philippines be able to compete effectively in world commodity markets. But this was an alternative firmly dismissed by senior administration figures, who argued that for the Philippines now to compete successfully in primary markets would require her to compete against countries with extremely low wages and harsh working practices (specifically Java, India, Formosa, Malaya, Sumatra), and thus would demand a most dramatic reduction in the standard of living of Filipinos, with the certain prospect of social unrest and violent protest;[37] that for the Philippines to remain predominantly a primary exporting country would imply her continued subservience to the industrial economies, in particular, given the weakening of ties with the United States, subservience to the rising industrial power of Japan.[38] These were indeed strong arguments for the determined pursuit of industrialisation.

The primary instrument of government-driven industrialisation was the National Development Company, whose legal powers, financial resources and management were substantially strengthened from the opening of the Commonwealth period.[39] The industrial efforts of the NDC were concentrated in three areas. First, it increased the production capacity of the Cebu Portland Cement Company to some 425,000 kilograms a day (in 1940), two and a half times the initial (1924) capacity of the concern.[40] Increased capacity at the government cement plant was accompanied by an expansion at Vicente Madrigal's Rizal Cement Company.[41] Second, the NDC, through a subsidiary, the National Food Products Corporation, established a canning plant at Guagua, in the province of Pampanga, north-west of Manila.[42] Beginning production in early 1939, the plant had an annual capacity of 5.4 million cans and canned bañgus (fish) and a variety of vegetables and fruits. Construction of a further cannery, in Capiz on the island of Panay, canning bañgus, was under way in early 1941.[43] As a complement to this emerging industry, in 1938 the NDC established a tin-can factory in Manila, pressing cans from imported tin sheets.[44] And third, the NDC founded a major cotton textile mill in Manila, production beginning in mid-1939. The primary purpose of the concern was to prepare yarn for the domestic hand-weavers (in northern Luzon) but the plant also contained weaving, bleaching, dyeing and printing divisions to produce finished textiles.[45] Supplies of raw cotton were secured almost solely through imports from the United States (although a major expansion of domestic cultivation was envisaged);[46] in addition substantial quantities of grey cloth were imported to maintain production in the bleaching, dyeing and printing divisions of the mill.[47] On its opening the NDC mill possessed 10,000 spindles and 104 mechanical looms, but this was increased in 1941 to 20,000 spindles and 500 looms.[48] With the initial capacity it was estimated that the mill would reduce Philippine cotton textile imports by 10 per cent, but it was anticipated that with the expansion of the plant this would (by the mid-1940s) rise to about 30 per cent.[49]

Some measure of the extent of import-substituting industrialisation in the Philippines at the end of the 1930s can be drawn from the census of 1939.[50] But two preliminary observations are required. The census did not fully capture the industrial employment created by the NDC, for some of the NDC plants (the Guagua cannery and the textile mill) did not come into operation until after the census enumeration. Second, the census return for certain 'manufacturing' occupations (notably 'Shoe and slipper manufacture', said to employ 20,271) combined employment in small workshops with (the concern here) employment in modern factories. Noting those points, the following table is offered simply to indicate scale.

TABLE 1: Employment in selected modern industry, manufacturing for the domestic market, January 1939

Lime and cement manufacture	1,687
Textile manufacture	289
Breweries	523
Liquor and beverage manufacture	311
Dairy products manufacture	448
Fish, sea products, pineapple, fruit and vegetable canning	388

Source: Philippines (Commonwealth), Commission of the Census, *Census of the Philippines: 1939* (Bureau of Printing, Manila, 1940-3), vol.2, p.489.

A further indication is provided by the estimate of gross national product in 1938 (broken down by economic sector) included in an appendix to the report of the Joint Philippine-American Finance Commission, presented in 1947.

TABLE 2: Gross national product in 1938

Economic Sector	Millions of pesos	Per cent
Agricultural crops and their products[a]	482	41.4
Livestock and products	52	4.5
Forest products and building	60	5.1
Fisheries	60	5.1
Mining	72	6.2
Manufacturing not elsewhere included[b]	30	2.6
Value added to consumers' goods imports[c]	137	11.8
Services not elsewhere included[d]	270	23.3
	1,163	100.0

[a] Includes the processing of agricultural products (p.10).

[b] Manufacturing other than the processing of agricultural products (p.10).

[c] This would appear to include principally wholesale and retail trade services (p.10).

[d] Includes domestic and personal services, transportation and communication, government and education, professions.

Source: *Report and recommendations of the Joint Philippine-American Finance Commission*, 7 June 1947. United States, 80th Congress, 1st Session, House Document no.390 (Government Printing Office, Washington, 1947), p.103.

Taken together, these tables firmly indicate that by the close of the 1930s the Philippines had achieved only the most modest degree of import-substituting industrialisation. Certainly there is no evidence of the major industrial expansion which occurred in Latin America in that decade.

III

Undoubtedly a major part of the explanation for the failure of the Philippines to experience substantial industrial expansion in this period lies in its internal structures, notably the essential identification of elite interests with the land. However, the remaining pages of this paper will seek to emphasise another perspective: to argue that during the 1930s the external circumstances of the Philippines provided a markedly less powerful stimulus to import-substituting industrialisation than apparently was the case in Latin America. There are three considerations here which require discussion.

First, the Philippines appears to have suffered (at most) only a modest decline in real import capacity through the depression years, for export earnings remained remarkably buoyant during the collapse in world trade. A crucial influence here was the privileged position enjoyed by Philippine sugar exports in the American market, its importance vividly demonstrated by comparing the experience of Philippine exports in this period with that of sugar exports from the other major producer in South-East Asia, Java. In both economies sugar was the principal export, in 1926-8 accounting for almost 29 per cent of Philippine export income, almost 42 per cent of Javanese.[51] But while Philippine sugar entered the depression protected in its huge metropolitan market, Javanese sugar, shipped principally to markets in Asia (notably India), where no privilege could be anticipated, found no such security.

TABLE 3: Sugar exports, the Philippines and Java and Madura, 1926-36

	The Philippines		Java and Madura	
	kilogram	peso	kilogram	guilder
1926	411,231,545	64,459,268	2,001,041,318	269,609,319
1927	553,324,007	100,591,919	2,337,612,446	365,322,260
1928	569,937,628	95,985,879	3,069,295,214	375,796,158
1929	695,000,000	106,488,000	2,981,252,064	311,586,081
1930	743,979,730	104,480,000	2,838,123,949	254,271,579
1931	752,932,232	99,926,210	1,864,819,310	129,338,031
1932	1,016,568,150	119,603,769	1,887,996,849	99,253,696
1933	1,078,652,571	128,666,851	1,389,083,666	62,127,189
1934	1,152,840,733	130,909,161	1,388,453,785	45,461,939
1935	516,232,686	65,981,359	1,410,261,097	35,983,936
1936	899,838,367	123,874,644	1,010,331,960	34,094,966

Sources: Philippine Islands, Dept of Commerce and Communications, Bureau of Commerce and Industry, *Statistical Bulletin of the Philippine Islands*, 1928, p.151; G.B. Sansom, *Department of Overseas Trade. Trade conditions in the Philippine Islands* (HMSO, London, 1933), pp.9, 13, 37; Philippines (Republic), Dept of Commerce and Industry, Bureau of Commerce, *Summaries of Philippine Foreign Trade 1931 to 1949* (Manila, 1949), p.23; Netherlands India, Departement van Landbouw, Nijverheid en Handel [from 1933 Departement van Economische Zaken], Centraal Kantoor voor de Statistiek, *Jaaroverzicht van den in- en uitvoer van Nederlandsch-Indië*, issues for 1926-36.

This table makes its point clearly. For Java the average annual value of sugar exports in the period 1931-6 was a mere 20 per cent of the average annual value in the pre-depression years 1926-8: for the Philippines the average annual value of sugar exports in the period 1931-6 was 28 per cent *higher* than the average annual value in the years 1926-8.[52] Philippine export earnings were further sustained in the depression years by the rapid emergence of a major new export, gold.

TABLE 4: Gold exports (ore and bullion, in pesos), 1931-40

1931	7,534,253	1936	22,454,209
1932	10,072,242	1937	28,654,468
1933	9,700,971	1938	61,013,588
1934	11,668,802	1939	71,756,413
1935	15,360,409	1940	75,800,161

Source: Philippines (Republic), Dept of Commerce and Industry, Bureau of Commerce, *Summaries of Philippine Foreign Trade 1931 to 1949* (Manila, 1949), p.49.

In aggregate terms, the average annual value of Philippine exports in the period 1931-6 was 76 per cent of the average annual value in 1926-8: the comparable figure for Java was a mere 28 per cent.[53]

Second, in the depression decade the Philippines possessed neither tariff nor exchange autonomy with respect to her dominant trading partner, the United States. Under the Tydings-McDuffie Act the free import of American manufactures into the Islands was to be maintained until July 1946, while in this period the exchange was held at US$1=2 peso (as it had been since the early years of American administration).[54] In brief it was not open to the Philippines, even in the Commonwealth period, to employ tariff restriction or currency devaluation to stem the import of American manufactures competing with fledgling local industry. It was of course open for the Philippines to employ tariffs against non-American manufactures. But (and this is the third consideration) that defence was simply inadequate against the recently emerged, penetrating industrial might of Japan. Thus despite tariff restriction,[55] in the early- and mid-1930s Japanese manufactures (most notably cotton textiles) sold significantly more cheaply in the Philippines than American manufactures, which entered free of duty. Two principal forces were at work here: the raising of American domestic prices by the incoming Roosevelt administration which, with the US$/peso rate fixed, increased the peso price of American manufactures, and the sharp devaluation of the yen against the peso (by approximately 40 per cent by 1934), which dramatically reduced the peso price of Japanese manufactures.[56] In the immediate pre-depression years, 1925-8, Japan had accounted on average for 23 per cent (by value) of cotton textile imports into the Philippines, the United States for 55 per cent.[57] In 1935 Japan's share had risen to almost 43 per cent, the United States' had fallen to a little over 44 per cent: at this point the expansion of Japanese textile imports was reined back by quota agreement between Japan and the United States.[58] And it might be added that the essential ineffectiveness of the Philippine tariff with respect to a range of imports from Japan in this period not only left major segments of the local market (and thus, where it might emerge, local industry) largely unprotected against Japanese manufactures but also meant that Japan's industrialists had relatively little incentive to establish manufacturing plant in the Islands. Thus it is important to note that in the 1930s

Japanese investment in manufacturing industry in the Philippines fell far short of their investment in the extractive sectors - in mining, timber extraction, commercial fishing, the cultivation of abaca.[59] Manufacturing investment was limited principally to two relatively modest textile factories (established, it may be noted, as quota restrictions were threatened and then imposed against Japanese cotton piece goods imports), three canvas rubber shoe factories, fish canneries (here tariff restriction appears to have been influential), a plant for the manufacture-assembly of bicycles, and a brewery (the Balintawak Beer Brewery: here again tariff restriction was an important influence).[60]

The weakness of nascent Philippine import-substituting industrialisation in the 1930s in the face of (principally American and Japanese) manufactured imports is well illustrated by the experience of perhaps the two most firmly established local industries in that period, the manufacture of beer and of cement. The essential data are presented in Tables 5 and 6.

Both these industries (it will be remembered) enjoyed a considerable degree of non-tariff protection against all imports, as well as tariff protection against all except imports from the United States. Yet beer imports rose modestly from the early 1920s to the mid-1930s as local production held constant; and rose sharply in the second half of the 1930s as local production markedly expanded. In the later 1930s imported beer took a larger share (in some years a considerably larger share) of the Philippine market than it had a decade earlier. (The return of American beers to the Philippines following the end of Prohibition appears to have been an important influence here.) In contrast, cement imports did fall dramatically from the opening of the 1930s as local production (held constant in the second half of the 1920s) began to rise; but, again, increased sharply in the later 1930s as local production markedly expanded. In brief, despite their considerable advantage in the local market (despite indeed a marked expansion of production in the second half of the 1930s), these two prominent import-substituting Philippine industries were in the depression decade far from establishing an unassailable position against imports. One further, quite distinct point might be drawn from these tables: it is clear that the principal stimulus to these important local industries came with the advent of the Commonwealth administration in 1935 (and its more interventionist and expansionary economic policies),[61] not with the onset of world depression at the end of the 1920s.

TABLE 5: Beer: domestic consumption from domestic production, exports, imports 1920-40 (in litres)

	Domestic beer removed from factories for domestic consumption	Exports	Imports
1920	4,874,400	175,047	141,165
1921	3,643,841	39,871	119,510
1922	3,335,400	36,689	161,994
1923	2,795,747	49,316	179,582
1924	3,517,007	55,831	483,270
1925	3,436,400	56,988	364,803
1926	3,362,200	70,795	407,081
1927	3,638,800	152,260	386,375
1928	3,790,000	141,891	536,931
1929	3,820,882	53,550	756,832
1930	3,900,658	40,197	631,592
1931	3,789,200	32,781	544,911
1932	3,856,600	3,222	438,911
1933	3,776,200	524,469	487,773
1934	3,335,800	182,168	642,529
1935	3,340,800	104,258	1,023,112
	Domestic beer production		
1936	3,530,200	69,581	1,845,640
1937	4,089,600	59,114	2,242,661
1938	5,861,950	319,111	2,304,347
1939	5,833,400	193,584	1,445,416
1940	7,381,100	287,779	1,002,040

Sources: Philippine Islands, Dept of Commerce and Communications, Bureau of Commerce and Industry, *Statistical Bulletin of the Philippine Islands*, 1924, p.52, 1929, p.88; Philippine Islands, Dept of Agriculture and Commerce, Division of Statistics, *Statistical Handbook of the Philippine Islands 1932* (Bureau of Printing, Manila, 1933), p.176; Philippines (Commonwealth), Dept of Agriculture and Commerce, *Philippine Statistical Review*, *3*, 1 (1936), p.58; Philippines (Commonwealth), Bureau of the Census and Statistics, *Yearbook of Philippine Statistics 1940* (Bureau of Printing, Manila, 1941), pp.156, 208, 329; Philippine Islands (later Commonwealth), Dept of Finance, Bureau of Customs, *Annual Report of the Insular Collector of Customs*, issues for 1920-38.

TABLE 6: Cement: production and imports 1925-40 (in kilograms)[a]

	Production		Imports
	Cebu Portland Cement Company	Total	
1925	5,655,637		36,160,283
1926	60,177,190		33,180,852
1927	65,724,376		34,478,332
1928	64,879,961		61,070,104
1929	76,465,090		48,582,467
1930	74,643,936		57,928,229
1931	64,463,551	84,199,493	19,521,846
1932	65,370,206	94,124,056	4,027,880
1933	47,799,825	82,850,595	2,051,820
1934	60,932,423	95,468,436	5,848,911
1935	65,792,925	110,572,500	209,514
1936	76,734,853	132,607,095	927,207
1937	89,190,657		5,132,815
1938	102,563,474		27,231,031
1939	165,174,070		51,353,057
1940	190,433,453		764,428

[a] The figures for production are calculated on the basis 1 bag = 94 lb/42.63 kg.

Sources: *Cebu Portland Cement Company, 1922-1953* (Cebu Portland Cement Company, Manila, n.d.); *Industrial Philippines: a cross section* (Manila, 1953), p.131; Philippine Islands (later Commonwealth), Dept of Finance, Bureau of Customs, *Annual Report of the Insular Collector of Customs*, issues for 1925-38; Philippines (Commonwealth), Bureau of the Census and Statistics, *Yearbook of Philippine Statistics 1940* (Bureau of Printing, Manila, 1941), p.253.

IV

To summarise: for the Philippines, the sharp contraction in world trading activity from the end of the 1920s provided little stimulus for the expansion of import-substituting industrial production, primarily because the real import capacity of the Islands was sustained through the depression (principally a consequence of the privileged position enjoyed by Philippine sugar exports in the American market as well as the emergence of gold as a major new export) and because the absence of tariff and exchange autonomy (or, frequently, the essential ineffectiveness of those tariffs which were in place) left nascent local industry exposed to the dominant manufacturing might of the United States and Japan. If the crucial elements in depression industrialisation in Latin America were a sharply reduced capacity to import (while internal demand was sustained by expansionary macroeconomic policy) and exchange and tariff intervention to defend local manufactures, these conditions simply did not obtain in the Philippines. It is true that the pursuit of industrialisation became the dominant theme of government economic policy in the 1930s. But this occurred only with the inauguration of the Philippine Commonwealth in the middle of the decade; was born of the fear that political independence in 1946 would bring economic ruin to the Islands, then dangerously over-committed to agricultural exports dependent on the American market (and the related fear that an agricultural Philippines, on independence, would fall subservient to industrial Japan);[62] and, perhaps inevitably, could achieve little in the few years before war intervened.

NOTES

1 I wish to thank Norman Owen for his valuable comments on an earlier draft of this paper. I remain responsible for all errors of fact and interpretation.

2 R. Thorp (ed), *Latin America in the 1930s: the role of the periphery in world crisis* (Macmillan, London, 1984), p.2.

3 Thorp suggests a fall in real import capacity of 45 per cent between 1928 and 1932: ibid., pp.2, 331.

4 P.E. Abelarde, *American tariff policy towards the Philippines 1898-1946* (King's Crown Press, Morningside Heights, New York, 1947), p.215.

5 T. Friend, 'The Philippine sugar industry and the politics of independence, 1929-1935', *Journal of Asian Studies, 22,* 2 (1963), p.181.

6 It may need to be explained that the virtual free entry of Philippine exports into the American market (secured in the legislation of 1909 and 1913) was of direct advantage to Philippine producers only in the case of commodities which appeared in the United States' tariff schedules. Thus it was that both abaca and copra received no preferential access to the metropolitan market in this period, for they were on the American 'free list'. Preferential access was limited, in essence, to sugar from 1909 and to coconut oil and cordage from 1922 (as tariffs were raised against those commodities by the Fordney-McCumber Act). N.G. Owen, 'Philippine economic development and American policy: a reappraisal' in N.G Owen (ed), *Compadre colonialism: studies on the Philippines under American rule* (University of Michigan, Center for South and Southeast Asian Studies, Ann Arbor, 1971), p.109.

7 Owen, 'Philippine economic development and American policy', pp.110, 122.

8 Philippine Islands, Dept of Commerce and Communications, Bureau of Commerce and Industry, *Statistical Bulletin of the Philippine Islands* (hereafter cited as *SBPI*), 1928, p.151; Philippines (Republic), Dept of Commerce and Industry, Bureau of Commerce, *Summaries of Philippine Foreign Trade 1931 to 1949* (hereafter cited as *SPFT 1931 to 1949*) (Manila, 1949), p.23.

9 E.C. de Jesus, *The tobacco monopoly in the Philippines: bureaucratic enterprise and social change, 1766-1880* (Ateneo de Manila University Press, Quezon City, 1980); E.G. Raventos, *La Compañia General de Tabacos de Filipinas, 1881-1981* (La Compañia General de Tabacos de Filipinas, Barcelona, 1981).

10 D.F. Doeppers, *Manila 1900-1941: social change in a late colonial metropolis* (Ateneo de Manila University Press, Quezon City, 1984), pp.20-2.

11 N.G. Owen, *Prosperity without progress: Manila hemp and material life in the colonial Philippines* (University of California Press, Berkeley, 1984), pp.63, 160.

12 L.E. Gleeck, Jr., *American business and Philippine economic development* (Carmelo and Bauermann, Manila, 1975), pp.84-5; 'Manila Cordage Company', *Tribune* (Manila), XIV Anniversary [supplement], 17 June 1939; M.T. Colayco, *The ropemakers: the story of Manila Cordage Co.* (Manila Cordage Company, Manila, 1975).

13 *San Miguel Brewery* [Golden Jubilee, 1890-1940] (La Fabrica de Cerveza de San Miguel, Manila, 1940).

14 'The San Miguel Brewery', *Manila Times: first Annual Edition*, February 1910.

15 'Beer in the Philippines', *American Chamber of Commerce Journal* (hereafter cited as *ACCJ*), *13*, 4 (1933).

16 'Story of the Soriano business empire', *Manila Daily Bulletin* [fiftieth anniversary edition], 27 March 1950.

17 Philippine Islands, Dept of Finance, Bureau of Internal Revenue, *Annual Report of the Collector of Internal Revenue*, 1928, p.29.

18 'Story of the Soriano business empire', *Manila Daily Bulletin* [fiftieth anniversary edition], 27 March 1950.

19 Advertisement in *Manila Times: first Annual Edition*, February 1910.

20 C. Quirino, 'Philippine tycoon: the life and times of Vicente Madrigal (1880-1972)' (unpublished typescript, Manila, 1967: held in the American Historical Collection, Manila), pp.92-4.

21 S.R. Paterno, 'Cement industry in the Philippines', *The Commercial and Industrial Manual of the Philippines, 1937-38* (Manila, 1938), pp.321-3.

22 For details of Madrigal's extensive business interests in this period see Quirino, 'Philippine tycoon'; Yoshihara Kunio, *Philippine industrialization: foreign and domestic capital* (Ateneo de Manila University Press, Quezon City; Oxford University Press, Singapore, 1985), pp.109-12.

23 Philippine Legislature, *Official Gazette*, *17*, 22, 28 May 1919, pp.908-9.

24 *Cebu Portland Cement Company, 1922-1953* (Cebu Portland Cement Company, Manila, n.d.).

25 Paterno, 'Cement industry in the Philippines'.

26 *Cebu Portland Cement Company, 1922-1953*. Production in bags converted to kilograms with 1 bag = 94 lb/42.63kg.

27 Philippine Islands, Dept of Finance, Bureau of Customs, *Annual Report of the Insular Collector of Customs* (hereafter cited as *ARICC*), 1927, p.99; 1929, p.98.

28 A.W. McCoy, 'The Philippines: independence without decolonisation' in R. Jeffrey (ed), *Asia - the winning of independence* (Macmillan, London, 1981), p.43.

29 For a detailed consideration of the independence negotiations see T. Friend, *Between two empires: the ordeal of the Philippines, 1929-1946* (Yale University Press, New Haven, 1965), parts 2 and 3.

30 S. Jenkins, *American economic policy toward the Philippines* (Stanford University Press, Stanford, California, 1954), p.36.

31 Economic policy in the Commonwealth period is also considered in A. Gopinath, 'President Manuel Quezon and economic protectionism, 1935-41', *Philippine Studies*, *34*, 2 (1986), pp.129-45; Doeppers, *Manila 1900-1941*, pp.25-31 *passim*.

32 J.M. Elizalde, 'The industrial development of the Philippines' in H.A. Andrada (ed), *Ang Tibay silver jubilee souvenir book, 1910-1935: quarter century of progress* ([Ang Tibay, Manila, 1935]).

33 'National Development Company', *Tribune* (Manila), XIV Anniversary [supplement], 17 June 1939; 'Base metal deposit in Surigao reserved', Philippines Commonwealth, Dept of Agriculture and Commerce, *Philippine Journal of Commerce* (hereafter cited as *PJC*), *15*, 7 (1939), p.31.

34 Doeppers, *Manila 1900-1941*, p.28.

35 'Bubbles', *ACCJ*, *18*, 1 (1938), p.11.

36 'Industrialization', *Business and Finance*, June 1937; reprinted in *The Commercial and Industrial Manual of the Philippines, 1937-38*, pp.203-5. In 1939, 63.93 per cent of the company's sales was to the Bureau of Public Works and to provincial and municipal governments; in addition, part of the sales to dealers (25.45 per cent of the total) was destined for government contracts. Only 8.01 per cent was to private contractors. 'Cement firm makes P 986,171', *PJC*, *16*, 3 (1940), p.27.

37 Elizalde, 'The industrial development of the Philippines'.

38 S. Araneta, 'Balanced economy - our imperative need', *PJC*, *13*, 10-11 (1937), p.37.

39 S.R. Mendinueto, 'The first National Assembly and the national economy', *PJC*, *13*, 10-11 (1937), p.18; J. Yulo, 'Publicity in America', *PJC*, *15*, 8 (1939), p.32. The president of the NDC in the mid-1930s was Joaquin Elizalde, then head of one of the most prominent business families in the Philippines: towards the end of that decade, the chairman of the NDC board was Manuel Roxas, then Secretary of Finance but later to be the first president of the Philippine Republic.

40 *Cebu Portland Cement Company, 1922-1953*.

41 'Rizal Cement factory expanded', *PJC*, *15*, 1 (1939), pp.40, 44.

42 'Guagua canning plant of NDC started', *PJC*, *15*, 3 (1939), p.36.

43 'Rush government cannery building', *PJC*, *17*, 2 (1941), p.27.

44 'NDC will soon start operation of textile and canning factories', *PJC*, *15*, 1 (1939), p.44; 'Bubbles', *ACCJ*, *18*, 1 (1938), p.10.

45 'Cotton mill to start operation early next year', *PJC*, *14*, 8 (1938), p.25.

46 'Cotton goods', *ACCJ*, *19*, 8 (1939), p.16; 'Huge cotton project is envisioned', *PJC*, *15*, 4 (1939), p.31.

47 C. Balmaceda, 'Greater self-sufficiency in prime necessities', *PJC*, *17*, 8 (1941).

48 L.D. Stifel, *The textile industry - a case study of industrial development in the Philippines*, Cornell University, Southeast Asia Program, Data Paper 49 (Ithaca, New York, 1963), p.34.

49 'Huge cotton project is envisioned', *PJC*, *15*, 4 (1939), p.31; 'Anonas says home weavers safe', *PJC*, *15*, 7 (1939), pp.32, 40. It should be emphasised that the Commonwealth administration's industrialisation drive extended beyond the initiatives noted in this paragraph. For example there were further industrial initiatives which, although they may not have reached actual production in this period, certainly were well advanced by the time of the Japanese invasion. Notable here was an initiative (by the National Coconut Corporation, created in 1940) for the manufacture of carbon electrodes for batteries, insulating material, bags, rugs and mats from the coconut. Note should also be made of the administration's measures to strengthen the domestic market for local manufactures: securing its supplies from Philippine producers whenever possible (khaki cloth for the Philippine Army and Constabulary from the NDC mill, canvas shoes, cement from the Cebu Portland Cement Company); establishing (in October 1933) the Manila Trading Center to assist small local manufacturers in advertising and distributing their products; promoting popular loyalty to local manufactures, notably by sponsoring expositions of Philippine-made products and by conducting campaigns (in schools, on the radio and through public meetings) to inculcate a spirit of economic nationalism. Such

initiatives were extensively reported in the *Philippine Journal of Commerce*, published monthly by the Department of Agriculture and Commerce.

50 Philippines (Commonwealth), Commission of the Census, *Census of the Philippines: 1939* (Bureau of Printing, Manila, 1940-3). The census date was 1 January 1939.

51 *SBPI*, 1928, p.151; Netherlands India, Departement van Landbouw, Nijverheid en Handel, Centraal Kantoor voor de Statistiek, *Jaaroverzicht van den in- en uitvoer van Nederlandsch-Indië* (hereafter cited as *JNI*), issues for 1926-8.

52 The immediate explanation for the major surge in Philippine sugar export from 1932 is that the prospect of the imposition of an American quota on imports from the Islands (as part of the independence settlement) caused each sugar *central* and adherent planter to increase production in an attempt to obtain the largest possible share of the quota when those were allocated. The subsequent contraction (which in 1936 still left the volume and value of sugar exports clearly above the levels of the late 1920s) reflected the imposition of the quota under the American Sugar Act of 1934. T. Friend, 'The Philippine sugar industry and the politics of independence, 1929-1935', *passim*.

53 Philippines (Republic), Bureau of the Census and Statistics, *Yearbook of Philippine Statistics: 1946* (Bureau of Printing, Manila, 1947), p.347; *JNI*, issues for 1926-36.

54 Jenkins, *American economic policy toward the Philippines*, pp.36, 110-11.

55 For example in late 1933 Japanese cotton imports faced a tariff averaging 20 per cent *ad valorem*. 'Japan approaching America in Philippine piece goods trade', *ACCJ*, *13*, 12 (1933), p.11.

56 M.C. Guerrero, 'A survey of Japanese trade and investments in the Philippines, with special references to Philippine-American reactions 1900-1941', *Philippine Social Sciences and Humanities Review*, *31*, 1 (1966), p.24, n.27. Guerrero notes that the success of Japanese cotton manufactures in penetrating the Philippine market in the first half of the 1930s was due in addition to 'close delivery dates, small shipments and the presentation of very attractive designs' (p.24).

57 Guerrero, 'A survey of Japanese trade and investments in the Philippines', p.28.

58 Ibid., pp.25-7.

59 Ibid., pp.46-7.

60 Ibid., pp.42-7. See also G.K. Goodman, 'America's "permissive" colonialism: Japanese business in the Philippines, 1899-1941' in N.G. Owen (ed), *The Philippine economy and the United States: studies in past and present interactions* (University of Michigan, Center for South and Southeast Asian Studies, Ann Arbor, 1983), pp.37-62; G.K. Goodman, 'Japan and Philippine beer: the 1930s', *Journal of Southeast Asian Studies*, *1*, 1 (1970), pp.54-9.

61 Note might be made here of an important programme of concrete-road construction undertaken in the later 1930s. 'Construction of concrete roads to start soon', *PJC*, *14*, 6 (1938), p.14.

62 It is interesting to note that industrialisation programmes pursued in other parts of South-East Asia in the 1930s were also stimulated, at least in part, by concern over long-term economic problems essentially unconnected with the depression and its impact. In Netherlands India industrialisation was seen as a partial solution to the long-established problems arising from increasingly severe pressure of population on cultivable land on Java; in Siam it was seen as a means by which foreign domination of the local economy might be diminished. See Jack Shepherd, *Industry in Southeast Asia* (Institute of Pacific Relations, New York, 1941), pp.53-4, 130-2.

11

THE CONSEQUENCES OF THE POST FIRST WORLD WAR DEPRESSION FOR THE CHINA TREATY-PORT ECONOMY 1921-3

MARIE-CLAIRE BERGÈRE

In the spring of 1920 came the first signs of the business depression that set off a crisis of 'reconversion' in the Chinese treaty ports. This was a crisis of external origin, and reflected the difficulties of the major economic Powers in the aftermath of the first World War. It first reached China through foreign trade. By the summer of 1920, a heavy fall in exports and a reduction in imports ushered in an era of domestic stagnation which continued for the next three years. A British official report said: 'Both foreigners and Chinese merchants are unanimous: 1921 has been one of the worst years ever seen and the prospects for 1922 are hardly any better.'[1]

The crisis spread unevenly through the heterogeneous Chinese economy. China's very state of underdevelopment made it largely immune to the effects of the world depression: with rare exceptions, the peasant and his world were hardly affected. This fact, however, cannot be used to argue that there was a dichotomy between the modern sector, tied to the world market and governed by its fluctuations, and a traditional, protected and autonomous sector. For the fact is that, difficulties notwithstanding, the national industries (that is those enterprises in China owned by Chinese) continued to grow between 1921 and 1923.

I. THE WORLD DEPRESSION

It was not until 18 months after the war that a crisis of reconversion hit the major economic Powers. In England and France, demand had initially been stimulated by the needs of reconstruction and the revival of household consumption after years of shortages. But in these countries, which had been profoundly affected by the war, inflation took hold. Inflation threatened the United States too, but the first signs of a recession came with a fall in the stock market in the autumn of 1919. American flour and grain prices fell in early 1920. But it was in Japan that the crisis emerged with full severity, in the silk crash of March 1920.

Japanese foreign trade, shipping and industrial production had expanded greatly during the war. The post-war boom was particularly remarkable in silks, prices rising by 200 per cent between February 1919 and March 1920. It was in this market that difficulties first arose when American buyers, deterred by the price increases, temporarily stopped buying silks.[2] In Yokohama, silk stocks accumulated; traders, many of whom had taken loans in order to speculate in the silk market, began to sell their stocks at a loss in order to repay the banks. In March 1920, the Japanese government tried to curb market speculation by setting the bank rate at 10 per cent. In the stock market crisis that followed, the Mogi Bank, which had played a big part in financing the silk trade, was forced to close. The Japanese crisis had immediate repercussions on the New York Stock Exchange, for the Japanese government, which was determined to support the external value of the yen, began to sell the large dollar reserves it had accumulated during the war.[3] A violent depression now began. Similar difficulties in Britain were aggravated by the government's deflationary policies; gradually, every industrial nation began to suffer the effects of the crisis. There was an increase in the number of bankruptcies and in unemployment. International trade was greatly affected. Work slowed down in the shipyards. Many shipping companies were forced to lay up their vessels. The decline in trade concerned mainly imports into the industrialised countries, where markets were now closed to luxury articles and certain exotic raw materials, for example silk, tea and raw cotton. The crisis thus gradually spread from countries where it had started. It reached Latin America, Australia, India and finally China, which now discovered that the outlets for their exports to the industrial world had shrunk.

As we shall see later, the distinctive features of the Chinese economy limited the domestic consequences of the difficulties faced by her exporters. But during the same period, China's foreign trade had to cope with another crisis, one caused by international currency fluctuations, for the stagnation in exports arising from falling demand was paralleled in certain import trades by difficulties resulting from a fall in silver prices in the major stock markets.

Silver had risen swiftly during and after the war, its average annual price going up from US$0.51 per ounce in 1915 to $1.12 per ounce in 1919. This rise accelerated in early 1920: in New York, the price reached $1.37 in February. But the trend was reversed in March, and by early June the price was $0.80 per ounce. At the end of 1920 it settled at a level comparable to (though slightly above) that of the pre-war period.[4]

These sharp fluctuations in world silver prices caused similar fluctuations in the exchange value of the Chinese tael (Table 1).[5]

TABLE 1: Variations in the tael exchange rate at Shanghai in 1920 and 1921 (average monthly value of the tael in US cents)

	1920	1921
January	147.82	72.06
February	148.10	63.35
March	140.80	58.74
April	129.02	62.00
May	113.42	
June	98.97	
July	100.30	65.90
August	106.27	66.56
September	103.59	69.43
October	92.87	76.98
November	86.40	76.12
December	71.63	74.37

Source: Based on the monthly financial columns of the *Bulletin Commercial d'Extrême-Orient*, 1920-1. The *BCEO* was the official journal of the French Chamber of Commerce in China.

It was as if between the beginning of 1920 and the end of 1921 China had devalued its currency by about 50 per cent, except that the devaluation had not been decided upon by the Chinese government itself: rather it was the direct result of an international situation dominated by European and American initiatives.

The causes of the silver depreciation and hence of the devaluation of the Chinese tael must be sought firstly in Europe, and especially in the massive sales of silver that were made by Great Britain, Germany, France and Austria.[6] In 1922, for example, these sales were equivalent to more than a fifth of the world's annual output (192 million ounces).[7] Sales on such a scale could only further accelerate the fall in silver prices. Other factors weighed on the silver market, in particular a drop in the demand from India and China. When these countries had surplus trade balances, Western buyers paid them in silver. But India had poor harvests in the autumn of 1920, and its previous trade surplus turned into a deficit of about 956 million rupees in that year.[8] During the same period the Chinese trade deficit rose from 16 million to 220 million Tls. In brief, there was a greater supply of silver at the same time as a reduction in demand from the two countries that usually bought the largest quantities of it.

However, the demand for silver did not arise solely out of the necessities of trade. It was also fuelled by the requirements of the Mints. While the European countries gave up silver coinage after the war, Mexico began to buy silver for minting from 1920 onwards. In China the Mints were very active, especially the Canton Mint which used 60 million ounces of the metal in 1921 alone to make small-denomination coins, and in so doing absorbed a substantial portion of the silver imported into China (for example of a total 28,647 bars reaching Shanghai between September and December 1921, 11,640 bars were sent on to Canton).[9] But supplies also came from melting down old coins, so that the impact on the world silver market of Chinese minting operations was not proportionate to their volume.

The most effective curb on falling silver prices was undoubtedly the policy of the US Treasury which began to buy up silver on 16 June 1920. But the law stipulated that these operations could cover metal only from American mines (that is about 40 per cent of world output). Hence purchases had only a short-lived effect on world prices.

The fall in silver prices, and the consequent weakening of the tael against foreign, gold-linked currencies, drove up the prices of Chinese imports very sharply. This situation was not wholly disadvantageous to the Chinese economy in that the now prohibitive cost of imports gave some protection to a market that had no customs barriers, and that at a time when the depreciation of the tael might have stimulated exports. In 1920, however, Chinese exports were badly hit. As an observer noted: 'Despite the fact that a period of such low exchange should constitute an exporter's paradise, the conditions abroad are a stone wall against any activity.'[10] The heavy fall in the value of the tael was not enough to stimulate exports, or even maintain them at their previous level, in the face of rejection by the slump-ridden Western markets.

Thus the world depression meant for China both a decline in exports, which were deprived of their main outlets, and a crisis in imports, which were paralysed by a fall in the exchange rate, as violent as it was sudden.

II. THE FALL IN EXPORTS

1920 had begun with an unprecedented boom in trade, but ended amidst huge difficulties. The total value of trade, which was at a record 1,276 million Tls in 1919, reached 1,302 million Tls the following year (Table 2).

TABLE 2: Value of foreign trade at actual prices (in millions of Hk Tls)

	Exports	Imports	Total
1915	418	454	872
1916	481	516	997
1917	462	549	1011
1918	485	554	1039
1919	630	646	1276
1920	540	762	1302
1921	601	906	1507
1922	654	945	1599
1923	752	923	1675

Source: After C. Yang, H.B. Hau *et al.*, *Statistics of China's foreign trade during the last sixty-five years* (National Research Institute of Social Sciences, Academia Sinica, Nanking, 1931).

While the value of imports at actual prices continued to rise, that of exports fell from 630 million Tls in 1919 to 540 million in 1920. Calculated in constant prices, taking 1913 as the base, the fall was of the same magnitude, that is about 16 per cent (see Table 3).

TABLE 3: Value of main Chinese exports (1915-23) at actual and constant prices (in millions of Hk Tls)

	At actual prices	At constant prices (base 1913)
1915	336	339
1916	358	331
1917	358	337
1918	400	335
1919	522	453
1920	439	370
1921	481	382
1922	522	389
1923	585	418

Source: Based on figures from the China Inspectorate-General of Customs, *Annual Trade Report and Returns, 1920-31* (Shanghai, annual, 1920-31, 12 vols.) (hereafter *TR*), '1923, report on the foreign trade of China'.. The values at constant prices were calculated on the basis of the average price of each article in 1913. However, this calculation could be made only for about 75 per cent of Chinese exports, which explains the difference between the figures of Table 2 (column 1) and Table 3 (column 1).

The figures at constant prices give a clearer picture of the continuing slump, which began to lift only in 1923.

As Table 4 shows, not all export sectors were equally affected.

TABLE 4: Development of principal Chinese exports in 1913, 1919 and 1920 (quantities exported)

	1913	1919	1920
Beans (millions of piculs[a])	22,636	38,771	31,300
Grain "	4,037	10,200	12,315
Raw cotton "	739	1,072	376
Albumen and egg yolks "	156	606	423
Sesame "	2,056	2,839	2,056
Silk cloth "	34	39	37
Raw silk "	149	165	104
Tea "	1,442	690	306
Goatskins (thousands)	7,794	13,832	10,836
Flour (thousands of piculs)	119	2,694	3,961

[a] A *picul* or *tan* was equal to about 60.5 kg, and a *catty* or *chin* to about 605 g.
Source: *TR, 1920*, Report on the foreign trade of China.

Grain and flour were not affected by the general decline. This was also true of certain products (not included in Table 4) which accounted for only a very low percentage of total exports, but whose sales remained steady or grew; these were non-ferrous ores (zinc and antimony), cigarettes and coal. This partial ability to withstand the crisis was related to the fact that the export trade had become increasingly diversified from the beginning of the twentieth century. Of course, China was still a supplier of luxury or semi-luxury products like silk and tea, but now it also supplied basic requirements (for example, grain and flour to Europe, and soy-bean cake to Japan) which had to be satisfied regardless of the crisis. Moreover, recent industrial progress had found major outlets in the South-East Asian countries which bought Chinese cigarettes and textiles; and even Australia took some of the flour made in Shanghai.[11] Finally, the demand from the overseas Chinese communities for Chinese products (especially food items) did not appear to slacken, which explains the continued growth of exports of preserved foods, vermicelli etc. These were significant pointers to a difference between China and those colonial economies which specialised in the export of just one or two raw materials. Yet they were secondary phenomena which diminished but did not alter the main trend: that was determined by the main export products, silk, tea, vegetable oils, skins. For all of these the essential cause of declining prices in this period was the loss of markets.

The countries hit by the crisis cut down their imports or stopped them altogether. The sudden fall in China's raw cotton exports, from 1,072 million piculs in 1919 to 376 million in 1920, coincided with the difficulties faced by the Japanese cotton mills which were their main customers.[12] The reduced need for raw cotton was met to a great extent from stocks built up in foreign markets in the last months of 1919 and at the beginning of 1920, when speculation had been in full swing. These stocks were extremely high, and the tightness of bank credit forced their owners to reduce them in order to meet deadlines for loan repayments. These hasty sales were often made at a loss, and caused a general collapse in the prices of Chinese products in European and American markets, from which East Asia now could not hope for fresh orders. Within a few months, certain products lost more than half their value; sesame, priced at 70 shillings per hundredweight in early 1920, was selling at 30 shillings by the end of that year.[13] The prices of albumen, egg yolks and vegetable oils also fell swiftly (Table 5).

TABLE 5: Collapse in prices of Chinese products on the London market between October and December 1920 (in shillings)

	October 1920	December 1920
Dried eggs (per pound)	0.11	0.7
Albumen (per pound)	4.9	3.10
Vegetable oil (per cwt)	98	60

Source: *BCEO*, January 1921, p.44.

In the two key export sectors of silk and tea, the crisis took on the proportion of a catastrophe. France and the United States were the main buyers of Chinese silks, absorbing virtually all silk exports from Shanghai and Canton (cf.Table 6).

in 1920, activity picked up in 1921, although sporadically: orders were very irregular; they came mainly from the United States, and were for sheep's wool.[28] Wool orders were repeated in the following year; the Japanese demand for raw cotton revived; and ground-nut shipments to Europe picked up again.[29]

Although Hankow handled only 3.9 per cent of Chinese exports, its central location and ease of access made it a big transit market into which farm produce for export came from the neighbouring provinces of Szechwan, Hunan, Hupei and Anhwei. It was China's chief tea-exporting port and had been badly affected by the closure of the Russian market. With the world depression, other export items (vegetable oils, eggs, skins, sesame seed) were affected in turn. The depression set in from the summer of 1920, and lasted throughout 1921. From time to time, a few orders (for skins in particular) 'broke the silence of the market a little',[30] but transactions were rare and the five commodity exchanges decided to merge in early 1922 for lack of activity.[31] In the months that followed business revived, but very unevenly from one sector to another.[32] Skins continued to be in fair demand, but the vegetable oils market remained lifeless and when American demand finally revived in early 1923 the Chinese traders were unable to meet it, for the local producers and middlemen who worked for the big export houses had been hard hit by the crisis. Many were facing bankruptcy in the winter of 1920. The Shanghai silks and cocoons guild appealed to the Peking government for financial aid,[33] but although their appeal was supported by the French Chamber of Commerce in China and the Legation, nothing came of it.[34] For their part, Hankow's albumen and egg merchants sought the backing of the local Chinese Chamber of Commerce; they wanted their taxes reduced, and reported that several large albumen factories had closed.[35] But the worst-affected were undoubtedly tea traders and producers. They incurred heavy losses from 1918 to 1921, and many plantations were either put to other use or abandoned.[36]

However, contrary to what might have been expected, the prices of Chinese export items did not collapse. Of course there was a distinct easing of prices when the crisis broke: at Hankow in December 1920 it was noted that 'tael prices for most products of export continue weak'.[37] Skins quoted in the Chinese market at 45-50 Tls each in the spring were being offered at no more than 28-35 Tls by the end of that year.[38] But this fall was far smaller than the one then being experienced by Chinese goods in Western markets: for example, the price of sesame seed fell by about 56 per cent (from 70 to 30 shillings per hundredweight) in the London market but by barely 20 per cent (8 to 6.5 Tls per picul) in China.[39] A report in the autumn of 1920 said: 'Chinese new season products for exports are being offered at prices either the same or slightly lower than those of last year . . .'[40] Moreover, the price fall in China was short-lived. From 1921 onwards, as prices in Western markets remained very low, Chinese prices returned to their previous levels or even outstripped them. This happened, for example, with silk. In Shanghai, *tsatlees* (quality white silks produced in Chekiang) were worth 840 to 900 Tls per picul in April 1920; in May the price fell by 100 Tls. In June, it was 665-730 Tls. However, in September it climbed back to 680-760 Tls. This revival was confirmed in the spring of 1921, when the price ranged from 715 to 755 Tls. Similar trends can be observed in the price of wild silk (tussore) which fell from 500 Tls per picul (in spring 1920) to 340 Tls (in August 1920), and then rose gradually to 530 Tls in April 1921.[41] Probably the most striking price recovery was that of raw cotton (Table 8).

Thus the difficulties in the Western markets, which seriously affected the volume of transactions, had hardly any effect on the local prices of products exported by China. In the end, these high prices proved to be another obstacle to the revival of exports. In August 1921, the *BCEO* columnist noted that 'the prices of Chinese export products are still high locally, to the point where it is becoming impossible to do business'. In September 1922 he observed that the prices of 'Chinese raw materials have risen to levels which do not permit exports'.[42]

What was the cause of this apparently paradoxical rise? The explanations given by certain contemporary observers appear to be rather superficial. For example: 'Having accumulated money in their trade of the past few years, the native holders are not forced to sell';[43] or, 'Long isolation from the outside world . . . [has] not prepared the Chinese merchant to look to other countries and to general financial and commercial undercurrents. This unpreparedness is to be found in the current market prices of raw materials in China which are still high at a time when prices in other parts of the world are declining.'[44]

But apart from such psychological considerations, factors such as the depreciation of silver and the failure of the harvest should also be taken into account. Thus the devaluation of the tael managed to compensate to a great extent for the decline in the gold-linked prices quoted in Western markets. This happened, for example, with sesame seed and silk prices.[45] And the steadiness of cotton prices in 1920 can partly be explained by shortages after a poor harvest, especially in Hupei and Chihli provinces. In spring 1921, an estimated shortfall of 60 per cent in the cocoon harvest helped to keep silk prices firm in the Shanghai market.[46]

TABLE 8: Rise in raw cotton prices at Shanghai in 1921 and 1922 (prices expressed in Tls per picul)

	Tungchow cotton	Shanghai cotton
Dec. 1920	23	22
Jan. 1921	24	22.50
Feb.	25.25	22.50
March	23	22
April	23.25	22.25
May	25.25	23.50
June	25.70	25
July	28	25.50
Aug.	(no returns)	26.25
Sept.	37	32.50
Oct.	36	31
Nov.	32	28.50
Dec.	30	28
Jan. 1922	(no returns)	31
Feb.	34	30
March	35	35
April	(no returns)	33.25
May	35	(no returns)
June	(no returns)	34.50
July	32.25	32.50
Aug.	30.45	(no returns)
Sept.	29	27.50
Oct.	28.50	28
Nov.	31	30
Dec.	33.20	30

Source: Based on market price-lists ('Tableau général des cours') published each month in *BCEO* from December 1920. These were recorded prices and not averages.

The importance of local conditions, which in this case counterbalanced the effects of the international depression, was only one aspect of the key role played by the internal market in Chinese economic development. In the end it was the immense size and vitality of this market that formed a most effective barrier against the spread of the world depression, even in the vulnerable export sector. It was the very mass of consumers represented by the Chinese population that kept the country sheltered, or relatively sheltered, from fluctuations in foreign demand. Chinese commercial crops were largely integrated into the traditional sector, and their output was geared above all to the internal market. The steadiness of Chinese export prices in 1921-2 highlighted the fact that foreign outlets were of secondary importance, even in sectors like silk and vegetable oils. Goods which were meant for export but which foreigners could not now buy were consumed in the country itself.[47] In 1921, it was growing demand for vegetable oils from Chinese consumers that stopped prices from falling.[48]

In July 1920, when silk exports had come to a complete halt, consumption by traditional weavers 'developed to such an extent that prices in the interior were maintained at a high level'.[49] Thus, 'thanks to sustained demand from local consumers, producers were able to sell [silk] on the spot at prices well above those they could have got by exporting it to Shanghai'.[50] Of course, only a portion of the output was involved here, namely that of the traditional (hand-spinning) industry. Steam filatures had to cope with a more difficult situation; only sporadic offers from abroad in the winter of 1920 and the spring of 1921 enabled them to surmount the crisis. However, silk yarn from the traditional sector had usually been included in the volume of exports, and its disappearance from the market now facilitated the export of steam filature production. It might be tempting to conclude from this example that it was China's state of under-development that enabled it to stand up to the crisis. On the contrary, however, it would appear that the determining factor here was in fact development, the development for example of national cotton mills, which absorbed a growing proportion of China's raw cotton output, replacing Japanese mills,[51] and thus causing prices to rise. As for silk, it was the growth of semi-modernised manufactures that resolved the crisis of outlets. Growth in local industry was reported from Shantung province in 1922, and consular reports from Mukden noted that 'cocoons from Southern Manchuria, which earlier used to head for Chefoo, are now consumed within the territory as production and spinning has greatly expanded in recent years'.[52]

The crisis in Chinese exports revealed the colonial character of a sector dominated by fluctuations in European and American economic conditions. But this crisis spread only in exceptional cases to domestic trade and production. Whether this phenomenon is attributed to the archaic nature of China's economic organisation, the relative weakness of imperialist penetration, or (in a more likely explanation) to the vitality of the internal economy and its capacity for adaptation, this structural discontinuity limited the effects of the crisis to its immediate points of impact. Imports were among the sectors thus directly affected.

III. THE CRISIS OF IMPORTS

Imports, unlike exports, continued to grow when the world depression began. Their value in actual prices went from 476 million Hk Tls in 1919 to 574 million in 1920 and to 632 million in 1921. Calculated in constant prices, the trend was the same (Table 9).

But here the increase in the volume of imported goods does not point to growing prosperity, and indeed the Inspector of Customs at Shanghai felt that 1920 was a 'year of disappointments'.[53] It is true that Chinese merchants, stimulated by export price rises in Western markets and encouraged by an earlier favourable movement in the exchange, placed very big orders at the beginning of the year. But several months later, when those goods reached China, many traders were unable to take delivery. As more and more shipments arrived, the pace of transactions slowed down in the main import markets like Shanghai and Tientsin and, at times, came to a complete halt.

TABLE 9: Value of main Chinese imports at actual and constant prices, 1915-23 (in thousands of Hk Tls)

	At actual prices	Constant prices (base 1913)
1915	332,981	322,893
1916	375,348	328,585
1917	415,468	331,608
1918	411,232	284,244
1919	476,531	318,363
1920	574,725	339,397
1921	632,427	383,305
1922	687,252	465,553
1923	684,023	453,799

Source: *BCEO*, July 1924, p.289. The values at constant prices were calculated from the average price of each article.

In general, the difficulties in financing imports could be accounted for by the decline in the export trade and the consequent disappearance of profits. In the short term, other factors played a part in precipitating and worsening the crisis. Thus the rigidity that we have seen in export prices was not paralleled in that of import prices. The sudden depreciation of silver from April 1920, and the consequent weakening of the tael, led to immediate and proportionate increases in local prices of Western goods, as import contracts always stipulated prices in gold-linked currencies. Thus in May 1921, prices of imports in the Tientsin market were three times their level of the previous year.[54] The extent of the crisis can be better grasped by recalling that every import operation was also, and sometimes above all, an act of speculation, that is, speculation on fluctuations in the value of silver, and hence of the tael, over the several months and sometimes the year that separated the signing of the foreign order from the delivery of goods. The price in gold-linked currencies (francs, pounds sterling, US dollars) shown in contracts did not change, but its equivalent in taels could fluctuate considerably according to the rise and fall of world silver prices. Of course, Chinese merchants could have eliminated this element of uncertainty by setting their exchange rates in advance, when they signed contracts,[55] or by hedging, that is, by immediately buying foreign currency equal to the amount of their orders. But these operations were very rarely employed. An observer noted: 'Divorce speculation . . . from even those businesses that in foreign countries are sound merchandising investments, and all the interest is taken out of its conduction for a great many Chinese merchants . . .'[56] Chinese importers had benefited since 1915 from a swift rise in silver prices, the profits from which had supplemented normal business gains. They were therefore hardly prepared to adopt a more cautious policy. In August 1920, five months after silver prices had begun to fall, they were still refusing to hedge, and preferred to await a recovery of the tael, which was not forthcoming.[57] In December 1920, when the tael was valued at no more than US$0.71, goods reached the market which had been ordered in February and March when the tael had been quoted at more than $1.40. To take delivery, therefore, Chinese traders had to pay out twice the originally stipulated amounts.

The situation was all the more critical as there had been a great increase in the number of foreign orders, reflecting a propensity for speculation rather than the needs of the market.[58] The metal traders, for example, placed five orders where just one would have sufficed. Thus, at a time when the exchange was most disadvantageous, importers had to cope with unusually large consignments. Their orders would have been enough to meet normal demand for two years.[59] What is more, these orders had been placed when prices in Western markets had been at their highest.

In 1920, long delivery periods, combined with the suddenness and violence of the depression, prevented Chinese merchants from taking advantage of the later fall in the prices of European and American goods. With a sharply devalued currency, these traders had to pay for goods bought at the high prices of the preceding boom.

For many of them, the cost became prohibitive. They could not take delivery of the goods they had ordered, which, in the meantime, had become too costly to be absorbed by the local market. Hence stocks accumulated. In Tientsin, at the end of December 1920, European and American importing firms were asking for delivery to be taken of goods worth a total of five million taels. As difficult negotiations began between a group of foreign import houses and the main Chinese buyers, warehousing costs and interest continued to accumulate.[60]

During the same period, foreign importers in Shanghai had to cope with similar problems. More than 150,000 tonnes of metals and metal products (nails, bars, etc.) were piled up in their warehouses.[61] Such was the glut that ships often had to wait for several days before unloading, since no one knew where to store their cargoes. Some companies were forced to build new depots.[62]

The fact that stocks were thus tied up raised acute problems of financing, for it must be recalled that Chinese traders, including the biggest ones, worked with very little personal capital. They speculated on a rapid turnover of merchandise, and depended on the unsecured credits traditionally granted by the native banks (*ch'ien-chuang*). In normal times, the cohesiveness and solidarity of the merchant community limited the risks inherent in such practices.

However, the earlier boom had drawn many newcomers into business, people who lacked not only capital but also experience and reputation. They were people on whom the merchant community could exert little control. Thus many Chinese buyers now sought all ways and means to get out of commitments which they could not meet. Quarrels broke out over the quality of merchandise, as pretexts for not taking deliveries.[63] Many small traders had to close shop and declare themselves bankrupt; others preferred to bolt without warning, 'leave for Ningpo'[64] as the Chinese put it. In all such cases, the losses fell on the foreign import houses. Little accustomed to such practices, the houses condemned the 'crisis in Chinese business ethics': 'In the recent crisis which has ruined many European firms, there were no more than 10 per cent of Chinese buyers who met their commitments; the rest all fled forever, taking their money and families with them.'[65] This harsh judgement by 'one of the most honourable members' of the French Chamber of Commerce in China was confirmed by Anglo-American business which, as it happened, was worse affected. 'The proverbial honesty of the Chinese is on trial', said the columnist of *Millard's Review*.[66]

But the problem here was not really one of fine sentiments. What had come under threat was the efficiency of a still broadly traditional trading system which had been suddenly faced with the requirements and necessities of international transactions. 'Chinese business ethics' were founded on a certain conception of human relationships which brought cohesion to a community invested with the power of sanction. They relied also on a deep knowledge of the laws of the market, and on compliance with those laws. All these elements were removed or at least weakened by the mechanisms of modern international trade. The fixed, written contract replaced verbal promises and amicable arrangements. Business trends, governed by market fluctuations of external origin, became not only uncontrollable but also unforeseeable. The notion of business cycles, which was then beginning to hold the attention of Western theoreticians, was still foreign to the Chinese: 'The condition existing now is partially of a mental attitude',[67] said a local observer. Another hoped 'that the merchants of the country will gain a store of information that will be of assistance to them, should a similar emergency arise in the future'.[68] Thus, where Westerners criticised inexperience and lack of knowledge, the Chinese themselves pleaded unavoidable circumstances. The most reputable firms did not repudiate their contracts but admitted that they could not fulfil them. 'Although there have sometimes been ups and downs in the exchange rate, never in 70 years has the difference been so sharp . . . All importers, big and small, are today at the mercy of events and on the verge of going into bankruptcy.'[69]

To prevent the worst from happening, in June 1920 the Shanghai (Chinese) General Chamber of Commerce stepped in on behalf of the cotton goods traders and asked that the importing houses should extend the deadlines for taking delivery of goods then in transit or at their final destination, and that all contracts covering as yet unshipped merchandise should be cancelled.[70] But this was opposed by the British and American chambers of commerce in China, which were hostile to the idea of contracts being cancelled. Similar attempts by the local traders of Tientsin also failed. There, the foreign importing firms used the diplomatic and political pressure that had so often been employed by Westerners in the past.[71] At their request, the dean of the consular corps intervened with the provincial governor. But the latter was ignored when he advised the Chinese merchants to fulfil their contracts.[72] Compromise solutions were reached only after months of very difficult negotiations.

Two import sectors were particularly affected by the crisis: cotton goods and metals. The crisis in cotton fabrics affected the two main import markets, Shanghai and Tientsin. In Shanghai, the situation worsened after the foreign chambers of commerce refused to consider the Chinese traders' requests for leniency. There were numerous bankruptcies and closures in the summer and autumn of 1920.[73] The value of the tael continued to fall as increasing numbers of cotton-goods consignments, covered by previous contracts, reached the port.[74] In February 1921, the Cloth Merchants' Guild warned importers in a circular that, owing to the crisis, Chinese buyers were no longer in a position to meet their commitments. The circular again asked for the cancellation of all unexecuted contracts. The spring of 1921 brought a distinct improvement in the situation. A short-lived recovery of the tael and firmer demand from the interior, especially from Manchuria, made it less difficult to clear stocks. These continued to be liquidated at great loss, but fresh contracts were made with Britain and the United States at more realistic prices. Chinese firms which had been strong enough to withstand the losses of the previous months now did fairly good business.

In Tientsin, the difficulties lasted longer. Chinese traders placed foreign orders worth about 20 million Tls at the end of 1920 and in the spring of 1921.[75] But no deliveries were taken. Faced with the uncompromising attitude of the European firms, which wanted contracts to be executed in full, the 21 biggest Chinese cotton-goods merchants decided to halt all commercial operations pending a compromise.[76] In March, the foreign importers of cotton goods also came together in an association, and negotiations were conducted with very great difficulty. Finally on 17 September 1921, the two sides came to an understanding. The goods which had arrived but which had not been taken delivery of, were to be sold by an organisation that would be jointly controlled by the foreign importers and the Chinese negotiators. The foreign importers were to be paid the proceeds of the sales immediately. The difference between the market price and the invoice price was to be settled through interest-free promissory notes, for which payment would be spread over about ten years. The importers were to bear all additional warehousing and interest charges. Following this agreement, promissory notes were issued for about 2.4 million (Chinese) dollars, that is, about 40 per cent of the value of the pending invoices. This operation relieved the glut to some extent, but in 1922 it was noted that 'the unfortunate matter of piece-goods continues to weigh heavily on the market, and the uneasiness that it has created persists'.[77] Bitter feelings ran especially high among the European importers, who had to accept losses of up to 20 per cent of their incurred expenditure. 'If the lack of success of a speculative action can henceforth constitute a case of *force majeure* to the advantage of a buyer (who, moreover, keeps all the profit of fortunate transactions to himself), what is to be the condition of the seller?'[78]

The crisis in the metal imports market also arose out of speculation. But a further element here was the fact that, in the aftermath of the war, foreign and especially American producers strove above all to meet their own domestic needs, and made only irregular shipments to China, with lengthy delivery periods of one or two years. This relative shortage pushed Chinese traders to increase their orders, many of which they thought would be late in delivery. But contrary to expectations, American shipments became far more regular in 1920 and glutted the Shanghai market.[79] Imports of iron bars thus rose from 365,000 piculs in 1919 to 950,000 piculs in 1920; those of twisted bars from 54,000 to 261,000 piculs; and those of old horseshoes from 21,000 piculs to 162,000 piculs.[80] At the end of 1920, the metal traders were in the same position as the cotton-goods traders. They too sought to evade the terms of their contracts and refused to take delivery of consignments under various pretexts. But recovery came more swiftly for them. Trading in metals was more tightly organised than that in cotton goods. About ten Chinese wholesalers controlled the Shanghai market and its extensions into the Yangtze and the northern regions. It was they who set the prices and terms for the disposal of goods. In the spring of 1921, their guilds managed to come to an agreement with the foreign import companies and banks, under which no fresh orders were to be placed or accepted while existing stocks remained.[81] This arrangement proved to be an effective one, and business picked up in 1921.[82]

The similarities in behaviour between the Shanghai and Tientsin markets and between the cotton-goods and metals sectors arose from the conditions of external trade. The differences between the two ports, in the duration and seriousness of the crisis, were due above all to the fact that it was not equally possible for Shanghai and Tientsin to dispose of their imports in the interior market. The difficulties experienced in Tientsin were particularly acute, and to a great extent this was due to a fall in demand from the northern provinces, which had been hard hit by natural calamities in 1920. The partial closure of the rural market played an important role here. In contrast, the swift recovery of the metals sector resulted from the continued expansion of domestic industries. It was this internal expansion which, despite an unfavourable international situation, stimulated the growth of certain sectors: textile plants, electrical tools and construction materials.

With the return to freely available foreign supplies after the war, Chinese industrialists were at last able to get the equipment they needed to expand production. Past profits and a promising future played a more decisive role here than the unfavourable turn in the external economy. The entrepreneurs were in a hurry to exploit the full potential of the local market that the war had opened up for them, and did not hesitate to replace and extend their capital equipment as fast as they could. Imports of mechanical plant grew rapidly (Table 10).

TABLE 10: Growth in Chinese imports of mechanical plant between 1913 and 1921 (Value at actual prices in thousands of Hk Tls)

1913	7,258
1920	30,074
1921	70,521

Source: 'China's machinery market', *British Chamber of Commerce Journal*, *5*, 12 (1922), pp.404 ff.

The major part of this expansion was accounted for by textile machinery (Table 11).

TABLE 11: Growth in Chinese imports of textile machinery between 1913 and 1921 (Value at actual prices in thousands of Hk Tls)

1913	839
1920	6,927
1921	26,792

Source:'China's machinery market', *British Chamber of Commerce Journal*, *5*, 12 (1922), pp.404 ff.

Other import sectors also maintained a high level of activity in the middle of the depression; rolling stock ordered by the Chinese government just after the war was delivered during this period.[83] Indigo and artificial dyes began to be imported again, with Germany's return to the Chinese market.[84] And new items appeared on the list of imports, for example automobiles, which became widely used in the big urban centres, especially in Shanghai.[85]

The activity in these sectors ensured a continued growth of total imports, in spite of the fewer transactions in cotton goods and metals. This general trend throws light on the real character of this crisis, in that it was only partly one of imports; it was a crisis of finance and speculation rather than a commercial crisis. We might even ask if the difficulties encountered by China's foreign trade in this period were not largely due, as D.D. Patterson put it, 'to the fact that there is no cooperation among the banking institutions, foreign or Chinese, that can be utilized to ease the situation off gradually'.[86]

IV. THE BANKING SECTOR AND THE CRISIS

In Western markets, banks play a vital role in controlling the level of economic activity. Their policies for restricting and expanding credit, which generally follow the lending rates of the central bank, are designed to restore equilibrium to the market. This policy obviously assumes a certain discipline born of a spontaneous understanding on action in the common interest, and a compliance with government directives. The special conditions in which the financial market functioned in China ruled out such assumptions and actions. The fact that the market was not unified and the absence of a central bank made it impossible for the government to take action; in fact, government intervention in the financial market was against traditional Chinese practice. As for spontaneous solidarity, this could not spring up effectively in a community that was divided between local and foreign banks, and where the foreign banks maintained various relationships with their own governments that in themselves had divergent interests.

The banks most directly affected by the foreign trade crisis were the Chinese traditional banks known as the *ch'ien-chuang*, for they financed the movement of merchandise between the treaty ports and the interior. As their working capital was not very great, they used the deposits of their Chinese clientele as well as credits from the foreign banks. Whether they granted traders unsecured loans on trust or loans secured against merchandise in warehouses, their success depended essentially on the swift turnover of stocks: for it was on the disposal of merchandise that depended the solvency of their merchant customers and the recovery of their limited capital, which had to be circulated as rapidly as possible in order to be productive. Any major slowdown in trade could bring the activity of the *ch'ien-chuang* to a halt.

This is what happened in 1920 and 1921. The banks were in a tight corner because of the loans they had previously made to Chinese export traders whose merchandise glutted the warehouses of the treaty ports for want of foreign outlets.[87] The banks were also hurt by the insolvency of many cotton-goods traders who had been unprepared for the fall in the exchange rate.[88] The long-term financing of stocks of merchandise was not possible for the *ch'ien-chuang*, nor was it part of their function. As they were forced to recover their loans as fast as possible, they pushed the traders into over-hasty stock liquidations, which further clogged the market. This was the price at which most of the *ch'ien-chuang* managed to recover their investment. As many previous crises had done, this one highlighted the subordinate role of the *ch'ien-chuang*. These vital organs of transmission, linking the Chinese world to foreign entrepreneurs, were powerless to act; they reacted to market fluctuations instead of controlling them.

The crisis also affected certain foreign banks. It brought rivalries among them to the fore, and showed that there could be no real co-operation between them and Chinese financiers. Although it was only in exceptional cases that the foreign banks underwrote exchange risks in import-export contracts, they did not escape the difficulties that hit Chinese importers, for they financed the shipment of goods between foreign markets and the treaty ports. Now the Chinese traders' refusal to take delivery of new consignments forced these banks to extend their credit deadlines. The issue of the additional interest to be paid on these credits was the subject of very difficult negotiations between the Chinese and foreign business communities; in most cases, the foreign banks had to give up all hope of obtaining satisfaction.[89] Certain banks which had indulged in excessive speculation on the exchange rate now had very heavy payments to make. The Banque Industrielle de Chine (BIC) was unable to pay, and its crash on 30 June 1921 created a severe upheaval in the Chinese financial market. The BIC, established in 1913 with the backing of the Belgian group Empain, and the participation of the (English) Peking Syndicate, had appeared to be a sound institution, and the balance sheet of 30 June 1920 showed substantial profits. But from September 1920, the bank's main customers, among them the Societé Maritime et Commerciale du Pacifique, felt the effects of the crisis, and the BIC found it increasingly difficult to meet its obligations. Despite the assistance that it now received from a consortium set up around the Banque de Paris, the BIC was unable to put its house in order.[90] Subsequently, the BIC's management was severely criticised. Its director, Pernotte, was accused of engaging in fraudulent speculation on the franc/tael exchange rate. The collapse of the BIC was a serious blow not only to the reputation of France but to that of all the foreign banks. Many Chinese deposit-holders withdrew their money, and the local banks, which previously accepted foreign banknotes to keep as a reserve, now asked for silver. The unusual demand for silver that followed led to an extreme contraction in the market throughout the second half of 1921.[91]

In addition to causing these violent upheavals, the crisis sorely tested the real co-operation that had grown up in the Shanghai market between Chinese and foreign financiers. The Hong Kong and Shanghai Bank's attempts to maintain the local exchange value of the tael in the face of fluctuations in the value of silver, were upset by the Chinese speculators of Kiukiang Road who made massive sales of the metal.[92]

The modern Chinese banks, which played a much smaller role than the *ch'ien-chuang* and the foreign establishments in financing import-export operations, were inevitably less vulnerable to the crisis in foreign trade. But their fall-back position in Chinese government bonds was threatened by the difficulties of the Peking government, whose bankruptcy appeared to be imminent in early 1921. However, the caution of the Chinese bankers kept them relatively safe from the crisis.[93] Most of them managed to safeguard their interests. But their security was won only at the cost of a passive attitude. The banks suffered the effects of deteriorating business conditions without being able to contribute to an improvement in the situation. Their lack of means for action reduced them to a purely defensive position. Not only did they not intervene to support the commercial market, but they had to abandon or restrict some of their activities, notably the handling of deposits. The banks were no longer able to put the money entrusted to them to advantage. They were able to find opportunities neither in the business market nor in government loans. Money accumulated, unused, in their coffers. Deposits were accepted only with reluctance, and interest rates were appreciably diminished.[94]

Yet there was money in China, and lots of it. Z.S. Bien, manager of the Tientsin branch of the Bank of China, felt that the central government would be able to find 30 million to 100 million Chinese dollars without difficulty if its authority were better established.[95] But the capital that China had accumulated through the post-war boom remained unutilised. It was out of this situation that a most extraordinary wave of speculation arose in Shanghai, which had seen so many speculative waves, a phenomenon that Chinese historians have called the 'Stock Exchange Storm' (*Hsin-chiao-feng-ch'ao*).[96]

There were no Chinese stock exchanges just after the first World War. The traditional business network sufficed for commodity transactions. As for shares, there were as yet very few since there were few purely Chinese stock companies. When Chinese capitalists wished to invest in foreign or joint (Chinese and foreign) companies, they confined themselves to operations on the (foreign) Stock Exchange in the International Settlement.[97] The first Chinese exchange, whose creation was authorised by the Peking government in 1915, restricted itself to transactions in State-issued bonds.[98] However, with the development of foreign trade and with industrial expansion, the need to create stock and commodity exchanges began to make itself felt. This idea was first put forward by Sun Yat-sen, and big capitalists like Yu Hsia-ch'ing soon took an interest in it. In the end they were forestalled by Japanese entrepreneurs who set up the first commodity exchange in China, the Shanghai Exchange,[99] in 1916 with financial support from the Mitsui group. The Japanese challenge was rapidly taken up, and in July 1919 a stock exchange proclaiming itself to be purely Chinese was established, the Shanghai Stock and Produce Exchange (*Shang-hai Cheng-chuan Wu-p'in Chiao-i Suo*), of which Yu Hsia-ch'ing was president.[100] The undertaking was borne on a wave of anti-Japanese sentiment. It very soon proved a success, and swiftly brought forth rival ventures. Thus raw cotton, yarn and cotton cloth exchanges were set up in the spring of 1921.[101] The new establishments were founded with increasing rapidity. By the summer of 1921, Shanghai had 50 stock exchanges.[102] By the following winter, it had 140.[103] From Shanghai the movement quickly spread to the other treaty ports, including Hankow and Canton.

The expansion of these stock exchanges mobilised large amounts of capital. The total capital invested in the creation and expansion of the Shanghai stock exchanges was estimated in August 1921 at several hundred million Chinese dollars.[104] Growth on this scale was quite disproportionate to the needs of the market. These stock exchanges, most of which traded mainly in their own shares, were purely speculative undertakings.[105] They were created on the Japanese model; their role was to guarantee trading operations on which they took a percentage. Hence they were revenue-earning enterprises.[106] When they traded in commodities, they almost always undertook forward transactions; accounts were settled without transfers of goods. But the stock exchanges usually confined themselves to trading in their own shares, the value of which increased even before a profit had been declared.[107]

The presence of a host of such exchanges had an unsettling effect on both the commercial and the financial markets. Speculation distorted commodity prices by creating a purely fictitious demand. This happened in Shanghai in the summer of 1921 when the price of raw cotton (Tungchow cotton) rose to 29.25 taels per picul on the Shanghai Stock and Produce Exchange, while its value in the market was no more than 26 taels. The command exercised by the stock exchanges over available capital deprived regular business of resources. Money became scarcer in the Shanghai financial market. In the autumn of 1921, the interest rate in Shanghai reached a record level of 0.70 per 1,000 per day (i.e. 25 per cent a year).[108] The tightening of credit combined with rapid inflation recalls the rubber crisis of 1910,[109] except that vigorous action by the Chinese authorities[110] prevented the market from collapsing in 1921-2.

The decisive factor in the recovery was undoubtedly the attitude of the Chinese banks themselves. To the extent that they usually made unsecured loans on trust, the traditional-style banks (*ch'ien-chuang*) were the most exposed to the wave of speculation; they had virtually no means of controlling the capital they lent. But they were exceptionally cautious; they called for the closure of the stock exchanges,[111] maintained loans at a prohibitive rate of interest in order to preserve their capital, and forbade their staff, employees and administrators from investing in the stock exchanges.[112] Thus the worst was averted. From December 1921 the stock exchanges started closing, going into voluntary liquidation or changing over to banking activities. Speculation gradually died down during the first six months of 1922.[113]

The Shanghai financial market, with its diversity of traditional and modern, Chinese and foreign establishments, thus offers an example of an incompletely integrated organism. It was sufficiently cohesive to dispel the immediate danger of the speculative crisis; but it could not, unlike banking sectors elsewhere, provide a solid, permanent link between capital and commercial and industrial firms. This incapacity helped to prolong and worsen the commercial crisis, which had originally affected only certain relatively limited sectors. Dragged down by the slackening pace of the Western economies, the Chinese economy did not have the former's institutional resources with which to shield itself. The retreat of the banks in the face of the business crisis left the market in a crippled condition, and promoted the movement of capital towards speculation, which was all the more dangerous as there was abundant capital. Hence the paradoxical situation of the Shanghai market at the end of 1921: a market richer than ever in capital, but in which the bank interest rate had reached 25 per cent per annum.

V. CONTINUED PROSPERITY OF THE NATIONAL INDUSTRIES

While many factories in the West had to reduce their production or even close down, Chinese industries maintained a vigorous growth which outlasted the exceptional conditions of the post-war boom. Profits continued to be very high in most sectors, as is shown by the reports of the Shanghai Chamber of Commerce.[114] In 1921, the big Ho-feng cotton mill in Ningpo made a profit of 700,000 Chinese dollars, a figure almost equal to its capital of 900,000 Chinese dollars.[115] These results fuelled the optimism of industrialists who 'firmly believe that the demand for articles of Chinese make . . . was not just a short-lived episode brought about by the unusual situation of the big industrial countries'.[116] Expansion continued in 1920-2, at a pace which was barely slower than that of the boom years of 1919-20. In 1921 alone, 42 new plants and factories, six of them textile undertakings, opened in Shanghai.[117] This expansion involved relatively well-established industries in China,[118] textiles, matches, flour and cement. It came about partly through the development of existing companies. In Nantung, Chang Chien, the director of the Ta-sheng mills, planned to expand the equipment in his factories; in the spring of 1921 he was awaiting delivery of 4,000 spindles and 3,000 looms from England, preparing to open his company's seventh mill and hoping to set up a big weaving plant.[119] In 1922 the Pao Heng Company set up its third cotton mill with a capital of 3 million Chinese dollars and 50,000 spindles.[120] In Ningpo, the big Ho-feng cotton mill also made major plans for extension.[121] In 1921

China's biggest cement undertaking, the Ch'i-hsin (Chee Hsin) Company, increased its investment to triple its capacity.[122] But the success of these companies aroused competition, and there was an increasing number of new firms.[123]

This stage of industrial expansion was also marked by the appearance of industrial sectors which until then were little represented in China. While shipping companies were laying up their vessels all over the world, Shanghai's shipyards were in full spate, working to meet a heavy local demand for light-draught vessels intended for inland navigation.[124] The engineering industries also grew rapidly; small workshops were opened, and big companies founded, like the *I-chung Chi-ch'i Kung-ssu* (the I-chung Mechanical Company), set up in 1922 by the cotton-mill owner, C.C. Nieh, with the help of Shanghai capitalists.[125] Another rich entrepreneur, M.Y. San, who had made a fortune in sweets and confectionery, tried to give China a modern sugar industry. Cane farming and cottage-industry refining were then in decline, and China had to import increasing quantities of sugar, 550,000 tonnes in 1918.[126] By disrupting trading relations between the industrial powers and their sugar-producing colonies, the World War had given China an opportunity to enter the market, an opportunity which its capitalists had not seized.[127] It was the big British refineries of Hong Kong, owned by Jardine Matheson and by Butterfield and Swire, that had made the most of the situation, and their huge profits acted as a stimulus to Chinese initiative. With the aid of Shanghai's biggest industrialists, Chang Chien, C.C. Nieh and C.T. Wang, M.Y. San organised the National Company of Chinese Sugar-Refineries in 1921, with a capital of 5 million Chinese dollars,[128] and tried to propagate sugar-beet farming in the northern provinces.[129] As a rule, new manufactures did not emerge through the mobilisation of capital on such a scale. Rather, they came through an increase in the number of small undertakings: soap-mills, paper-mills, factories to make industrial paints or oil-lamps.[130]

The development of Chinese industries during this period can also be gauged by the increased distribution of their goods in the domestic market, along with a concomitant fall in certain imports. This trend towards the substitution of foreign articles by local ones was pronounced in the case of cotton yarn; in Chungking (Szechwan), the Customs report for 1922 noted an increase in the local purchase of Chinese yarn; in Foochow (Fukien), Shanghai yarn almost completely replaced Indian yarn.[131] The decline was less severe in the other regions of China, and the Manchurian provinces under Japanese influence were not affected (Table 12).

TABLE 12: Imports of foreign yarn (by volume) into China from 1913 to 1920-2 (1913 = 100)

	North-east	North	Centre	South	Whole of China
1913	100	100	100	100	100
1917-19	119.6	74.1	48.2	64.3	59.2
1920-2	167.6	61.8	27.6	67.0	48.7

Source: Yen Chung-p'ing, *Mien-fang-chih shih-kao* [A short history of cotton industries in China], 3rd edn (K'o-hsueh Ch'u-pan-she, Peking, 1963), p.141.

Similarly there was a growing domestic market for cigarettes, matches and hosiery made in Chinese factories, to the detriment of imported articles.[132]

This industrial expansion, right in the middle of the world depression, highlights the essentially national character of Chinese commercial undertakings. With some exceptions they were independent of foreign markets, and their development between 1920 and 1922 was aimed above all at satisfying internal demand.

On industrial development of this type, the world depression could have only a limited effect. Falling prices or falling foreign demand could hardly affect industry in a country that contained both its raw materials and its customers. Through political events, however, the world depression did have repercussions on China's infant industry, but its repercussions were beneficial. By curbing the productive forces of the main industrial powers, and by postponing their aggressive return to the Chinese market, the world crisis enabled China's capitalists to continue to enjoy the relative monopoly that the war and then the necessities of European reconstruction had given them. Thus international circumstances gave Chinese industry the protection that the government's weakness had earlier failed to provide.

The consequences of the post first World War depression for the modern sector of the Chinese economy thus appear to have been marked but fairly localised; the only activities directly affected were those with links to foreign trade. This resistance to the world depression did not flow simply from the dispersed character of China's economic structures; it can also be explained by the national character of its modern enterprise. It was the consequence of both underdevelopment and development. Hence, to appreciate the expansion of its modern sector, it is not sufficient to study only the international economic situation. In China, the latter played a role only in combination with agricultural cycles from which the economy continued to derive its basic rhythms.

NOTES

1 *Dept of Overseas Trade, Report on the commercial, industrial and economic condition of China in July 1922* by H.H. Fox (HMSO, London, 1922), p.8 (hereafter referred to as *DOT, Report, July 1922).*

2 G.Clark, 'The business depression in Japan', *China Weekly Review*, (CWR), 17 July 1920. See also G.C. Allen, *A short economic history of modern Japan*, pp.97-102.

3 During the war, Japan enjoyed a big trade surplus which was settled in gold until the US placed an embargo on the export of this metal in 1917. The Japanese government and the Bank of Japan then accumulated huge currency reserves in New York, estimated at 1,343 million yen towards the end of 1919.

4 Cf. C.F. Remer, 'Price maintenance and the silver market', *CWR*, 2 October 1920, pp.217 ff.

5 The tael was the traditional unit of account, defined by a certain weight of silver (37-38g) and by the fineness of the metal. This definition varied from region to region and from sector to sector. The customs tael (Hai-kuan liang), abbreviated to Hk Tl, was used by the Customs Administration in all the treaty ports. It represented 38.34g of pure silver, equivalent to 17.79 French francs in 1920.

6 Cf. 'La baisse de l'argent en 1920', *BCEO*, financial column for February 1921, pp.30 ff.

7 Cf. R. Buchan, 'China and the silver situation', *CWR*, 30 June 1923 (special supplement on finance and banking).

8 Cf. R. Buchan, 'China and the silver situation'; and League of Nations, *Mémorandum sur les balances des paiements du commerce extérieur, 1910-1923* (Geneva, 1924), p.73.

9 Cf. *Bulletin Commercial d'Extrême-Orient* (*BCEO*), September 1921, pp.38-9 and the financial pages of the magazine's subsequent issues.

10 D.D. Patterson, 'China's commercial today', *CWR*, 12 March 1921, p.73.

11 *CWR*, 16 October 1920; and 'The trade of China, 1920', *CWR*, 11 June 1921, p.73.

12 The fall in raw cotton exports also coincided with the expansion of China's cotton mills.

13 'The trade of China', *CWR*, 11 June 1921, p.73.

14 Cf. Tsing Tung-chun, *De la production et du commerce de la soie en Chine* (Paul Geuthner, Paris, 1928), p.139.

15 League of Nations, *Mémorandum sur l'industrie de la soie naturelle* (Geneva, 1927).

16 Cf. Tsing Tung-chun, *De la production*, p.138; and League of Nations, *Mémorandum sur l'industrie de la soie naturelle*.

17 Weekly quotation from the *Bulletin des Soies et des Soieries et Moniteur des Soies* (hereafter *BSSMS*) (price per kilo in francs).

18 *Compte-rendu des Operations de Conditions Publiques des Soies de Lyon pendant les Années 1920-1921.*

19 'Le marché de la soie à Shanghai: revue de l'état du marché en 1921', *BCEO*, February 1922, pp.39-42; and Tsing Tung-chun, *De la production*, p.150.

20 '1922-nian Shang-hai chih ssu-shih chuang-k'uang' [The state of the Shanghai silk market in 1922], *Yinhang Choupao* [Bankers' Weekly] (hereafter *YHCP*), *7* (1923), pp.10-12.

21 Cf. B. Torgashev, 'The export market for Chinese tea', *CWR*, 11 February 1922, pp.461-2. Cf. also 'Hua-ch'a ch'a-k'ou mao-i fu-hsing chih chi-hui' [The circumstances of the renewal of the China tea export trade], *Nung-shang Kung-pao* [Official Bulletin of Agriculture and

Commerce], *10*, 11 (1924), pp.16-18.

22 B. Torgashev, 'La crise du marché du thé chinois', *La Chine*, no.16 (15 September 1922), pp.1381-8.

23 *BCEO*, December 1920, p.37; and *BCEO*, January 1921, p.44.

24 The silk export year began and ended in June.

25 *BCEO*, January 1922, pp.35-6.

26 *BCEO*, June 1922, pp.38-9.

27 *BCEO*, July 1922, p.43; August 1922, p.43; September 1922, p.43; October 1922, p.43.

28 *BCEO*, November 1921, p.51.

29 *BCEO*, September 1922, pp.50-2 and January 1923, p.59; and *Chung-wai ching-chi chou-k'an* (English title: *Chinese Weekly Economic Bulletin*), no.4, 31 March 1923, pp.6-9.

30 *CWR*, 1 January 1921, p.284.

31 S.J. Schneider, 'T'ung oil, 1900-1924: an export trade in the central China setting', (Harvard Seminar Paper).

32 'Han-k'ou shang-yeh kai-k'uang chi shang-yeh pu chen chih yu-lai' [The commerce of Hankow in general and the causes of the business slump], *YHCP*, no. 307, 17 July 1923, pp.15-18.

33 *CWR*, 27 November 1920, p.726.

34 'The silk year in China 1920-1921', *BCEO*, July 1921, p.6.

35 *CWR*, 18 December 1920, pp.154-5.

36 B. Torgashev, 'The export market for Chinese tea', *CWR*, 11 February 1922, p.462.

37 *CWR*, 18 December 1920, p.154.

38 *CWR*, 11 June 1921, p.74.

39 *CWR*, 11 June 1921, p.73.

40 *CWR*, 16 October 1920, p.330.

41 'The silk year in China 1920-1921', *BCEO*, July 1921; and *Chinese Economic Bulletin*, 1 July 1922, p.3.

42 *BCEO*, September 1921, pp.36-7; and *BCEO*, October 1922, p.43.

43 *CWR*, 16 October 1920, p.330.

44 *CWR*, 16 October 1920, p.331.

45 *CWR*, 11 June 1921, p.73; and *BCEO*, 27 July 1921, p.7.

46 'Le marché de la soie à Shanghai', *BCEO*, February 1922, p.39.

47 *BCEO*, January 1922, pp.35-6.

48 *Chinese Economic Bulletin*, 8 July 1922, p.2.

49 'The trade of China, 1920', *CWR*, 4 June 1921, p.14.

50 'Le marché de la soie à Shanghai', *BCEO*, February 1922, p.39.

51 'The trade of China, 1920', *CWR*, 4 June 1921, p.14. See also *BCEO*, April 1922, pp. 35-6: 'Chinese raw cotton is rising constantly despite large quantities of imports from India. This shows the enormous progress made by the China cotton industry.'

52 *BCEO*, September 1922, p.53.

53 China, Maritime Customs, *Returns of Trade and Trade Reports* (hereafter *TR*), *1920*, Report from Shanghai.

54 *BCEO*, September 1921, p.41.

55 This so-called indent system of exchange was practised through the foreign banks, which had a monopoly of international exchange operations. Chinese historians believe that the system was more advantageous to the foreign banks than to local traders. Cf. Wang Ching-yü, 'Shih-chiu shih-chi wai-kuo tsai hua yin-hang shih-li ti k'uo-chang chi ch'i tui Chung-kuo t'ung-shang k'ou-an chin-jung shih-ch'ang ti k'ung-chih' [The growth of the influence of foreign banks in nineteenth-century China and their control over the money market of the treaty ports], *Li-shih Yen-chiu* [Historical Research], 1963, no. 5, pp.51-74.

56 D.D. Patterson, 'Unscrambling legitimate business and unwise speculation', *CWR*, 13 November 1920, pp.571-5; quoted from p.572.

57 *BCEO*, June 1921, pp.42-3.

58 Contemporary Chinese commentators acknowledged that these orders partly caused the crisis, and that local traders were responsible for them. Cf. 'Yang-huo-pang k'ung-huang p'ing-i' [An impartial discussion on the imports crisis], *YHCP*, *5*, 12 (1921).

59 *CWR*, 13 November 1920, p.572.

60 *BCEO*, September 1921, p.41.

61 *BCEO*, December 1920, p.37.

62 *CWR*, 13 November 1920, p.572.

63 D.D. Patterson, 'When is the commercial revival coming?', *CWR*, 1 January 1921, pp.239 ff.

64 *CWR*, 11 December 1920, p.69 and 12 February 1921, p.582.

65 *BCEO*, October 1921 (letter to the editor), p.15.

66 *CWR*, 5 March 1921, p.5.

67 D.D. Patterson, 'China's commercial today', *CWR*, 12 March 1921, p.74.

68 *CWR*, 13 November 1920, p.573.

69 Letter from the Association of Traders in Foreign Commodities for the Maintenance of the Financial Market (Yang-huo Chin-k'ou Chin-yung Wei-chih Hui), addressed to the French Consul-General in Shanghai, and forwarded to the French Chamber of Commerce; quoted in *BCEO*, December 1920, p.3.

70 *CWR*, 5 March 1921, p.5, and *Politique de Pékin*, 27 June 1920, p.537.

71 For example during the 1910 crash. Cf. M-C. Bergère, *Une crise financière à Shanghai* (Mouton, Paris, La Haye, 1964), p.63.

72 *CWR*, 5 March 1921, p.5.

73 'Le commerce de la Chine en 1920', *BCEO*, August 1921, pp.3-4.

74 *CWR*, 13 November 1920, p.572, and 12 March 1921, p.74.

75 'T'ien-chin huo-pang yü wai-kuo yang-hang cheng-ch'ih pu-hsia ch'ing-hsing chih yen-chiu' [Study on the circumstances of the conflict between the traders and foreign firms of Tientsin], *YHCP*, *5*, 12 (1921).

76 *BCEO*, February 1922, p.42.

77 *BCEO*, February 1922, p.42.

78 'Le marché de Tientsin', *BCEO*, November 1921, pp.50-1.

79 *TR*, *1920*, Report from Shanghai.

80 *CWR*, 13 November 1920, p.572.

81 *CWR*, 12 March 1921, p.74.

82 Nevertheless, the volume of metal imports into Shanghai in 1921 was appreciably

smaller than in the previous year. In all, their value fell from 32 million to 22 million Hk taels. The need to liquidate stocks came in the way of new contracts being signed. Cf. *TR, 1921*, Report from Shanghai. However, this fall in imports into Shanghai had little impact on the total value of metal imports into China. From 61.5 million Hk taels in 1920, their value fell to 60 million in 1921. It is true that the depreciation of the tael masks a more serious retreat here, as appears clearly when the quantities imported are examined: 5.5 million piculs of iron and steel in 1920; 4.1 million in 1921. Cf. *TR, 1921*, Report on the Foreign Trade of China.

83 *DOT, Report, July 1922*, p.44.

84 *BCEO*, 21 December 1921, p.44; and D.D. Patterson, 'China's trade outlook brightening', *CWR*, 2 July 1921, pp.216 ff.

85 *TR, 1920*, Report from Shanghai.

86 D.D. Patterson, 'Present commercial trends in China', *CWR*, 9 April 1921, p.292.

87 *Politique de Pékin*, 9 January 1921, p.6.

88 *CWR*, 23 July 1921, p.386.

89 Especially in Tientsin, at the September 1921 settlement referred to above.

90 J.N. Jeanneney, 'Finances, presse et politique. L'affaire de la Banque Industrielle de Chine', *Revue Historique*, 514 (1975), p.377-416.

91 *TR, 1921*, Report from Shanghai.

92 *North-China Herald (NCH)*, 27 November 1920, p.611.

93 Cf. table of profits for the (modern) Chinese banks in Peking during the 1921 financial year, *La Chine*, no.1, 15 August 1921, pp.56-60.

94 'Untangling China's finance', *CWR*, 23 April 1921, pp.397 ff.

95 Cf. *Shang-hai ch'ien-chuang shih-liao* [Research materials on the history of Shanghai's *ch'ien-chuang* banks] (hereafter *SCSL*) (Shang-hai Jen-min Ch'u-pan-she, Shanghai, 1960), p.117.

96 'A gambling mania', *CWR*, 23 July 1921, p.386.

97 *NCH*, 12 June 1915, p.772.

98 *NCH*, 6 April 1918, p.13.

99 *CWR*, 22 January 1921, p.419.

100 *NCH*, 7 February 1920, p.346, and *SCSL*, pp.117-18. See also 'First stock exchange in Shanghai opened', *CWR*, 10 July 1920, p.363.

101 *CWR*, 12 March 1921, p.94, and *NCH*, 9 July 1921, p.108.

102 Cf. A.L. Anderson's report to the Conference of British Chambers of Commerce in China (November 1921) quoted in *BCEO*, January 1922, pp.11-14, 'La speculation à Shanghai'.

103 *NCH*, 10 December 1921, p.178.

104 *CWR*, 6 August 1921, p.528.

105 The cotton yarn and cloth exchange set up by H.Y. Moh provided regulation and information which were appreciated by all industrialists and traders concerned. But this was an exceptional case.

106 'A gambling mania', *CWR*, 23 July 1921, p.386.

107 *CWR*, 2 July 1921, p.250; and She Yao-shu, 'Lun chiao-i-suo chih shi-pai yuan-yin' [The causes of the failure of the Chinese stock exchanges], *Shang-hai Tsung-shang-hui Yüeh-pao* [Monthly Journal of the Shanghai General Chamber of Commerce], 2, 8 (1922), pp.8-13.

108 *SCSL*, pp.634-40 (the figures in this table give the maximum prices in each month). Cf. also *BCEO*, August 1921, p.39; September 1921, pp.38-9; November 1921, p.46.

109 *NCH*, 13 August 1921, p.475.

110 *CWR*, 20 August 1921, p.638.

111 *YHCP*, *5*, 18 (1921), p.140.

112 *SCSL*, pp.120-1 (text of the joint decision by the guilds).

113 *BCEO*, January 1922, p.36; February 1922, p.35; March 1922, pp.32 ff. See also *Chinese Economic Bulletin*, 25 March 1922, p.9; 22 April 1922, p.6; 6 May 1922, p.4; 13 May 1922, p.8; 22 July 1922, p.7.

114 'Profits of business enterprises in Shanghai in 1921', *Chinese Economic Bulletin*, 4 March 1922, pp.3 and 4. Cf. also 'Jen-hsu nien-ko-yeh yin-yü t'iao-ch'a' [Inquiry into the profits of various branches of business in 1922], *Shang-hai Tsung-shang-hui Yüeh-pao*, *3*, 3 (1923).

115 *TR, 1921*, Report from Ningpo. On the business of the cotton mills in 1923, cf. 'Min-kuo shih-i-nien-du ko sha-ch'ang ying-yeh pao-kao' [Business report of cotton-mill enterprises for the 1922 financial year], *Shang-hai Tsung-shang-hui Yüeh-pao*, *3*, 5 (1923).

116 *DOT, Report, July 1922*, p.28.

117 *Chinese Economic Bulletin*, 25 March 1922, pp.3 and 4.

118 The number of installed spindles (both Chinese and foreign) in China rose from 1.6 million in 1918 to 3.48 million in 1922. Cf. H.D. Fong, *Cotton industry and trade* (2 vols., Chihli Press, Tientsin, 1932), vol. 1, p.8. In 1922, there were 2.7 million spindles owned by Chinese industrialists. Cf. inquiry by Chinese Cotton Millowners' Association, published in *Chinese Economic Bulletin*, 4 October 1924, p.4.

119 *CWR*, 18 December 1920, p.164.

120 *Chinese Economic Bulletin*, 18 March 1922, p.11.

121 *CWR*, 11 December 1920, p.108.

122 *TR, 1921*, Report from Chinwangtao.

123 'China's progress in industry', *CWR*, 25 December 1920, p.223 (provides statistics on new firms registered by the Ministry of Agriculture and Trade).

124 *TR, 1921*, Report from Shanghai.

125 *Shang-hai min-tzu chi-ch'i k'ung-yeh* [Shanghai's national mechanical industries], (2 vols. Chung-hua Shu-chü, Peking, 1979), 2nd edn, vol. 1, pp.203-56.

126 Hsiao Liang-lin, *China's foreign trade statistics, 1864-1949* (Harvard University Press, Cambridge, Mass., 1974), p.68.

127 'Les industries du sucre en Chine', *La Chine*, 1 October 1922, pp.1405 ff.

128 *CWR*, 13 August 1921, p.580.

129 *CWR*, 23 April 1921, p.438.

130 On the establishment of soap factories, cf. *Chinese Economic Bulletin*, 4 February 1922, p.7; 18 March 1922, p.10; 6 May 1922, p.7; 13 May 1922, p.10; 12 August 1922, p.4; 2 September, 1922, p.7; and *NCH*, 1920, supplement published on the paper's seventieth anniversary (inserted after p.332 of the issue of 24 July 1920). On the paper-mills, cf. *CWR*, 12 March 1921, p.10; 18 December 1920, pp.164-5. Among others, there was a huge project promoted by the Chairman of the Guild of Paper Merchants in Shanghai to set up a company with a capital of 1 million Chinese dollars. A preliminary technical mission was sent to Europe to collect information on the industries there (*CWR*, 11 December 1920, p.108). On

the industrial paint factories, cf. *NCH*, 1920, supplement quoted above.

131 *TR, 1922*, Reports from Chungking, Foochow.

132 *TR, 1922*, Report from Amoy. Foreign-made matches disappeared through competition from Chinese matches; the growth of the local match industry increased shipments to the interior, to the detriment of Japanese imports. According to the Report from Tientsin, shipments of Chinese cigarettes to the interior grew at a steady pace. 1919: 46,900 piculs, 1920: 50,000 piculs, 1921: 56,000 piculs, 1922: 80,894 piculs.

12

THE WORLD DEPRESSION AND THE CHINESE ECONOMY 1930-6[1]

RAMON H. MYERS

We do not have any detailed study of China's economic development between 1929 and 1936, when world depression spread from North America and Europe to the developing world. Yet conventional wisdom claims that the Chinese economy suffered greatly because of that economic setback.[2] More recent scholarship has tried to alter this interpretation.[3] But the standard studies on this period argue that world depression caused the Chinese economy to contract after 1931, greatly reduced domestic prices, and induced a tremendous outflow of silver from the country.[4] The combined effects of these developments not only produced economic hardship for the small modern sector, but spread into the hinterland, greatly devastating the agrarian sector.[5]

What precisely happened to the Chinese economy between 1929 and 1936? This essay offers a new interpretation of the world depression's impact on China's economy by referring to several studies that have recently appeared and reassessing previous scholarship on the subject. Section I examines the salient features of the early modern economic growth that spread from the city-ports into certain sections of the hinterland before 1930. Section II describes the major economic trends in the country between 1930 and 1936 as depression deepened in world markets. Sections III and IV review economic conditions in the urban and rural sectors to show what complex changes were taking place in China's economy. A conclusion offers some general remarks about the economy's development during the period of the great world depression.

I. THE CHINESE ECONOMY BEFORE 1930

The Shimonoseki Treaty of 1895 concluded the first Sino-Japanese War, forced the imperial court to initiate economic reforms, and opened the door to foreign investment and trade. Even though the Ch'ing empire collapsed in 1911, the rapid expansion of city-port trade and investment continued to facilitate the development of urban networks along the coast and up the Yangtze river as far inland as Chungking. In Manchuria and the five northern provinces, new railway lines linked the hinterland to the port cities. A new wave of commercialisation spread through many districts of the countryside. Several years later, the first World War stimulated an even greater economic boom, and the production of goods and services led by a modern manufacturing sector continued to expand during the 1920s, despite natural disasters, urban strikes and riots.

Although estimates of economic growth between around 1915 and the early 1930s are based on fragmentary data, they indicate that a modest spurt in economic growth had taken place. Gross domestic product probably increased at an annual rate of around 1.0 per cent, and per capita growth at 0.33 per cent.[6] The agricultural sector appears to have expanded at around 0.8 per cent per annum, manufacturing at 1.9 per cent, and services at 1.0 per cent. By the mid-1930s the structure of the economy had been slightly changed, compared to the years of the first World War: agriculture's share of GDP had declined from 66.0 to 62.9 per cent; manufacturing's share had risen from 16.1 to 18.9 per cent; and services' share of GDP had risen slightly, from 17.9 to 18.2 per cent. The network of city-port activities that constituted the modern sector had expanded to account for 27.4 per cent of GDP, but the traditional sector still made up 72.6 per cent. In spite of the modern growth spurt that had occurred, probably nine out of ten persons still lived and worked in villages to derive their livelihoods from farming, handicraft, commerce and services.

The money supply had greatly expanded to facilitate this new growth. All transactions in product and factor markets depended upon copper cash, silver and paper notes. Although gold remained a store of value, bankers and businessmen used it primarily in foreign trade transactions. Households used copper cash and silver for transactions, and both currencies could be exchanged in the money markets. Silver was also used for large transactions and served as a basic standard of account as well as a store of value. Because of the active role of both native and modern banks, the supply of paper notes greatly increased during the period from around 1913 to the end of the 1930s. S.R. Wagel noted that 'the capital of all the native banks in Shanghai rarely exceeded Tls. 1,000,000, while in 1914 it was even less - being only Tls. 600,000 - it is simply marvellous to think that these institutions helped carry on a business of nearly Tls. 250,000,000 in Shanghai alone'.[7] Foreign banks also issued their own notes, as did the Chinese provincial banks. Just as customers expected to convert these notes into silver on demand, so did foreign traders export or import silver whenever the price of silver changed in different international markets.

Looked at in this way, China's banks constituted a free-wheeling, highly competitive financial system. No central bank controlled these banks. The latter consented to converting into silver, upon demand, the notes they issued to their customers. They used commodities, real estate and foreign exchange to back their liabilities (made up of bank notes and deposits). They relied upon arbitrage in different markets, created loans, issued notes, and offered deposits for their customers. Although the law stipulated that bank notes be backed by 60 per cent 'cash' (silver, gold, foreign exchange) and 40 per cent securities, the authorities rarely enforced that ruling. This banking system rapidly responded to demands for currency, giving the economy a resilience and flexibility it might otherwise not have had. As we will note below, its behaviour during the 1930s was symptomatic of the characteristics just cited.

Because markets were highly competitive and offered easy entry and exit, prices for goods, services and factors of production were very flexible. Officials might try to intervene and influence prices when foodgrains became scarce, but otherwise they refrained from trying to control prices. Businessmen also recognised that no seller or buyer could command enough economic power to corner the local or regional market and dictate prices. While all markets appear to have had these highly competitive characteristics, some sections of the country still remained independent of the modern sector, maintaining their own special cycles of economic activity. We lack information about the extent of Chinese market integration, particularly its integration with the international market, so we might view this huge, complex economy as having both independent and integrated markets, which coexisted in ways still not clearly understood.

After the 1890s, foreign trade created new business opportunities for the Chinese. As relative commodity prices began to change, merchant capitalists began to perceive new profit opportunities that had not existed before. They began organising putting-out systems in villages to weave cloth, produce carpets, reel silk, process tea, make grass mats, manufacture matches, grind flour, etc. These putting-out systems began spreading into numerous rural districts where they had not existed before.[8] Most importantly, merchant capitalists used these new systems to integrate the village economy with the modern sector located in the city-ports. At the same time, new factories using machinery and electrical power began appearing in the city-ports to sell for both domestic and foreign markets.

These developments facilitated greater commercialisation of agriculture.[9] More farmers began to allocate their labour to the production and sale of industrial crops. More households could employ their women and teenagers for putting-out contract work to earn more income. Villages and regions favoured by the direct spread effects of trade and industry in the city-ports benefited most of all, but other areas that could supply food-grains or raw materials to these regions experiencing commercialisation and industrialisation also benefited. These developments, naturally, depended upon stability and peace. If local administrations had to raise taxes; if warlord armies confiscated crops, carts, and labour animals from the farmers; if areas devastated by natural disasters received no assistance from the county or provincial bureaucrats, then economic activity declined and great hardship became commonplace. Whenever these disasters occurred, China's population, already very large, suffered severe unemployment and deprivation because so many areas and their markets were closely connected with other markets. Therefore, a random disturbance experienced in one district might produce a deadly ripple effect in one or more markets far away. In this way, external shocks to one part of the economy could have a multiplier effect that expanded unemployment and misery manyfold elsewhere in the economy.

By the late 1920s, China's exports probably amounted only to between 3 and 4 per cent of GDP.[10] In other words, foreign trade was still a very small fraction of total economic activity; yet the 48 city-ports that conducted trade after 1913 had become rapidly integrated with the international market. For example, South-East Asian rice markets had become closely integrated with markets along the Chinese coast, as well as inland up the great Yangtze river.[11] At the same time, the city-ports had become mini-Hong Kong centres that generated a rapid, expanding commercialisation of agriculture, as well as the reorganisation of handicraft and services in many parts of all major regions. As a result, too, of improved transportation and communications, these highly competitive markets within China had begun to generate a tremendous domestic demand for goods and services. Domestic demand probably played a much more powerful role in influencing supplier response in the city-ports than did the minuscule foreign trade that linked those same city-ports to the world market.[12] Yet the businessmen in these centres were definitely sensitive to price changes in both the domestic and world markets. To be sure, certain areas that specialised solely in production for the world market - suppliers of silk and tea, for example - were highly dependent upon demand and supply changes in those same markets. But domestic suppliers had achieved greater flexibility to market in different regions of the economy as well as through foreign trade channels. A more integrated national economy, in other words, had begun to take form.

This was the complex Chinese economy, then, that had evolved by the time the Great Depression began to make its impact felt worldwide. In order to show the pattern of economic development in the 1930s, we must first examine the available economic indicators.

II. THE CHINESE ECONOMY, 1930-6

National income estimates for China in the 1930s show that all sectors advanced, and when these trends are compared with those for the period between the first World War and the early 1930s, economic growth appears to have slightly accelerated.

These trends pertain to mainland China inclusive of Manchuria. Although Japan seized Manchuria in 1931-2, Japanese investment and management did not really begin to change the economy of that region until 1937 and after. Therefore, the economic indicators cited below for China inclusive of

Manchuria appropriately reflect the long-term economic modernisation under way and still continuing in the 1930s.

Table 1 presents the annual values and their indexes for sectoral shares of gross domestic product during 1931-6; the annual rate of sectoral growth has been derived by estimation only for 1931 and 1936.

TABLE 1: Trends in sectoral shares of GDP, 1931-6 (billions[a] yuan in 1933 prices with index = 100)

	Agriculture		Manufacturing		Services		GDP	
Year		(index)		(index)		(index)		(index)
1931	18.01	95.64	5.36	97.63	5.20	101.16	28.57	96.97
1932	18.97	100.74	5.44	99.08	5.06	98.44	29.47	100.03
1933	18.83	100.00	5.49	100.00	5.14	100.00	29.46	100.00
1934	16.59	88.10	5.21	94.89	5.10	99.22	26.90	91.31
1935	18.19	96.60	5.56	101.27	5.34	103.89	29.09	98.74
1936	19.35	102.00	5.96	108.56	5.63	109.53	30.94	105.02
Annual growth rate, 1931-6								
	0.98%		2.11%		1.55%		1.55%	

[a] Thousand millions.

Source: K.C. Yeh, 'China's national income, 1931-36' in Chi-ming Hou and Tzong-shian Yu (eds), *Modern Chinese economic history* (Institute of Economics, Academic Sinica, Taipei, Taiwan, 1979), p.97. These estimates cover Manchuria but not Taiwan.

We observe that GDP advanced at an annual rate of 1.55 per cent, declining only in 1934, largely because of the poor harvest. The manufacturing sector grew at 2.11 per cent per annum, and services expanded more moderately at 1.55 per cent. Both sectors' growth rates exceeded those of previous decades. The agricultural sector grew at almost 1.0 per cent annually, with output stagnating in two years, declining in one year, and then sharply increasing in the other three years. Clearly, the modern sector grew rapidly and, while the traditional sector did not stagnate, its growth was much slower and fluctuated much more than the other two sectors. This finding is confirmed by the estimates of various sub-sectors of the economy in Table 2.

The estimates for mining and manufacturing in Table 2 show rapid growth for the modern sector, but the estimate of agricultural output growth confirms the trend already noted in the value-added sectoral estimate in Table 1.

TABLE 2: Economic indicators for the industrial and agricultural sectors, 1930-6 (for all indexes, 1933 = 100)

Year	(1) Coal-mining output for modern mines (1,000 tons)	Index	(2) Industrial production of 14 commodities (1,000,000 yuan)	Index	(3) Agricultural production of 10 commodities (1,000 yuan)	Index
1930	18,680	89.36	754.4	85.5		
1931	19,948	95.42	809.7	91.8	9,969,494	94.56
1932	19,049	91.12	814.2	92.3	10,373,367	101.11
1933	20,904	100.00	882.0	100.0	10,256,072	100.00
1934	24,287	116.18	908.7	103.0	9,168,742	89.39
1935	25,699	122.93	945.0	107.2	9,798,156	95.53
1936	29,368	140.40	1,042.9	118.2	10,268,149	100.01
Annual growth rate, 1930-6	7.81%		5.51%		(1931-6): 0.98%	

Sources: (1) T. Wright, *Coal mining in China's economy and society, 1895-1937* (Cambridge University Press, Cambridge, 1984), p.10. Includes Manchuria but not Taiwan, and covers only large mines. (2) J.K. Chang, *Industrial development in pre-Communist China: a quantitative analysis* (Aldine Publishing Company, Chicago, 1969), p.131. Includes Manchuria but not Taiwan. (3) Price data for 10 crops obtained from Ta-chung Liu and Kung-chia Yeh, *The economy of the Chinese mainland: national income and economic development, 1933-1959* (Princeton University Press, Princeton, NJ, 1965). For rice, p.330; for wheat, p.332; for millet, p.333; for sorghum, p.335; for barley, p.337; for maize, p.336; for potatoes, p.340; for soy-beans, p.342; for rapeseed, p.345; for cotton, p.347. Crop production data obtained from Chang Yu-i (comp), *Chung-kuo chin-tai nung-yeh-shih tzu-liao* [Materials on modern Chinese agricultural history] (San-lien Shu-tien, Beijing, 1957), vol.3, p.922. Weighted price and output data cover Manchuria but not Taiwan.

We observe that the new estimate by Tim Wright for coal production in modern mines shows a whopping 7.81 per cent annual rate of growth, even higher than J.K. Chang's industrial output growth rate of 5.5 per cent. These two economic indicators include economic activity in Manchuria. These growth rates for specific industries of the modern sector show a more rapid growth rate than those in Western countries in the same period.

If we focus only upon the modern sector and subdivide it into seven industries, we observe the same rapid growth in the estimates compiled by a distinguished Chinese economist after the second World War. These estimates are based on value-added measures for seven sub-sectors of the modern economic sector. In Table 3 we note that growth was particularly rapid in the electrical energy industry, modern banking, postal services, modern manufacturing and telecommunications.

TABLE 3: Estimates of value-added growth for seven sub-sectors of the modern sector, 1931-6 (1933 = 100)

	(1) Minerals and metal-lurgical products	(2) Modern manufac-turing industries	(3) Electrical power	(4) Rail-ways	(5) Telecom-munications	(6) Postal services	(7) Modern banking
1931	102.68	104.99	84.88	110.01	103.61	85.28	89.60
1932	102.27	99.49	84.88	96.21	103.36	87.64	89.60
1933	100.00	100.00	100.00	100.00	100.00	100.00	100.00
1934	104.07	96.47	109.30	110.84	100.54	108.94	117.84
1935	119.33	110.00	116.62	119.67	115.92	116.99	126.24
1936	109.94	133.99	122.09	120.04	117.30	136.29	147.57
Annual growth rate, 1931-6	1.36%	4.90%	7.42%	1.74%	2.47%	9.72%	10.40%

Sources: (1) Ta-chung Liu, *Chinese national income, 1931-1936: an exploratory study* (Brookings Institution, Washington, DC, 1946), p.52, which provides gross value-added estimates of production at current prices for nine minerals and metallurgical products. (2) Ibid., p.49. Based on gross value-added estimates; includes all firms (Chinese and foreign; private and public) in the modern sector. (3) Ibid., p.44. Based on gross value-added estimates. (4) Ibid., p.42. Based on gross value-added estimates. (5) Ibid., p.43. Based on gross value-added estimates. (6) Ibid., p.43. Based on gross value-added estimates. (7) Ibid., p.53. Based on gross value-added estimates.

The above estimates show that considerable economic growth occurred, especially in the modern sector, between 1930 and 1936, when the worldwide depression had deepened. As the modern economic sector continued to expand rapidly and vigorously, even agriculture expanded slightly. What happened to China's foreign trade during this same period?

By 1929 Manchuria accounted for 32.3 per cent of China's total exports and 17.9 per cent of total imports. Manchurian foreign trade accounted for 24.3 per cent of all China's foreign trade. After 1932, Manchuria's trade became diverted primarily to Japan because of imperial Japan's takeover of that region; consequently, we must adjust for Manchuria's foreign trade to evaluate China's foreign trade in the 1930s and before. When we reconstruct China's foreign trade to exclude that of Manchuria, and deflate imports and exports for price changes, we have the results presented in Table 4.

TABLE 4: Deflated exports and imports for China excluding Manchuria (1,000 Haikwan taels)

Year	Value of imports	Index (1913=100)	Value of exports	Index (1913=100)	Total value of trade	Index (1913=100)
1913	524,833	100.0	335,699	100.0	860,532	100.0
1920	385,750	73.5	348,968	103.9	734,718	85.3
1926	640,588	122.0	392,180	116.8	1,032,768	120.0
1927	528,461	100.7	422,622	125.9	951,083	110.5
1928	626,198	119.3	424,067	126.3	1,050,265	122.0
1929	664,960	126.7	404,661	120.5	1,069,621	124.2
1930	641,928	122.3	355,734	105.9	977,662	113.6
1931	671,597	127.9	353,218	105.2	1,024,815	119.1
1932	549,396	104.6	261,078	77.8	810,474	94.1
1933	503,613	95.9	323,698	96.4	827,311	96.1
1934	439,016	83.6	308,094	91.7	747,110	86.8
1935	429,770	81.8	329,064	98.0	758,834	88.1
1936	398,056	75.8	325,875	97.0	723,931	84.1

Source: All trade data were obtained from the annual Maritime Customs' reports for China. After deducting exports and imports through Manchuria's ports, mainland China's total exports and imports were deflated by the Nankai export and import price indices found in Chi-ming Hou, *Foreign investment and economic development in China, 1840-1937* (Harvard University Press, Cambridge, Mass., 1965), p.232. Trade data for 1933-6, denominated in yuan, were converted to Haikwan taels at the rate of 1.558 yuan = 1 Haikwan tael.

From the above table, we first note that trade grew modestly in the late 1920s; the total value of trade declined in 1932; and then imports continued to fall while exports returned almost to their 1930-1 level.[13] The fall in imports from 1932 was partly due to China's recovery of its tariff autonomy and the rapid tariff increases after 1930 like those of other countries. Exports did not exhibit any tendency to fall in 1932-6. Therefore, although total trade did show a moderate decline after 1931 due to the gradual fall in imports, that trade did not collapse, because exports remained fairly stable.

Secondly, we do not detect any major trend of trade expansion after 1913. Trade rose moderately from around 1913, but fell after the first World War. It rose moderately in the late 1920s, then fluctuated, exhibiting the 1930s trends mentioned above. Foreign trade certainly was not a powerful engine for domestic development. If it had been, its rate of growth would have greatly exceeded the growth of GDP, as was the case for the export-led countries of the Pacific Basin after the second World War. Internal trade, however, had become a more powerful force in generating economic development.

We can gain some appreciation of that robust growth of internal trade from the data taken from the Maritime Customs records. These records naturally omit the enormous domestic native trade taking place; they record only the merchandise traded on ships that Customs officials inspected travelling between the treaty ports, destined for domestic consumption. These records, therefore, cover only a fraction of the huge amount of domestic commerce that actually took place, but will serve as a rough proxy of the change in volume of internal trade. Even so, the following table shows how rapidly domestic trade was expanding when viewed from the perspective of the Maritime Customs records. In Table 5, data have been assembled for select years to show the overall trade (exports, imports, and inter-treaty port trade). The foreign trade and inter-treaty port trade for Manchuria have been deducted from overall and inter-treaty port trade. All trade figures have been deflated to adjust for price changes.

TABLE 5: Overall trade, foreign trade, and internal trade for selected years, 1913-36 (1,000 Haikwan taels)

Year	Overall trade	Index	Foreign trade	Index	Internal trade	Index
1913	1,043,203	100.0	860,532	100.0	182,671	100.0
1916	943,420	90.4	758,500	88.1	184,920	101.2
1920	1,019,277	97.6	734,718	85.3	284,559	155.7
1930	1,338,380	128.2	977,662	113.6	360,718	197.4
1936	1,429,991	137.0	723,931	84.1	706,060	386.5

Sources: Data were obtained from the China Maritime Customs Returns for relevant years. Trade data are deflated by the price index contained in Chi-ming Hou, *Foreign investment and economic development in China, 1840-1937* (Harvard University Press, Cambridge, Mass., 1965), p.232. Manchuria trade data have been excluded from all three categories of trade. Foreign trade includes the value of net imports and net exports. Internal trade includes all trade flows between treaty ports and is net of foreign trade. Overall trade comprises both these categories.

From Table 5 we observe that the growth (in real terms) of internal trade for China proper had nearly doubled between 1913 and 1930, increasing at an annual rate of 4.07 per cent per annum. Foreign trade (in real terms) fluctuated over that period, and by 1930 was only 13 per cent above the level for 1913. But between 1930 and 1936, when foreign trade declined by some 25 per cent, internal trade rose by a whopping 95 per cent (an annual growth rate of 11.7 per cent per annum).

If internal trade grew so rapidly in the 1930s and the real value of exports did not decline, except in 1932, then what happened to domestic prices? In late 1931 the domestic price level in the major city-ports finally began to decline. Wholesale prices had been on the rise during the 1920s, but in the third quarter of 1931 they began to fall, and they continued to decline until late 1935, when prices then rose, on a sustained basis. In the summer of 1934 wholesale prices had jumped briefly because of a drought in the central provinces which had adversely affected the harvest. But the forces of deflation still proved too powerful, and prices slumped even further in certain districts. We can review these price trends in Table 6.

TABLE 6: Wholesale prices in six Chinese cities and Hong Kong 1930-July 1936

	Shanghai	Tientsin	Canton	Nanking	Hankow	Tsingtao	Hong Kong
Number of commodities in index	154	106	190	106	111	121	85
1930[a]	114.8	115.9		100.0	100.0	100.0	
1931	126.7	122.6	112.6	106.1	114.5	107.6	134.7
1932	112.4	112.9	113.8	100.8	112.4	103.6	120.7
1933	103.8	100.6	104.5	92.2	98. 9	94.9	102.1
1934	97.1	91.8	94.3	80.6	89.0	86.9	92.3
1935	96.4	95.4	84.6	80.4	89.3	89.4	76.8
1936[b]	106.0	108.5	102.8	96.5	110.6	107.4	98.9

[a] Base year differs for the seven city price indices. Shanghai index of 100=1926; Tientsin=1926; Canton=1926; Nanking, Hankow and Tsingtao=1930; Hong Kong=1922.

[b] Price index represents the average of first seven months of 1936.

Source: A.B. Lewis and Lien Wang, 'Wholesale prices in different cities in China and in Hong Kong, 1930 to 1936', *Economic Facts*, no.2 (1936), pp.95-7.

For Shanghai wholesale prices in 1934 were 27.4 per cent lower than in 1926. For Hankow they were 28.3 per cent lower, and for Tsingtao and Tientsin they were 23.6 and 28.6 per cent lower respectively.[14] Shanghai grain prices in 1934 had fallen to their 1920 level; the price of hens' eggs was equal to their price in 1900; the price of coal was only 13 per cent above the 1900 price.[15] The overall wholesale price index for 154 items in Shanghai was 8 per cent lower in 1934 than in 1921. Similar price falls could be observed for Tientsin and other large cities.

Why did prices decline so sharply for four years, even while the modern sector's growth continued to expand rapidly? The Chinese economy had become more tightly integrated with the international market after the 1870s. Therefore price formation in much of China had become heavily conditioned upon that integration. External or exogenous factors, notably the world price of silver and international commodity prices, exerted increasing influence upon domestic price formation. The process by which these external factors influenced domestic prices was as follows.

Because silver was the primary medium of exchange in China, changes in the international price of silver influenced how China could trade with the rest of the world. When silver became widely demonetised after the 1850s, the dollar or sterling price of silver greatly declined. This made Chinese exports cheaper and her imports more expensive, thus putting upward pressure on domestic prices. The decline in silver price continued through most of the early twentieth century until 1932, from when within four years the price of silver in the international market more than doubled. This appreciation in the price of silver was associated with a very substantial outflow of silver from China after 1932, as Table 7 shows. The appreciation also exerted the opposite influence on prices within China. But the changing price of silver was not the only factor affecting domestic prices.

TABLE 7: Import and export of silver, 1926-37 (US $1,000)

	Import	Export	Balance
1926	59,873	19,438	+40,435
1927	56,510	11,595	+44,907
1928	79,280	3,739	+75,540
1929	77,715	9,986	+67,728
1930	47,180	16,354	+30,822
1931	25,801	10,350	+15,451
1932	21,166	23,664	-2,497
1933	20,912	24,662	-3,749
1934	3,593	88,294	-84,720
1935	3,958	25,341	-21,382
1936	1,366	73,757	-72,390
1937	125	83,808	-83,682

Source: Hsiao Liang-lin, *China's foreign trade statistics, 1864-1949* (East Asian Research Center, Harvard University, Cambridge, Mass., 1974), pp.128-9. Data on pp.128-9 converted to US dollars at exchange rate values given on p.192. The above data do not include smuggling of silver which, if included, would considerably increase the value of outflows.

Chinese commodity prices were also influenced by world commodity prices. If world commodity prices rose, as they did from the 1870s until the first World War, these increases were transmitted into the Chinese market economy.

Although world commodity prices began to decline after 1929, between 1929 and 1931 the effect of this on Chinese prices was offset by the continued depreciation of silver; consequently Chinese prices still rose. In 1932-3, however, falling international commodity prices and the sudden appreciation in silver both put substantial downward pressure on domestic commodity prices. For the first time since China began to trade extensively in the world economy (after the 1870s), a major price deflation had occurred. Although international commodity prices began to recover in 1933, domestic prices continued to fall until the end of 1935 because of the more powerful influence exerted through the appreciation of silver. When silver flowed out of China after 1932 and domestic prices fell, did the money supply also decline? Had the money supply also declined, it would be most unlikely that the output of goods and services could have risen, as earlier tables have indicated. In fact, recent research by Thomas Rawski has shown that the money supply expanded over this period. Although the component of the money supply made up of silver contracted, the inside component, comprising bank notes and deposits, expanded and more than offset the decline in the silver stock, as Table 8 shows.

TABLE 8: Rawski's money supply estimates: 1910-36
(year end totals, million yuan)

	Silver		Copper	Bank notes	Bank deposits	Total money supply	
	1A	1B	2	3	4	5A	5B
1910	880	1934	413.7	114.3	807.4	2,215.4	3,269.4
1915	1,035	2,089	382.2	209.7	786.5	2,413.4	3,467.4
1920	1,225	2,279	350.7	282.2	1,242.9	3,100.8	4,154.8
1925	1,581	2,635	319.2	547.5	1,985.5	4,433.2	5,487.2
1930	2,200	3,254	287.7	956.3	3,392.1	6,836.1	7,890.1
1931	2,271	3,325	281.4	896.9	3,591.5	7,040.8	8,094.8
1932	2,289	3,343	275.1	924.4	3,880.8	7,369.3	8,423.3
1933	2,275	3,329	268.8	978.8	4,290.6	7,813.2	8,867.2
1934	1,995	3,049	262.5	1,108.9	4,620.9	7,986.5	9,040.5
1935	1,703	2,757	256.2	1,413.5	5,460.1	8,832.8	9,886.8
1936	1,391	2,445	250.0	2,438.6	6,394.2	10,473.7	11,527.8

Source: T.G. Rawski, 'Estimates of China's money supply, 1910-1936', unpublished, p.43.

In fact, according to a recent reinterpretation by Brandt and Sargent of the influence of American silver policy on China, the outflow of silver after 1932, and especially between 1934 and 1936, did not exert any negative influence on the Chinese economy.[16] On the contrary, with bankers and merchants engaged in currency arbitrage (obtaining silver in China; exchanging it for US dollars and sterling in New York or London; buying more Chinese currency to buy silver; and repeating the cycle), the Chinese economy gained a windfall.

To conclude: the decline in prices after 1931 was the product of changes in world prices, and the rising price of silver in the international market. Yet at the same time the money supply continued to rise. All major economic indicators show that economic activity was rising except for the decline in total foreign trade (caused principally by the decline in imports). Domestic trade greatly expanded, except in areas where violence disrupted the centres of supply and modern transport facilities. But even in these areas, suppliers were frequently able to divert their market surplus by traditional modes of transport - of waterways, mule-hauled carts, and wheelbarrows - so that trade continued. Let us now examine the economic conditions in the cities, then review circumstances in the village economy.

III. URBAN CHINA, 1930-6

Although in 1935 the Nanking government really controlled only about two provinces, Chekiang and Kiangsu (and exerted minimal control in another eight), its budget spending did affect urban and transport developments in these two large provinces of east-central China.[17] Between 1929 and 1936 Nanking government spending rose about 250 per cent, but about one-fifth of its spending had to be covered by borrowing, or by floating bonds which were purchased mainly by banks and businessmen.[18] The impact of such spending upon cities was considerable. For example, as Nanking's population rose from 360,000 in 1928 to over 1,000,000 in 1935, the city was rapidly transformed, as the following report in a 1933 Shanghai newspaper relates.[19]

> Since 1927, when 50 new buildings were erected at a cost of a little over $1,000,000, according to figures of the Municipal Government, more than 4,000 buildings have been erected at a total cost of $26,220,000. Much building activity has been necessitated by the remarkable growth in the population, which standing at nearly 600,000 has practically doubled in five years.

By early 1933 Nanking's largest avenue, Chungshan Road, extended twelve kilometres outside the city to the mausoleum of Dr Sun Yat-sen.

By 1932 Shanghai was considered the sixth or seventh largest port city in the world, clearing 37 million tons of shipping. There were an estimated 1,781 factories; four waterworks delivered 45 million gallons of water annually, and five electric power plants served the city. The International Settlement area alone generated around 46.5 million Shanghai taels or 15.8 million US dollars in land rent each year. One report contended that the 'aggregate of individual incomes in Shanghai is certainly not much less than Tls. 300,000,000 per annum.'[20] In 1932 the January incident of Japanese troops attacking Chapei, a Chinese district of Shanghai, led to the closing of the Shanghai stock market and all major banks for roughly three months. But economic activity picked up in 1933 when 'industry recovered to approximately what might have been expected had there been no disturbance'.[21] Business activity in 1934 continued to be brisk, leading one Shanghai commentator to state, 'The general conclusion can be reached from these data that Shanghai in 1934 is continuing to grow. Its volume of industrial production has steadily increased and, while the trend is not as rapid as in certain years, it is substantial and steady.'[22]

But the building and real estate boom that had reached a high pitch during 1934 spluttered toward the year's end, and in Shanghai a 'depression really began to set in in the autumn and at the close of the year was serious'.[23] This brief setback was described in the following terms.[24]

> For Shanghai the year was one in which depression deepened to extreme acuteness. The uncertainty over silver and, above all, the general world position caused a marked falling off in trade. This was not mitigated by marked activity in certain local industries - mainly miscellaneous textiles. Nor was the further erection of large apartment houses, hotels and other considerable urban dwelling taken to reflect prosperity. Indeed, toward the end of the year a drastic reduction in rents was expected, owing to the keen competition among the owners of apartment houses and the like.

By the middle of 1935, however, Shanghai's economy was again on the upswing. The cigarette industry's production was up, and the output of cotton yarn rose.[25] Economic growth continued strongly into 1936. In that year a commentator pointed out, 'It is an encouraging sign that failures and suspensions of business firms dropped from 41 in October, 1935, to only 13 during the corresponding period this year.'[26]

If Nanking and Shanghai were not really adversely affected by the world depression, neither were other cities in east-central China. West of Shanghai in Kiangsu province lay Wusih city and the county of the same name. In late 1932 a roving reporter described that area:[27] 'Electric lights are found in all the large villages, supplied from the same central plant which gives a 24 hr service to the city and which is situated near Changchow.' Further south, in Chekiang province, the villages in the environs of Ningpo also appeared to be prospering in 1932.[28]

> When this writer arrived in Ningpo, four years ago, a trip to the adjacent country towns and villages meant the hiring of a special boat at an exorbitant price. Now the network of canals in the district is traversed by steam tugs, towing as many as ten canal boats in a long chain, and one can get to almost any place for thirty or forty cash.

The city of Ningpo seemed to be flourishing.[29] 'As a result of private enterprise, many new buildings have been erected in the city, the majority of them being of the 'Jerry built' type - lath and plaster and a few bricks.'

But prosperity was not just concentrated in east-central China, although evidence for that concentration was certainly most conspicuous. Swinging northward to eastern Honan in 1932, one traveller pointed out that much new urban building was in evidence.[30]

> The last two years have seen a much greater show of prosperity than before. In the city many new shops are being built whereas old fronts are being renewed. In the village at the railway station many new compounds presumably for houses are being erected at the present time.

Finally, even with the great outflow of silver in 1934, we cannot find any mention in the Shanghai press of the damaging influence of the world depression or of the silver outflow upon Shanghai's economy.[31]

Throughout the years 1932-6 businessmen's confidence had greatly improved. The expansion of cotton production throughout North China since 1930 had encouraged many entrepreneurs to add new capacity to the textile industry.[32] By early 1937 new paper mills were being set up in Shanghai. The Yung Li Company issued debentures amounting to $15,550,000 to establish the manufacture of sulphate of ammonia, and $1,000,000 for establishing the Tien Li Chemical Works.[33] New plants were also being erected in Canton, and there was much road-building taking place in Kwangtung province.[34]

The great Yangtze flood of 1931 had caused considerable economic uncertainty and difficulty.[35] But the Japanese military intervention in Shanghai in January 1932 was alone responsible for the financial difficulties in the city and the closing of the stock market for the next three months. In late 1934 and 1935 a brief recession in Shanghai had brought about some bank failures. Because many Shanghai banks had invested in the 1933-4 real estate boom, their deposits and reserves allegedly fell from 22.7 to 18.3 million yuan, and the number of banks declined from 68 to 50.[36] But aside from these minor setbacks, economic modernisation continued in the urban sector of the east-central provinces, as well as in many other parts of China. If much of the urban sector fared so well, what of the rural sector during these same years?

IV. THE RURAL SECTOR, 1930-6

When modern growth had first originated in the city-ports, their networks had extended only into a limited number of rural markets to affect the village economy. While the farmers so affected had benefited greatly from modern economic growth, other areas had benefited more slowly or not at all. Such a differentiated, large rural economy, therefore, would be influenced in very complex ways by the unprecedented decline in prices after 1932. We first examine how the fall in prices might have affected the agrarian economy; then we develop a typology to describe three patterns of agricultural development during the 1930s.

When prices fell in 1932, some farm prices fell more rapidly than others, but nearly all farm prices fell more rapidly than the prices of goods produced in the city-port sector and marketed throughout the countryside. Farmers highly dependent upon the proceeds earned from marketing key crops whose prices had declined in the extreme, experienced some decline in cash earnings. For example, in Shantung, where many farmers greatly depended upon marketing wheat, their primary cash crop, the price per 100 catties was 5 yuan in 1929, rose to 7 yuan in 1930, and to 9 yuan in 1931, but then fell to 5 yuan in 1932 and to 3.5 yuan in 1933.[37] Again, in the silk and tea districts of central and south-east China, where farmers had produced primarily for export, the decline in export sales in the 1930s forced them to reduce the acreage devoted to export crops, thereby reducing their cash proceeds. In Shun-te county of Kwangtung, for example, 'the farmers had formerly allocated about 10 per cent of their land to cultivating mulberry trees, but by 1933 about one-third of that land had become idle'.[38]

Where specialisation and exchange had made many farmers more dependent upon the market, the sudden adverse movement in the terms of trade had forced many households to borrow, so that in some areas rural indebtedness mushroomed between 1933 and 1936. In 1933 crop reporters for the Nanking government had noted that 'about 56 per cent of the farmers are in debt, and the average annual rate of interest is 34 per cent'.[39] When debt rose, many households had to reduce their outlays for ceremonial functions. In his study of Kaihsien kung village, south of Lake Tai in Kiangsu, Fei Hsiao-t'ung reported that a 30 per cent fall in income had occurred because of the reduced sale of silk. That income loss had forced villagers to reduce their spending for marriages, funerals and the birth of children.[40] The rise in rural debt had also forced many households to mortgage their land; between 1934 and 1935 the households mortgaging their land had increased in 16 out of 22 provinces.[41] Many households also sold their land, and rising land sales further depressed land prices. In Chengting in Hopei province, for example, farm land values in 1934-5 had fallen to a level equivalent to their 1905 values.[42] What occurred in Chengting had also taken place in other parts of China.[43]

But where farm proceeds had declined, land and labour costs were also falling. Because factor markets were highly competitive, factor prices were flexible downward when commodity prices were falling. Under these conditions, therefore, not all farmers were so adversely affected. Farmers whose costs had fallen were still able to supply the same quantity to markets and make ends meet. We do not know in quantitative detail how these complex price and cost changes affected farmers throughout this huge, differentiated economy; but there is another way to evaluate economic change in these farming communities, and that is to use descriptive types to show local rural conditions during the period.

In the first descriptive type, the village economy continued to experience specialisation and trade, because political conditions remained stable and rural markets remained integrated with networks of the city-port sector. In this type of village economy, agriculture, handicraft and services were closely connected by trade and credit with the modern sector located in the city-ports. Because investment and spending in the modern sector continued strongly in the 1930s, trade with the agrarian economy flourished and economic activity in these rural areas prospered. These same areas may also have benefited from new road and railway construction in this decade. Perhaps as many as 150 million people were involved in these integrated markets and received the above-mentioned benefits arising from urban, modern economic growth.

The second type of village economy experienced little or no change during these years, and life continued as usual. We do not know what proportion of China's interior fell into this category, but many areas distant from waterways, railway lines and road networks were not connected with the national market system. Their economic activity neither expanded nor declined in this period.

The third type of village economy comprised those areas which were adversely affected by severe weather fluctuations like floods or droughts, in which farmers lost their reserves and had to sell their property and migrate in order to survive. There were also areas in the direct path of bandits or warlord armies, to which farmers lost their livestock, carts and even their sons and farmhands. These areas could be excessively taxed at the same time. We will refer to this type of village economy as one experiencing random shocks that reduced the surplus which farmers could market.

Taking examples of our first type of economy, the following description of conditions in central Shantung, around Tsinan city, in late 1933 suggests that many cities within the modern commercial network enjoyed prosperity, as demonstrated by the abundance of new consumer goods.[44]

> Regarding the general living standards of the people, the last two years have seen considerable growth in the use of potato, which can be bought at quite distant markets. Electric torches, barbed wire, and especially bicycles have become much more common. Rubber shoes and galoshes have a ready

> sale. Chinese barbers have clippers and do ladies' hair-dressing with up-to-date chairs and other equipment. School girls go about with skirts and bobbed hair.

These conditions pertained to urban centres, but what of the surrounding countryside? In the rural districts of central Shantung, the spread of tobacco cultivation had enabled farmers to maintain, or even expand, their income.[45] 'Owing to the prices obtainable for good tobacco leaves being much in excess of those for grain produce, large tracts of land in Shantung are now used for growing tobacco plant.' And when these conditions occurred in the context of good harvests, as had been true of this region, the following results could be observed.[46] 'The last year's crops have been abundant - both spring and autumn. Taxes have been lowered and so the farmers are content and prosperous'. In the spring of 1935, a correspondent for the *North-China Herald* reported favourable developments in rural areas along the Fukien, Kiangsi and Anhwei provincial borders, as compared to the difficult years of the early 1930s when KMT troops had battled with Communist insurgents.[47]

> There is brightness in the countenance of the people in contrast to the care-worn look of recent years . . . The revolution of transport is simply astounding and distances remain as a word but hardly survive as a fact. The craze for modernism is making great transformations for the convenience of the travelling public and the old time inn is giving place to the up-to-date hotel. Passing through the county of Linche, it was interesting to learn that begging was prohibited. On the streets of the county town not a beggar is to be seen.

In the province of Hunan, where peace prevailed, General Ho Chien had eradicated opium cultivation and had 'carried out a programme of road-construction with the result that communications have been improved. Places which formerly were a week's journey from Changsha are now within reach of a twenty-four hour motor ride'.[48] These transport improvements had facilitated the marketing of a greater surplus, so that farmers began to receive direct benefits from such road-building.

But the historical record for this decade also indicates that many areas never changed. In other words, such areas never experienced either the new modernisation impulses or the random disturbances mentioned above. Some sections of rural China simply remained the same as in previous decades, neither improving nor declining. Here is a brief description of northern Kiangsu in the spring of 1937, based on a Christian church survey of Hsuchowfu, which had only six government schools in an area of 100 square miles.[49] 'There was no New Life Movement, nor any mass education among 40,000 farmers, while road building had lapsed.'

Roughly three out of every four farmers owned their land, and all households were registered under the *pao-chia*, a type of community surveillance system formerly used in imperial China. While harvests had fluctuated, the majority of people appeared to just get by as they had in the recent past.[50] 'It is commonly said that although last year's crops were largely failures owing to the floods, and though the people are able to afford wheat flour, yet not more than five per cent really go hungry or are undernourished.' Similarly, when a news reporter returned to Kaifeng, a large city in central Honan province, he found little had changed over the past few years.[51] 'Kaifeng showed few signs of growth or improvement since I was there three years ago.'

Turning to our third type of village economy, increasing banditry and excessive taxation in these same years had made the life of farmers miserable. E.B.Copland described farmers' reactions toward official taxation in rural Honan in 1936 as follows:[52] 'Farmers feel that they get nothing from the Government except demands for taxes, and almost no services for what they pay.' Official demands for village labour on road construction, etc., without payment, was another burden on the villages of northern Honan. Conditions became so bad that 'most people do not remember such widespread distress as we see in this region since the years of the great famine in 1920-21. Beggars have never been so numerous'.[53]

Some rural areas were also adversely affected by the decline of nearby urban centres. Take, for example, the case of Hankow, on the Yangtze river far inland from Shanghai. Because of banditry and Communist insurgency in Hupei province, Hankow's commerce stagnated in 'the first eight months' of 1932.[54] C.D. Dixon, Chairman of the British Chamber of Commerce in Hankow, reported that '40 per cent of the Chinese hongs and shops have closed their doors and gone out of business, and in most cases rents are six months in arrears'.[55] Rural areas dependent upon Hankow's commerce suffered as a consequence.

But in rural areas where excessive rain or drought had occurred, the farmers suffered much more. Here is what one observer wrote about Tatung county in Kweichow province in late 1932.[56]

> The whole countryside is armed there and farmers came fully armed to market . . . The harvest generally seems to be poor this year and in Tsing-chen district is still largely unreaped on account of the consistently wet weather. Nevertheless, the farmers are busy planting opium where and whenever they can get the sod turned.

Severe drought had hit parts of Shensi province. In spring 1933 the reports from Shensi cited severe famine conditions within the large triangular area embracing Hancheng on the Yellow river, southward to the mouth of the Wei river, and from Hancheng south-westward to Fengsiang. The following observations on two areas within this triangle show that people had perished from famine.[57]

> It is not an exaggeration to give an estimate of from 2/3 to 4/5 of the houses having been torn down and the material sold so as to enable the owner to buy food for the family . . . In the city of Wukung, only a few carts are to be found. Village dogs, fowls, and nearly all animals throughout the parts that Dr Kelly visited had perished.

Similarly in Szechwan, for those counties located between the two major urban centres of Chungking and Chengtu, the lack of rain in late 1936 had brought the countryside to the verge of famine.[58]

> The country is in a desperate condition through drought, no rain practically since the summer. Crops have failed and one heard nothing but how to get sufficient to eat and to keep body and soul together . . . I had the impression that the villages along the big road were flourishing places, but this journey has given me a different impression. There is little in most of them, but tumble down mat or grass shacks.

Further south, in Kwangsi province's Jung county, a researcher reported in his diary that a series of disasters, including very bad harvests, had created conditions of near-famine.[59]

> As a consequence of unemployment and poverty the land prices per mow have fallen from 250 to 150 yuan; rural wages per worker have fallen from 50 to 25 cents; the interest rate for 10 dollars' silver has doubled from 20 to 50 catties of coarse grain. In the spring of 1935 around 60 to 70 per cent of the village households were eating a thin rice gruel with sweet potatoes, taro and barley hulls to support life. Some families even ground roots into a powder to make a starchy soup to assuage their hunger. This prosperous area had become transformed into a community bordering upon famine.

Thus, in those rural areas where random disturbances had adversely affected the agrarian economy and where a general price decline had occurred, villagers were compelled to sell land and incur debt.

Therefore, when economic conditions had deteriorated, births sometimes declined and the death rate increased. The following table shows some interesting demographic trends for a rural area that had suffered from the outbreak of disease as well as a decline in farm prices.

TABLE 9: **Birth and death rate by economic status of 4,579 rural families, Kiangyin, Kiangsu (September 1931 - August 1934)**

Economic status	Births per 1,000				Deaths per 1,000			
	1931-2	1932-3	1933-4	1931-4	1931-2	1932-3	1933-4	1931-4
Rich	37.3	34.7	34.6	35.5	26.5	32.3	33.9	30.9
Well-to-do	50.6	46.3	44.9	47.2	39.6	31.0	49.3	40.0
Poor	48.5	44.1	37.9	43.6	46.6	39.6	56.0	47.3
Total	48.3	44.1	40.0	44.2	42.8	36.1	52.0	43.6

Source: Tsai-Djang Chen and Chi-ming Chiao, 'Birth and death rates in Kiangyin registration area', *Economic Facts*, no.1 (1936), p.67.

From the above we note that the birth rate steadily declined and the death rate rose between 1933 and 1934. These researchers offered the following explanation for the trends they had detected.[60]

> The steady decline in the birth rate was probably due to the decline in farm prices, the decline in the marriage rate, and epidemics of cholera and malaria. Declining farm prices meant decreasing farm incomes, causing many married people, especially the young people, to go out without their families to hunt for jobs.

The annual population growth rate for Kiangyin county was 0.06 per cent between 1931 and 1935, compared to 1.09 per cent in the 1920s.[61] Complex economic decline, the outbreak of disease, and random disturbances adversely affecting the harvest, could interact to reduce the growth of population.

V. CONCLUSION

This essay has presented a new interpretation of economic development in China during the 1930s, when the Great Depression engulfed the advanced countries and caused the great decline in world trade. Contrary to the conventional wisdom in standard works dealing with Chinese economic development during this period, widespread economic decline did not take place. This alternative interpretation is based on new statistical estimates, unpublished research by various scholars now in progress, and the historical record.

Before 1930, China's city-port sector began experiencing modern economic growth as foreign trade and foreign investment increased. Waves of Chinese entrepreneurs established new factories and businesses in the city-ports and began developing new trade networks with the great agrarian economy. The gradual restructuring of the handicraft and service sectors in the hinterland was also associated with the rapid commercialisation of agriculture and the expansion of inter-regional trade.

As sections of the domestic economy became integrated with the international market, businessmen in the city-ports were able to make profits by taking advantage of price changes in the highly competitive domestic and international markets.[62] The appreciation of the exchange rate after 1931 transmitted falling world prices into the domestic market. But a revolution in banking had made possible the expansion of bank deposits and note issue that facilitated this rapid economic growth.[63] Because of the continued economic growth of the modern sector and the expansion of the money supply, the outflow of silver from China in 1934-5 did not adversely influence the economy, as so many have asserted.

Our economic indicators show that the modern urban sector continued to expand over the period, with rising per capita income and employment. Although imports began to decline after 1932, chiefly because the Nanking government had begun to impose tariffs after 1928, exports held their own between 1932 and 1936. In spite of the dislocating effects of Japan's seizure of Manchuria in 1931-2, China's domestic trade continued to grow, helped to some extent by the goods and services formerly traded with Manchuria being diverted to other regions.

The most spectacular economic event after 1932 was the great decline in domestic prices. This new trend was due to a number of factors. First, falling world prices were transmitted into Chinese markets through the competitive trading networks that integrated the two market systems. Second, the appreciating exchange rate also transmitted falling world prices into domestic markets. Finally, the expansion of output and domestic trade during these same years continued. Equally as important as the great decline in wholesale and retail prices was the decline in factor prices. Because factor costs, principally land prices and labour wages, were flexible downward, households and entrepreneurs could still make ends meet even when market proceeds had declined.

When we refer to the historical record of the period, then, we do not observe signs of depression such as massive unemployment in the cities or in many parts of the countryside. Where information indicates that rural misery occurred, we can usually find specific reasons for it: poor harvests, banditry or warlordism. China simply did not experience any national economic depression as the world depression deepened.

NOTES

1 I am grateful for the critical remarks offered by Professors Christopher Howe and David Fieldhouse and other participants in the Conference on the Economies of Africa and Asia during the Inter-War Depression, held at the School of Oriental and African Studies, 12-14 December 1985. But I owe the greatest debt to Dr Loren Brandt, whose basic disagreements with my original approach and interpretation compelled me to retreat and agree with his general argument that China's economic growth continued through the 1930s and was not really affected by the Great Depression and the outflow of silver after 1934.

2 This is the interpretation advanced in L.E. Eastman, *The abortive revolution: China under Nationalist rule, 1927-1937* (Harvard University Press, Cambridge, Mass., 1974), ch 5. Eastman states that the 'cities, however, were partially shielded from the full brunt of the depression' (p.187). Yet, like many others, including this author, he blames American silver policies for driving the Chinese economy into a second and deeper phase of depression (see p.186). For a similar argument about the role of silver outflow, see R.H. Myers, *The Chinese economy, past and present* (Wadsworth, Belmont, California, 1980), pp.176-7. Milton Friedman and Anna Jacobson Schwartz make the same argument. See *A monetary history of the United States, 1867-1960* (Princeton University Press, Princeton, N.J. 1963), p.699. Many Chinese sources also argue the same interpretation.

3 See P.K.T. Sih (ed), *The strenuous decade: China's nation-building efforts, 1927-1937* (St John's University Press, New York, 1970), particularly chs 3-8.

4 This interpretation is presented in works cited in n.2.

5 For a good source on the effects of the depression, as well as of other factors, upon the rural economy, see Chang Yu-i (comp), *Chung-kuo chin-tai nung-yeh-shih tzu-liao* [Materials on modern China's agricultural history] (San-lien Shu-tien, Beijing, 1957), vol.3. This useful compendium of historical materials presents a vast amount of selected materials on the decline of the rural sector. Readers of this work must exercise great caution in citing this evidence, because much of it has been taken out of context and the work ignores considerable historical materials that cite favourable developments in the countryside during the 1930s.

6 The estimates in this paragraph are derived from K.C. Yeh, 'China's national income, 1931-36' in Chi-ming Hou and Tzong-shian Yu (eds), *Modern Chinese economic history* (Institute of Economics, Academia Sinica, Taipei, Taiwan, 1979), p.107. More recently, Thomas G. Rawski has compiled new estimates for economic growth during the Republican period (1911-49) and found China's growth in the 1930s to be even higher than estimated by K.C. Yeh.

7 S.R. Wagel, *Finance in China* (Garland Publishing, New York, 1980), p.286.

8 For a good description of this process in sections of Shantung and Hopei provinces in North China after the 1880s, see Minami Manshū Tetsudō Kabushiki Kaisha, Chōsabu [Research Bureau, South Manchurian Railway Company], *I-ken tofugyō chōsa hōkokusho* [An investigation report of the native cotton cloth industry of Wei county] (place of publication unknown; probably published in 1942), pp.257-82.

9 For a review of the accelerated commercialisation of agriculture, especially in North China after the 1890s, see R.H. Myers, *The Chinese peasant economy* (Harvard University Press, Cambridge, Mass., 1970), ch 11. For a different interpretation of the impact of this commercialisation upon rural households, see P.C.C. Huang, *The peasant economy and social change in North China* (Stanford University Press, Stanford, California, 1985), ch 16.

10 R.F. Dernberger estimates that in the 1920s Chinese exports as a proportion of GDP came to 7.3 per cent. His estimate is based upon the average GNP for 1931-6 in T.C. Liu's 1946 national income study. I believe that Dernberger's estimate is too high. If we convert the value of mainland China's 1933 exports to yuan and add the yuan-value of exports leaving

Manchuria in that same year, as a percentage of K.C. Yeh's GDP estimate for 1933 we obtain a value of around 4.6 per cent. See Dernberger's estimate in D.H. Perkins (ed), *China's modern economy in historical perspective* (Stanford University Press, Stanford, California, 1975), p.27.

11 L.Brandt, 'Chinese agriculture and the international economy, 1870-1930s: a reassessment', *Explorations in Economic History*, no.22 (1985), pp.168-93. Brandt's unpublished findings, soon to be submitted for publication, also confirm the new interpretation advanced in this essay.

12 Loren Brandt's unpublished estimates for domestic trade, as reflected in intra-treaty port trade, and for export growth show that after 1913 domestic trade was expanding more rapidly than exports. This finding is also supported by evidence presented in Table 5.

13 Previous analyses of China's trade between 1930 and 1936 are extremely confusing. First, various authors have not separated the trade statistics for Manchuria and the rest of China. Second, they have not deflated the import and export series for price changes. See in particular the discussion of foreign trade trends in 1926-36 in Yu-kwei Cheng, *Foreign trade and industrial development of China* (University Press of Washington, DC, Washington, DC, 1956), p.70. See also the many articles on quarterly foreign trade trends during the 1930s in such Chinese journals as *Cheng-chih Ching-chi Hsüeh-pao*.

14 See Sheng Chün and Li Kan, 'Ching-chi k'ung-huang fa-sheng ch'ien-hou chih pi-chiao wu-chia' [A comparison of prices before and after the economic depression], *Ching-chi-hsüeh Li-k'an*, 7, 2 (1936), p.126.

15 Hsu Tao-fu (ed), *Chung-kuo chin-tai nung-yeh sheng-ch'an chi mao-i t'ung-chi tzu-liao* [Statistical materials for modern China's agricultural products and foreign trade] (Jen-min Ta-ch'ang-she, Shanghai, 1983), pp. 99,98,93.

16 See L. Brandt and T.J. Sargent, 'Interpreting new evidence about China and U.S. silver purchases', *Working Papers in Economics*, E-87-3 (Domestic Studies Program, Hoover Institution, Stanford University, Stanford, California, 1987), pp.1-35.

17 For discussion of the extent of Nanking government control over various provinces, see Hung-mao Tien, *Government and politics in Kuomintang China, 1927-1937* (Stanford University Press, Stanford, California, 1972), p.180.

18 A.D. Young, 'China's fiscal transformation, 1927-1937' in P.K.T. Sih (ed), *The strenuous decade: China's nation-building efforts, 1927-1937* (St John's University, New York, 1970), p.102. Between 1929 and 1937 government expenditures nearly doubled, and by 1938 they had risen a further 28 per cent.

19 P. Finch, 'A capital in the making', *North-China Herald*, 22 February 1933, p.316. For further evidence of Nanking's spectacular economic growth, see 'Nanking's growth', *North-China Herald*, 25 December 1935, p.505. One commentator stated, 'One of the most impressive manifestations of Nationalist China is the vigorous and healthy growth of Nanking as a capital, not only in regard to industrial, municipal and government developments but in the increase of population'.

20 'Shanghai', *North-China Herald*, 29 March 1932, p.473.

21 'Growth of Shanghai industry', *North-China Herald*, 5 December 1934, p.395.

22 Ibid., p.395.

23 'China in 1934', *North-China Herald*, 2 January 1935, p.35.

24 Ibid., p.35.

25 *North-China Herald*, 6 January 1937, p.24.

26 Ibid., p.24.

27 'Wusih', *North-China Herald*, 9 November 1932, p.236.

28 'Ningpo', *North-China Herald*, 9 November 1932, p.236.

29 Ibid., p.237.

30 'Eastern Honan', *North-China Herald*, 16 November 1932, p.275.

31 'Currency reform', *North-China Herald*, 15 January 1936, p.85. Even this editorial made no mention of the dire effects of the world depression or silver outflows upon the business life of Shanghai.

32 Hatchi Zenjirō, 'Shina membōshikigyō no gendankai' [The current stage of China's cotton spinning industry], *Mantetsu Chōsa Geppō*, *15*, 12 (1935), p.4 for a table comparing the growth of spindles between 1929 and 1934 for the US, England, Germany, Japan, India and China. Only the last three countries expanded capital stock in the cotton textile industry.

33 'China's industrial progress', *North-China Herald*, 13 January 1937, p.81.

34 'Improvement in Kuangtung', *North-China Herald*, 20 January 1937, p.125. We also learn that 'the road system in the province, too, is being well attended to . . . bridges are to be built and the surface re-laid'.

35 The unprecedented rainfall in central China throughout early 1931 had, by mid-year, created an inland sea '900 miles long with an average width of forty miles', directly affecting 50 million people. 'Review of the year in China', *North-China Herald*, 5 January 1932, p.30.

36 Wei Yu-fei, 'Shang-hai ti hui-hua ch'ien-chuang' [The credit banks of Shanghai], *Tung-fang Tsa-chih*, *33*, 17 (1936), p.107.

37 Chang Yu-i (comp), *Chung-kuo chin-tai nung-yeh-shih tzu-liao* [Materials on modern China's agricultural history] (San-lien Shu-tien, Beijing, 1957), vol.3, p.622. This is an extremely useful compendium of historical materials, but readers must be very careful in using the evidence in this work. Items have been taken out of their historical contexts, and virtually all sections have been selected according to a Marxist interpretation of China's modern agricultural history.

38 Ibid., p.627.

39 A.B. Lewis, 'China's silver problems and their possible solution', *Chinese Affairs*, *6*, 10 (1934), p.222.

40 Hsiao-tung Fei, *Peasant life in China*, 5th impression (Routledge and Kegan Paul, London, 1962), p.203. Prior to 1930 the villagers had been able to finance recreation and ceremonial activities, but these outlays had greatly declined during the 1930s because of the income loss from the failing silk industry.

41 Chang Yu-i, *Chung-kuo*, vol.3, p.766.

42 W.Y. Yang and Lu Sheng-hwai, 'Analysis of prices of farm crops in Chengting, Hopei, 1907-1937', *Economic Facts*, no.11 (1938), p.540.

43 A.B. Lewis, 'China's silver problems', p.222. Lewis offered the following observation. 'Because of the low value of farm produce, farm land values have fallen about 20 per cent, according to crop reporters; but many farmers cannot sell their land even at that price. When farm real estate is falling in price, credit is hard to obtain. Creditors lose when prices fall, not only because they are unable to collect, but also because the property which was pledged as security declines in value'.

44 'In China today', *North-China Herald*, 9 November 1932, p.235.

45 Ibid., p.235.

46 Ibid., p.236.

47 'Change over the countryside', *North-China Herald*, 17 March 1935, p.451.

48 *North-China Herald*, 26 April 1933, p.123.

49 'Little progress in northern Kiangsu', *North-China Herald*, 17 March 1937, p.451.

50 Ibid., p.451.

51 'Impressions of Kaifeng', *North-China Herald*, 22 July 1936, p.166.

52 E.B. Copland, 'Rural bankruptcy problem', *North-China Herald*, 29 April 1936, p.210.
53 Ibid., p.210.
54 'Hankow's courage', *North-China Herald*, 26 April 1933, p.123.
55 Ibid., p.123.
56 *North-China Herald*, 7 December 1932, p.395.
57 'Shensi famine', *North-China Herald*, 8 March 1933, p.390.
58 *North-China Herald*, 7 February 1937, p.265.
59 Chang Yu-i, *Chung-kuo*, vol.3, p.794.
60 Tsai Djang-chen and Chi-ming Chiao, 'Birth and death rates in Kiangyin registration area', *Economic Facts*, no.1 (1936), pp.66-7.
61 Ibid., p.69.
62 L. Brandt, 'Chinese agriculture and the international economy, 1870-1930s: a reassessment', *Explorations in Economic History*, no.22 (1985), pp.168-93.
63 T.G. Rawski, 'Estimates of China's money supply, 1910-1936', unpublished.

SUBJECT INDEX